M000239649

To my beloved companions on the first year of the Regional Council of the Bahá'ís of the Midwestern States. It has been a joy to serve with you during the inaugural term of this wonderful institution. I will forever treasure my memories of you.

With love for you always,

~ Your Brother Roi

This book is dedicated to

Shoghi Effendi

who sacrificed everything so that the Bahá'í world community
would be able to stand on its own spiritual feet and walk
the path created by Bahá'u'lláh
and made clear by 'Abdu'l-Bahá

Shoghi Effendi Through the Pilgrim's Eye

Volume 1
Building the Administrative Order, 1922–1952

Earl Redman

GEORGE RONALD
OXFORD

George Ronald, Publisher
Oxford
www.grbooks.com

© Earl Redman 2015
All Rights Reserved
Reprinted 2016

A catalogue record for this book is available from the British Library

ISBN 978–0–85398–588–4

Cover design: Steiner Graphics

CONTENTS

PREFACE

At the beginning of January 1922, a young man of twenty-four was stunned by the news that he had been appointed the head of a world-wide Faith and had been given divine assistance in order to do his job. Shoghi Effendi later said that his first thought was that 'when they read the Master's Will to me, I ceased to be a normal human being'.[1] Within a very few months, he found himself confronting such crises as the theft of the keys to the Shrine of Bahá'u'lláh, the appropriation of the House of Bahá'u'lláh in Baghdad, and the treacherous rebellion of well-known Bahá'ís. Struggling to handle the deluge of challenges, he escaped into the mountains of Switzerland where he cut himself off completely from everything except his spiritual fight to overcome his human frailties. He left as Shoghi Effendi, but when he returned, he was the Guardian. The pressure of his job was so intense and persistent that almost every year he would feel compelled, forced, to seek solitude in order to recharge his spiritual batteries for the trials ahead. He requested secretarial help several times over the years, but except for short-term assistance, his calls went unanswered. As a result, Shoghi Effendi did almost everything himself and many pilgrims and members of the Holy Family worried about the exhaustion that was commonly obvious in his face. Following in the footsteps of 'Abdu'l-Bahá was the most difficult task in the world.

When I entered the room of 'Abdu'l-Bahá in the House of the Master in 2007, I had no idea that I would ever write a book about any aspect of Bahá'í history. Then, for forty-five minutes, I was lost in the presence of 'Abdu'l-Bahá and, as Howard Colby Ives said after meeting 'Abdu'l-Bahá in New York, 'life has never been quite the same since'. When I began to search for stories about 'Abdu'l-Bahá in 2010, I found far more than I had expected. The Master was not just an inspiring person from the pages of Bahá'í history books, but a phenomenal Spiritual Being who directly reflected the light of Bahá'u'lláh. After writing *'Abdu'l-Bahá in Their Midst*, I could not stop my study of that tremendous Soul. That book covered the period from His departure from Haifa in 1910 to his return to Haifa in 1913. This continued delving led to the book *Visiting 'Abdu'l-Bahá* – not yet published – which chronicled His life and the reactions of those who met Him in Akka and Haifa from 1898 to 1921. The ending of that book necessarily included looking into the reactions of Shoghi Effendi as he found himself unexpectedly declared the Guardian of the Faith of Bahá'u'lláh.

Before I began researching the lives of 'Abdu'l-Bahá and Shoghi Effendi, I did not realize what a seismic shift had happened in 1922 after the passing of the Master. I knew that, unlike 'Abdu'l-Bahá, Shoghi Effendi wore Western clothes and did not go to the mosque. 'Abdu'l-Bahá had come to Akka as a prisoner and an exile and, as Amatu'l-Bahá Rúḥíyyih Khánum has written, was seen 'as the saintly protagonist of a great spiritual philosophy of universal brotherhood, a distinguished notable among other notables in Palestine. By sheer force of personality He had dominated those around him.' Shoghi Effendi, on the other hand, 'knew he could never do this in the circumstances surrounding him at the outset of his Guardianship, neither had he any desire to do so'. He also knew that one of his primary tasks was to win recognition for the Faith of Bahá'u'lláh as a recognized world religion.[2]

As I read pilgrims' notes, I noticed a huge difference between those of 'Abdu'l-Bahá's time and those of Shoghi Effendi's. The pilgrim notes of people who visited 'Abdu'l-Bahá were almost invariably focused on 'Abdu'l-Bahá as a father figure and on His spiritual power. But 'Abdu'l-Bahá was the last 'father figure'. During all previous Dispensations, humanity was always centred around a pope, archbishop, pastor, rabbi, priest, or mulla. Shoghi Effendi said that it was time for humanity to grow up. Prior to Shoghi Effendi, 'Abdu'l-Bahá had been the 'father figure' for the Bahá'ís of the world, but now it was time to change. The Bahá'ís, said the Guardian, should be centred on Bahá'u'lláh and building the world civilization which is the hallmark of His teachings. He avoided acting as a father, signing his letters 'your true brother', and not allowing his photograph to be circulated or his birthday celebrated.[3]

'Abdu'l-Bahá had embraced the station of a father to the Bahá'ís as when He told Fanny Knobloch in 1908 that 'As a father who loves his children; as a teacher who loves his pupils and desires that they make progress, so I hope that you will make progress.'⁴ Of His spiritual power, the pilgrims wrote about their uncontrollable tears, of falling involuntarily at His feet and of being totally mesmerized by Him.

I didn't recognize the full impact of the change until I read pilgrim notes from a Canadian, Emeric Sala, written in 1937. One day, Shoghi Effendi asked him,

> Since after the martyrdom of the Báb the authority of the Faith was passed on to Bahá'u'lláh, and after his passing to 'Abdu'l-Bahá, to whom was it transferred after the ascension of 'Abdu'l-Bahá?⁵

My immediate answer, like Emeric's, was the Guardian. But Shoghi Effendi said no. And again like Emeric, my next guess was the Universal House of Justice. Again Shoghi Effendi said, no. And like the baffled pilgrim, I felt quite confused. The Guardian responded to Emeric's confusion by asking whether the Bahá'ís were reading his letters – the answer, he said, was clearly stated in his letter titled *The Dispensation of Bahá'u'lláh* (and now included as a chapter in *The World Order of Bahá'u'lláh*). Shoghi Effendi had divided the letter into four parts: the Báb, Bahá'u'lláh, 'Abdu'l-Bahá and, not Shoghi Effendi, but the Administrative Order. This last part, he said, was composed of both the Guardian and the Universal House of Justice. They had the authority, not the Guardian alone.

Shoghi Effendi did leave an impression on those who visited him – just not in the same way that his Grandfather did. Amatu'l-Bahá Rúḥíyyih Khánum wrote:

> In 1956, a pilgrim recorded, accurately and shrewdly, her impressions of the Guardian: 'His face is beautiful, as it is so pure in expression and so impersonal, yet at the same time tender and majestic . . . I saw large grey-blue eyes . . . His nose is a combination of what it was in the pictures of him as a little boy – he still looks much like that! – and the sort of ridged nose of the Master. His years seem no more than forty-eight instead of sixty. He had a small, greying moustache, tightly clipped. His mouth is firm and pure, his teeth white and beautiful. His smile is a precious bounty . . . He is completely simple and direct. He himself does not demand all this deference, but just to be in his presence makes one feel absolutely

"weak and lowly". The Guardian is ever courteous and does not lose patience with questions of the immature. However, he is not reticent about letting people know which questions are important, and which are not, and which will be answered later by the International House of Justice . . .' She said Shoghi Effendi presided over the table 'so simply and yet with kingly mien – as only a great king can be simple! . . . I felt as if he were like a great powerful locomotive, pulling behind him a long, long string of cars, laden – not with dead-weight exactly – but sometimes pretty dead! This weight is the believers who have to be pushed, or pulled, or cajoled, or praised at every moment to get them into action. The beloved Guardian sees far in advance the needs, the lack of time, the obstacles and problems. He is actually hauling us all along behind his guiding and powerful light. Like a locomotive too – he can go straight ahead, fast or slow down, but he CANNOT deviate his course, he MUST follow the track which is his divine Guidance. He gives one the sense of being a perfect instrument – very impersonal, but hypersensitive to every thought, or atmosphere. He cannot be swayed in his thought. He is not influenced in the least by friendship, preference, money, hurting or not hurting feelings. He is absolutely above all that . . . The Guardian also made it very clear that now is not the time to dwell on the esoteric part of the teachings – on the contrary, we must be ACTIVE and positive, and get the Ten Year Crusade completed . . . He talks and comments, and then arrives at the end and suddenly folds his napkin neatly, rises from his chair . . . impossible to describe or convey in the least the luminosity and beauty of the Guardian. If he smiles at you – or looks with that swift penetrating gaze – it is a thrilling and soul-stirring feeling . . . always his discourse is about the Cause, and it stays with the theme of getting the Ten Year Crusade accomplished. He shows elation when there is good news, and goes into a deep depression when there is bad or evil news . . . Although he loves appreciation expressed in regard to the beauty of the Gardens and the Shrines and their planning, the Guardian seemed to shun personal praise or being thanked for anything . . . we were trying desperately to fix his beloved countenance for all time in our memories, and not to lose one single shading of his expression, always impersonal, sudden and varied and surprising . . . Alas, Shoghi Effendi's "radiant nature" has all too often been clouded over and saddened by the unwisdom of the friends, or their flagrant disobedience, or disregard of his instructions. Frantically one wonders who has not failed him in one way or another!'[6]

Those who were not adherents of the Bahá'í Faith were also impressed with the Guardian. Marcus Bach was a writer and a professor of religion who went searching for the truth in 1953. That search led him to Haifa and Shoghi Effendi. For a Christian, it was an eye-opening interview:

Whatever kind of man he was, he had drawn together into one procession many races, creeds, and minds. Great people and little people were marching with him toward the citadel of a united world. Rich and poor were finding a common ground, in senti-ment, at least. Strong and weak were joining hands and hearts in an idea. His Eminence was leading them onward to what he called a 'world-girding mission' and they knew what he meant . . .

I saw coming through the adjoining room a small, dark-com-plexioned man, dressed in Western attire but wearing a fez. His clean-shaven face and slender figure registered indomitable strength . . .

Quietly he took me at once into the heart of the Baha'i Cause and though I had heard much of this before from members of the faith, it was a new experience for me to meet a religious leader who was not defending one Book, but, rather, Books; who had no argu-ment for one Messiah, but for Messiahs; who was not pointing out one way, but ways to God . . .

This, then was the man I had come to see, a beardless prophet, one who might have been a successful businessman, artist, or teacher; an intense and vital man, whose all-seeing eyes always read my thoughts in advance, whose sharp mind had a ready answer the moment my questions were asked . . .

He spoke . . . in words tinged with poetry and power. He spoke in melodious, faultless English, with a firm and staunch authority as if what he had to say was said by divine right. He blended the vast run of world events for the past century into the hub of the 1863 proclamation that Baha'u'llah had come to do God's work and will . . .

. . . He had no other purpose than to see his mission accomplished.

xiii

Build the faith! Resist the enemies of the Cause! Trust in God! The divan on which he sat might have been a throne; his words, the words of a king.

But the thing that struck me most as our meeting progressed was his unquestioned devotion to the Galilean. He was fully as faithful to Jesus as he was to Baha'u'llah. Any basis for understanding the Baha'i concept would have to start with the premise that Shoghi Effendi was a thorough-going Christian in the philosophical, if not the theological sense . . .

To the Guardian the relationship between Jesus and Baha'u'llah was consistently unvarying. The world, he recalled, had rejected Christ. It was again seeking to reject the Splendor of God. But as the Prophet of Nazareth seized and conquered the minds of men, so the Prophet of Teheran was conquering, too . . .[7]

Shoghi Effendi spoke to many people and they wrote down what he said. As in all such cases, these recollections must be taken in the spirit of pilgrim notes – interesting and thought-provoking highlights from the Guardian's talks, but not any part of the Bahá'í Sacred Text. Unlike 'Abdu'l-Bahá, Shoghi Effendi could talk with pilgrims in English, which eliminated one potential source of confusion, translation, but the words those pilgrims recorded, and which are used in this book, are what they remembered later, when they wrote in their diaries.

Regarding the notes taken by pilgrims at Haifa. The Guardian has stated that he is unwilling to sign the notes of any pilgrim, in order that the literature consulted by the believers shall not be unduly extended . . . This means that the notes of pilgrims do not carry the authority resident in the Guardian's letters written over his own signature. On the other hand, each pilgrim brings back information and suggestions of a most precious character, and it is the privilege of all the friends to share in the spiritual results of these visits.[8]

Most of what Shoghi Effendi is reported to have said in this book are pilgrim notes and not authoritative. Only those quotations from him, extracted from his published works carry the full weight of his authority. In contrast, the quotations extracted from what people wrote while visiting Shoghi Effendi mostly come from personal diaries and letters initially written in longhand, though many were later typed. Since the pilgrims were primarily writing for themselves and their friends and not for publication, their writings not uncommonly contain typographical errors, grammatical stumbles, and missing punctuation, apostrophes and accents. Quoted text throughout this book has been left exactly as it was written by the pilgrims in order not to change their meaning or emotion.

This book is coloured primarily by the viewpoints of Western pilgrims because the materials available to me came dominantly from books, pilgrim notes and other sources written by Westerners in, or translated into, English. Only a few pilgrim notes written by Eastern Bahá'ís were found translated into English. Undoubtedly, there is a wealth of material written by Iranian, Iraqi, Indian and other non-English-speaking visitors to Shoghi Effendi, but they weren't available to me in a language I could use. Hopefully, this book will inspire other writers fluent in Persian or Arabic to write and publish similar books based on the experiences and remembrances of those pilgrims.

ACKNOWLEDGEMENTS

Writing about history is a like a game of hide and seek. There are an amazing number of sources, but they are commonly not easy to find. Several people greatly aided my search for stories and information. Lewis Walker, of the United States National Bahá'í Archives, provided me with about 700 pages of pilgrim notes, many of which I had not seen referenced in print before. The words of the pilgrims helped give a much fuller description of the Guardian and activities at the Bahá'í World Centre. Dr Duane Troxel, of The Heritage Project of the National Spiritual Assembly of the United States, provided me with searchable scanned copies of the *Bahá'í World*, *Star of the West*, *Bahá'í News* and other Bahá'í source books. He also provided audio files containing pertinent talks, and a host of other interesting documents. Suzanne Mahon, of the National Spiritual Assembly of New Zealand, scanned and sent letters and biographical information about members of the first group from New Zealand to go on pilgrimage, which allowed me to give fuller descriptions of those early Bahá'ís. Rowshan Mustafa, a Bahá'í in Tunis who is very knowledgeable about the Faith in Egypt, graciously contributed stories from his life-time of experience, including some from his father, Knight of Bahá'u'lláh Muhammad Mustafa.

Keith Munro, John Goggins and Maurice Sabour-Pickett read through drafts of this book and provided many helpful comments on organization and clarity. Their suggestions led to much editing, resulting in a much better book. Maurice, as he did in my earlier book, went through the text with his fine-toothed comb, uncovering all those typos, inconsistencies and grammatical aliens that I can never find. Larry Staudt and Nancy Korn also helped find typos. I must also include Karl Schoeppe, former Alaska ferry captain, for his constant supply of corn tortillas, a commodity unavailable in Ireland. The consequent enchiladas fuelled my work and kept me fired up.

May Hofman, as my editor at George Ronald, was a great help in making my masses of words into a coherent book. She was particularly helpful in clarifying the Guardian's teaching plans. When May suggested a change or an addition, I paid attention because she was almost always either right (for changes) or perceptive of what would improve the book (with additions). Her help was greatly appreciated.

And last, but not lastly, I must once again thank my wife, Sharon O'Toole, for all her support and help while the seemingly endless book writing was going on. She is accumulating an amazing number of gold stars in her virtues book.

WHO IS SHOGHI EFFENDI?

Bahá'ís know that Shoghi Effendi is the grandson of 'Abdu'l-Bahá, Who is the son of Bahá'u'lláh, the Manifestation of God for this time. Many will also know that his father was related to the Báb, thus uniting the two Manifestations of God. But who, really, is this person whom the British Palestinian authorities initially called 'the Boy', but whom they later would go to for advice?

Shoghi Effendi was only twenty-four when he became the Guardian of the Cause of God and charged with guiding the affairs of a world-wide Faith. Most Bahá'ís, understanding the spiritual guidance he would receive, immediately supported him and were obedient. Some, who saw only a very young man, but could not see his spiritual connection to the source of all knowledge, insisted that he follow their advice. When he did not, they rebelled, somehow forgetting 'Abdu'l-Bahá's explicit statement in His Will and Testament that the 'youthful branch', Shoghi Effendi, was now the Interpreter of the Word of God and under the 'care and protection of the Abhá Beauty, under the shelter and unerring guidance of the Exalted One':

> O my loving friends! After the passing away of this wronged one, it is incumbent upon the Aghsán (Branches), the Afnán (Twigs) of the Sacred Lote-Tree, the Hands (pillars) of the Cause of God and the loved ones of the Abhá Beauty to turn unto Shoghi Effendi – the youthful branch branched from the two hallowed and sacred Lote-Trees and the fruit grown from the union of the two offshoots of the Tree of Holiness, – as he is the sign of God, the chosen branch, the Guardian of the Cause of God, he unto whom all the Aghsán, the Afnán, the Hands of the Cause of God and His loved ones must turn. He is the Interpreter of the Word of God . . .
>
> The sacred and youthful branch, the Guardian of the Cause

of God, as well as the Universal House of Justice to be universally elected and established, are both under the care and protection of the Abhá Beauty, under the shelter and unerring guidance of the Exalted One . . . Whatsoever they decide is of God. Whoso obeyeth him not, neither obeyeth them, hath not obeyed God; whoso rebelleth against him and against them hath rebelled against God; whoso opposeth him hath opposed God . . .[1]

This passage encompasses all Bahá'ís. The Aghsán were the relatives of Bahá'u'lláh, the Afnán were the relatives of the Báb, and the friends were the rest of the Bahá'ís.

In his very early years, Shoghi Effendi asked 'Abdu'l-Bahá to give him his own name so that he would not be confused with his cousins. 'Abdu'l-Bahá gave him Rabbani for a surname, meaning 'divine'. In that time, most surnames were commonly derived from the place a person came from, such as Abu'l-Qásim-i-Khurásání, who was Abu'l-Qásim from the province of Khurasan, or the name of a prominent person in the family.[2]

'Abdu'l-Bahá had many years of training under His Father to develop His spiritual powers, but although Shoghi Effendi had served as the Master's secretary for a year and a half before his departure for England in 1920, he was unexpectedly and abruptly thrown into the deep end of the pool. He quickly amazed everyone at how well he could swim. Though the Guardianship came as a complete surprise to him, Shoghi Effendi had from childhood shown the qualities he would need to fulfil his destiny. Amatu'l-Bahá Rúḥíyyih Khánum said:

He always as a child had those qualities needed in a Guardian. He was studious, devoted to the teachings. He used to memorize them. He was passionately devoted to the Master.

Once the Master came into a room and found the Guardian alone memorizing tablets. The Master asked him what he was doing. The rest of the family was downstairs drinking coffee or tea and talking. 'Abdu'l-Bahá looked out of the window at them and said to Shoghi Effendi, 'I don't want you to be like them.'

Shoghi Effendi asked 'Abdu'l-Bahá if he might go and study in England. He had been serving the Master as interpreter and sometimes as Secretary. When he went to England with the Master's permission he never dreamed it would be the last time he would see his beloved Grandfather. The object of his going was to perfect his English so he could translate the Writings of Bahá'u'lláh.[3]

The young Guardian's future had been understood as early as 1910 when Dr Josephine Fallscheer saw the young man. As she talked with the Greatest Holy Leaf,

the son-in-law (the husband of the eldest daughter of Abbas Effendi), entered the room, evidently for the purpose of taking leave of the Master. At first I did not notice that behind the tall, dignified man his eldest son, Shoghi Effendi, had entered the room and greeted his venerable grandfather with the oriental kiss on the hand. I had already seen the child fleetingly on a few other occasions. Behia Khanum had recently informed me that this young boy of perhaps twelve years of age was the oldest direct male descendant of the family of the Prophet and destined to be the only successor and representative (vazir) of the Master. As Abbas Effendi spoke in Persian regarding some matter to Abu Shoghi (the father of Shoghi Effendi), who was standing in front of Him, the grandson, after greeting us politely and also kissing the hand of his great aunt, remained near the door in a most respectful attitude. At this moment a number of Persian gentlemen entered the room and greetings and leave-takings, comings and goings, took place for a quarter of an hour. Behia Khanum and I withdrew to the right near the window and in lowered voices continued our conversation in Turkish. However, I never removed my eyes from the still very youthful grandson of Abbas Effendi. He was dressed in European summer clothes, with short pants but long stockings that came up above his knees and a short jacket. From his height and build one would have taken him to be thirteen or fourteen . . . In the still childish face the dark, already mature, melancholy eyes struck me at once. The boy remained motionless in his place and submissive in his attitude. After his father and the man with him had taken their leave of the Master, his father whispered something to him as he went out, whereupon the youth, in a slow and measured manner, like a grown up person, approached his beloved grandfather, waited to be addressed, answered distinctly in Persian and was laughingly

3

dismissed, not however, without being first permitted the respectful kiss on the hand. I was impressed by the way the youth walked backwards as he left the room, and how his dark, true-hearted eyes never for a moment wavered from the blue, magical glance of his grandfather.

Abbas Effendi rose and came over to us and we immediately stood up, but the Master urged us to take our seats again and Himself sat down informally on a stool near us, or rather facing us. As usual in silence we waited for Him to speak to us, which He did shortly: 'Now my daughter,' He began, 'How do you like my future Elisha?' 'Master, if I may speak openly, I must say that in his boy's face are the dark eyes of a sufferer, one who will suffer a great deal!' Thoughtfully the Master looked beyond us into space and after a long time turned His gaze back to us and said: 'My grandson does not have the eyes of a trailblazer, a fighter or a victor, but in his eyes one sees deep loyalty, perseverance and conscientiousness. And do you know why, my daughter, he will fall heir to the heavy inheritance of being my Vazir (Minister, occupant of a high post)?' Without waiting for my reply, looking more at His dear sister than at me, as if He had forgotten my presence, He went on: 'Bahá'u'lláh, the Great Perfection – blessed be His words – in the past, the present and forever – chose this insignificant one to be His successor, not because I was the first born, but because His inner eye had already discerned on my brow the seal of God.

'Before His ascension into eternal Light the blessed Manifestation reminded me that I too – irrespective of primogeniture or age – must observe among my sons and grandsons whom God would indicate for His office. My sons passed to eternity in their tenderest years, in my line, among my relatives, only little Shoghi has the shadow of a great calling in the depths of his eyes.' There followed another long pause, then the Master turned again to me and said: 'At the present time the British Empire is the greatest and is still expanding and its language is a world language. My future Vazir shall receive the preparation for his weighty office in England itself, after he has obtained here in Palestine a fundamental knowledge of the oriental languages and the wisdom of the East.' Whereupon I ventured to interject: 'Will not the western education, the English training, remould his nature, confine his versatile mind in the rigid bonds of intellectualism, stifle through dogma and convention his oriental irrationality and intuition so that he will no longer be a servant of the Almighty but rather a slave to the rationality of western opportunism and the shallowness of every day life?' Long pause! Then Abbas Effendi 'Abdu'l-Bahá rose and in a strong and solemn voice said: 'I am not giving my Elisha to the British to educate. I dedicate and give him to the Almighty. God's eyes watch over my child in Oxford as well – Inshallah!'[4]

Rúḥíyyih Khánum explained the relationships between the Manifestation of God, Bahá'u'lláh, the Perfect Exemplar, 'Abdu'l-Bahá, and the Guardian, Shoghi Effendi:

Bahá'u'lláh was the Prophet. He did everything and said everything that was necessary for the world at present. The Master was the embodiment of His powers and teachings. He put an ingredient into the world of service in the true sense, of goodness, and a religious life in its highest form which is imperishable. Then something else was needed; this is where . . . a lot of people, including members of the Master's family and some of the Bahá'ís, have fallen down in their perspective of things. They wanted a second 'Abdu'l-Bahá – a series of patriarchal repeats in the form of the Guardians. But God seems to have had another idea. The strongest impression I always get of Shoghi Effendi is of an object travelling unidirectionally with terrific force and speed. If Bahá'u'lláh shone like the sun, and the Master gently went on radiating His light, like the moon, Shoghi Effendi is an entirely different phenomenon, as different as an object hurtling towards its goal is from something stationary and radiating. Or one could liken him to a chemical. Bahá'u'lláh assembled everything that we needed, the Master mixed everything together and prepared it; then God adds to it <u>one element</u>, a sort of universal precipitant, needed to make the whole clarify and go on to fulfil its nature – this is the Guardian . . . he is made 'exactly to fulfil the needs of the Cause – and consequently of the planet itself – at this time.'[5]

In 1954, Shoghi Effendi laid out the history of religious evolution in his ten-stage 'majestic process':

the vast, the majestic process, set in motion at the dawn of the Adamic cycle . . . a process which commenced six thousand years ago, with the planting, in the soil of the divine will, of the tree of divine revelation, and which has already passed through certain stages and must needs pass through still others ere it attains its final consummation. The first part of this process was the slow and steady growth of this tree of divine revelation, successively putting forth its branches, shoots and offshoots, and revealing its leaves, buds and blossoms, as a direct consequence of the light and warmth imparted to it by a series of progressive dispensations associated with Moses, Zoroaster, Buddha, Jesus, Muḥammad and other Prophets, and of the vernal showers of blood shed by countless martyrs in their path. The second part of this process was the fruition of this tree, 'that belongeth neither to the East nor to the West,' when the Báb appeared as the perfect fruit and declared His mission in the Year Sixty in the city of Shíráz. The third part was the grinding of this sacred seed, of infinite preciousness and potency, in the mill of adversity, causing it to yield its oil, six years later, in the city of Tabríz. The fourth part was the ignition of this oil by the hand of Providence in the depths and amidst the darkness of the Síyáh-Chál of Ṭihrán a hundred years ago. The fifth, was the clothing of that flickering light, which had scarcely penetrated the adjoining territory of 'Iráq, in the lamp of revelation, after an eclipse lasting no less than ten years, in the city of Baghdád. The sixth, was the spread of the radiance of that light, shining with added brilliancy in its crystal globe in Adrianople, and later on in the fortress town of 'Akká, to thirteen countries in the Asiatic and African continents. The seventh was its projection, from the Most Great Prison, in the course of the ministry of the Center of the Covenant, across the seas and the shedding of its illumination upon twenty sovereign states and dependencies in the American, the European, and Australian continents.[6]

The seventh stage was 'Abdu'l-Bahá's ministry and his travels to the West. This was the 'projection' of the Light of Bahá'u'lláh into the West. The passing of 'Abdu'l-Bahá marked the end of that stage and the naming of Shoghi Effendi as the Guardian began the eighth stage, distinguished by the building and slow maturation of the Bahá'í Administrative Order:

The eighth part of that process was the diffusion of that same light in the course of the first, and the opening years of the second, epoch of the Formative Age of the Faith, over ninety-four sovereign states, dependencies and islands of the planet, as a result of the prosecution of a series of national plans, initiated by eleven national spiritual assemblies throughout the Bahá'í world, utilizing the agencies of a newly emerged, divinely appointed Administrative Order.[7]

The period of time covered in this book, therefore, is that eighth stage, when Shoghi Effendi slowly built up the Administrative Order, trained it through a series of national teaching plans, then used it to 'diffuse' the Faith over the world according to 'Abdu'l-Bahá's *Tablets of the Divine Plan*. While many of his letters to Bahá'í institutions, communities and individuals have been published and are thus available for study, his personal interactions with the Bahá'í pilgrims to the Holy Land during this time are more scattered. The accounts here show how the primary objective of the Guardian all through this stage was to prepare the world for the ninth stage, the Ten Year Crusade:

The ninth part of this process . . . is the further diffusion of that same light over one hundred and thirty-one additional territories and islands in both the Eastern and Western Hemispheres, through the operation of a decade-long world spiritual crusade . . .[8]

This 'further diffusion' illuminated every country and territory of the world and was designed to lead to the tenth stage, which was to begin with the election of the Universal House of Justice and wherein the Light of Bahá'u'lláh was to 'penetrate' to every corner of the world:

the tenth part of this mighty process must be the penetration of that light, in the course of numerous crusades and of successive epochs of both the Formative and Golden Ages of the Faith, into all the remaining territories of the globe through the erection of the entire machinery of Bahá'u'lláh's Administrative Order in all territories, both East and West . . .[9]

THE ASCENSION OF 'ABDU'L-BAHÁ

The passing of 'Abdu'l-Bahá and the arrival of Shoghi Effendi in Haifa was an important transition for the young Bahá'í Faith. The Master's passing will be covered in some detail in the final chapter of *Visiting 'Abdu'l-Bahá* by this author (forthcoming in 2016). This chapter summarizes those events.

With the passing of 'Abdu'l-Bahá, all of the work fell upon the Greatest Holy Leaf. Her first task was to inform the world. To Roy Wilhelm in the United States, she wrote 'His Holiness Abdul-Baha ascended to Abha Kingdom.'[1] To Tehran, 'Light of Covenant transferred from eye to heart, day of teaching, unity, self sacrifice.'[2] The funeral was held on 29 November at 9 a.m. John Bosch wrote:

> By 8 oclock the house, the yards, the garden were full of mourners . . . Mírzá Jalal, the son of the King of the Martyrs, called me to help him to carry the casket, of white wood & zinc lined, from the north room into the room where Abdul Baha was & four of us lifted the body of the Master into the casket. The body was wrapped in four or five thicknesses of most beautiful white silk. First in casket was placed a silk comforter of the finest quality with a small pillow for his head to lay on.
>
> The best Attar of Roses was sprinkled over the white silk & the two ends of the comforter were laid over the body & then the cover was placed on the casket. At 5 minutes to 9 oclock we picked up the casket & carried it on our shoulders to the center room of the house, where a short talk was given by a Mohammedan priest & at 9 silently the funeral procession started, taking about an hour & a half walking up the Mount Carmel road to the Tomb of the Báb.
>
> Never has there been such a procession, comprising of men of all nations of all walks in life, rich & poor, representing all creeds.

About 40 carriages were waiting but only 5 were occupied, as everybody wanted to honor [Him] in walking after the remains of the Master . . . Arriving at the tomb several speeches were given in four languages. Real Bahai speeches.

The casket was brought within the tomb about 11:30.

It is estimated that about 3000 people attended the funeral.[3]

The mourners included the 'High Commissioner of Palestine, Sir Herbert Samuel, the Governor of Jerusalem, the Governor of Phoenicia, the Chief Officials of the Government, the Consuls of the various countries resident in Haifa, the heads of the various religious communities, the notables of Palestine, Jews, Christians, Moslems, Druses, Egyptians, Greeks, Turks, Kurds, and a host of his American, European and native friends.' Shoghi Effendi estimated that as many as 10,000 people were there.[4]

Shoghi Effendi and Lady Blomfield described the funeral procession:

This impressive, triumphal procession was headed by a guard of honour, consisting of the City Constabulary Force, followed by the Boy Scouts of the Moslem and Christian communities holding aloft their banners, a company of Moslem choristers chanting their verses from the Qurʾan, the chiefs of the Moslem community headed by the Mufti, a number of Christian priests, Latin, Greek and Anglican, all preceding the sacred coffin, upraised on the shoulders of his loved ones. Immediately behind it came the members of his family, next to them walked the British High Commissioner, the Governor of Jerusalem, and the Governor of Phoenicia. After them came the Consuls and the notables of the land, followed by the vast multitude of those who reverenced and loved him.[5]

When the procession arrived at the Shrine of the Báb, the casket was placed in front of the Tomb and all those involved gathered around. Then nine speeches were made, none by a Baháʾí, but by Muslims, Christians, Jews and others. When the speeches were over, Sir Herbert Samuel, the British High Commissioner of Palestine, 'holding his hat in his left hand, knelt down and kissed, for the last time, the shawl that covered the casket, and all those who were present did the same.'[6]

The caretaker of the Shrine of the Báb, ʿAbbás Qulí, was a strong man. The day before 'Abdu'l-Bahá passed away, the Master asked him a strange question: 'You are a strong man. Could you not carry me away to a place where I could rest? I'm tired of this world.' When the casket was taken into the Shrine, there was only room for one person to descend into the crypt. The casket was placed on 'Abbas Qulí's shoulders and he, alone, carried it down to its final resting place.[7]

After the passing of the Master, food was distributed to between fifty and a hundred of the poor at the same place where 'Abdu'l-Bahá met the poor every Friday. Then on the seventh day, 4 December, corn was passed out to a thousand of the poor in His name.[8] Everyone who asked was given forty pounds of corn.[9]

On 6 December, the ninth and last official day of mourning, 140 pilgrims went to the Shrine of Bahá'u'lláh.[10] Mírzá Muḥammad-'Alí, the Arch-breaker of the Covenant, was so bold as to go to the house of the Master, but the Greatest Holy Leaf turned him away. The disgruntled Muḥammad-'Alí then wrote to various newspapers 'calling the Bahais to turn to him, quoting extracts from the Covenant of His Holiness Bahá'u'lláh. The Bahai Assembly of Cairo answered him, and exposed his claim to leadership . . .'[11]

'Abdu'l-Bahá's passing on 28 November was a surprise to many, though he had made a number of hints about it to those around Him. To 'Abdu'l-Bahá's oldest grandson, Shoghi Effendi, however, it was completely unexpected. He was at Balliol College, Oxford, studying so that he could become a better translator for the Master. 'Abdu'l-Bahá had specifically asked Shoghi Effendi's parents to send him a cable that he should return to Haifa immediately. Worried that a cable requesting his urgent return would unnecessarily worry their son, they sent a letter instead. It did not arrive in time, so when the Master left the physical plane, Shoghi Effendi was not there.

The Greatest Holy Leaf sent a cable to Major Wellesley Tudor-Pole on 29 November that read simply: 'His Holiness 'Abdu'l-Bahá ascended Abhá Kingdom. Inform friends.' Tudor-Pole immediately called Shoghi Effendi and asked him to come quickly to his office. When the young man arrived, Tudor-Pole was not in. The cablegram lay open on the desk and Shoghi Effendi saw the name of 'Abdu'l-Bahá so he read it. He promptly collapsed. After a couple days of recovery in the home of Helen Grand, a Canadian Bahá'í who lived in London, Shoghi Effendi went to stay with Dr Esslemont and began to make plans to return to

Haifa. Though he did not know what lay ahead, a letter he wrote was prescient:

> The terrible news has for some days so overwhelmed my body, my mind and my soul that I was laid for a couple of days in bed almost senseless, absent-minded and greatly agitated. Gradually His power revived me and breathed in me a confidence that I hope will henceforth guide me and inspire me in my humble work of service. The day had to come, but how sudden and unexpected. The fact however that His Cause has created so many and such beautiful souls all over the world is a sure guarantee that it will live and prosper and ere long will compass the world! I am immediately starting for Haifa to receive the instructions He has left and have now made a supreme determination to dedicate my life to His service and by His aid to carry out His instructions all the days of my life.[12]

Delayed by passport problems, Shoghi Effendi did not arrive in Haifa until 29 December 1921, accompanied by Lady Blomfield and his sister, Rúhangíz. Mercifully, the Greatest Holy Leaf, who had by that time read 'Abdu'l-Bahá's Will and Testament and knew what was about to descend upon the unknowing Guardian, let him grieve in the House of the Master for three days before allowing him to read about his future.

1922

'TELL THE FRIENDS, TIME WILL PROVE THAT THERE HAS BEEN NO MISTAKE'

It was a heart-broken Shoghi Effendi who arrived in Haifa on 29 December 1921. 'Abdu'l-Bahá, who had passed to the Abhá Kingdom a month before, was not there to meet him. Louise Bosch, however, was and heard his arrival:

> Then I heard what must have been his footsteps coming up to the front door and coming in; when he gave – I don't know how to describe that cry – an outcry of greatest grief – pain – *ache*. It was *loud*. And then I remained in the room. Although I did not see Shoghi Effendi I knew for certain it was he . . .[1]

At that point, the young Shoghi Effendi had no idea what was in store for him or how dramatically his future had been changed. Only the Greatest Holy Leaf and Munírih Khánum, 'Abdu'l-Bahá's sister and wife, respectively, knew. On the day after the Master's funeral, they had opened the strong box containing the Will and Testament. The box contained a sealed letter, stained from dampness, addressed to Shoghi Effendi.[2] The two women opened the letter to see if there were any directions on 'where to bury the Master or what, for a waiting, despairing Bahá'í world, His instructions might be. Thus they found out that Shoghi Effendi was the Guardian even before he did . . .'[3]

For three days, the Greatest Holy Leaf and Munírih Khánum kept the secret from the distraught young man, allowing him some time to recover. During that time, John and Louise Bosch said 'he came over to lunch at the Pilgrim House and was full of plans of what needed to be done at that crisis of the Faith.'[4] But then the young man was given the letter addressed to him and Louise wrote that

> from the third day on, I didn't see him. Then on the fifth day past sunset I went over, and what I saw I shall never forget. He was coming out of a room and walking through the door of the Most Exalted Leaf's room. He was like an old man, bent over and he could barely speak, but he shook hands with me, and looked at me for a moment. He spoke like a person who cannot hear anything now or doesn't want to see any one now. He was wholly changed and aged and walking bent and he had a little light or candle in his hand. I think he said to me, 'It is all right.'
>
> But I saw something terrible had happened. He had reacted just the way the Family had known he would. That's why he didn't come back to the Pilgrim House. He got ill. He couldn't eat; he couldn't drink or sleep.
>
> After the first three days had passed and he had seen the Will he couldn't at all accept it. He seemed to make such remonstrances that his mother felt called upon to recite to him a history of a similar time after Muḥammad when one of the Holy Imáms would not serve. So Shoghi Effendi's mother said: 'Are you going to repeat the history of that Imám, who also felt he was not qualified?'[5]

Shoghi Effendi was just twenty-four years old and, though he had spent much of his life in the company of 'Abdu'l-Bahá, he had only expected to be one of His translators.[6] He had gone to Oxford specifically to improve his English for this task. His fellow students at Oxford saw him as a hard-working but fun-loving companion. One noted that Shoghi Effendi loved to play tennis: 'He was ambidextrous and switched his racket from one hand to the other for a volley . . . but not in a grimly earnest manner. On the contrary he was laughing . . . most of the time.' Another wrote that he was 'friendly and easy to get on with and enjoyed laughter . . . and liked making friends.' Yet another said the young Bahá'í was 'irrepressibly cheerful, always on the point of laughter, and bouncing around . . . Wherever he was, spirits were high.'[7]

Suddenly, he was placed in the previously unknown station of

Guardian of the Faith. The Greatest Holy Leaf and Munírih Khánum, his great-aunt and grandmother, stood firmly behind him, bowing down to the authority given Shoghi Effendi by 'Abdu'l-Bahá as the Guardian of the Faith and authorized interpreter of the Writings[8] and supporting him through their example.

So it was that, having lost his beloved grandfather, 'he found that the burden which had rested first on the Báb, then on Bahá'u'lláh, and then on his beloved grandfather, 'Abdu'l-Bahá, had fallen with all its weight on his shoulders'. The new Guardian said, 'The day they read me the Will and Testament I ceased to be a normal human being.' He had expected that 'as he was the eldest grandson, it might fall to his lot to be requested by the Master, posthumously naturally, to open any documents of instruction and communicate them to the Bahá'ís.' But Shoghi Effendi began to arise and to meet the challenge and Rúhíyyih Khánum later wrote that 'the always personable and noble young man, now, and ever increasingly as the years went by, had the stamp of kingship in his face, his manner, his walk and gestures'.[9]

It was a challenging time not only for Shoghi Effendi, but also for the Bahá'í community, both in the Holy Land and across the world. 'Abdu'l-Bahá had been well known and highly venerated and had the wisdom of the years – he had been forty-eight when He was appointed the Centre of the Covenant. He had also had many years during which Bahá'u'lláh prepared him for the future. His daughter Rúhá Khánum told Effie Baker that

> Baha'u'llah received so many letters. He would give them to 'Abdu'l-Baha to answer. 'Abdu'l-Baha would bring the answers and read them to him. Baha'u'llah would be pleased and praise 'Abdu'l-Baha for the way in which he answered them. (Rouha Khanum) told how 'Abdu'l-Baha would go to a room in the Inn (across from the house where Baha'u'llah was imprisoned for seven years) called Master's drawing room. Here he would receive people, Baha'is and non-Baha'is and give them advice both spiritually and materially. At twelve o'clock [He] would come and have lunch with Baha'u'llah and tell him all that transpired during the morning. [He] would go to the Barracks in the afternoon and write in little room (sentry box for soldier). Had no room where he could go to write privately. He would come back and again go and visit and help people.[10]

Emogene Hoagg and Lady Blomfield

Emogene Hoagg, who had been living in Haifa since 1920 but was in Egypt when 'Abdu'l-Bahá died, returned to Haifa on 23 December 1921 to find Dr and Grace Krug, Fred and Lorol Schopflocher, John and Louise Bosch, Johanna Hauff and Ethel Rosenberg already there. Emogene felt 'A great loneliness!'. On the 26th the Schopflochers left and Ethel had set up a Christmas tree in the Pilgrim House. She had brought presents for the children, which created great excitement.[11]

Lady Blomfield arrived with Shoghi Effendi on the 29th; it was her first visit to Haifa. As Shoghi Effendi struggled to understand his new role, Lady Blomfield looked beyond these troubles to where she was, at the Bahá'í World Centre, and felt its spiritual power. She had never seen the Shrine of the Báb before and she was impressed:

> it is a large beautiful room with precious Persian rugs on the floor – lovely branched candlesticks give a subdued light with their wax candles; on either side of this room there is an arch, leading into a room for men and another for women. Lovely Persian rugs cover these floors also – the spiritual atmosphere cannot be described, it can only be felt. Prayers are chanted as we kneel or stand. There is nothing tawdry or forced or insincere – oh the Majesty of a sacred simplicity! In which the worship of hearts seems to vibrate and ascend.[12]

The gloom was pierced now and then by rays of humour and light. Lady Blomfield talked with the women of the Holy Household about the manners and customs of British husbands. This excited the women:

> They wanted to hear what British husbands' manners and customs were. When I told them, they said 'Do write it all down and let us have it translated into Arabic, to show to our husbands!! or better still would you write to our men and talk to them.' I replied that it would give me great pleasure but that I should not be able to re-educate them with one or two talks and I should certainly rather antagonize them!![13]

Lady Blomfield was glad to have friendly faces around her during this difficult time. Lotfullah Hakím, whom she had known in England, was also there. She was entranced by Fujita, the only other attendant living in the House of the Master, and she described him as 'a nice intellectual Japanese man with hair *en brosse* and long mustache, just like an old Japanese print. He cooks such things as do not come from the Master's house and serves the meals with the help of Lotfullah.'[14]

A memorial feast

On 6 January, forty days after the passing of 'Abdu'l-Bahá, the Bahá'ís held a memorial feast at both 'Abdu'l-Bahá's house and the home of Rúḥá Khánum for two hundred guests. Lady Blomfield wrote that the

> long tables were decorated with trailing branches of Bougainvilliers [sic]. It's lovely purple blooms mingle with the white narcissus, and with the large dishes of golden oranges out of the beloved Master's garden made a picture of loveliness in these spacious lofty rooms, whose only other decoration was the gorgeous yet subdued colouring of rare Persian rugs. No useless trivial ornaments marred the extreme dignity of simplicity.[15]

The guests began to arrive at 11 and by 1 p.m. all were present. The women had done all the planning, but the men did the serving. Emogene noted: 'What a feat to serve 200 guests at one time!' and added 'the real force was behind "the veil".'[16]

At one point during the commemoration, Shoghi Effendi led everyone to the Shrine of 'Abdu'l-Bahá, where he chanted. Afterwards, the men went to one room in the Eastern Pilgrim House and the women went to another. Shoghi Effendi went with the women and asked them to sing *Nearer My God to Thee*, obviously a favourite of his since he asked various pilgrim groups over the years to sing the hymn. Catharine Nourse, who was a youth of seventeen at that time, remembered the moment:

> Here we were standing, trying to put on our very best manners and behave ourselves perfectly and the Guardian asked the American women to stand up and sing *Nearer My God to Thee*. And nobody knew the words. We did know the song, the tune, but we nearly went wild. I can see Mrs Krug's face yet. If he'd asked her to climb up in the sky, I don't think she'd have any more of a problem. Well,

we did it and the Persians are very sweet, they never laugh . . . and they were very humble and I will never ever forget that. Talk about an embarrassing moment.[17]

The next day, 'Abdu'l-Bahá's Will and Testament was read in public. Emogene wrote that the pilgrims were

rather unexpectedly . . . called to hear the Testament of the Master read. It took almost two hours, with an extra Tablet included. Much sobbing & weeping when he referred to the hardships endured from the Nakazeen [the Covenant-breakers]. Much feeling when he mentioned that Shoghi Effendi would be the head of the Cause. Many expressions of loyalty, and I believe great comfort is felt that the Beloved has left for us a head and thereby strengthened the solidity of the Cause.[18]

Fujita also described the scene:

Will of . . .'Abdu'l-Bahá read in Number seven. In the center of the hall! That room! Oh, we had the biggest . . . meeting there. All sitting on floor. A prominent Bahá'í, from Egypt, he read the Will, right in the corner, and everybody faced, and everybody sat around, even the Nakazeen, some of the Nakazeen was among us, violator. Very touching ceremony. Oh, from early in morning, we had a meeting . . . to go some time, to circulate all the Will of 'Abdu'l-Bahá. Every time mention . . . Shoghi Effendi's name, everybody arise. Very respectable, very. That's why the Shoghi Effendi is [to] be Guardian of the Cause. That day family, back in that tea room now. See, the gentlemen and the ladies are all segregated. They know, behind the curtain, they all know. The Will of 'Abdu'l-Bahá was read, everybody consented, Shoghi Effendi is the Guardian of the Cause. That's final, nobody object, and then after the passing 'Abdu'l-Bahá, the reign of Guardian, Shoghi Effendi.[19]

The pilgrims

In early January, a group of fourteen pilgrims arrived from Persia. They had only learned of the passing of 'Abdu'l-Bahá when they approached

Haifa. It had taken them two months riding on donkeys, mules, camels and third class on trains and ships. Lady Blomfield wrote, 'Their grief is terribly pathetic.' Meeting Lady Blomfield, they said, 'our master has been to your country, your house – but not to our country, only in the Celestial Realm, shall we see our Adored one face to face'.[20]

Catharine Nourse was there with her mother, Elizabeth, and brothers, Boyce and Phillip. Catharine had at one time, when 'Abdu'l-Bahá was in Washington, sat on his knee and had attended children's classes with Stanwood Cobb, Paul Haney (who much later became a Hand of the Cause) and Mary Maxwell.[21] Boyce, Catharine and Phillip greatly enjoyed John Bosch. John had a long white beard and moustache and Catharine said he looked like a saint. Saint he might have been, but he also knew the worldly desires of young people and would take them down the road each day and buy them sweetmeats at the various shops.[22]

One day, when Shoghi Effendi had been at the Shrine of the Báb, he decided to walk back to the House of the Master. The Bahá'ís all followed him at a respectful distance as if he were a 'king among kings as he walked down the mountain'. When they reached the house, Shoghi Effendi asked Boyce Nourse if he would like to walk in the garden with him. As the two strolled through the garden, Shoghi Effendi's young companion asked if he could take his picture, to which, unexpectedly, the Guardian said yes. The photo he took, which is reproduced in the book *The Priceless Pearl*, shows the Guardian holding a handkerchief filled with violets that he had picked at the Shrine and which he was taking to the Greatest Holy Leaf. He had picked a second bunch that he presented to Elizabeth Nourse to take back to America: the first gift from Shoghi Effendi to America. Those violets were preserved and later given to the National Archives.[23]

For Lorol and Fred (Friedrich) Schopflocher, Bahá'ís just a single year, pilgrimage was a life-changing visit for them both, but especially for Fred. He became extremely attached to the new Guardian, but it was 'through Fujita, in a moment of immense spiritual emotion, Fred became confirmed in his faith'.[24] He would later be appointed a Hand of the Cause of God.

Isabel Rives was also on pilgrimage during this time. Just before she left, Shoghi Effendi invited her to a meeting at noon that Sunday at the Shrine of Bahá'u'lláh. In dismay, Isabel said that she could not attend because her ship sailed at that exact hour. She wrote that Shoghi Effendi 'sent messengers hither and yon and called the Meeting for 12 Saturday so I could be present'. There were both American and English pilgrims there at the time and most of them boarded the train that morning, nearly filling their 3rd class coach. Shoghi Effendi had asked them to sing *Nearer My God to Thee* at the Shrine so they rehearsed on the ride over. Following the local mores, all of the women were veiled, but since the coach was filled with Westerners, they all had their veils up over their heads – until the conductor came through when 'down went the veils, with a bang, as soon as he was out of sight, up they went again'.[25]

Once in the Shrine, Shoghi Effendi chanted with his face transformed: 'he looked like an angel, and he certainly chanted like one.' Then the American and English pilgrims sang. Many flowers had been placed in the Shrine and Shoghi Effendi collected some. One, a tea rose, which he said was 'Abdu'l-Bahá's favourite, he gave to Isabel. When she returned to Washington, she gave a petal to each of those present at a meeting.[26]

As January wore on, the pilgrims began to depart. John and Louise Bosch left on the 17th and Johanna Hauff had gone on the 29th.[27] When John and Louise Bosch were about to depart, a ray of sunlight came from Louise:

> Louise wanted an Eastern street costume and veil such as the ladies of the Household then wore, in deference to the time and place. Riḍváníyyih Khánum helped to make it and they dressed her in it. Few sights were funnier to Easterners than a Western woman trying to wear the veil. They led Louise, striding along in her wrapping, to a room where she found the ladies at prayer. An aunt of the Guardian's said: 'You must go and see Shoghi Effendi.' Then she opened a door to the next room and announced through the crack: 'A Turkish lady wishes to see you.' Feeling like a child in fancy dress, Louise went in. 'I stood maybe four or five feet from his bed. He sat up in the bed and when I could not contain my laughter he said, 'Oh, it's Mrs. Bosch,' and he pointed to my shoes. Then he laughed a little and I and his aunt laughed. She told me this was the first time Shoghi Effendi had even smiled since his return.
>
> The last words that Shoghi Effendi spoke to Louise when she and John took leave of him were: 'Tell the friends, time will prove that there has been no mistake.'[28]

Curtis Kelsey and Fujita go to Cairo

While the Nourse family was still in Haifa, Elizabeth Nourse asked Shoghi Effendi if there was something she could do for him. Many years later Catharine Nourse described what happened next. He said 'Yes, there is. You could take Curtis Kelsey and Fujita to Egypt and give them a vacation.' Catharine continues the story:

> Now, those of you who know Fujita, he used to be the chauffeur for Mrs True when they were all very young . . . And when he was in Haifa, 'Abdu'l-Bahá went to him one day and started pulling his chin and He said, 'I'm going to give you a beard.' So every day, 'Abdu'l-Bahá pulled his chin and pretty soon he had a nice beard down to about here and it made him look very distinguished . . . He was quite a gentleman. He walked with a cane and he wore a little bowler hat, a British top hat. Oh, he was very meticulous and he dressed beautifully . . . Both of my brothers were very tall and we went to Egypt and we took Curtis Kelsey and we took Fujita. We stayed at the Shepheard's Hotel, that's one of the big hotels in Cairo and when we went in to dinner every night, people stood and watched us and watched us.[29]

On the first evening, just as Curtis and Fujita were settling in to their luxurious hotel room –a complete contrast to their simple accommodation in Haifa – they received a note from their benefactress asking them to join her for dinner. Fujita immediately opened his suitcase and pulled out a tuxedo. In his small room in Haifa, Fujita had a huge trunk full of clothes – he had been quite the partyer before becoming a Bahá'í. Occasionally, Fujita would open the trunk, look at the clothes, and exclaim, 'Look, all dressed up and no place to go!' Now, he had a place to go and wear his tuxedo.[30]

When Curtis, Elizabeth and Fujita reached the lobby, Fujita took charge,

> his tuxedo tails almost touching the rich oriental rugs. As he approached the dining room, one of the hotel's elegantly dressed butlers, standing erect, opened the thick oak doors. It was a majestic entry. The only thing missing was a series of trumpet fanfares and

the roll of the drum. Terribly self-conscious, Curtis walked down the aisle after Fujita, who was bowing to the left and then to the right. The men on both sides stood and bowed back, sensing that Fujita was some sort of royal figure from the orient.

No sooner had they been seated, than a butler approached Fujita and whispered something in his ear. Fujita arose and proceeded to the door, again bowing to the left and then the right, the gentlemen on both sides responding in kind.

As Fujita entered the lobby, he was greeted by a large Persian who swept him into his arms and kissed his beard.[31]

When Fujita had started to grow the beard, 'Abdu'l-Bahá told him that people would one day put him up on a table to kiss that beard. When other Bahá'ís in Cairo learned that Fujita was there, they arranged a meeting which Fujita attended. Catharine Nourse remembered:

> He met with the men one evening in a meeting where the women weren't allowed to go and he was very embarrassed when he came out to us and he said that they done just what 'Abdu'l-Bahá had said. They had stood him on a little card table and all the Persians had come around and kissed his beard because 'Abdu'l-Bahá had given it to him . . .[32]

Translating the Will and Testament

Emogene Hoagg began working with Rúḥá Khánum translating the first part of the Will and Testament into English on 15 January. Mírzá Muḥammad Khán joined them the next day. Emogene said the work was 'very difficult', but by the 22nd they had completed the first section.[33] On 7 February, Emogene worked with Shoghi Effendi for five hours typing up the Will and Testament. On 24 February she was retyping the completed translation for Shoghi Effendi.

The first challenges

The world gave Shoghi Effendi little time to adjust to the immense burden his grandfather had placed on his shoulders. The young Guardian, still reeling from the twin shocks of the passing of 'Abdu'l-Bahá and his appointment as the Guardian of the Cause, was almost immediately buried under an avalanche of problems. His first major challenges as Guardian were the theft of the keys to the Shrine of Bahá'u'lláh at Bahjí, attacks by Covenant-breakers, and the loss of the Most Great House, the House of Bahá'u'lláh, in Baghdad.

On 30 January 1922, just one month after Shoghi Effendi's arrival in Haifa, Mírzá Muḥammad-'Alí, the Arch-breaker of the Covenant, had twenty of his supporters, led by his brother Badí'u'lláh, forcibly steal the keys to the Shrine of Bahá'u'lláh from the caretaker, Abu'l-Qásim Khurásání. Mírzá Muḥammad-'Alí had similarly taken possession of the Mansion of Bahjí after the death of Bahá'u'lláh in 1892 and now he was using the passing of 'Abdu'l-Bahá to wreak more havoc. He had initially tried to gain possession of the Shrine of Bahá'u'lláh by invoking Islamic law. That failing, he tried again, claiming it to be his right as the brother of 'Abdu'l-Bahá. Both attempts were tossed out by the British. So he stole the keys, thinking that a 24-year-old youth wouldn't have the gumption to challenge him. This uproar forced the British Governor of Akka to demand the keys and to post guards at the Shrine.[34] Shu'á'u'lláh, Mírzá Muḥammad-'Alí's son, arrived from America after having sent out letters calling for the Bahá'ís to support his father, whom he declared to be the new Centre of the Covenant.[35]

The British apparently didn't place much stock in such a young man as Shoghi Effendi as the replacement of Sir Abbas Effendi, calling him 'the Boy'.[36] In their official gazette, the *Palestine Weekly*, the authorities let it be known that they

> understand that in the will of the late Sir Abbas Effendi provision is made for the convocation by his grandson, Shoghi Effendi, of representative Bahais from the various countries of the world. They hope that this assembly will express an authoritative opinion on all points of disagreement, including the question of the custody of the Shrine at Acre.[37]

But 'the Boy' refused to be intimidated by his much older nemesis or by the British authorities. Within a year, through Shoghi Effendi's patient efforts the British authorities had determined that the Shrine of Bahá'u'lláh was, indeed, rightfully the property of the Bahá'ís and the keys were returned.[38]

As in all Bahá'í transitions, Covenant-breaking quickly raised its ugly head. People reacted to the naming of Shoghi Effendi as the Guardian of the Faith in many ways; most by immediately accepting his station because of 'Abdu'l-Bahá's Will and Testament. Some watched and waited to see how Shoghi Effendi would do, but some long-time, dedicated followers of Bahá'u'lláh rose up against him. The first to reject Shoghi Effendi in the West was 'Abdu'l-Bahá's long-time secretary, Ahmad Sohrab. Nell French, one of the earliest American Bahá'ís who was then living in Pasadena, California[39] was the person who told Ahmad Sohrab the contents of the Will and Testament of 'Abdu'l-Bahá. She later wrote that he became intensely agitated, 'his face black, and pacing back and forth, he exclaimed: "This cannot be. Shoghi Effendi knows nothing about the Cause. He was never with 'Abdu'l-Bahá as I have been. I am the one who should have been appointed."'[40]

'Abdu'l-Bahá had sent Sohrab with Mírzá Abu'l-Faḍl as his servant and cook when the great teacher went to the United States in 1901. Ahmad Sohrab's climb to and over his own personal precipice began in 1904 when 'Abdu'l-Bahá told him to leave America with Mírzá Abu'l-Faḍl. He refused to leave and stayed in America. But because he learned English, Ahmad Sohrab became one of 'Abdu'l-Bahá's interpreters when He travelled through North America and Europe in 1912 and 1913, and then served as one of His secretaries in Haifa.[41] 'Abdu'l-Bahá kept those with dubious loyalties close to Himself.

Because of his incessant letter writing and translating, Ahmad Sohrab had gained renown throughout the West. In 1919 he returned to America. Upon hearing of 'Abdu'l-Bahá's passing and Shoghi Effendi's elevation to Guardian, Sohrab began demanding that the Universal House of Justice be established. When Shoghi Effendi began to create local and national spiritual assemblies instead, Sohrab started actively working against him. In 1929, he joined with the wealthy Julie Stuyvesant Chanler to create the New History Society. Though he didn't question the authenticity of the Will and Testament of 'Abdu'l-Bahá, he preached that Shoghi Effendi had 'erred in his function as the Guardian of the Faith'. In 1954, angry about the successes of Shoghi Effendi's Ten Year Crusade, he returned to Haifa and tried to join forces with the remains of the Covenant-breaking community, going so far as to denounce 'Abdu'l-Bahá Himself. Ahmad Sohrab's New History Society did not survive his death in 1958.[42] His wife and daughter 'completely severed all relations with him, indeed so humiliated and disgusted were they by his conduct that they changed their surname'.[43]

Another prominent Bahá'í, this one in the East, was 'Abdu'l-Ḥusayn Ávárih, who had written an authoritative history of the Faith and whom Shoghi Effendi sent to Europe to strengthen the believers soon after he arrived in Haifa. Ávárih was one of the well-known Bahá'ís called to Haifa in March 1922 to consult with Shoghi Effendi. Believing that Shoghi Effendi should immediately establish the Universal House of Justice, Ávárih was not happy when Shoghi Effendi first chose instead to develop the base of the Administrative Order, the local and national spiritual assemblies, before forming the Universal House of Justice. In January 1923, Ávárih went to England and then Egypt. There he began to push his point of view so hard that the Spiritual Assembly of Cairo wrote to Shoghi Effendi, who invited Ávárih to come to Haifa to talk about the problem. Ávárih was in no mood to acquiesce to the notions of someone so much his junior, and even questioned the authenticity of 'Abdu'l-Bahá's Will and Testament. He begrudgingly accepted it as authentic when Shoghi Effendi showed him the original. Ávárih then met the Greatest Holy Leaf and insisted that the Universal House of Justice be established and was 'reported to have uttered a veiled threat that if his demand were not acted upon, he would have no choice but to arouse the Bahá'ís of Persia to rebel against the Guardian'.[44]

Returning to Persia, Ávárih proceeded to cause so much dissension that in May 1924 the Spiritual Assembly of Tehran wrote to Shoghi Effendi about him. When Ávárih saw that he was getting nowhere with his complaints, he wrote to members of 'Abdu'l-Bahá's family, 'saying that there had been misunderstandings and suggesting that if Shoghi Effendi were willing to arrange an annual income for him, he would alter his attitude and stop his activities against the Covenant of Bahá'u'lláh.' That failing, he wrote several letters asking for rein-statement as a Bahá'í but expressed no repentance for his actions, and Shoghi Effendi ignored them. Finding himself isolated and impotent, he was reduced to writing letters to Shoghi Effendi using 'offensive language and vowing to destroy the Faith of Bahá'u'lláh altogether'.[45] He ended up attacking not only Shoghi Effendi, but also 'Abdu'l-Bahá and Bahá'u'lláh 'in the foulest terms'. Like Ahmad Sohrab's wife, Ávárih's wife also cut herself off completely from her errant husband.[46]

The House of Bahá'u'lláh in Baghdad

In Baghdad, since the passing of Bahá'u'lláh in 1892 the House of Bahá'u'lláh there had remained in the possession of a series of custodians and unfortunately had not been well maintained. In 1920, when the British Mandate was established in Iraq and religious freedom appeared to be secured, 'Abdu'l-Bahá authorized extensive repair work to be done on the house under the direction of Ḥájí Maḥmúd Qassábchí.[47] Ḥájí Maḥmúd had learned of the Faith when a Bahá'í in Baghdad gave him the *Star of the West* and the *Kitáb-i-Aqdas*. He became a staunch believer and supported the Cause financially, particularly the legal costs of defending the House of Bahá'u'lláh.

The renovation activity attracted the attention of the neighbouring Shi'as and, after the death of the custodian, Muḥammad Ḥusayn Bábí, they sued for possession on the grounds that he had no heirs. This suit over ownership came about because

> [i]n view of the lack of security which prevailed under the former system of government and the constant hostility of the Shiahs, Bahá'u'lláh decided never to reveal his ownership of the dwelling-houses in question, which to all appearances remained the property of one of his disciples, and for the same reasons the sect abstained from using the dwellings for the exercise of their religion, thus refraining from drawing attention to the sacred character which they attached to the property.[48]

Then in February 1921, the Shi'a petition was granted and the Bahá'ís were evicted. The Minister of Justice, however, overturned the ruling in April and the Bahá'ís regained possession. Then on 23 November a second suit was decided in favour of the Shi'a claimants. This allowed the Shi'as to apply to the Peace Court in early 1922, but before the court could rule, the claimants,

> by threatening a disturbance of the public peace, . . . prevailed upon King Faysal to give an illegal personal order to the Governor of Baghdad to evict the Baha'is from the houses, and to confiscate the keys – these instructions being given in the teeth of a protest from the British High Commissioner. After this, 'the case passed from

court to court and was finally brought before the Court of Appeal at Baghdad, which, by a majority of four (the native members) to one (the British Presiding Justice), decided in favour of the plaintiffs (the Shi'ah)'. This judgment was pronounced by the Mandatory Power – in the comments on the Bahá'í petition which it submitted to the Permanent Mandates Commission – to be not only unsustainable and contrary to law, but also to be under suspicion of having been influenced by political considerations.[49]

In *The Priceless Pearl*, Amatu'l-Bahá Rúḥíyyih Khánum wrote that:

In 1922 [22 February] the government took over the keys of the House in spite of the assurance King Feisal had given that he would respect the claims of the Bahá'ís to a building that had been occupied by their representatives ever since Bahá'u'lláh's departure from Baghdad; His Majesty, for political reasons, now went back on his word and in 1923 the keys were most unjustly delivered once again to the Shi'ahs.[50]

In July of the next year, the Bahá'ís asked the Peace Court to grant them possession of the buildings, which it did on 20 December 1923. The elation of the Bahá'ís was short-lived, however, because the Council of Ministers, with the approval of King Feisal, ordered that the property not be returned until ownership could be proved.

Rúḥíyyih Khánum noted:

When the Guardian was informed of this flagrant miscarriage of justice he immediately mustered the Bahá'í world to take action: he sent nineteen cables to various individuals and national bodies . . . His instructions were that the Bahá'ís should cable and write their protest at this decision to the British High Commissioner in Iraq. Persia and North America – where the Bahá'í communities were numerically strong – were informed that in addition to every local Assembly voicing its protest directly, the National Assembly should not only contact the High Commissioner, but protest directly to both King Feisal of Iraq and the British authorities in London . . . He put the proper phrases into the mouths of those he advised, the eastern friends being told to 'fervently and courteously', 'in firm considerate language', earnestly appeal 'for consideration of their spiritual claims to its possession' and to the 'British sense of justice', while the western believers were informed that 'effective prompt action urgently required . . . protesting vigorously against Court's glaring injustice, appealing for redress to British sense fairness, asserting spiritual claims of Bahá'ís . . . declaring their unfailing resolve to do their utmost to vindicate their legitimate and sacred rights.'. . .

The exchange, during a six-month period, of well-nigh a hundred cables, in addition to a continual correspondence with various agents working to safeguard the Most Holy House, testify in bulk and substance to Shoghi Effendi's preoccupation with this problem. One of his first acts, on receiving the news of the decision of the Supreme Court, was to cable the High Commissioner in Baghdad that: 'The Bahá'ís the world over view with surprise and consternation the Court's unexpected verdict regarding the ownership of Bahá'u'lláh's Sacred House. Mindful of their longstanding and continuous occupation of this property they refuse to believe that Your Excellency will ever countenance such manifest injustice. They solemnly pledge themselves to stand resolutely for the protection of their rights. They appeal to the high sense of honour and justice which they firmly believe animates your Administration. In the name of the family of Sir 'Abdu'l-Bahá 'Abbas and the whole Bahá'í Community Shoghi Rabbani'. On the same day he cabled the heart-broken Keeper of Bahá'u'lláh's House: 'Grieve not. Case in God's hand. Rest assured.'. . .

Shoghi Effendi, however, did not accept defeat so lightly and never rested until the case of the Holy House was brought before the League of Nations Permanent Mandates Commission, in November 1928; the Mandatory Power had upheld the right of the Bahá'ís to the possession of the House, and the Mandates Commission recommended to the Council of the League of Nations that it request the British Government to make representations to the Iraqi Government to redress the denial of justice to the Bahá'ís in this case. The Bahá'ís continued to press the matter from 1928 until 1933, but to no avail because the instruments for enforcing the decision were lacking and the power of the Shí'ahs inside Iraq was such as to cause the entire question to be dropped by the Iraqi Government, whenever that decision was pressed upon it.[51]

A gathering of supporters

Though these initial challenges were daunting, support began to arrive quickly. Muḥammad Taqí Iṣfahání, who had for many years been resident in Egypt and whose home there had been visited by 'Abdu'l-Bahá, appeared soon after the passing of the Master and spent forty days looking at the situation. He was worried that Shoghi Effendi could be vulnerable to attacks by the Covenant-breakers, so began writing a defence of the Bahá'í Faith. He wrote several volumes before he realized that the new Guardian was perfectly able to defend the Faith himself 'and locked away his own work'. He was posthumously named a Hand of the Cause by Shoghi Effendi in 1946.[52]

'Alí-Aṣghar Qazvíní also arrived shortly after 'Abdu'l-Bahá's passing and immediately offered the Guardian his services. For the next twenty-five years 'Alí-Aṣghar served Shoghi Effendi:

> His functions were many: he become lovingly known as 'Mu'allim' or 'teacher' as he used to instruct the Bahá'í children in the Persian language and writing and in the teachings. His pupils included members of the household, of the community, and young servants in need of instruction. He was the Postman of the Guardian; day after day, year after year, going to and from the Post Office in the heat of summer and the storm of winter, with all the heavy and important correspondence and cables of this World Center. He was the ever-vigilant watchman of the home of the Master, keeping the household accounts, solicitous of its every interest, the friend of every friend of the Guardian, the enemy of every enemy of the Cause . . .
>
> It was a touching sight to see him, stooped with age, almost blind with myopia, his hair and beard turning white, going faithfully about his duties, carrying the heavy brief case of mail back and forth from the Post Office; serving the Guardian's guests tea; bringing the cakes for the Feast Days; even on occasion bent double with the bread for the entire house on his back, during the war days when it was rationed and all the complicated cards were in his trustworthy hands.[53]

Fáḍil-i-Mazindarání, one of the most erudite Bahá'í teachers, who had returned from two years teaching and guiding the Bahá'ís in America at the direction of 'Abdu'l-Bahá, was there when Shoghi Effendi arrived:

It was as though he brought an ocean of hope, activity and longing to serve and to sacrifice. No sooner did he arrive than he began to write to all parts of the Bahá'í world. One who met him saw in him the same will, the same love, the same tenderness, the same over-powering desire to serve that he saw in 'Abdu'l-Bahá.[54]

1922

A GATHERING OF THE LEARNED

It didn't take long before those with spiritual eyes began to see the wisdom of 'Abdu'l-Bahá's appointment of Shoghi Effendi as the Guardian. Lady Blomfield wrote:

> Shoghi Effendi is taking up his charge with a deep sincerity and dignity, in one so young it is very touching. One sees more and more the wisdom of the Beloved Master's choice. If he were not so entirely selfless, pure-minded and humble, the tremendous power and influence might mislead him. His mentality is great, his vision so universal, and his wisdom so astonishing as to seem miraculous. Of course, he is informed with the Spirit of the Master, and all the people needed for his helpers are being drawn here from the uttermost ends of the earth.[1]

Lady Blomfield was referring to the group of deepened, sincere and knowledgeable Bahá'ís Shoghi Effendi had called to Haifa from the United States, England, Germany, France and Persia.

Shoghi Effendi convened a group of well-known and knowledgeable Bahá'ís from both West and East to consult on a plan of action. From Iran, the erudite Faḍíl-i-Mazindarání (Jináb-i-Fáḍil), who had been sent by 'Abdu'l-Bahá to America in 1917 to help deepen the believers, had returned to Haifa in 1920 and was still there when the Master died. Ávárih, the prominent teacher and scholar, arrived later. From Burma came Siyyid Mustafa Roumie. The Westerners called included: Laura and Hippolyte Dreyfus-Barney, who arrived from France on 18 February; Americans Mountfort Mills, Roy Wilhelm and Mason

Remey; Consul and Alice Schwarz from Germany; Major Wellesley Tudor-Pole, Lady Blomfield and Ethel Rosenberg from England; and Emogene Hoagg, who was living in Haifa at the time. Jean Stannard, Corinne True and her daughter Katherine, who arrived on 27 February, and Ruth Randall were also there.[2] These were all long-time, deepened believers who had spent a considerable amount of time with 'Abdu'l-Bahá over the previous two decades.

Ethel Rosenberg had met 'Abdu'l-Bahá in 1901 on her first pilgrimage, then returned to Akka again in 1904 and 1907. Lady Blomfield had become a Bahá'í in 1907 and had acted as 'Abdu'l-Bahá's hostess during much of His visit to England in both 1911 and 1913. She had accompanied the bereaved Shoghi Effendi to Haifa from London. Major Tudor-Pole had gone to Egypt in 1911 specifically to meet 'Abdu'l-Bahá and was then involved in His visit to England in 1911 and 1913. The Master stayed at his Clifton Guest House in Bristol on two occasions. Tudor-Pole had also been instrumental in ensuring 'Abdu'l-Bahá's safety at the end of the First World War. Laura Barney, who married Hippolyte Dreyfus in 1911, had made her first pilgrimage to Akka in 1900. Over the next seven years, she made several more visits to the Master which resulted in the book *Some Answered Questions*. Hippolyte Dreyfus went on pilgrimage and met 'Abdu'l-Bahá in 1901 and 1902 and translated some of the Bahá'í Writings directly from Arabic to French. The Dreyfus-Barneys made two more pilgrimages to visit the Master in 1919 and 1920. Emogene Hoagg had met the Master for the first time in 1900 in Akka. She saw Him again when He was in America in 1912, then followed Him to Egypt and Haifa the next year. She stayed in Haifa until mid-1914 and was again a resident in Haifa in 1920.[3]

Mountfort Mills and Roy Wilhelm arrived on the morning of 21 February and were met by Hippolyte Dreyfus and Mírzá Jalál. Ruth Randall's steamer was in Haifa Bay when the two men stepped ashore, but she didn't reach dry land until the afternoon. Mills had first met 'Abdu'l-Bahá in Paris in 1911 and had been very involved with His journey through America. In early 1921, he went on pilgrimage and met the Master one last time. He was to become the Guardian's legal counsel and 'trouble-shooter' during the next decade. Roy Wilhelm had first met 'Abdu'l-Bahá in Akka in 1907. In 1912, he had offered his home in New Jersey to the Master where He hosted a Feast. In 1951, Shoghi Effendi would appoint Roy Wilhelm a Hand of the Cause.

On 22 February, Shoghi Effendi called Mountfort Mills, Roy Wilhelm, the Dreyfus-Barneys, Mírzá Jalál, Dr Lotfullah Hakím, Rúḥí Effendi, Ruth Randall and Munavvar Khánum to what Roy called an 'interesting gathering'. That evening, there was a meeting of about fifteen men, including an 'elderly gentleman who is the son of Subhi Ezel' (a son of Bahá'u'lláh's Covenant-breaking half-brother, Mírzá Yaḥyá). Roy was happily surprised to see that 'even the children of former enemies are now accepting the Cause'.[4]

The next morning, some of the well-known visitors met the illustrious women of the Holy Household, the Greatest Holy Leaf (Bahíyyih Khánum), the Holy Mother (Munírih Khánum, 'Abdu'l-Bahá's wife), and four of the Master's daughters. Roy Wilhelm was much impressed by the Greatest Holy Leaf, noting that her face 'possesses wisdom, tenderness, and power'. The women emphasized that Shoghi Effendi 'must now be regarded as a young and tender shrub, and must be carefully nurtured and protected by all the friends of God. He is at times almost overcome by the thought of his great responsibilities which so suddenly have been placed upon him.'[5]

Roy wrote that Shoghi Effendi was

a most interesting character study. He is, I presume, about twenty-three, small of stature, a singular sweetness of countenance and character, possessing extraordinary brilliance of mind and perception, it seems to me, for one of his years. His quickness too is remarkable. He makes it constantly evident that he wishes authority to rest in the body of the Bahá'ís at large. It seems to me that we should as far as possible shield him from the multitudinous perplexities which continually were presented and pressed upon 'Abdu'l-Baha from all quarters of the globe else his sympathetic mind will be so overburdened that his health may not be equal to the strain, and in any event his time and attention diverted from the most important matters – of bringing into operation the terms of the Will and Testament.[6]

While Shoghi Effendi appeared to be settling into his new role, Lady Blomfield worried about him, too:

I am alert to keep away depressing, whining apes. I say, 'Oh don't pay any attention to that donkey. I will write to him.' 'But Ladyee, perhaps he isn't quite yet a donkey.' I always try to make him laugh, but it is too pathetic! His only recreation is translating some Tablet or prayer written in wonderful classic, mystic Arabic – enough to weary the brain of a well-fed savant with nothing else to do![7]

Some of those who consulted with Shoghi Effendi were initially worried about 'Abdu'l-Bahá's choice. Emogene's early comment was, 'I am so disheartened and trust that the Beloved will protect and guide His choice.' When Mountfort Mills arrived, he was at first 'afraid the giving of authority into the hands of one would bring great trouble. Imagine putting intelligence against the divine knowledge of the Master!' Hippolyte Dreyfus-Barney, too, was worried. But these attitudes changed as they learned more about the young man chosen by the Master.

In the evening of 23 February, Roy Wilhelm and others were invited to a meeting to welcome about twenty newly arrived Persian pilgrims. Roy was highly affected by the gathering, noting,

> These pilgrims represented various religions and classes – some were light, others dark – some were merchants, others landowners or farmers – there were various kinds of costumes – some had red fezes, some black, some tall others short – one or two big turbans, another the head covering and bands, like the Sphinx. But their faces all shone. They expressed great love for us and asked us in turn to send their affection to America . . .[8]

After the meeting, the Greatest Holy Leaf sent Mountfort and Roy a Bahá'í 'bouquet', consisting of the whole top of a mandarin orange tree with about fifty mandarins, 'large, juicy and not only sweet and flavory but as fragrant as the rose'. Roy joked that 'I'm sure Mountfort would not want you to know how many of these wonderful fruits he surrounds in a day – for myself I do not usually eat more than three or four at a time – several times a day.'[9]

Mountfort Mills wrote about his confidence in the young Shoghi Effendi:

> We met Shoghi Effendi, dressed entirely in black, a touching figure. Think of what he stands for today! All the complex problems of the

great statesmen of the world are as child's play in comparison with the great problems of this youth, before whom are the problems of the entire world . . .

We received his joyous, hearty hand grasp and our meeting was short. A bouquet was sent to our room in the form of a young tree filled with nectarines or tangerines. It was brought by Mr. Fugeta. We awoke without any sense of sadness. That feeling was entirely gone. The Master is not gone. His Spirit is present with greater intensity and power, freed from bodily limitations. We can take it into our own hearts and reflect it in greater degrees. In the center of this radiation stands this youth, Shoghi Effendi. The Spirit streams forth from this young man. He is indeed young in force, form and manner, yet his heart is the center of the world today . . .[10]

On 26 February, the Bahá'ís held a memorial service for Helen Goodall, who had passed away a week before in California. She was one of the early Californian Bahá'ís and had hosted 'Abdu'l-Bahá during part of His stay there. Shoghi Effendi attended and chanted a Tablet the Master had revealed for her daughter, Ella Cooper. Lady Blomfield, Lotfullah Hakím and Emogene Hoagg served refreshments that included three dishes of sweet biscuits the women had made.[11] Ethel Rosenberg, Laura Dreyfus-Barney, Roy Wilhelm, Mountfort Mills and many Persian pilgrims attended.[12]

Soon after the memorial, some interesting news arrived from Ishqábád. Apparently Lenin, the Russian leader, had demanded to know about the Bahá'í Faith and had written: 'Inform me of what your religion consists! If I find it false, I will destroy your Temple . . .' When the Bahá'ís informed him of the principles of the Faith, Lenin sent back a courteous letter which said, 'This is from God.'[13] Unfortunately, Lenin died in 1924 and by 1928 his successor, Stalin, began a persecution of the Bahá'ís in Ishqábád that resulted in the government's seizure of the House of Worship and the near eradication of the Bahá'í community there.

Corinne True and her daughter Katherine arrived in Haifa on 27 February. 'Mother True' had first gone on pilgrimage in 1907 and, while there and much to her surprise, 'Abdu'l-Bahá had placed her in charge of the American House of Worship project in Wilmette, which up to that time had been managed by the House of Spirituality, the early version of the Local Spiritual Assembly. That had changed her life:

Being given the responsibility for the Temple was extremely challenging, particularly as a woman in a country where women did
not yet have the opportunity to vote. Because of the marked indi-
vidualism of those days in the Bahá'í community, there were many
'philosophical' differences. The Bahá'ís of that time were immature in the ways of the Faith and 'Abdu'l-Bahá used Corinne True
to begin a transformation of the Bahá'í community. 'Abdu'l-Bahá
encouraged her to consult with the House of Spirituality . . .

Corinne True wanted a nation-wide committee to develop the
Temple plans so that it would not be just Chicago's Temple, but
America's (which at that time also included Canadian believers).
When 'Abdu'l-Bahá enthusiastically approved of this plan, things
moved forward. The next thing 'Abdu'l-Bahá did was send the
Americans a Tablet in which He stated that women should be on
the new national committee. With this directive, the Bahá'í Temple
Unity was created and three women, including Corinne True, were
elected to the Executive.[14]

Corinne True had expected to be impressed by Shoghi Effendi and
she was. She had worried about the possibility of Covenant-breaking,
but it appeared to her that Shoghi Effendi was protected in those early
days. He recognized the potential problems, but he didn't allow them
to affect the way the Faith was administered. Shoghi Effendi had taken
the reins of authority and those around him listened when he spoke,
not just because of his station, but also because what he said made
sense. The young Guardian faced not only the potential problem of
Covenant-breaking, but also the political and social problems of a new
Palestine with British-approved Jewish immigration causing greatly
increased tension between the religious groups. Shoghi Effendi did not
have the luxury of taking time to learn his new job. Corinne noticed
that the Guardian commonly didn't get to bed before 3 a.m. and was
back at work only three hours later. She also noticed that the Greatest
Holy Leaf was always close by and that he consulted her often.[15]

After Corinne went to the Shrines of the Báb and 'Abdu'l-Bahá, she
wrote that

to our astonishment we found two large pictures of the American or
'Mother Mashreq'ul Azkar' (as named by Abdul Baha) hanging on

the walls of the two rooms used by the pilgrims who visit the shrine. These are the only pictures on those sacred walls and were placed there by the Center of the Covenant, himself.

Members of the Master's family repeatedly told us of his love for the model of this Mashreq'ul Azkar and that they had heard him tell the architect, Mr. Louis Bourgeois, that its design had come to him from Baha'Ullah.[16]

On 4 March, Lady Blomfield, Ruth Randall, the Nourse family, Corinne True and Emogene Hoagg, along with members of the Holy Family, went to the Shrine of Bahá'u'lláh. Ruth wrote that

The sun shone down through the glass roof, and the garden was green and lovely. The American friends stood together in the little alcove, and so we could see Shoghi Effendi as he approached the Threshold. One could never forget his face. The expression of adoration and humbleness, combined with a great majesty, cannot be put into words.

Then he chanted and of course, his voice is heavenly, but there, it was surely the voice of an angel singing.[17]

Then Shoghi Effendi surprised the Western pilgrims, just as he had done to the group at the forty-day commemoration, by requesting they sing the hymn, *Nearer My God to Thee*. They were better prepared this time, but emotions became a problem. Ruth Randall began to sing, but the tears and sobbing from the women of the Holy Family were infectious and soon Lady Blomfield, Emogene Hoagg and Corinne True were all sobbing in accompaniment. Ruth wrote: 'How to sing! Well, I controlled my emotions and when I started my voice was very unsteady, but when everyone joined in, I found courage, and Shoghi Effendi was very pleased. It was a very impressive few minutes . . .'[18]

Mason Remey's demons

Mason Remey arrived on 10 March. He had learned of Shoghi Effendi's request when Carrie Kinney called him on the phone and he immediately suspected that it was a trick of the Covenant-breakers. He cabled the new Guardian to confirm the call. Once on his way, Mason wrote that he 'dreaded reaching Haifa' because 'Abdu'l-Bahá was not there. Mason had first met the Master in 1901. He wrote:

> By experience I had known that He was my salvation and my protector, and that what ever happened, and what ever mistakes I made, He would guard and care for me and guide me to His path. However, with Him not there a certain dread hung over me – almost a fear – and as the train rounded the promontory of Carmel and I could look up the mountain and see the Holy Tomb of The Báb, where I knew they had laid the Master's body, my heart sank deep within me.[19]

Within an hour of Mason Remey's arrival in Haifa, Shoghi Effendi greeted him. Mason had last seen him eight years previously and was surprised to find a man 'young in years but premature in poise and depth of spirit and of thought'. He was struck by his similarity to 'Abdu'l-Bahá

> in the shape of poise of his head, his shoulder, his walk and his general bearing. Then I felt the terrible weight and responsibility which had been placed upon that young boy. It seemed overwhelming that he, whose life was just starting, so to speak from the human worldly standpoint, should have had this great responsibility and care thrust upon him, a weight, which would so consume him and place him aside by himself as to eliminate from his life the freedom and joy of the human side of life, which, though not eternal, has a certain call for each of us human beings.[20]

The Guardian gave him a copy of the Will and Testament and asked him to study it carefully.

The next morning, Mason walked up to the Shrine where he found 'Abbas Qulí putting fresh flowers at the thresholds of the inner chambers. He was impressed by the lighting:

> Curtis Kelsey, who went to Haifa from America in order to install electric light plants at the Holy Tombs and in the Bahá'í Colony, has made an artistic arrangement in his wiring of the Tombs upon Mount Carmel and one quite in harmony with the style and character of

the buildings. The black iron lamps hang as formerly, suspended from the high, vaulted ceiling, but he has reversed the shades, thus giving the effect of an indirect lighting system. The venetian iron candelabra, in the inner shrine of the Báb, which the Master permitted me to make and place there some years ago, is still hanging as before, with its nine tall candles, save that in the central sanctuary lamp, where formerly there hung a glass oil container with a floating wick, there is now an electric bulb. A very powerful electric light is placed on the exterior of the tomb, directly above the main doorway to the north. This is lighted every evening and it forms a focal point on the mountainside and is visible for many miles out at sea.

Several times, in the night, after the household had quieted, Lotfullah Hakim and I climbed up the mountain to the Tomb of the Master, for a few moments of prayer before the door of the Shrine which at that late hour was invariably locked though lights from within might have led one to imagine the building to be open. As is customary in the Orient, burial shrines of importance are kept illumined by night. The Bahá'í sacred Shrines are never left in darkness.

I wish that I might adequately describe the spiritual experience of those nocturnal pilgrimages. The beauty of the spot is beyond description in words. In the clear, scintillating moonlight of the Orient the eye can see for many miles. From this Holy Tomb, Mount Hermon, with its cap of snow, seventy or eighty miles distant, was distinctly visible in the clear moonlight. About the Tomb are fragrant trees, shrubs and flowers. On still nights, when there was little wind, the air would often be heavy with the fragrance of orange blossoms as we knelt on the doorsill pouring out our hearts in prayer and supplication . . .[21]

Curtis Kelsey had come to Haifa in 1919 at the instigation of Roy Wilhelm. Roy was sending over electrical power plants to light the Shrines of the Báb and Bahá'u'lláh and he wanted Curtis to set it up. When Curtis arrived, he found himself working with a Persian electrician, Ḥusayn-i-Kahrubáyí, whose only English word was 'okay', while Curtis's only Persian word was 'yes'. But they created a system that worked efficiently enough to get the job done well.[22]

A few days after his arrival, Mason received a telegram from Houghston McBain saying that he and his mother would be arriving in Haifa soon. Mason had met the McBains on the steamer to Egypt and they had become so interested in the Faith that they changed their schedule in order to visit Haifa. Shoghi Effendi gave Mason the privilege over the next three days of escorting them to Bahjí, Akka and the Shrine of the Báb. They found that the Most Great Prison had been converted by the British into a prison and was 'swarming with prisoners'. Mrs McBain enjoyed the company of the women of the Holy Family on at least two occasions.[23]

Mason went with the McBains to the Garden of Riḍván and was dismayed to find it in a 'most deplorable state of dilapidation':

> Fences down – seats and benches falling apart and bridges unsafe, while the great voiliaire, built out over the river where the white peacocks were formerly kept, had collapsed and part of its superstructure had fallen through the flooring into the water. The flowerbeds had been kept up, however, and were a mass of blossoms, but dry rot was attacking many of the trees – in fact the two great mulberry trees beneath which Baha'u'llah used to sit were quite riddled by decay and seemed to be so far passed hope that the gardener had set out two new trees near by, hoping, he explained to us, that these would eventually grow to take the place of the older ones.[24]

Shortly after Mason's arrival, Consul Albert and Alice Schwarz reached Haifa from Stuttgart. They had met 'Abdu'l-Bahá in Stuttgart in 1913 and then had the bounty of having Him stay at their health spa in Bad Mergentheim. Albert was later called 'Germany's outstanding pioneer worker' and named a Disciple of 'Abdu'l-Bahá by Shoghi Effendi.[25] Only one other German, Johanna Hauff, had been able to make a pilgrimage to Haifa before and the Schwarzes were very 'joyful and happy'. Albert spent some of his time there making sketches of the Bahá'í holy places.[26]

One Sunday, Ethel Rosenberg, Emogene Hoagg, Rúḥangíz Khánum, Lotfullah Hakím and Mason Remey rode up Mount Carmel in the carriage. At one point, they found an old cannon. When they discovered that it still swivelled on its mount, Rúḥangíz Khánum and Emogene climbed aboard the gun and Lotfullah and Mason spun them around. When Rúḥangíz Khánum suddenly saw some other people walking towards them, she 'descended in great haste from her perch, lowering her veil as she did so' and sought refuge in the carriage.[27]

On 21 March, Naw-Rúz, all the pilgrims gathered at the House of the Master to view the portraits of the Báb and Bahá'u'lláh. For this viewing, however, a photograph of 'Abdu'l-Bahá was added for the first time. After viewing the portraits, the pilgrims moved to 'Abdu'l-Bahá's room and Mason Remey remembered that:

> Flowers had been placed here and there – the room was just as it had been while He had been there. The light filtered into the chamber through the closed blinds and plain white curtains falling upon the bedstead . . . Here the grief of the friends overflowed though always restrained. I was one of the last to enter the room – Emogene Hoagg and I were there together and for a few moments we knelt in prayer while our tears flowed in silence.
>
> Later on in the middle of the afternoon we all gathered at the Pilgrim House on Mount Carmel for tea before visiting the Holy Tombs. Shoghi Effendi was there and he led the group to the Tomb. He poured rose water on our hands as we entered the shrine. Visiting the tomb of the Báb first, we all stood while Shoghi Effendi chanted a prayer of visitation. Then we all went to the Master's tomb where we seated ourselves in Oriental fashion on the floor while two of the friends chanted in melodious voices from the Holy Words. After this we withdrew one by one from the building going down the mountain singly and in small groups.[28]

Mason's arrival was not welcomed by everyone. Ruth Randall complained directly to Shoghi Effendi and Hippolyte Dreyfus mentioned that Mason was 'good for sending out letters', possibly an allusion to Mason's attempt in 1918, as a member of a Committee of Investigation, to warn about what he viewed as wide-spread Covenant-breaking in the American Bahá'í community. When many in the American Bahá'í community had rejected his opinions, Mason's ego was bruised.[29] Then when his design for the Temple at Wilmette was rejected in favour of one by Louis Bourgeois, his feelings of persecution increased, pushing him to go so far as to claim that the selection proved that 'the Master's policies were so overthrown'.[30] In that first conversation, Shoghi Effendi had brought up the subject of disunity by saying that it was

his wish that all the past should be entirely wiped out and forgotten, and with the exception of those whom the Master had pronounced as violators that all should be received by all the friends. He said that Fareed, Khierllah, Shuah Ullah and Kirchners were to be avoided, but that _____ were received by all and really loved with true Bahá'í affection and the past obliterated. Then in addition to this he said that the believers were to be very mindful and when anyone stirred up trouble it was to be reported to the Assembly of Spiritual Consultation to solve – quietly and without general talk.[31]

Mason had been asked by some Bahá'ís in America to bring up this exact topic, but the newly installed Guardian had answered before he could ask. Unfortunately, Mason had a difficult time wiping out his memories of when he had chaired the Committee of Investigation and what he saw as the opposition to its conclusions. In 1934, he wrote a document called *The Violation in Chicago* in which he complained bitterly about those who had disagreed with him and went so far as to name names.[32] After he left Haifa, Mason wrote:

in my inner thoughts a change was taking place, and this change began to objectify to me during the days of my voyage. Since the fall of 1917 a struggle had been on in the Cause in America. This had first been generally felt at the time of the violation at Chicago when a partial split formed over the Kirchner affair – a split which was never really healed, and which latterly has continued as a widening difference between those friends who champion 'Reality' and its policy of supporting certain people as against those people who stand with the Washington and Chicago Assemblies against those people and their doings. Of late this has become a breach between the people of the New York Assembly upon one hand, and Chicago upon the other hand – the other assemblies throughout the country for the most part siding with Chicago.

These and many other matters I reflected over during the voyage and now before landing I have quite definitely made up my mind that I must get away from all this discord in order to find that peace of soul so necessary for Baha'i Service.[33]

Mason also wrote that he did not know the Guardian very well:

I feel that personally I know Shoghi Effendi but slightly and that from this personal standpoint there is no particular friendship nor affinity between us of which I am aware – nevertheless, I am conscious of a very deep spiritual devotion to him because of the Master's Testament which is all the greater in its spiritual intensity because it lacks the human element which is changing and ephemeral. Although often I could neither understand nor follow in thought the reasons why Shoghi Effendi made certain decisions, nevertheless at all times I had an intense desire to serve him, to do his bidding and to support him in making his way as easy and tranquil as possible.[34]

From being a frequent visitor to the Holy Land, Mason Remey would return to Haifa only when called by Shoghi Effendi to be part of the International Bahá'í Council in late 1950.

Consulting with the architect

The state of the Riḍván Garden was one of the myriad problems the Guardian faced, but he was already making plans to renovate many sacred Bahá'í places. He consulted with Mason Remey, who was a well-known architect in America, about a possible shrine for Bahá'u'lláh. One of the Guardian's initial ideas was to place the Shrine of Bahá'u'lláh above that of the Báb. Mason explained his concept:

His thought was a high dome upon the elevation of land adjoining the Tomb of The Báb directly south [uphill] where stands the cypress trees beneath which Baha'u'llah used to sit. Under this dome would be the tomb of Baha'u'llah, while a little way lower down the mountain to the north from the Tomb of the Báb would be the tomb of Abdul Baha, the three tombs to be so composed that they would form one composition in the grouping upon the three levels.[35]

At one point 'Abbas Qulí, the caretaker of the Shrine of the Báb, joined them and said that 'Abdu'l-Bahá had on three occasions emphatically stated that no one should be buried near the Shrine of the Báb. The next day, 'Abbas Qulí brought a rough sketch of the Master's plan for the Shrine. 'Abdu'l-Bahá wanted three more rooms to be added to the existing Shrine to make it square. Then a roofed arcade with columns was to be built over the structure. On top of that was to be a second storey with nine rooms with the centre room being capped by a 'dome of importance'. The eight rooms surrounding the dome were to connect one to another so that pilgrims could walk around the central chamber.[36]

Shoghi Effendi also talked with Mason about the future Mashriqu'l-Adhkár, the House of Worship, to be built on Mount Carmel. The Guardian preferred the promontory of Mount Carmel, close to the monastery. He envisioned nine terraces descending the steep mountainside to the plain below.[37] Shortly before Mason left Haifa, Shoghi Effendi took him to the plain between Haifa and Akka to look for another possible site for the future Shrine of 'Abdu'l-Bahá. They stopped at the halfway house, then walked a quarter to a half mile inland to a point about halfway between the shore and the railroad. Shoghi Effendi envisioned a piece of land about one square mile, covered with trees and crossed by waterways and lakes with the Shrine in the middle in the style of the Taj Mahal. Shoghi Effendi was motivated to look at this site because 'Abdu'l-Bahá had once mentioned His wish to be buried on the sands of the beach half way between the Shrines of the Báb and Bahá'u'lláh.[38] The final decision, Shoghi Effendi said, was to be left to the Universal House of Justice.[39]

On another evening, Mason went with Shoghi Effendi and a few others to the Pilgrim House. When they arrived, Shoghi Effendi, placed a package on a table and carefully unwrapped it. It was the original Will and Testament of the Master. Mason wrote:

> We stood about the table as he reverently laid the package thereon, carefully unfolding the envelope from a silk handkerchief in which it was wrapped. As he took the three Tablets from the cover we saw that each was in the handwriting of the Master – written, as Shoghi Effendi called our attention to witness – without hesitation or correction and signed by the Master in several places. We stood with bated breath in the presence of this document of documents in which is contained the wondrous plan for the spiritual organization of the Cause of God and our guidance for a thousand or thousands of years.

The substance of the Testament was, of course, most unexpected. No one could have anticipated its wonderful ordinances. But as one studies it and imbibes its thought he sees at once that no other plan could have been made for guarding and preserving the Cause save the one which the Master has given in his Will. Never have I read anything which gave me the joy and the inspiration that this holy document produced in my heart. It filled my heart with the assurance that the Cause was safely guarded. It gives us a fixed direction toward which to turn and a permanent center about which we all are to revolve so long as we are in this world.[40]

This is an interesting reaction from one who, in 1960, tragically broke that Covenant by declaring himself to be the second Guardian. To his own detriment, Mason learned exactly how that document he had so admired that night would safeguard the Cause of God against his own future perfidy.

The Tablets of the Divine Plan become the guide

The young Guardian strongly encouraged all the Westerners to carefully study the Will and Testament of 'Abdu'l-Bahá, and began illuminating the importance of the divinely appointed Administrative Order of the Faith. He pointedly noted that the 'local Spiritual Assemblies are responsible for the spiritual affairs of the Cause in their respective centres and that likewise the Convention and the executive Committee [of Bahá'í Temple Unity] are responsible for general spiritual matters.'[41] Lady Blomfield was highly impressed with the young Guardian's rapidly increasing strength and wisdom:

it is so wonderful as to be miraculous. These men here, experienced in the world as they are, are amazed at the wisdom he shows in the administration of the cause. Such tasks!! And he is only 24. Such a sweet simple-pure-minded boy, trained all his life by the Master who says in His Testament, 'Oh Friends, take care of Shoghi Effendi. Let not the dust of despondency shadow his radiant nature!!' It is really a sacred trust.[42]

Evidently, most of the Guardian's consultations about the immediate future of the Faith primarily involved Mountfort Mills, Roy Wilhelm, the Dreyfus-Barneys, Lady Blomfield, Major Tudor-Pole and the Schwarzes. Mason Remey was not involved except peripherally. Others had been called from Persia and India, but had not arrived in time to be part of the consultations with those from the West.[43]

The consensus of opinion of everyone, except the Guardian, appeared to be that the Universal House of Justice should be elected as quickly as possible. The Governor of Haifa, Colonel Sir Stewart Symes, and his wife visited Shoghi Effendi one afternoon. Badí Bushrui, his private secretary, and a few others including the Western believers were with him. The visitors and pilgrims gathered at Mírzá Jalál's home and a prime topic of conversation was the claim of Mírzá Muḥammad-'Alí. The Governor expressed the hope that the Universal House of Justice could be formed as the authoritative Bahá'í organization, saying that its establishment would allow the issue of the ownership of the Shrine of Bahá'u'lláh to be 'removed from the status of a family quarrel and placed on the firm legal basis of a permanent religious organization.'[44] The group also discussed the seizure of the House of Bahá'u'lláh in Baghdad.[45]

But on 5 March, Shoghi Effendi, with that intuitive spiritual power bequeathed to him by the Master, began his work by first constructing the foundation of the World Order formulated by Bahá'u'lláh and 'Abdu'l-Bahá. He wrote that there was a

> vital necessity of having a local Spiritual Assembly in every local-
> ity where the number of adult declared believers exceeds nine, and
> of making provision for the indirect election of a Body that shall
> adequately represent the interests of the friends . . .[46]

He intuitively understood that before the dome (the Universal House of Justice) could be built, the building (the National Spiritual Assemblies) had to be raised; and that before the building could be erected, a strong foundation (Local Spiritual Assemblies) had to be prepared. So, within two months of having been named the Guardian of the Cause of God, Shoghi Effendi set the Bahá'í world on a road previously unsuspected by the mass of the believers, one that would lead to the future World Order of Bahá'u'lláh. By April Shoghi Effendi had set in motion, not the election of the Universal House of Justice as promoted by those who looked upon his age as a sign of immaturity, but the building of an administrative order that would, in the fullness of time, allow that body to be elected. When he sent Ethel Rosenberg back to the United Kingdom, Roy Wilhelm, Mason Remey and Mountfort Mills to America, and Consul Albert and Alice Schwarz to Germany, he gave them all the task of developing National Spiritual Assemblies.[47]

Shoghi Effendi's guide became his Grandfather's *Tablets of the Divine Plan* that called for the spiritual conquest of the planet. The Guardian began implementing the first five of 'Abdu'l-Bahá's Tablets immediately. These called for the movement of Bahá'ís into those parts of North America where there as yet were no Bahá'ís. Pioneers were asked to go into 'virgin' states and provinces, and, in states and provinces that did have Bahá'ís, into towns and cities where no Bahá'ís lived. He encouraged those pioneers to raise up Local Spiritual Assemblies and he began educating the National Spiritual Assemblies, once elected, on how to manage the local ones. Shoghi Effendi was building the Bahá'í Administrative Order from the bottom up. He also extended this plan to other countries with Bahá'í communities.

Shoghi Effendi made it clear that he was not the Master and that things were changing. He wore Western clothes and did not go to the mosque. In one of his letters, he wrote: 'It is difficult to break with some of the customs and traditions of the past, and familiarize the vast number of Bahá'ís, so diverse in their outlook and conception, with the necessary changes and requirements of this new phase in the history of the Cause.'[48] He illustrated the depth of the changes when, one day, a group of Muslim muftis (clergy) arrived to pay their respects. The Guardian excused himself because he was very busy at that time. Some of the family reminded him that 'Abdu'l-Bahá had always received these muftis and feared that they would be offended if they were not seen. The Guardian replied that the 'time had passed for such considerations and that he must devote himself undivided to the Cause'.[49] As Amatu'l-Bahá Rúḥíyyih Khánum later explained:

At the time of the ascension of Abdu'l-Bahá I don't think it would be an exaggeration to say that the community of Bahá'ís was made up of Christian Bahá'ís, Moslem Bahá'ís, Buddhist Bahá'ís, and so on. Everyone in the world has just so much force, just so much work they can do. 'Abdu'l-Bahá had given all His force and had accomplished all He could for the Faith. Then came the young Guardian. The Guardian has made us Bahá'ís. He separated us from the old roots. He saw to it that we put down roots firmly in the teachings of Bahá'u'lláh. A father is loving and patient with his children. When the elder brother takes over he has less paternal patience and much more brotherly discipline. We got this from Shoghi Effendi.[50]

Comings and goings

During all this time, pilgrims came and pilgrims went. Mason Remey left Haifa in early April and Shoghi Effendi gave him a small package containing an amazing gift. Inside were some strands of Bahá'u'lláh's hair and dried blood. The Guardian also gave him some partially burned candles from the Shrine of 'Abdu'l-Bahá to give to the delegates at the upcoming National Convention.[51]

One day, an American pilgrim named Clarence Welsh arrived. He had been invited by 'Abdu'l-Bahá and had spent a year working to save enough for his pilgrimage. Even so, he had had to travel steerage class, the cheapest possible, and was dismayed to find that he had arrived too late to meet the Master. He had brought a camera and a large supply of film and hoped to defray his expenses selling photographs when he returned home.[52]

At some point, Lady Blomfield began to develop the idea of writing a history of the Faith. She began collecting stories from those around her in Haifa. In this she was strongly encouraged by Shoghi Effendi. The result was the book *The Chosen Highway*.[53]

On 24 March, Lady Blomfield and the Dreyfus-Barneys took a week-long trip to the Damascus area. The trip didn't get off to a good start: somewhere in Lebanon, the car broke down in the desert. While Hippolyte Dreyfus, the chauffeur and their guide became mechanics, the two women walked ahead. A group of Bedouin women, 'handsome after one got used to the tattoo marks covering their chins', tried to entice them to their tents. Finally, the car appeared over the sand hill, with the guide dressed in 'voluminous trousers, beautiful purple jacket and wonderful head gear of purple and blue green striped silk' riding on the step. Before reaching them, the ladies watched the car ford the Kashon River, 'now quite a formidable rapid stream, with booby trap holes in it', with three of its wheels disappearing beneath the water before it managed to surmount the far bank. 'However, all was well and we went on gaily.'[54]

Roy Wilhelm departed on 25 March, followed soon afterwards by Mountfort Mills, Consul and Mrs Schwartz and Mason Remey. Emogene Hoagg left on 28 March.

1922

THE FIRST RESPITE IN SWITZERLAND

On 5 April, Shoghi Effendi left Haifa for Europe in order to compose himself for what he knew was to come. Just before leaving, the Guardian appointed nine people to form the Haifa Spiritual Assembly. Initially, this body was created to work with the Greatest Holy Leaf to care for the Cause while he was gone. It continued to function until 1938 or 1939, primarily sending out a newsletter, called the Haifa News Letter, which contained material from Shoghi Effendi about the activities of the Faith from around the world.[1]

Later recounting his reason for leaving, Shoghi Effendi told Leroy Ioas that

> I had in mind that 'Abdu'l-Bahá would give me the honor of calling the great conclave which would elect the Universal House of Justice. I thought in His Will and Testament that that was probably what He was instructing to be done. But he said, instead of that, I found that I was appointed the Guardian of the Cause of God. I didn't want to be the Guardian of the Cause.
>
> In the first place, I didn't think that I was worthy. Next place, I didn't want to face these responsibilities . . . I didn't want to be the Guardian. I knew what it meant. I knew that my life as a human being was over. I didn't want it and I didn't want to face it.
>
> So remember, I left the Holy Land, and I went up into the mountains of Switzerland, and I fought with myself until I conquered myself. Then I came back and I turned myself over to God and I was the Guardian. Now, he said, every Bahá'í in the world, every person in the world, has to do exactly the same thing . . . Every

Bahá'í must fight with himself and conquer himself. And when he has conquered himself, then he becomes a true instrument for the service of the Cause of God – and not until that. And he won't achieve his greatest success until he has done it.[2]

Rúḥíyyih Khánum later said that

he had to go to a sanatorium he was so ill. He went and walked for hours and hours in the mountains. All of those early years of his Guardianship when he went to Switzerland in the summers because he was absolutely broken down; he couldn't stand any more of his problems and his burdens. He used to go walking in the mountains . . . sometimes fourteen to sixteen hours a day, day after day . . . just to lose himself and to try, perhaps, in physical exhaustion to quiet the clamour of his thoughts and his heart. He passed eventually through that period of intense sufferings, and as 'Abdu'l-Bahá said in His Will that he may grow to be a fruitful tree, he grew in stature, in greatness, in experience, and all his innate qualities began to be manifested to the Bahá'í world.[3]

On 7 April 1922 the Haifa Spiritual Assembly received a letter from the Greatest Holy Leaf saying that

the Guardian of the Cause of God, the chosen Branch, the Leader of the people of Bahá, Shoghi Effendi, under the weight of sorrows and boundless grief, has been forced to leave here for a while in order to rest and recuperate, and then return to the Holy Land to render his services and discharge his responsibilities.[4]

Shoghi Effendi himself wrote to the American Bahá'í community saying,

This servant, after that grievous event and great calamity – the ascension of His Holiness 'Abdu'l-Bahá to the Abhá Kingdom – has been so stricken with grief and pain and so entangled in the troubles (created) by the enemies of the Cause of God, that I consider my presence here, at such a time and in such an atmosphere, is not in accordance with the fulfilment of my important and sacred duties.

For this reason, unable to do otherwise, I have left for a time the affairs of the Cause, both at home and abroad, under the supervision of the Holy Family and the headship of the Greatest Holy Leaf – may my soul be a sacrifice to her – until, by the Grace of God, having gained health, strength, self-confidence and spiritual energy, and having taken into my hands, in accordance with my aim and desire, entirely and regularly the work of service, I shall attain to my utmost spiritual hope and aspiration.[5]

In her efforts to manage the affairs of the Faith during Shoghi Effendi's absence, the Greatest Holy Leaf had the full support of Munírih Khánum.[6]

Shoghi Effendi left with a cousin and initially went to Germany to consult doctors. Rúḥíyyih Khánum remembers him saying that they were very disturbed because he had almost no reflexes. Then the traumatized young Guardian discovered the high mountains. He stayed in a small room in the home of a Mr Hauser in Interlaken, Switzerland. Rúḥíyyih Khánum, in *The Priceless Pearl*, wrote:

This man was an old Swiss guide in whose house on the main street Shoghi Effendi had rented a tiny room, the attic under the eaves, for which he paid about one franc a night. The ceiling was so low that when his uncle-in-law, a big man, came to see him, he could not stand upright. There was a small bed, a basin and a pitcher of cold water to wash with. Interlaken is in the heart of the Bernese Oberland and the starting point for innumerable excursions into the surrounding mountains and valleys. Often long before sunrise Shoghi Effendi would start out, dressed in knee breeches, a Norfolk jacket and black wool puttees on his legs, sturdy mountain boots, and a small cheap canvas rucksack on his back and carrying a cane. He would take a train to the foot of some mountain or pass and begin his excursion, walking often ten up to sixteen hours, usually alone, but sometimes accompanied by whichever young relative was with him; they could seldom stand the pace and after a few days would start making their excuses. From here he also climbed some of the higher mountains, roped to a guide . . . His longest walk, he said, was forty-two kilometres over two passes. Often he would be caught by the rain and walk on until his clothes dried on him. He had a deep love of scenery and I believe these restless, exhausting hour after hour marches healed to some extent the wounds left so deep in his heart by the passing of the Master.

Shoghi Effendi would tell me of how he practically never ate anything until he got back at night, how he would go to a small hotel . . . and order *pommes sauteés*, fried eggs and salad as these were cheap and filling, go home to his little room under the eaves and fall into bed exhausted and sleep, waking to drink a carafe of the cold mountain water, and sleep again, until, driven by this terrible soul-restlessness, he arose and set out again before daybreak . . . He never travelled other than third class . . . If he travelled by night he would sleep on the hard wooden benches, his head on his rucksack, more than those who travelled with him could stand.[7]

During a few of these Swiss retreats, Shoghi Effendi had a bicycle and would cycle over the passes. Rúḥíyyih Khánum wrote that she always wondered how he returned from those trips safely with his 'verve, audacity and lack of mechanical sense . . . He had very little feeling for machines, being a typical intellectual . . .[8] These bicycles were not the modern multispeed machines ridden today, but one-speed, heavy and solidly built. The caption to a photo of Shoghi Effendi with his bicycle in the snow in *The Guardian of the Bahá'í Faith* reads: 'ON TOP OF THE WORLD. His bicycle – the poor man's car – became a favourite of Shoghi Effendi. He sometimes climbed the highest passes in Switzerland, pushing it up and riding down.'[9]

Genevieve Coy

Genevieve Coy arrived in Haifa on 1 June 1922 on her way to becoming the director of the Tarbíyat School for Girls in Tehran. The previous director, Lillian Kappes, had passed away the year before and 'Abdu'l-Bahá had requested that the American Bahá'í community find a replacement for her. At the 1921 American Annual Convention, Genevieve, 'a specialist in the education of gifted children and teacher of psychology in one of the great State Universities, who this spring took her Ph.D. at Columbia University, New York,' was confirmed in the post. She spent the next year learning Persian and departed New York on 10 May 1922.[10]

Genevieve had met 'Abdu'l-Bahá in Haifa in 1920. Though neither He nor His successor, Shoghi Effendi, were present when she arrived this time, she found her pilgrimage deeply spiritual and full of memories of the Master. While on the train passing through Palestine, she commented on the

Green fields, many flocks of black goats, many herds of black and white cattle, herdsmen in tattered garments . . . Trees with long green leaves, along some small brook – white melons ripening in the fields – the blue, blue sea breaking in whitest foam on the yellow sand! And then the curve of Mount Carmel, Acca white in a misty distance, and the Tomb of the Bab on the mountainside. It all seems a dream from which I must awaken soon – to be here again in this blessed land! The air is fragrant with many flowers, the breeze is cool and sweet – God's peace breathes about one.[11]

Lotfullah Hakím met her at the station and took her to the Pilgrim House. It was like a home-coming, seeing its 'high-ceilinged rooms – the faint fragrance that greets one – the cleanliness – the tiled floors, the beautiful rugs.' She noted that 'the two gateways are covered with a riot of bougainvillea, masses of dark-red blossoms, hundreds of them, almost hide the green leaves. If I stand at the window I can look up to the Tomb and the Mosafer Khaneh, halfway up the mountainside.'

The next morning Lotfullah met her at six o'clock and together they hiked up to the Shrines of the Báb and 'Abdu'l-Bahá. The caretaker, 'Abbas Qulí, opened both Shrines for them and, leaving their shoes, they entered

first the Tomb of the Bab. To be again in that place, at that threshold in prayer – what words can tell what it means to one's heart and spirit? It is so perfectly natural and easy to pray there. One's prayer knows no weariness. One realizes God so near, that one needs make no effort to find Him. 'Love divine, all love excelling' becomes the supreme reality. Prayer for all the friends in America, all the Bahais, prayer with all the devotion of my spirit for the dear ladies of the Master's household and for Shoghi Effendi, that the divine love may bring them perfect comfort and spiritual joy!

And then we went into that room which I had never before

entered – the Master's shrine. In physical furnishings it is like that of the Bab. The outer room is slightly larger, I think, and the outer door is not directly in line with the inner door. Lovely rugs are on the floor, copies of one or two Tablets are on the walls. I stood at the outer doorway a long time, trying to realize the meaning of the place to which I had come. Then I knelt at the inner threshold a moment – afterwards a little away from it. Mirza Lotfullah placed on the threshold the jasmine flowers that he had brought in from the garden. We prayed silently for a long time. The Master's spirit dwells there in peace and love. What one feels, or how, I do not know. It is the triumph of life. I suppose for those who were here at the Master's funeral, who saw his body laid in that room, there must be associations of great sadness and loneliness with that spot – but for those who come to Haifa to find his love and his service in the lives of the friends, for those the Tomb of the Master is a place of joy. One knows as never before the victory of life that never ceases, but only changes its form. Words cannot suggest it. It is one of the gifts of God that He sends to those who long for union with the Beloved One.[12]

When they left the Shrine, 'Abbas Qulí invited them to his house for tea. He then took them up to the little room on top of his house that had been especially built for 'Abdu'l-Bahá. The view looked to the north, south and west and included the valley of Achor, the slopes of Mount Carmel and the Shrine. The caretaker explained that

Here, in this little room the Master used to stay; often at night the friends would hear him walking about on the house-top, chanting. Here he used to receive the notables of the town and country. In the room is the bed the Master used to use, and also the chair, in which he used to sit out in front of the Tomb, when meetings were held there. Above the bed are now hung many pictures of the Master, alone, and with groups of friends. Abbas Gholi talked to us for quite a long time about the Master and the days he had spent there near the Tomb. He told about the building of that upper room. The Master had said that he would like a room there near the Tomb. He asked Abbas Gholi if he could not build him one, and the care-taker of the Tomb said, yes, where would the Master like to have it. The

Master suggested that he would like to have it on the top of the house. Abbas Gholi said that the walls of the house were not strong enough to have another story built on top of them. Then the Master said that he would like to have it built in the garden, or above the Tomb. Abbas Gholi said that much excavation would be required for that. Finally the Master said, 'Never mind; do not trouble about it.' Not long after that one of the friends had built for the Master a little room on top of the stable, at the Master's house. Then the Master said to Abbas Gholi, 'Could you not build a house like that on the roof', and he said 'Oh, yes.' The Master said, 'But I thought that you told me you could not build a room on top of your house' So Abbas Gholi said, 'But a small room like that would have thin walls, and that could easily be built.' The Master smiled and said,' Very good!', and so the room was built.[13]

Genevieve loved the Greatest Holy Leaf, who at that time was struggling under the loss of the Master and the demands of guiding the Bahá'í Faith in the absence of Shoghi Effendi. Genevieve would visit her every night and massage her back.[14]

On 6 July, Genevieve, Fujita and Ḥusayn-i-Kahrubáyí drove to Bahjí with Isfandíyár, 'Abdu'l-Bahá's long-time carriage driver. Ḥusayn was going out to charge the batteries at the Shrine. They arrived at about 8 p.m. and were welcomed by the caretaker, Abu'l-Qásim, his helper and an Arab policeman, who was stationed there by the authorities to keep the peace since the Covenant-breakers had stolen the keys to the Shrine. Abu'l-Qásim spoke English fairly well so Genevieve complimented him on the beauty of the gardens around the Shrine of Bahá'u'lláh. He answered, 'Yes, it is the garden of Baha'Ullah, and therefore it must be beautiful!'[15]

When they went to the Shrine, it was illuminated by the lights installed by Curtis Kelsey and Ḥusayn-i-Kahrubáyí earlier in the year. Genevieve was very impressed by how the lighting was done: 'The thing which seemed to me most beautiful about the lighting was that the lights were so placed that they shone out from under a fern in the center of the little inner garden. The light came out soft and green through the fronds of the fern.' After prayers, Ḥusayn turned on all the lights which, Genevieve said, 'made me think of Abdul Baha's comment, when he was in America, that Baha'Ullah always loved light.' Fujita also showed her a bronze vase made by Tiffany, inset with jewels and cloisonné work (a pattern of blue and yellow enamel and wire) sent by the American Bahá'ís in commemoration of the Master's visit to their country.[16]

The next morning, Isfandíyár drove Fujita and Genevieve to Akka and to the House of 'Abbúd. From there, they wandered through the bazaars, stopping at one shop where they encountered a very old Bahá'í who had been Bahá'u'lláh's cook when He lived in the prison. Then they continued to the House of 'Abdulláh Pá<u>sh</u>á. From there, it was a short distance to the Most Great Prison. When they arrived, the British were in the midst of a huge renovation project and most of the interior of the Prison

> was cut off by a barbed fence, and beyond that was a garden. The great reservoir in the center had been whitewashed and was as white as new snow! Everywhere was cleanliness and order. About the reservoir were planted a circle of eucalyptus trees which were higher than a man. And in the corners were flower gardens in a very flourishing condition . . . There were a number of soldiers about, resting or looking after the garden. We were not permitted to go inside the wire fence, so we did not see the rooms at the end of the barracks. The rooms that Baha'Ullah and the family occupied are in good condition, clean, and apparently not used by the soldiers.[17]

The beginnings of the Administrative Order

On 6 June, Shoghi Effendi's emphasis on developing the Administrative Order resulted in the creation of the All-England Bahá'í Council, with members chosen to represent the three Bahá'í centres in the country at that time, London, Manchester and Bournemouth. The body included Dr John Esslemont, Ethel Rosenberg, Edward Hall, George Simpson, Albert Joseph, Jacob Joseph, Virginia Thornburgh-Cropper, Claudia Coles, Helen Grand, 'Mother' George and Miss Fry. Within a year, this group, as noted by Shoghi Effendi in *God Passes By*, would be converted into one of the first National Spiritual Assemblies in the world.

Stanwood and Nayyan Cobb

Stanwood Cobb and his wife, Nayyan, arrived in Haifa during the summer. He had twice previously been on pilgrimage, in 1908 and

1910, and spent time with 'Abdu'l-Bahá. This time neither the Master nor Shoghi Effendi were there, but that didn't diminish the impact of being in the Holy Land. He wrote:

As for our nine days in Haifa, they were days naturally full of spiritual inspiration. I was especially privileged in visiting on several occasions the Holy Family, a favor not hitherto granted to male pilgrims to Haifa. They told us intimate details of the life and passing of Abdul Baha; – how he refused every comfort which his family tried to secure for his last days, how upon his death he had hardly one change of clothing. Anything above this amount of clothing he had always given away. Thus his life stands out as a beacon light, pointing to others the way of service.

We made many visits and prayers at the tombs of Abdul Baha and of the Bab. From the beautiful garden surrounding the tombs we looked down the mountain side to the sea, already perceiving in our imagination the glorious parkway which shall one day rise from the Mediterranean to the Holy Tombs. Even now the authorities of Haifa are planning to construct such a boulevard, thus fulfilling the prophecy of Abdul Baha . . .

I will mention two experiences while at Haifa, experiences of the inner spiritual life which I shall never forget. One of these experiences came from the extraordinary privilege I had, while visiting the Bahje or tomb of Baha'Ullah, of sitting in the armchair in the chamber of Baha'Ullah, where Abdul Baha so often sat looking out over the plains of Acca to the sea. For just a minute I sat in this chair, and for just that minute I was abstracted from all worldly sensation and lifted to the plane of the Kingdom. Such a heavenly peace flowed about me as I had never experienced before, not even when in Abdul Baha's presence. It was a feeling not only of peace but of exaltation, as being above the distractions and anxieties and dangers of this world. Clearly I was on another plane of being, though physically upon this earth. It was such a wonderful experience that I silently beckoned my wife, who was sitting on the couch, to exchange places with me. While in the armchair, she felt this same uplift and supreme happiness. On the couch we both had, on the other hand, merely the feeling of spiritual peace such as belongs to this earth plane at its best. Truly we had for that supreme moment rested with heavenly souls upon the fields of God. No wonder that martyrs sing as they approach the moment of their release from the cage of life!

The other experience that I referred to was that of beholding for the first time the photograph of Baha'Ullah. As I gazed upon his countenance, so massive and so full of majesty and power, I felt that adoration and devotion which led them to become his humble followers while he was a prisoner in a penal colony, and which inspired these ardent followers to spread his gospel throughout the world, – 'with a thousand longings sacrificing themselves to the Eternal Beloved'.

It was not a feeling of personal devotion which swept over me. It was rather an awe and worship of the majesty of the law which Baha'Ullah personified. As I looked into that Face I perceived the import and power of that Message which he brought for the healing of the nations. I realized that his laws were divine laws, as were those of Moses, only far greater and destined to be the foundation of a divine civilization. Before the awful majesty of such a law, as incarnated in Baha'Ullah, one could but prostrate oneself, body and soul; and feel that the greatest privilege this life afforded was to work to help bring this civilization to pass.

Such was the power of Baha'Ullah, conveyed even through a photograph. And when his sacred shoes were put into my hands I heard as it were the footsteps of them echoing around the world, the footsteps of One from the mountain-top bearing good news. I had prayed at the tomb of Abdul Baha to have a clearer realization of the station of Baha'Ullah. My prayer had been graciously answered.[18]

The pilgrim notes of both Genevieve Coy and Stanwood Cobb are quite interesting in that neither expresses great disappointment over not meeting Shoghi Effendi. Both emphasize the great spirituality they found within the Shrines. During the time of 'Abdu'l-Bahá, most pilgrims came with the intense desire to meet the Master and then to go to the Shrines. Almost immediately upon taking on the task of being the Guardian, Shoghi Effendi began to move the believers away from being personality-centric, as was the case in the time of 'Abdu'l-Bahá, to being more focused on spirituality, the Manifestations Who founded the Faith, and on the World Order they had begun. It was the beginning of a maturation process that continues today.

Shoghi Effendi's return

As the months went by and Shoghi Effendi remained out of touch in Switzerland, the Greatest Holy Leaf became increasingly worried about his absence. Finally, she sent a few family members to Switzerland to look for him and beg him to return. So, it happened that one day as Shoghi Effendi returned from one of his soul-cleansing hikes, he was very surprised to encounter his mother and another relative on a street in Interlaken. She tearfully told him of the distress of the Greatest Holy Leaf and begged him to return.[19] The *Star of the West* announced his return:

> Shoghi Effendi, after a six months' absence, returned to Haifa on Friday afternoon, December 15th, in radiant health and happiness and resumed 'the reins of the office' of Guardian of the Bahai Cause, committed to him in the Will and Testament of Abdul Baha.[20]

The Guardian's first letters hinted at his struggles and their successful outcome:

> To have been unable, owing to sad circumstances over which I have had no control, to keep in close and constant touch with you, the beloved children of 'Abdu'l-Baha, since His passing from this world, is to me a cause of sad surprise and deep and bitter regret.[21]

> To have been unable, owing to unforeseen and unavoidable circumstances, to correspond with you ever since you entered upon your manifold and arduous duties is to me a cause of deep regret and sad surprise![22]

> Now that my long hours of rest and meditation are happily at an end, I turn my face with renewed hope and vigor to that vast continent the soil of which is pregnant with those seeds that our beloved master has so tenderly and so profusely scattered in the past. Prolonged though this period has been, yet I have strongly felt ever since the New Day has dawned upon me that such a needed retirement, despite the temporary dislocations it might entail, would far outweigh in its results any immediate service I could have humbly tendered at the Threshold of Bahá'u'lláh . . .

Bereft of all news whatsoever during my hours of restful seclusion, I now feel the more the thrill of the various tidings, few but indeed promising, that have been awaiting my return to the Holy Land.[23]

1923

Shoghi Effendi loved light and did not like gloomy places. Amatu'l-Bahá Rúḥíyyih Khánum said that his own room was always brightly illuminated. He ensured that the Shrines were well-lit and that the stair from the German colony to the Shrine of the Báb was bathed in light. Early in 1923, he had a very bright light placed over the door of the Shrine of the Báb. Residents of the town made fun of the light and it caused one fanatical Christian named Dumit 'to erect, some years later, on the roof of his building, which stood not far from the Tomb of the Báb, a large illuminated cross, an object which, far from irritating Shoghi Effendi, he described as a flower in the button-hole of the Shrine!'[1]

A year after becoming the Guardian, it was obvious to Shoghi Effendi that he needed secretarial help with his work. In January, he wrote to the Bahá'ís in London saying, 'The presence of a competent assistant in my translation work at present in Haifa would be most welcome, and highly desirable and I submit this matter to the members of the Council that they may consider the matter of sending for a time one of the English friends who would attend with me to this all-important work.' No one arose to fill this need.

A girl's school

Munírih Khánum had always had an interest in the education of girls and, one day, had begged 'Abdu'l-Bahá for a school for Bahá'í children. The Master pointed at Mount Carmel and told her that

> This long mountain will be covered with schools, hospitals and Pilgrim Houses. All that has been foretold will come to pass . . . There is a piece of land opposite the Holy Shrine. 'Abbas Gholi, the

owner, at the Feast of Ridvan offered it as a gift. and it was accepted. We must purchase all the adjoining land. That is a good location for a school. It has beautiful scenery and pure air, and is near the Holy Shrines.[2]

Edith Sanderson, who had been one of the earliest Bahá'ís in Paris, was in Haifa at that time and asked permission to help. Mason Remey drew up a plan for the school. In 1923, Munírih Khánum, in an article in *Star of the West*, wrote that they had a large piece of land and about £1,500, but still needed a considerable amount more. As an incentive, she wrote that every contribution to the girls' school would receive a receipt signed by Díyá'í'yyih Khánum, Shoghi Effendi's mother, and the three other daughters of 'Abdu'l-Bahá, Rúḥá Khánum, Túbá Khánum and Munavvar Khánum.[3]

An engineer and an architect examined the project to estimate the costs and advised that it would be better to buy a house with about five rooms first in order get the school under way before building a bigger structure.[4]

An opponent

The Reverend William McElwee Miller, a long-time missionary to Iran, visited Shoghi Effendi in 1923. He had met a former teacher of the Guardian and, learning that Shoghi Effendi had become the head of the Bahá'í Faith, decided to visit him on his way to Jerusalem:

> I was given a card of introduction which I could present when I stopped in Haifa on my way to Jerusalem . . . When I presented the card, Shoghi Effendi, the Guardian of the Cause, received me cordially, gave me tea, and I had a pleasant and profitable visit with him. Next morning early, when I went for a walk up the side of Mt. Carmel, I stumbled on a Baha'i shrine, where some Persians were having breakfast. They had heard about my coming, so they welcomed me, gave me tea from their samovar, and I felt I was back in Persia. They took me into the shrine of Abdu'l-Baha, son of Baha'u'llah.[5]

Miller passed through Haifa again in 1925, but did not visit Shoghi Effendi.[6] By 1931, Miller concluded that the Bahá'í Faith was 'a dying

movement' and that 'It is only a matter of time until this strange movement
. . . shall be known only to students of history'.[7] After many frustrating
years trying to teach Christianity to the Muslims in Iran, Miller became
very critical of the Bahá'í Faith. While he had very little success in his
endeavours to convert the Iranian Muslims, the Bahá'í Faith progressed
rapidly. In 1974, he wrote a book that was purportedly a history of the
Bahá'í Faith, but was in reality a virulent attack on the Faith.[8]

First National Spiritual Assemblies

In March, Shoghi Effendi explained the basic method of electing a
National Spiritual Assembly and called for the election of National
Spiritual Assemblies 'where conditions are favourable' and the commu-
nity has 'grown and reached a considerable size, such as America, Great
Britain and Germany'.[9] The Bahá'ís of the British Isles erected one of the
first pillars of the Universal House of Justice with the election of what
Shoghi Effendi accepted as the first true National Spiritual Assembly
in the world, in April. Those elected to serve included Lady Blom-
field, Virginia Thornburgh-Cropper, Eric Hammond, Ethel Rosenberg,
George Simpson, 'Mother' George, Edward Hall, Jacob Joseph and Dr
John Esslemont.[10]

National Spiritual Assemblies were also elected in India and
Germany. Following an election at Riḍván, the Executive Committee
in India asked Shoghi Effendi if they could change their name to the
National Spiritual Assembly to be in conformity with England and
America.[11] The Guardian approved the change and the National Spiritual Assembly of India was born. Narayenrao Rangnath Shethji, known
as Vakíl, was elected the first chairman.[12]

The German Bahá'ís had held their first national convention in September 1922. The 57 delegates met and first nominated 23 people for
election. From this group, they elected nine in a secret election. Shoghi
Effendi confirmed that these nine were the first official National Spiritual Assembly of Germany.[13]

North America would not have an 'official' National Spiritual
Assembly until 1925. The United States and Canada had had the Bahá'í
Temple Unity body for many years, but it was more focused on building
the American Mashriqu'l-Adhkár, with a secondary job of coordinating
national Bahá'í activity.[14]

Inspired problem solving

Shoghi Effendi, as a man, was very humble. He always travelled simply and stayed in inexpensive accommodation. But Shoghi Effendi, the Guardian of the Cause of God, had a different standard. An example of the interaction between his personal humility and his station is how he solved the problem of Western ladies not standing when he entered a room. In Western society, men stood when others entered, but women usually remained seated and simply extended their hand to be shaken. This caused Shoghi Effendi the man no problem, but he was never just a man; he was the Guardian and that station required a higher level of respect. The freedoms of Western women were a trial for many Eastern men and watching a woman refuse to stand when the Guardian entered a room was more than they could bear. To solve this problem, Shoghi Effendi just made sure that he was always in the room first. That way, the women were always standing when introduced to him and he could show them to their seats. No decree was needed.[15]

May and Mary Maxwell

May Maxwell had been devastated by the passing of 'Abdu'l-Bahá and by early 1923 was very ill and weak. In March, she, along with her 12-year-old daughter, Mary, and her maid, Athala Burke, left Canada on a very slow journey to the Holy Land, taking two months because of her condition. May was still 'in mourning and inconsolable' and it fell to her young daughter to handle all the travel arrangements. They arrived on 29 April. May was greatly uplifted when, upon her arrival, Lotfullah Hakím gave her a recently discovered Tablet written to her by the Master shortly before His ascension.[16]

For May, the pilgrimage was both a physical and a spiritual resurrection. From the time of the passing of 'Abdu'l-Bahá, she had suffered a complete emotional and physical breakdown so severe that her husband and daughter both feared for her life and sanity. Her husband, Sutherland, thought that the only thing that could revive her was to go on pilgrimage and meet the Master's successor. Rúḥíyyih Khánum later wrote that 'it was Shoghi Effendi who literally resurrected a woman who was so ill she could still not walk a step and could move about only in a wheel chair'.[17] At times while in Haifa, knowing what she was thinking, the Guardian would say, 'Mrs Maxwell, the thoughts you are thinking are not true.' [18]

One of the most important concepts that May learned when talking with Shoghi Effendi was that the Guardian did not want the Bahá'ís to focus on his personality, but on the 'Infinite Sun of Truth, to the Báb, Bahá'u'lláh and 'Abdu'l-Bahá.' When pilgrims visited 'Abdu'l-Bahá, He tended to be the centre of their attention, but Shoghi Effendi was changing this focus from the person to the higher spirituality of the three central Figures of the Faith. [19]

It was 12-year-old Mary's first pilgrimage. She was particularly affected by the 'spirit of service' where 'a Queen or a beggar woman would be met with the same loving sweetness.' She wrote that 'Indeed it was this divine normality that really confirmed me here as a little girl of twelve years.' [20] Mary's introduction to Shoghi Effendi was less dignified than she would have liked. She was highly protective of her mother because of her mother's poor health. May and Mary were in the Pilgrim House, May in her room and Mary in the living area, when a young man entered. The young man asked if he could see Mrs Maxwell. Mary was

a tall girl for her age, fully grown and physically well-developed already. She said she pulled herself up to her full height and, looking him squarely in the eyes, asked to know, with considerable dignity and aplomb, who it was who wished to see Mrs. Maxwell. The young gentleman meekly replied, 'I am Shoghi Effendi', upon which she turned tail and fled into her mother's room in mortified embarrassment. Hiding her head, as she used to say 'like a puppy', beneath her mother's pillows, she could only point to the door and gasp, 'He—he—is—there!' when her mother asked what the matter was. And when May Maxwell found out who it was behind the door, she said, 'Pull yourself together, Mary, and go and invite him in.' [21]

Mary's high spirits were only temporarily checked. One day she was riding in the car with Shoghi Effendi, returning from Bahjí. The car's canvas top had been rolled back and the 12-year-old jumped up and sat on the folded-up top to have the wind in her face. When Shoghi Effendi warned her not to fall out, Mary insisted that she would not. 'Intoxicated with the morning,' she watched hundreds of little white crabs scurry away from the car as it drove down the beach. [22]

One day, Shoghi Effendi called Mary and May to his bedroom. They found him in bed, unshaven and with 'hollows down under his eyes almost to his chin'. He was so weak that he couldn't get out of bed. He said, 'Mrs Maxwell, it is no use. I can't stand it. I'm going away.'[23] Long-time Bahá'ís had begun to challenge his leadership and, exhausted by the immense volume of physical work and mental strain, Shoghi Effendi escaped from Haifa in June and sought some restoration of health and solace in the high peaks of the Alps. It was much more than a vacation from the soul-numbing work of guiding the world-wide Faith of Bahá'u'lláh and defending that which was sacred to it. Rúḥíyyih Khánum describes the trip as 'a complete break, a fleeing into the wilderness, a soul-searching, a communion with himself and his destiny in order to find the strength to go back and assume the duties of his high office'. As he had the previous year, he cut himself off completely from his work, calling his absence 'forced and prolonged' and sought the 'solitude of the high mountains of Switzerland'. He returned in November 1923, and the letter he wrote to the American believers on the 14th of that month said he had returned from a 'forced' absence.[24]

Before he left, the Guardian suggested that May and Mary spend the time of his absence in Egypt, which they did, staying in both Port Said and Ramleh (near Alexandria). It was a very difficult time for May and, now being away from the Guardian, she often felt hopeless. Mary, on the other hand, greatly enjoyed herself by collecting animals. By November, she had a cat, a rat, two dogs, a hen (she did have two, but they ate one), several birds and a snake.[25]

When Shoghi Effendi returned to Haifa in November and learned of May's continuing disability, he called them back. Actually, he sent three telegrams. One was sent on 19 November and simply said, 'Most welcome'. The second, which he sent ten days later, said 'Desire to see you'. The last, sent on 28 December, repeated 'Most welcome' but added 'Eager to meet you'. May and Mary then returned and stayed in Haifa until the end of February 1924.[26]

While in Port Said, Mary had learned to do a dance called the Egyptian 'shimmy' and the Greatest Holy Leaf asked her to perform it. So, the young Mary, 'in full costume with kohl around her eyes and a drum under her arm', danced and sang before Baḥíyyih Khánum, who laughed so hard that her faced was streaked with tears.[27]

Shortly before she left, May was with several members of his family when Shoghi Effendi came in. He told her that 'You are most fortunate to be so near the Greatest Holy Leaf, bodily close to her. I hope that you will be able to receive something of her spirit to take to the friends in America. Her spirit is the remedy for all their troubles.'[28] May concluded her writing with the following:

> Again we are at Bahje – the strip of intense blue sea, the distant lapping of the waves, the sunlit olive orchard and that all-surrounding peace and stillness broken only by the occasional soft note of a bird, and into this outer chalice of nature pours continually the emanations of the Shrine, a subtle, divine afflatus, permeating earth and air and sky, so that one feels that here and on Mount Carmel alone, earth is connected with heaven.
>
> On this holy mountain the soul frees itself from earthly entanglement and the cloudy mortal atmosphere is dispelled in the beaming rays of light and truth.
>
> Such divine thoughts and feelings are engendered in the human heart near these Holy Shrines as cannot find their true expression in words, but must be translated into the beauty of character and into a life wholly dedicated at the altar of God.
>
> In closing I want to say to all my loved brothers and sisters that Shoghi Effendi's hopes and wishes for us, his explicit instructions are contained in his Epistles to America, but that in sharing with you these notes and impressions – alas! so inadequate – it is my hope to bring us all nearer to that glorious life of servitude and sacrifice, to the beloved Guardian of the Cause of God, the visible Sign of our invisible Lord.[29]

Mary witnessed on one occasion the highly protective feeling that the Greatest Holy Leaf had for Shoghi Effendi. She was totally dedicated to him. One evening, the men were gathered in the central hall with the Guardian. May and Edith Sanderson were also there, seated by Shoghi Effendi, but Mary sat with the women, including the Greatest Holy Leaf, in an adjacent room which had the door open so they could hear what was being said. Suddenly, one of the believers threw himself at Shoghi Effendi's feet, overcome with emotion, causing a bit of an uproar. The Greatest Holy Leaf, not being able to see what was happening and only hearing excited voices, leaped to her feet with a cry, calming down only when she learned that nothing was amiss.[30]

During the second visit, May had extensive talks with the Guardian which she summed up in a document called *Conversations with Shoghi Effendi*:

Shoghi Effendi discusses the affairs and conditions of the Cause with astonishing openness and frankness, he does not like secrecy and told us many times that this openness, frankness and truthfulness among the friends constitutes one of the great remedies for many of our difficulties, and he sets us the example of free and open consultation.

With a modesty and simplicity which one must see in order to appreciate, because it is foreign to our American temperament, he invites suggestion and consultation from the visiting friends and from those around him.

He listens to every suggestion with the utmost courtesy and seriousness and then brings to bear upon it the light of his wonderful lucid mind, his clear all-comprehensive thought, his powerful and penetrative judgment.

The spirit of criticism is abhorrent to Shoghi Effendi, he will not permit a breath of criticism of one believer of another and although he wants to hear the truth of every matter this must be based on sincerity of purpose. He instantly detects the least insincerity of motive or effort to influence him in any way.

He is never influenced or swayed in the divine authority with which God has vested him, but exercises a perfect protection and tender guardianship over every soul.

In speaking of a certain matter which was troubling him at the time he said, 'You see I wish to know the motive behind these actions,' and then with his beautiful young face full of laughter, 'I do not like to be put off and put off and have the matter delayed and when they are dealing with an impatient person like myself it becomes very difficult' . . .

One day in discussing the question of submission to the authority of the Spiritual Assemblies Shoghi Effendi said: 'The Master has not left any latitude for personal opinion, it is not a matter of reason, it is a matter of faith.

'Some of the instructions and commands may seem unreasonable, but if we believe we have faith in them and the sign of faith is obedience. The whole question resolves itself into a matter of faith and obedience is the proof of faith, it is the result of faith, if we do not obey it is because we have not faith in the commands of the Master.

'I cannot see it in any other way.

'When a certain believer was here the question was put to the Master very plainly; supposing that in a Convention the will of the majority, the decision of the majority is against my individual conscience, suppose that my conscience cannot agree with their decision, must I submit my conscience to the will of the majority? . . .

'The Master answered that the individual conscience must yield to the majority. He left no room for doubt on this point. He not only gave the command, but He explained the reason for it. He said that if each one followed his own conscience there would be no result, confusion would reign as no two consciences agree, therefore we must follow the will of the majority.'

The energy of our Guardian is inexhaustible, and as he retires at one or two o'clock in the morning, his working day is very long.

His strength and vigour never flag, the stress of work, the magnitude of the complex problems pouring in daily in voluminous mail from every corner of the earth seem to serve to renew his forces, the progress of the Cause is reflected in his joy, his buoyancy, his eager enthusiasm and absorbed interest.

But when the welfare or progress of the Cause is menaced through the lack of love and harmony among the believers in any part of the world, when this sad news reaches him, his divine happiness suffers eclipse, his strength ebbs away . . .[31]

May also illustrated his busy schedule:

With his dazzling smile He left us, saying: 'I am very busy. My time is full. Now I must go with Mirza Azizullah Khan and go through some writings and papers. At three o'clock Miss L (an American pilgrim) is coming to see me. She is leaving tomorrow and I want to talk with her. Then Mons. R (a pilgrim from India) is coming. Then I have to go over the manuscript of Mirza Mahmood, an important book he is writing on the Cause. Afterwards I go to the Shrine on

Mount Carmel to oversee the excavating, the garden and the new pump which is sending water to the upper level. I will attend the men's meeting tonight and before retiring go through all my mail.'[32]

The water pump

The pump that Shoghi Effendi referred to was for bringing water to the gardens at the Shrine of the Báb. Watering these gardens around the Shrine of the Báb was not easy, but Shoghi Effendi solved the problem in his methodical way. The House of the Master had a well on its south side that produced very good water which was initially hauled up with a rope, bucket and pulley. Later a windmill was installed to raise the water. To get water from the well to the gardens around the Shrine, Shoghi Effendi searched Haifa for iron pipe, coming up with pieces of varying diameters, which required many adapters. Finally, he had a pipeline from the well all the way up to the Shrine, but the windmill wasn't powerful enough to push the water up so he installed an electric pump. Then he had water for the gardens.[33]

Roy Wilhelm was very aware of what Shoghi Effendi needed and when he learned that the Guardian needed a pump to water the gardens, he promptly contacted Curtis Kelsey about buying one. Curtis found a pump costing US$2,000, but when he called Roy, Roy was too ill to talk with him. In order not to delay the purchase, Curtis took out a loan and bought the pump himself, though he was not sure how he would pay back the money if Roy didn't recover very quickly. Then, out of the blue, Leroy Ioas, the Treasurer of the National Spiritual Assembly, called and said that the Guardian had told him to send Curtis a check for $10,000. Curtis wasn't overly surprised that his loan had been covered, knowing about divine assistance, but he couldn't figure out what the extra $8,000 was for. He found out over the next few years as Shoghi Effendi requested that he buy a pickup truck, an automobile, 3,000 feet of hose, cable and various other things to be shipped to Haifa. Before he was done, Shoghi Effendi had sent $40,000 which Curtis put in a special checking account. After buying all these things, the Guardian wrote and told Curtis to close the checking account. When Curtis checked how much money was left, he was amazed to discover that the account held all of three cents. Though Shoghi Effendi never saw any of the monthly bank statements, he seemed to know exactly what was in the account. Curtis sent Shoghi Effendi a 3-cent postage stamp when he closed the account.[34]

A lesson in humility

At some point after the passing of 'Abdu'l-Bahá, Mírzá Maḥmúd Furúghí, a Baháʼí from Khurasan in Persia, arrived on pilgrimage. During his first week in Haifa, Mírzá Maḥmúd heard nothing from Shoghi Effendi except descriptions of the institutions of the Faith and how the Baháʼís could strengthen them. This was not what he had come to hear. One day, he was finally alone with the Guardian, so he asked: 'Beloved Guardian, during the time of the Master, he often bestowed verbal and written honorifics, but so far your honeyed tongue has not granted any such favours.' Shoghi Effendi, 'with a winning smile and in utmost kindness and affection' responded with another question: 'For example, what title was granted to you?' 'He addressed me as the general of 'Aramram Army,' replied Mírzá Maḥmúd. The Guardian humbly said, 'I am one of the soldiers of this army. What can I say?' The answer left Mírzá Maḥmúd speechless, so he quietly left the Guardian and went up to the Shrine of the Báb. There, he prostrated himself and begged for forgiveness for his ego-prompted question, praying, 'Please forgive me; I was ignorant, now I know.'[35]

Amelia Collins

Milly (Amelia) Collins and her husband, Thomas, came to Haifa at some point during the year. They were very well off and since Thomas liked to travel by freighter, they sailed to Egypt where they did the fashionable thing and sailed up the Nile. Thomas was not a Baháʼí, but in deference to his wife they also went to Haifa.

At first, Milly and Thomas tried to stay in a hotel, but Shoghi Effendi invited them to stay at the Pilgrim House. When Milly first met the Guardian she said, 'he was just a young man then, full of determination to carry forward the great work entrusted to his care. He was so spontaneous, so trusting and loving and outgoing in the buoyancy of his beautiful heart.'[36] One evening, Shoghi Effendi gave Milly some papers and asked her to study them. The papers were all about the Baháʼí Administrative Order and not about prayer and purification as she had hoped. Abu'l-Qásim Faizí later wrote that 'before attaining the presence of the beloved Guardian her sole aim was to learn from him some truths about prayer, and purification of the soul and heart'. According to Faizí, she told him that:

'To me he was a door into the world beyond, and through him I longed to have a glimpse of that wondrous world. Therefore, with great eagerness and anticipation I hurried to my room, opened the papers, and read and read.

'The next day when I saw him, his first question was, "What did you think of the papers I gave you to read."'

At this point dearest Milly always used to stop, to tell us the following:

'I started my spiritual life on a basis of truth and frankness. Whatever I felt in my heart, whether right or wrong, I would say without fear of consequence. Now I was standing before the person who could read the innermost recesses of my heart and soul. How could I speak anything but the simple truth? Those papers contained nothing but explanations and elucidations of the World Order of Bahá'u'lláh and how it should be established in the world. And I desired only to know about prayer and glimpses of the world beyond. Therefore, I could only answer the Guardian's question with these words, "What shall I say? I did not understand anything!"'

Here again, she would pause and look deeply into the faces of the friends and say:

'Do you think he reproved me for this? Never. On the same day, in the afternoon, he told me that the Master had walked often in these lanes and streets near His House, and the Guardian invited me to go walking with him. As we were walking together he spoke of nothing except the same subjects he had written about in the papers he had given me to read. But with what a voice and with what sweetness! Words cannot describe them. He explained the details with such patience, as a father would to a child. But my idea was still lurking in my mind, and I was constantly thinking to myself that soon he would speak the words that would, each one, open a door into the mysteries of prayer and the world of the spirit which I longed so much to know more about. How can we, insignificant and weak as we are, understand the plans of God? We are confined to our humble and limited circumstances, unaware of what He may have in store for us. The Guardian, who was beginning to delineate the spiritual foundations of the Kingdom of God on earth, began to educate me in the administrative principles of the Faith in spite of my own desires.

'When I returned to America I went directly to the National Convention and arrived during the reading of that very message from the beloved Guardian which he had given me to read in Haifa. I found myself called to the front, and the words that I spoke came from some deep well of consciousness. That afternoon's walk with Shoghi Effendi and those exalted statements heard from no less a person than 'Abdu'l-Bahá's successor, were like seeds that that dear teacher had implanted in my mind and heart, and now each one was bursting forth into expression of these new ideas.

'And later, wherever I went, I found that the friends had received that same letter, and that they, and the members of the Spiritual Assemblies, were busily engaged in discussing it. Sometimes there were clashes of thought and misunderstanding, and these, I found, I had been prepared by the beloved Guardian to explain and throw light upon. I had been given by him that which was necessary for the service and advancement of the Cause, and not that which would satisfy only my own selfish desires.' [37]

Though Thomas Collins was not a Bahá'í, he was entranced by the Guardian. One day he looked at the unfinished Western Pilgrim House. In 1919, Ruth and Harry Randall had given a sum of money for the construction of a large, twenty-room pilgrim house to replace the old one across from the House of the Master. Mason Remey drew up the plans and construction had started, but the initial funds were not sufficient to complete the building and work had come to a halt by the time Shoghi Effendi became the Guardian. After passing the unfinished building for several days, Thomas became angry and said, 'How can the Bahá'ís see an unfinished building every day in front of the Guardian's eyes? You [speaking to Milly] will see that the building is brought to completion.' Since he was not a Bahá'í, he couldn't make the donation, but he could ensure that Milly did, so Milly and seven other Bahá'ís contributed enough so that the Western Pilgrim House was completed by December 1925.[38] When Thomas passed away, he left his entire fortune to her, knowing full well that she would give it to the Faith. Though he never declared himself to be a Bahá'í, he was very proud of Milly because she 'had the courage to do something different'.[39]

Commemoration of 'Abdu'l-Bahá's passing

The anniversary of the passing of the Master was commemorated in Haifa:

> In a calm and quiet night, brightened by the silvery rays of the moon, gathered 'Abdu'l-Bahá's sorrow-stricken faithful ones, to commemorate the night of His last farewell. On the cistern by the Tomb sat His fervent servants; below them flickered the dying lights of Haifa, and above head shown in full magnificence the star bespangled heavens. It was in the mid-watches of such a night that with sorrow and fervour the servants turned unto their dear Master so near and yet so far away; and with a deep feeling of that bitter loss they supplicated help and guidance from their Lord. A word or two from Shoghi Effendi made them feel the Master nigh, and made them realise as never before that it was only in following in His steps, and in living the life that He had, that we can prove our faithfulness to our Master's Cause.[40]

Genevieve Coy

Genevieve Coy was back in Haifa in late December. She noted that Shoghi Effendi had lunch with the pilgrims at the Western Pilgrim House almost every day and talked about the different problems connected with Faith in various parts of the world. She said he

> was quite ready to listen to the opinions of others, and often questions those at table as to what they think about certain questions. He speaks very directly and frankly, with a very dynamic quality. He has a quick sense of humour, and occasionally says things that might seem a wee bit sarcastic, if one did not clearly realize the kindness in his attitude. But he evidently sees people, and their abilities and defects, very clearly. One feels very clearly his wisdom, his capacity and his power. He is very simple and friendly, so that one feels free to ask him all kinds of questions.

We have talked a great deal about Spiritual Assemblies. He evidently feels that the local and national assemblies are still in a very crude stage, and that until they begin to function more adequately it would be unwise to attempt to organize the Universal House of Justice.[41]

1924

Pilgrims

The year 1924 saw the return of Siegfried (Fred) Schopflocher, Ali-Kuli Khan with his wife Florence, and Dr John Esslemont. Claudia Coles made her first pilgrimage. It was also a year during which the violence against the Bahá'ís in Persia was inflamed.

Genevieve Coy was still in Haifa as 1924 began. On 3 January, Shoghi Effendi asked if she would care to walk up to the Shrine of the Báb with him. It was a leisurely walk, with Shoghi Effendi stopping now and again when he wanted to make sure she understood one point or another. Arriving at the Shrine, they walked about in the gardens while he talked about his plans for the future development of the terraces. Then they entered the Tomb. They were the only ones there and after a time, Shoghi Effendi chanted 'slowly and with wonderful sweetness'. The chanting brought back the memory of her first visit three years earlier when she had been with the Master. She remembered how tired His face had seemed. Now she was listening to His successor and she wondered:

> What is it in Shoghi Effendi that so wins one's devotion? He is so simple, so young, so unassuming. And yet he had a power to win one to the Cause, and its service, that is little short of miraculous. It is not that I see the Master in him, but more that his devotion to the Master is contagious.[1]

Through his visits in 1924 and 1925 Fred Schopflocher developed a close relationship with Shoghi Effendi, who referred to him as 'My beloved Fred, that living torch, lit by the spirit of our departed Master' and as a 'zealous and promising disciple of 'Abdu'l-Bahá'. He noted that Fred had a 'clear understanding of, and entire devotion to, the interests' of the Bahá'í Faith.[2]

Claudia Coles had been given permission by 'Abdu'l-Bahá to come on pilgrimage in 1910. For some reason, she had not be able to go on that occasion, but she was able to go in March 1924. She left London and arrived in Haifa on 14 March, where she joined Helen Grand, who had travelled over from New York. Shoghi Effendi had left for Switzerland shortly before they arrived, but they were able to enjoy the presence of the Greatest Holy Leaf. Helen Grand wrote that

> I shall never forget our first walk through the Master's garden, where He had spent so many hours making it beautiful with every flower one could imagine, arbored walks, growing with exquisite white and yellow roses, trees bearing golden fruit. The beauty of it all is beyond the power of a pen. The garden is steeped with memories of 'Abdu'l-Bahá and one feels His continued Presence, making it truly a Holy Garden, where prayers, night and day, have been offered to God for the 'Brotherhood of the World' and the unity of the nations.
>
> Every evening we walked upon Mount Carmel to the Tomb of 'Abdu'l-Bahá and spent an hour or more in the twilight; the great silence and peace were deeply wonderful.[3]

The murder of Major Robert Imbrie

In Iran, Bahá'ís were being targeted for death during the Islamic month of Muharram by a clergyman bent on increasing his power and influence. Having previously been held in check by their own government, a leadership struggle between power-hungry men allowed the clergy access to dominance and influence.[4]

Major Robert Imbrie was the American Vice-Consul, and as the danger escalated Susan Moody and Elizabeth Stewart, American Bahá'í doctors who ran a clinic for women, went to see him on 8 July with their concerns. He immediately offered to stay at their home that night, but they did not think that was necessary. The Major did, however, insist that they inform the Iranian police. The Major himself called the police and told them in no uncertain terms that he would hold them responsible if the women were harmed. When the women returned home, they saw two armed guards at their door. At nine that night an unruly mob gathered and began shouting obscenities. When the mob approached the house where Susan and Elizabeth were hiding with their light off, suddenly a force of armed police arrived and forced the crowd away.[5] Susan wrote that during the night, 'the homes of all Bahá'ís which had been threatened by stoning, looting, or by insulting language, were guarded and the general looting or slaughter was intercepted'.[6]

Ten days later, on 18 July 1924, Major Imbrie was brutally murdered and this brought great worry to Shoghi Effendi. It was caused by superstition, bigotry and power politics. According to an article in the *New York Times*:

> About a month ago a native was rumored to have lost his sight at a well immediately after having uttered the name of Abbas Effendi ['Abdu'l-Bahá], the late spiritual leader of the Bahá'ís. The well thereupon became a shrine and was visited by crowds of Moslems, who started anti-Bahá'í demonstrations without any attempt by the authorities to stop them.
>
> A few days ago the well was said to have been poisoned and Bahá'ís were reported to have done it. Attempts were made to find the alleged culprits and the place became still more crowded.
>
> On Friday morning Major Imbrie and Seymour, his companion, visited the place to take photographs. They were warned not to approach the well, as women were present.
>
> Accordingly, they desisted and entered their carriage. Then shouts were raised that they were the Bahá'ís who had poisoned the well. Stones were thrown, and the carriage was followed by a crowd. Finally it was stopped and the two Americans were dragged out and attacked by the mob with sticks and stones. Soldiers were seen in the crowd and the police made only feeble efforts to rescue the Americans.
>
> Major Imbrie, who was unarmed, did his best to defend himself until he became unconscious from a blow on the skull, evidently delivered with a sabre. While he was lying on the ground a stone broke his jaw. He was finally carried to the police hospital, but the mob forced its way into the operating room and continued to attack him. He received more than forty wounds.[7]

Immediately after the attack, Susan and Elizabeth rushed over to comfort Mrs Imbrie at the residence of the American Consul, who said that her husband had 138 stab wounds on his body. Every day for the next few days, the two Bahá'í women spent time with Mrs Imbrie. Martial law was quickly established by the government and that was all that protected the Bahá'ís in the area from mob violence. The murder marked, however, the renewal of persecution of the Bahá'ís in Iran. For the three weeks following the murder, Susan and Elizabeth had no visitors at their clinic and few of their patients returned, so after a time, they left the country, planning to return at a later date.[8]

Ali-Kuli Khan and Florence

Just as passions burst into flame, Ali-Kuli and Florence Khan, on their way to Haifa, arrived in Tehran. The Khans had had an exciting life since their previous pilgrimage eighteen years before, in 1906. After World War I, Ali-Kuli Khan had been at the Versailles Peace Conference with the Persian delegation, then served his country as head of the Persian Embassy in Constantinople. In 1922, he became the Grand Master of the Court of the Crown Prince of Persia, followed a year later by the post of the Plenipotentiary to the Five Republics of the Caucasus for Persia.[9] Life at such high political altitudes had been extremely difficult, and by 1924 the Khans had determined that their destiny lay in the West, so they were passing through Tehran on their way to see Shoghi Effendi and then return to America. On the very day that Major Imbrie was murdered, they were to have taken tea with him and his wife, and were shocked 'to receive a hurried word from her that he had been killed by a mob in the streets'.[10]

Leaving Tehran on 23 October, the Khans headed for Haifa, driving through Baghdad, Damascus and Beirut.[11] They arrived in Haifa by car on 30 October. A much-relieved Florence wrote:

Praise God with us that He has delivered us from that distant land [of Persia], and greatest of all Divine Bounties for us, has brought us here, to the blessed Shrine of 'Abdu'l-Bahá and to the feet and service of Shoghi Effendi. At last we are freed from wasting our lives on a barren soil . . . the hands of the friends in that distant land are really manacled, and while they can and do serve the Cause continuously and zealously, and the Cause is progressing, yet there are some forms of service which are utterly futile, as things go at present.[12]

When they arrived in Haifa, they went to the House of 'Abdu'l-Bahá and were almost immediately brought into the presence of Shoghi Effendi, who was meeting with the Haifa Spiritual Assembly. Florence's daughter, Marzieh Gail, summarized her mother's notes:

> This was the usual Thursday meeting of the Haifa Spiritual Assembly, and all were gathered in the Master's reception room. Shoghi Effendi occupied the lower end of 'Abdu'l-Bahá's divan, the upper end having been the place of 'Abdu'l-Bahá – the place now vacant, marked only by His folded up shawl, and a small pillow of rose-colored velvet, embroidered with 'Abdu'l-Bahá's initials in gold, just as He had put aside these things for the last time, not very long before . . .
>
> 'The Valí (Guardian) of the Cause is a young and energetic man. He is stately, dignified, and his shining face reflects purity and love.' She told of his tact, brilliance, quick and gentle wit as he sat with visiting friends at the daily luncheon in the Western Pilgrim House. 'The kindly wisdom of his eyes. The powerfully developed forehead . . . Most unobtrusively he makes vivid suggestions, shows how conditions may be bettered in individual Bahá'í Centers. "Travel and teach," he urged.'
>
> Of his clothing, she reported that 'He wears a tall, black Persian hat, a black suit, a black European outer coat to his knees.' Rúḥá Khánum told her that Shoghi Effendi had only one or two suits. There were of fine materials, as was his felt hat, and he was always fresh and immaculate, like 'Abdu'l-Bahá, though in semi-Western garb, and seeming to many Americans like a young American executive – although none of those could match his English. 'We are not Eastern or Western,' he told the believers, 'we are Bahá'ís.'[13]

She also describes Florence's talks with Shoghi Effendi:

> Asked the meaning of his name (Shawq, a word well known to mystics), he said musingly, 'Zeal, eagerness, yearning, especially yearning.'
>
> The Bahá'í world had never before heard the word Guardian in its Bahá'í meaning. All this was new in those days. The Master's Will had been known only about two years. 'He is indeed the heir,' Florence wrote, 'to the spiritual Kingdom established by Bahá'u'lláh.'

'It is undeniable that I am the Guardian,' Shoghi Effendi told her. 'I am under the protection of 'Abdu'l-Bahá.'

'Tell the believers I am their co-worker and their brother, their fellow-worker in the Cause.' . . .

At the daily luncheons where the Western visitors did not have to share him with other pilgrims, and at that time were permitted to take notes, he showed himself to be intensely interested in world affairs, knowledgeable about the affairs of each nation, and he eagerly discussed the affairs of the Faith all over the world.

Even in those early years he would share, at table, letters from far away traveling teachers, and was often deeply moved when they came from persons whose health was frail and their means few.

His writings were not to be called 'Tablets.' He continually wished to show that he was on a far different plane from the Master; his station was that of Guardianship; the Báb, Bahá'u'lláh, and the Master were all apart. If a pilgrim asked him to bless some memento to be taken home, he would lay it on the bed or in the unchanged bedroom where, in the Holy Household's home, the Master spent the last three days of His life and died – or else on the threshold in one of the Shrines. . . .

His great call was 'Action!' 'You say you loved 'Abdu'l-Bahá, then prove it,' he seemed to be telling the older believers. 'Arise and serve! Elevate personal character and behavior!' And he would remind the Bahá'ís that the Master in His Will and Testament asked them to look to the example of Christ's disciples. How they 'forsook all their cares and belongings, purged themselves of self and passion and with absolute detachment scattered far and wide and engaged in calling the peoples of the world to the Divine Guidance, till at last they made the world another world . . .'

Working continuously from morning to late in the evening and eating very little at these midday meals, he would quietly give the visitors his whole attention at the luncheon table and he never produced an impression of being in a hurry.

'His activity is amazing . . . The day of Shoghi Effendi is the day of action, of deeds, and good personal conduct and character – action and doing, not talking.' He wished the believers to bring forth a harvest after all the bounty showered upon them by 'Abdu'l-Bahá for so many long years. She wrote of the gardens he had already developed about the Holy Tombs, even palms and cypresses along the path, now leading straight up Mount Carmel from the avenue which extends down to the sea. 'Most marvelous of all, he has carried away the great boulders – which for ages have existed on Mount Carmel – between the Tomb of the Báb and the avenue. Except for a small strip, over-priced by its owner, all the land from the Tomb down to this avenue at the base of the mountain belongs to the believers. He has created this new and broad and noble approach straight up the mountain side, and lined it with fast-growing fan-palms and flowers, and all this in so brief a time.' It was typical of Florence that to her these great boulders symbolized the obstacles – human evils, selfishness, worldliness – which the Guardian would clear away from the path of the Faith . . .

His method of teaching was not to be harsh or disapproving, but rather to understand, and often to suggest some better conduct with a smile. If he wished to advise, he might comment on something he approved of in another believer. For instance, he told Marzieh that every morning on awakening, 'Azíz Bahádur would read some of the *Hidden Words*. *Hidden Words*, 'Abdu'l-Bahá has said, is our 'standard and criterion of judgment . . .'[14]

Florence was entranced by the Greatest Holy Leaf; she wrote of her 'sacrifice in continuing on amongst us, her encouraging sweet courtesy so like 'Abdu'l-Bahá's . . . the peerless daughter of Bahá'u'lláh, the first and most wonderful woman ever born into this world'. When Shoghi Effendi returned from England, he had no room of his own in the House of the Master so he stayed in Rúhá Khánum's house. The Greatest Holy Leaf had two rooms built for him on the roof of the House of the Master, but Shoghi Effendi said that there was no money available to furnish them. One day, when Laura Dreyfus-Barney took the matter into her own hands and went downtown and bought some basic furniture and a floor covering, he gave in and changed his residence. Although the Guardian was generous with funds for others, he was extremely frugal for himself.[15]

Even though Shoghi Effendi had been the Guardian for less than three years, the Khans were disturbed to see an arrogance creeping into the attitudes and manners of his relatives. Shoghi Effendi later referred to this in *God Passes By*, writing how during the four years after the passing of 'Abdu'l-Bahá, arrogance 'created an irreparable breach within the ranks of Bahá'u'lláh's kindred, [and] sealed ultimately the fate of the great majority of the members of His family . . .'[16] Florence noted that Westerners would probably not have seen the early signs, but they were visible to those Easterners who looked. Marzieh Gail's example in *Arches of the Years* was Suhayl Effendi, the Guardian's cousin. One day, Suhayl was sitting next to the teenage Marzieh at the luncheon table. Persian etiquette dictated that Suhayl should have refrained from superfluous conversation while the Guardian was present; instead he carried on a conversation with Marzieh. This one-sided conversation was also pointed. Shoghi Effendi had adopted a transliteration system for converting Persian names into English that had been established by a group of Orientalists at an international conference, and Suhayl began making fun of the choice, in essence criticizing the Guardian. When Shoghi Effendi did not appear at the next day's pilgrims' luncheon, some learned a lesson, though others did not.[17]

Shoghi Effendi commonly took a long afternoon walk around Mount Carmel at 4 o'clock and would frequently invite Khan to go with him. These walks were not for the unfit and, as Gail wrote, 'except for the privilege of being with him, could exhaust the most tireless'.

On many days, the Khans would walk up to the Shrine of the Báb in the evening and would enter the chambers.

They would find them softly lighted by electric chandeliers, and wall-lights shining through gold-glowing, Tiffany globes – appropriate, Florence wrote, because 'Abdu'l-Bahá loved best the yellow rose – better than the white or red – and here the light was a diffused and spiritual, soft yellow glow. Usually Shoghi Effendi would chant 'Abdu'l-Bahá's Visitation Tablet, and no one can tell befittingly of his chant. The solemn, unaffected sweetness and power of it, the total lack of sentimentality or studied, clerical 'pear-shaped tones'. No one could ever have loved 'Abdu'l-Bahá the way Shoghi Effendi loved him, and the Guardian stood there in his Grandfather's very presence, outside the inner room of the Shrine, chanting prayers of which the Master says, 'It will be even as meeting Him face to face.' The prayer which asks for selflessness, and asks repeatedly to be dust in the path of God's loved ones. In those days a family member had hung a great portrait, the Taponier photograph of 'Abdu'l-Bahá, on an inner wall of the middle room, and His eyes looked loving down on those who came. (This large picture, perhaps as being contrary to Aqdas laws forbidding pictures and statues in Houses of Worship, and placed there before Shoghi Effendi's return, was removed after a time.)[18]

Shoghi Effendi commonly went to the Shrines with the pilgrims. Before entering, everyone would remove their shoes and there would be two piles of dusty footwear, one at each door. The Guardian's shoes were always conspicuous for being well polished and neatly placed. For the Eastern pilgrims at that time, the Shrines were segregated. Women used the rooms on the east and the men those on the west. Western pilgrims weren't so restricted, though Shoghi Effendi would commonly pray in the east room. Florence wrote that the Guardian would stand when he chanted the Tablet of Visitation, but pilgrims were free to stand, kneel, or bow at the threshold as they felt moved to do. For Adele Mills, the wife of Mountfort Mills, who was unwell, Shoghi Effendi had a chair placed.

Keith Ransom-Kehler once entered the Shine thinking that she was alone. She said,

> I entered on the women's side and I thought the whole building was empty. I set about praying, and when I pray they know there is something doing in Heaven. I knelt down, I sobbed, I cried out. Then all of a sudden I looked across at the men's side and found that a whole group of Eastern pilgrims was quietly observing me.[19]

The Guardian emphasized that he was the Guardian and, though he had the unerring protection of 'Abdu'l-Bahá, he did not have the same station. When talking and corresponding with the friends, he was always their 'fellow worker' or their 'true brother'. He rarely allowed his photograph to be taken. Though Shoghi Effendi repeatedly said that he did not have the same station as his Grandfather, people who entered his presence quickly realized that he was very different from those around him.[20]

When the Khans made their first visit to the Shrine of Bahá'u'lláh, Shoghi Effendi went with them and 'poured a special scent into their cupped hands . . . not the usual attar, but a rare, enchanting perfume'.

At the threshold, Shoghi Effendi chanted the Tablet of Visitation, then took the family into the Mansion. They were surprised to find that it was like a museum of the Faith,

> for here they saw not only treasures and beautifully executed murals, but contemporary records and photographs of Bahá'í achievements, and a model of the . . . House of Worship at Wilmette – a great lamp shedding its soft light in the central upper court. A large calligraphy on one wall was by Mírzá Muḥammad-'Alí, arch-breaker of Bahá'u'lláh's Covenant, a man who burned with never-ending hatred of his half-brother but who, when he made this calligraphy, was still within the Faith.[21]

Dr John Esslemont

During the summer of 1924, Dr Esslemont was in Scotland when his health began to deteriorate. He was advised to leave Scotland before the winter. Shoghi Effendi sent him a letter inviting him to Haifa; he arrived on 21 November. Upon his arrival, he immediately began taking Persian lessons and when Jessie Revell arrived in December was already translating passages from *Nabíl's Narrative* and helping Shoghi Effendi translate the *Tablet of Aḥmad*.

Jessie was very impressed with Shoghi Effendi's helper:

> It seems he lived to serve and comfort others. I can see the mental picture of him now one day in Haifa – he had invited me to accompany him to the Shrine of the Báb and 'Abdu'l-Bahá on Mount Carmel and early one morning together we prayed there for the whole world – this memory will be with me throughout all the worlds of eternity; on our way back we saw 'Azizu'lláh Khán S. Bahádur, sitting in the sun and very, very sad because he was ill and could not serve Shoghi Effendi as he had been doing. Dr. Esslemont sat beside him, encouraged and cheered him, and while they sat together, I took a picture of them. 'Azizu'lláh Khán's face became happier because of Dr. Esslemont's comforting presence and words.
>
> Dr. Esslemont was so very thorough and efficient in everything he did. He would work for hours over the translation of a single word in order to get the best shade of meaning. He was always

trying to find a way to make Shoghi Effendi's duties lighter and to serve him more and more wherever possible.[22]

Shoghi Effendi was back in the Holy Land by 24 September, after six months away. He wrote:

> I return to the Holy Land with an overpowering sense of the gravity of the spiritual state of the Cause in the world. Much as I deplore the disturbing effect of my forced and repeated withdrawals from the field of service, I can unhesitatingly assure you that my last and momentous step was taken with extreme reluctance and only after mature and anxious reflection as to the best way to safeguard the interests of a precious Cause.
>
> My prolonged absence, my utter inaction should not, however, be solely attributed to certain external manifestations of unharmony, of discontent and disloyalty – however paralysing their effect has been upon the continuance of my work – but also to my own unworthiness and to my imperfections and frailties.[23]

Mountfort and Adele Mills were in Haifa in November, spending several weeks there. There were about ten pilgrims in Haifa at the time and more were expected.[24]

The National Spiritual Assembly of Egypt was formed in December.[25]

1925

The International Bahá'í Bureau in Geneva

Jean Stannard was in Haifa in February after several years of working in the East. She was thinking of moving to Lausanne, Switzerland, but wanted to ask Shoghi Effendi. When she asked Him what he considered to be the most important place for her to go, he immediately replied, 'Geneva'. Surprised at the unexpected answer, she nevertheless went as directed. Geneva at that time was the centre of international movements and Mrs Stannard quickly established the International Bahá'í Bureau, which she integrated into the group of movements active in that city. Shoghi Effendi's vision of the Bureau was that it was to be a communications centre between Bahá'í groups internationally.

The Bureau was soon augmented by Martha Root and the two women industriously began giving lectures and entertaining guests. Martha Root managed to have the Esperanto Congresses of 1925 and 1926 held in the Bureau's rooms and it was at one of these that Lydia Zamenhof, daughter of the inventor of the Esperanto language, first learned about the Bahá'í Faith. Lydia became a strong Bahá'í; she perished in a Nazi extermination camp during the Second World War.

Mrs Stannard largely paid for the operation of the Bureau herself until 1927, when failing health and finances forced her to reduce her involvement. Julia Culver took up the challenge of financially supporting the Bureau and conducting its affairs. Emogene Hoagg joined her in 1928. Shoghi Effendi stressed the importance of the Bureau, defining its activities in 1931:

> Geneva is auxiliary to the Center in Haifa. It does not assume the place of Haifa, but is auxiliary. It exercises no international authority;

87

it does not try to impose, but helps and acts as intermediary between Haifa and other Bahá'í centers. It is 'international' because it links the different countries; it is like a distributing centre.[1]

John Esslemont

By February of 1925, Dr Esslemont was Shoghi Effendi's English-language secretary and was helping him with the *Hidden Words* and other Writings of Bahá'u'lláh. Watching the young Guardian, Dr Esslemont observed:

> The love and trust which the believers felt towards the Master seems now to be extended in full measure to Shoghi Effendi, and his quiet, humble, wise and loving handling of his manifold duties makes one feel that he is truly inspired by the Spirit of the Master, and that the high traditions of leadership of the movement are being worthily sustained . . .
>
> Shoghi Effendi like the Master has an extremely sensitive nature. Signs of disunity among the friends or of disobedience to the teachings affect both his spirits and his physical health in a marked degree, while evidences that the friends are working unitedly sincerely and selflessly have a correspondingly cheering and helpful effect . . . Some of the friends insist on addressing him as 'Our Lord' or "Our Master' and the like. This he dislikes and disapproves. He wishes to be known simply as Shoghi Effendi or as the Guardian of the Cause, titles by which the Master referred to him. He wishes us to show our loyalty to the Cause by lives of service and not by extravagant expressions of personal adulation, by deeds and not by words.[2]

Dr Esslemont, however, spent the two weeks between 11 and 28 March in hospital with an attack of pleurisy, a complication of his tuberculosis. During his hospitalization, Martha Root arrived as a pilgrim. Together they studied Esperanto and she found Dr Esslemont to be an excellent teacher.

Martha quickly saw the tremendous workload that Shoghi Effendi carried and noted:

Dr. Esslemont helps him a great deal, but Dr. has been very ill, he came out of the hospital to his room last week and could walk out a little each day. Then he had a relapse and is now in bed. His health is very frail but he is so precious to the Cause with his writing, his Persian, his help in translating. Please let us pray for him strength to serve longer.[3]

When John Esslemont returned from the hospital, he was still very weak and after consultation with Shoghi Effendi and his doctors, it was decided that he should spend the summer in a cool and dry place. He was invited by Victoria von Sigsfeld to stay at Hüsli, Finsterlingen, in the Black Forest of Germany and in late May he accepted and travelled there with Mrs Lowell. While there, he worked with his hostess on the German translation of his book, *Bahá'u'lláh and the New Era*.[4] Dr Hermann Grossmann was there at the same time.[5] Dr Esslemont stayed there until September.

Corinne True, Effie Baker, Martha Root, and the New Zealand pilgrims

When Corinne True arrived in February Shoghi Effendi told her she could stay for as long as she liked. She noted that the Greatest Holy Leaf had built the Guardian an apartment on top of the House of the Master with an office, a bedroom and a bath. On the walls of his office, Shoghi Effendi had

maps of different countries, marked with red ink and dots for every city where there are Baha'is. You can see right away in what part of the country the work is being done. Germany and Australia are doing more for the Cause, it is spreading fast in those two countries, more so than in any other country. Shoghi would be very happy when we can get matters established and relieve him of a great deal of work that should be taken care of by the different assemblies. He has a tremendous correspondence. He dictates letters and then adds a few words by hand.[6]

'Mother' True was impressed with developments in the city of Haifa. She said that many tourist ships were coming to the port and that Thomas Cook, the international travel agency, had opened an office and asked Shoghi Effendi if they could take tourists to see the Shrine of the Báb and the gardens. This he allowed, so many tours were coming. On Sundays, many of the local people came to the Shrine, as many as five hundred, though few entered the building, and then only on special request.[7]

Martha Root had arrived in Port Said on 8 March and spent several days waiting for a ship bearing the first pilgrims from Australia and New Zealand. At 6:30 a.m., Effie Baker, Margaret Stevenson, Sarah Blundell and her daughter and son, Ethel and Hugh, were all surprised to see Martha and three Egyptian Bahá'ís, Muhammad Mustafa, Mahmoud el Nouchoucaty and one other, come on board.

Effie, the first woman to become a Bahá'í in Australia, had first heard about the Faith from Hyde and Clara Dunn in late 1922. The effect on her was instantaneous:

> Hearing this [a quote from Bahá'í scripture] I thought, 'I must listen to what this speaker has to say.' . . . After the principles, Mr. Dunn gave a short account of the history of the Bahá'í Faith and . . . I went immediately and declared myself as accepting the Bahá'í message.[8]

Effie was an artist, a photographer and a crafts maker (known in Australia as the 'Toymaker') and had been travel-teaching with Hyde and Clara Dunn in 1923. In 1924 she went to New Zealand with Martha Root where she learned that the four New Zealand Bahá'ís were planning to make their first pilgrimage. At that time, Effie was suffering from blood poisoning caused by many years of using lead-based paints and wetting her paint-brush with her tongue. She thought that the three-month voyage to Haifa would do her good so, when invited to join them, she accepted. It would be eleven years before she saw her native Australia again.[9]

Sarah Blundell had first heard about the Faith in New Zealand from *The Christian Commonwealth* newspaper in 1911, which carried a story about 'Abdu'l-Bahá's visit to London. Hyde and Clara Dunn visited New Zealand in 1924 and Sarah held a meeting in her house for those whom she thought might be interested. Soon afterward, Sarah became a Bahá'í.[10] Two of Sarah's seven children, Ethel and Hugh, also had an interest in spiritual matters. Ethel had been searching for the Truth from a young age. One day after being sick for a time, she had gone to a room to pray:

while sitting there feeling rather down-hearted, I said to myself 'Why can't I be well?' As I sat there wondering, suddenly I saw before me a cliff, up which was a zig zag path and I saw myself walking up that path. Then – at the top of the cliff, there came a beautiful silver light, and in that light, stood an Eastern man! He had white hair and beard, a white headdress and robe. He stooped down and held my right wrist in his hand, with a warm firm grasp. I thought 'If he is helping me up that cliff, why have we not clasped hands?' Then the Eastern man spoke! He said 'God has hold of you, you do not have to hold onto God!' These words had a stirring effect on me, they reversed my ideas and relaxed my tense thinking. The light and the Eastern man had gone, but not so the effect of his words.

One morning, a year or two later the Postman delivered our mail and among this was our paper 'The Christian Commonwealth'. On opening this I saw a photo of my 'Eastern man', His name 'Abdu'l-Baha'. It was stirring to read of His long imprisonment with His Father, Baha'u'llah in the most great prison of Acre. I longed to know more.

Some years later, in 1924, Mr. and Mrs. Hyde Dunn visited Auckland. The great moment for me came after listening to Mr. Dunn's first address . . .[11]

In Port Said, the pilgrims breakfasted together on the ship, then went ashore to fight their way through Customs with the aid of English-speaking Muhammad Mustafa, who worked at the telegraph office. Martha Root had a letter from someone that enabled them to get through Customs without a bag being opened. That done, they were taken to their hotel where they were met by Munavvar Khánum, the youngest daughter of 'Abdu'l-Bahá and wife of Mírzá Ahmad Yazdi, and the group had lunch together. Afterwards, Muhammad Mustafa offered to go with them as far as Kantara on the western side of the Suez Canal, where they switched to the Haifa train, a change requiring them to be rowed across the Canal. His help was greatly appreciated when they had to go through Customs before boarding the Haifa train. The group crossed the Canal at 7:30, but didn't leave for Haifa until midnight.[12]

The pilgrims arrived in Haifa at 10 a.m. on 13 March, and Fujita met them at the station. Effie noted that he was certainly 'a good Bahá'í General and soon had the little band of happy pilgrims marshalled and in order'. The group was quickly installed in the Pilgrim House, where they were greeted by Corinne True. Shortly before lunch, the new pilgrims met with Shoghi Effendi and Effie noted that

> it was a wonderful meeting. His step is quick and decisive also his manner of speech but the sweetness of his countenance and the bright alert expression of his eyes conveys to you a wonderful tenderness of heart which radiates to you such graciousness and simplicity you feel at once at your ease, as if a weight has been removed from your heart and a great peace reigns. You feel a great happiness in his presence.[13]

Margaret Stevenson also remembered that first meeting:

> After a rest and lunch we were taken by Mrs True over to Abdul Baha's House to visit Shoghi Effendi. He gave us a very warm welcome in the room where Abdul Baha used to welcome the friends, and after talking to us for a while, he went out of the room and sent the ladies in – the Holy Mother (Abdul Baha's wife) and one of her daughters. They too gave us a very warm welcome and said how they had been looking forward to our coming. It seems they were so afraid that after the passing of Abdul Baha that the friends would not come to see them, and so they are so delighted to welcome them. They gave us tea before we left, in beautiful little glass tumblers on a glass saucer and little Persian cakes.[14]

Margaret noted that all the pilgrims stayed in the Pilgrim House. The residents at that time included Sarah, Hugh and Ethel Blundell, Effie Baker, Corinne True, Mountfort Mills, Miss Horn (who arrived from Stuttgart on 27 March)[15] and Dr Esslemont. Meals were cooked in the House of the Master, overseen by members of the Holy Family. Margaret wrote that

> the food is beautifully cooked. Everything is cooked in Abdul Baha's house and sent over. They cook for about 80 people, I was afraid I might not like the Eastern dishes but they are very nice, just a bit too rich, but nice to eat. The trouble they go to is wonderful, sometimes 4 or 5 courses for dinner.[16]

Margaret was also very taken with Fujita, saying 'Fujeta waits beautifully' (meaning that he served the food well) and 'is a wonderful man, so obliging and always so happy. He is so jolly too many a joke we all have'. The New Zealanders had brought some seeds they gave to Fujita, which delighted him.[17]

Martha Root saw that the load Shoghi Effendi carried was phenomenal and searched for a way to help him. Later she wrote to friends saying 'After praying about it . . . I thought if we could each write him a little note of love and appreciation and urge him to take a little change during the hottest weather, we would be remembering what 'Abdu'l-Bahá told us about Shoghi.' She described the Guardian as

> so spiritually beautiful. Every time I am with him I am so HAPPY! He radiates joy and love to everybody. His mind seems all comprehensive, he grasps the big problems and always knows just what to do; his translations are great – but he tries to dictate letters and perhaps add a few lines and doing this for all the world is taking his strength just terribly . . . it is not giving him time for the other big questions which are crowding. You have no idea how many letters come asking questions. He wishes all to write, his joy is to hear the news of the Cause, but it is the ANSWERING that is going to kill him . . .[18]

After lunch, Corinne True took the new arrivals for a walk down Carmel Road. That evening, Effie saw the light illuminating the Shrine on the mountain and was told:

> Just after it was installed, some ships were coming into port and they were so confused with the light. Looked on their chart and couldn't pick it up. They had the lighthouse on Mount Carmel and the one at Acca, but not this new one, so they were afraid to come in and stayed out at sea till daylight. They complained about the confusion, but the British Government instead of ordering the light to be removed had it marked on the chart.[19]

On Saturday 14 March, Mrs True took the group up past the new Western Pilgrim House to the Shrine of the Báb. The work on the new Pilgrim House, started by Harry and Ruth Randall in 1919, was completed with funds by Amelia Collins and others by December 1925. This is the same building that was later the first Seat of the Universal House of Justice in 1963.[20]

The visit to the Shrine of the Báb was a powerful one for Martha. She wrote:

> The stately Persian Bahai caretaker took us to a bench. He took off his shoes. We did the same and then he led us to the door & into the Tomb of the Báb. Upon the floor were soft, rich red rugs. Going to the threshold of the shrine he knelt in sublime devotion. One by one, our group of pilgrims bowed the forehead to the threshold and poured out a prayer of deepest gratitude. How it flashed upon the inner eye that His Holiness, the Báb, shot against the walls in Tabriz had heralded in the Coming of the Promised One of all ages! With what difficulty and danger had his precious remains been hid for years and then brought secretly to this holy mountain[,] the . . . home of the exiles! The millions who kneel and pray at this Tomb of the Báb will go forth to be heralds of this Bahai Cause and some, like Him, will be Martyrs to promote these teachings.[21]

'Abbas Qulí chanted the Prayer of Visitation. Afterwards, Effie noted:

> Every one who is visiting says what wonderful improvements Shoghi Effendi has made with the laying out of the gardens. If you could only see the rock and limestone that Mount Carmel is composed of, you would see what a stupendous work has been undertaken. He could only do one side because it was so expensive but four young Baha'i men offered their services free and are working there excavating the stone and carrying soil. It is a labor of love. How everyone serves[,] all one sees is a lesson to all. They prepare at the Master's House food for eighty and ninety people each day. Each one doing his share with such love and joy . . .[22]

Then the group moved to the adjacent Shrine of 'Abdu'l-Bahá, as Martha described:

> Then going to the other room in this divine house, the pilgrims bowed with foreheads at the threshold of Abdu'l Baha's shrine. But

94

He stood beside the pilgrims. This one heard Him say: 'Be happy! Be happy! Be happy!' and again 'Ye can always communicate with me through ["]Ya Baha El-Abha[,"]' And again came his words, 'Remember I am with you always, whether living or dead, I am with you to the end!'[23]

The next afternoon, the group visited the Eastern Pilgrim House near the Shrine of the Báb. Everyone in the group was asked to talk about the progress of the Faith in their countries. Effie said: 'You cannot imagine the pleasure and joy they get when news comes from the friends of other countries. Their faces just shine with light and devotion.'

They were also invited to a wedding on 15 March. All the women went to the home of 'Abbas Qulí and to visit and congratulate the bride. Margaret Stevenson described the wedding. The bride

looked very nice, but oh so shy. She was very pale and her hands were so cold – she had a beautiful dress on – white satin, embroidered with gold coloured sequins and beads – looked very handsome, then she wore a lovely veil of, I think, chiffon or ninon. After some talk we were asked to lead her to her bridegroom and I had the honour to give her my arm (just because I happened to be nearest to her). We took her to the bridal chamber where the bridegroom was waiting for her. He was standing near the door not looking at anybody. There were two chairs placed near the window and the bride was seated on one and the man who was to perform the ceremony which is very simple, brought the bridegroom to the other seat and joined their hands and said something which of course we could not understand. It was so strange to watch them – they were both so shy, when he was asked something – (I suppose if he would have her) he answered with his head turned from her and when she was asked, this, I suppose same question, she did not answer at all, but just turned her head over her shoulder – . . . and had to be asked again, when she did answer in a very subdued shy voice. Then some money was given to the bridegroom which he passed to her, for it is the custom that a man must give his bride money. After it was all over we said good bye to them and they were left alone for a while, and we went back to the other room and had Persian tea, cakes and sweets, after which we went home. (I forgot to say that each of us

took the bride a little gift.) When we were passing the room where
we had left the bride and bridegroom, he had gone over to the men's
meeting room and she had numbers of her friends round her.[24]

On 17 March the pilgrims went to Akka. The group consisted of Sarah,
Ethel and Hugh Blundell, Corinne True, Effie Baker, Fujita, Margaret
Stevenson and the cook and her daughter. After an hour's train ride,
they all climbed into 'Abdu'l-Bahá's carriage and visited the House of
'Abbúd and the Most Great Prison. When the group arrived at Bahjí,
they were joined by Mountfort Mills, Suhayl Effendi and 'Azízu'lláh.[25]
One of the highlights of the visit to Bahjí was talking with Rúhá
Khánum, who told them the Greatest Holy Leaf's story of their arrival
in Akka in 1868. Effie wrote in her notes:

> . . . the boat first came to Haifa. Landing, sea rough, the Turkish
> boat very dirty. They fixed up anything they could get to try and
> make a little privacy for Baha'u'llah who was very sick. There was
> no accommodation on the boat for them. They were put into small
> boat from the ship and rowed near shore. They carried the women
> and children on a chair. The people of Acca heard some prisoners
> were coming and were along the seashore to see them arrive. They
> numbered about seventy altogether (We saw the room they were put
> in for the first night. It was a privilege. Fugeta told us they rarely
> show it now. Of course the prison authorities allow you permission
> to visit the part of the Barracks where Baha'u'llah was imprisoned,
> but you cannot go without a permit.)
>   The Governor of the prison had no idea there would be so many
> and he did not know where to put them. Had no place ready for so
> many. There was no water except foul stagnant water from a round
> (?) well in the courtyard (which we also saw). They had to strain it
> through bits of cloth before they could drink it. They all got fever.
> Master nursed them. Greatest Holy Leaf couldn't drink, ill with
> fever . . .
>   When taken out of prison [1870] some Azeles [Covenant-
> breakers] came. They were much against the Cause. [After much
> persecution, a group of misguided Bahá'ís murdered three of the
> Covenant-breakers. The authorities then] took 'Abdu'l-Baha first
> and for three nights put him in dungeon with chains. Then they took

him to interview Baha'u'llah. He tried to hide the chains from his Mother's sight. [He] pleaded with them when they took Baha'u'llah to put him in the upper room and not the dungeon. They agreed. ['Abdu'l-Bahá] went into the dungeon himself and became ill from being in such a foul, damp place.

The last time he [Bahá'u'lláh] was brought before Court, he was commanded not to leave Acca. He said to them, 'I have news to make you happy. I am very happy this order is given. Now I really will have a good rest. My imprisonment is not my sorrow but the unfaithfulness of my followers.' She (Rouha Khanum) then told us how ['Abdu'l-Bahá] used to go and visit Baha'u'llah after he was allowed the freedom of the surrounding few miles of Acca and then went to live in the Palace of Behjeh, four or five miles out of the city. He used to go and see Baha'u'llah every Friday. Would put on [an] old Aba and go on foot, chanting prayers, praying slowly as if walking to his Beloved. Would rest in shade of old aquaduct with stone for a pillow (we saw the spot on the way to Behjeh).

Baha'u'llah would sit from early morning at his window watching for him and as soon as he saw [him] he would send the friends and pilgrims to meet 'Abdu'l-Baha, saying: 'The Master comes. Go and meet him!' It was a beautiful sight to see them meet. Such wonderful love, such kindness! 'Abdu'l-Baha would recount his work to Baha'u'llah. Then Baha'u'llah would direct his next week's work. Baha'u'llah would say, 'How happy you make me. You bring light and happiness to my heart.' Then Baha'u'llah would tell them all to leave the room and he and the Master would have a private talk for a while.

Baha'u'llah received so many letters. He would give them to 'Abdu'l-Baha to answer. 'Abdu'l-Baha would bring the answers and read them to him. Baha'u'llah would be pleased and praise 'Abdu'l-Baha for the way in which he answered them. (Rouha Khanum) told how 'Abdu'l-Baha would go to a room in the Inn (across from the house where Baha'u'llah was imprisoned for seven years [House of 'Abbúd]) called Master's drawing room. Here he would receive people, Baha'is and non-Baha'is and give them advice both spiritually and materially. At twelve o'clock would come and have lunch with Baha'u'llah and tell him all that transpired during the morning. Would go to the Barracks in the afternoon and write in little room (sentry box for soldier). Had no room where he could go to write privately. He would come back and again go and visit and help people.

(Rouha Khanum) spoke of the pilgrims coming on foot and the journey taking four and sometimes six months to complete. There were nine pilgrims once who came this way (Ismael, 'Abdu'l-Baha's gardener who is still living was one of them). They were very poor, nothing else to offer, they brought a white lily in a basin or pot and carried it on their heads, each taking their turn. Baha'u'llah said that when they offered it to him, 'It was the best present kings or queens could ever get,' though the valley of Behjeh was full of lillies, it was their love that counted . . .[26]

The next day, after visiting the Shrine of Bahá'u'lláh, they enjoyed the gardens 'Abdu'l-Bahá had created, then had lunch under two mulberry trees in the Riḍván Garden where Bahá'u'lláh and 'Abdu'l-Bahá used to sit. Following lunch, they returned to Haifa.[27]

On 21 March, the pilgrims took part in a second wedding and a Feast. At the Feast, Munírih Khánum gave each of the pilgrims a silk handkerchief and a ringstone blessed by 'Abdu'l-Bahá. The Western women had seats of honour with the Eastern men while the Eastern women met elsewhere. The *Newsletter* of the Haifa Local Assembly reported:

> Today as we were celebrating the Naw-Ruz Feast on Mount Carmel . . . our joy was intensified by the receipt of a cablegram from the Bahá'í friends in Auckland, New Zealand, extending to us love and greetings . . . This celebration was unique in that we had the pleasure of having with us representatives from practically all parts of the world: the first party of friends to visit the Holy Land from Australasia: Mrs Blundell, and daughter and son, Miss and Mr Blundell, Miss Stevenson, all from Auckland, New Zealand, and Miss Baker from Melbourne, Australia; Mrs Corinne True and Miss Martha Root from America. There are also pilgrims from India and Persia who have just arrived . . .[28]

The following day they visited the home of Badí Bushrui, a Bahá'í who was the Governor of Tiberias. Effie wrote that he was 'such a fine man.

His wife is very sweet and charming. They put on the phone record of the Master's voice. It was wonderful.' On 23 March, most of the group, except Martha, went to Jerusalem. Mrs Blundell had rented a seven-seater Studebaker car. A Bahá'í, Mr Tannous, who had a business taking tourists to Jerusalem with his 'Jerusalem Express' made all the arrangements.[29] They returned from Jerusalem via the Sea of Galilee to Haifa the following day.[30]

At the end of Effie's pilgrimage, on 31 March, she and the rest of the New Zealand group were shown the photograph of Bahá'u'lláh. Effie wrote that His was 'A wonderfully powerful face. To me the eyes were half-closed but they seemed to search one's heart and involuntarily the words came to one's lips "Oh! God forgive me!".' [31] Afterwards, wrote Margaret Stevenson,

> Shoghi Effendi had told us he would meet us up Mt Carmel, so after seeing the pictures we went up in Abdul Baha's carriage, Shoghi Effendi chanted for us and gave us flowers. Some of us walked home with him and he talked so beautifully. Soon after we got home he sent for Effie and me to say good bye – this time we went upstairs to his room where he does all His work and which looks right out on the big light on one Shrine. We had a lovely time and I asked him if He would read a prayer to us in English, which He did. He did read it so beautifully.[32]

Shortly after her departure, Rúḥí Afnán wrote to Sarah Blundell that the Greatest Holy Leaf, because of her health, had been unable to visit the Shrine of 'Abdu'l-Bahá for over a year. A short time later, however, she was able to visit the Tomb of her Brother. It was the first time she had seen the gardens that Shoghi Effendi had been so assiduously been developing, and they were a great and pleasant surprise for her, wrote Dr Esslemont.[33]

Martha Root stayed in Haifa for more than a month and spent considerable time in the company of the Greatest Holy Leaf and Dr Esslemont. Later, Martha wrote to him, urging him to teach Esperanto to Munavvar Khánum. He replied, 'I shall be very pleased to take on Monaver Khanum as an Esperanto pupil if she cares to start . . . I hope Monaver will turn out as satisfactory a pupil as yourself! I am proud of you.'[34] Shoghi Effendi was also proud of her. In a letter, he wrote that she was the 'nearest approach to the example set by 'Abdu'l-Bahá Himself to His disciples in the course of His journeys throughout the West'.[35]

A visitor

Sometime in April, Lady Dorothy Mills came to Haifa as part of a tour of Palestine and the Middle East. After returning home, she wrote a book called *Beyond the Bosporus*, in which she describes meeting Shoghi Effendi:

> He is a most charming young man, looking about thirty, small, slight featured, Persian in his general appearance, dressed in sober black robes, with composed and courteous manner. He seems to talk with every known language, and spoke to me with willing fluency and conviction of the aims of his movement . . .
>
> In the midst of the acrid, all-against-all atmosphere of Palestine, it was a rest to stroll leisurely round the little green garden, while its owner ran on in his smooth, cultured voice, and pulled the thorns from a huge bunch of roses that queer little wizened smiling Jap gardener gathered for me . . .
>
> Much of this [Bahá'í teachings] Shoghi Effendi expounded to me as we strolled round his rose-walled garden, with the picturesque metaphor and smile of his Persian forebears . . .
>
> They are a lovable and fascinating people, the Bahais: idealists who have dreamed a dream of peace that passes all understanding, who seek to bring relief to restless unhappy human hearts, who, by cooperation, would replace competition, and blend all races, religions, nations and classes into one harmonious whole. A beautiful dream, too good, it is feared, to come true in our present state of imperfection and atavistic crudity, but a dream that it is pleasant to come into contact with, as I did for a couple of hours, on a blazing April afternoon.[36]

First Dutch pilgrim

When Martha left Haifa, she returned briefly to Port Said where she met a Dutchman called Hajo Mesdeg. He had left his home in The Hague, Holland, and walked through Belgium and France to Italy where, pushed by 'an inward urge', he caught a Dutch cargo steamer to Egypt, arriving in Port Said. Before Mesdeg arrived, a well-known Bahá'í who lived in Port Said had a dream in which 'Abdu'l-Bahá came and gave him a Dutch cheese. He interpreted this as meaning that he would have a guest from Holland. He sent a local Bahá'í, Mahmood Effendi, to the ship where he encountered a tall, blond man, whom he invited to stay with his benefactor. Mesdeg had a card that read, 'On feet in search of Jesus Christ.' When Muḥammad Taqí asked him why he was there, Mesdeg said that he had heard that Christ had returned and he was looking for him. Muḥammad Taqí did not tell Mesdeg about the Bahá'í Faith, but told him to go to Haifa and meet Shoghi Effendi. While in Port Said, Mesdeg also met, in addition to Martha, Fred Schopflocher and a few other Bahá'ís. After spending time with the Bahá'ís and reading John Esslemont's book, *Bahá'u'lláh and the New Era*, he became a firm believer and determined to go to Haifa. He arrived there on 8 May and, fired up by his new beliefs, had translated an eight-page Bahá'í folder into Dutch by the next day. Dhikru'lláh Khádem saw Mesdeg at the Shrine of the Báb, with his face against the outside wall and tears streaming down his face.[37]

Mesdeg later wrote:

> I think about the great moments I spent in Acco and Haifa, about the peaceful strolls permitted to me by Shoghi Effendi, great grandson of Baha'u'llah and present leader of the Baha'is. Then we would walk on Mount Carmel, and suspend our conversation on philosophy, sexuality, religion and fanaticism to gaze at the far away snow-capped mountains of Judea or the sunset in the west. Then I think . . . of my kneeling down on Carmel at the graves of the Báb and his two prophets, father and son, (Father in Acco) my heavenly joys . . .[38]

Dhikru'lláh Khádem's first pilgrimage

Mesdeg was still in Haifa when the 21-year-old Dhikru'lláh Khádem, a future Hand of the Cause, made the first of six pilgrimages to the Bahá'í World Centre. He was so strongly attracted to the Guardian before going on his pilgrimage that he did not wait for his permission to arrive. When he came at the door to the House of 'Abdu'l-Bahá, the rashness of his actions suddenly struck him. As he was standing at the door overcome with remorse, Dr Esslemont and Mesdeg 'spotted him from a window in the Western Pilgrim House and quickly came out to welcome him. At the same time, one of the Bahá'ís recognized him and handed him the letter of permission that had been prepared that day and was about to be posted.'

Shoghi Effendi put him to work immediately – holding one end of a survey string while the Guardian marked the outline for the three additional rooms which were to be added to the Shrine of the Báb. When he left, Shoghi Effendi told him to tell the youth of Persia to study English and English literature. The young pilgrim was the first to put the suggestion in effect as he threw himself into the study of English. This later became invaluable to him when the Guardian had him translate materials from English into Persian. Before he left, Shoghi Effendi gave him a photograph of 'Abdu'l-Bahá with a rose.[39]

Egypt: Recognition of the Faith as an independent religion

In the meantime, momentous events concerning the recognition of the nature of the Bahá'í Faith as an independent religion were taking place in Egypt. In May, by losing a court case the Bahá'ís paradoxically won a great victory and another thorn in Shoghi Effendi's side was eased. It began in 1923 when two things happened. First, when Egypt began drafting its constitutional laws, there was much discussion about which religions to recognize. A committee was set up to examine the question and a judge of the Civil Courts, 'Abdu'l-Jalíl Bey Sa'ad, who was also a Bahá'í, wrote a series of articles emphasizing that all religions should be treated with 'equal freedom'. The committee passed the principle and theoretically it should have become law.[40]

The second thing that happened was that several Muslim women whose husbands had become Bahá'ís appealed to the courts for divorces, saying that their husbands had abandoned Islam. Cases were brought in 1923, 1924 and 1925. To resolve the cases, the Muslim Ecclesiastical Court had to examine the Bahá'í Faith and compare it to Islam. Their conclusion was:

All these prove definitely that the Bahá'í religion is a new religion, with an independent platform and laws and institutions peculiar to it, and show a different and contradictory belief to the beliefs and laws and commandments of Islám. Nor can we state a Baháʼí to be a Muslim, or the reverse; as we cannot say of a Buddhist or a Brahman or a Christian that he is a Muslim or the reverse . . .

. . . it is essential to maintain that he [Muhammad] was the last of the Prophets and that his laws are eternal and can never be abrogated or changed . . . To depart from Islám is heresy and this heresy may be either through a heretical statement or an untrue belief . . . This is the worst form of heresy, for it is the denial of Islám . . .

The religious law states that heresy dissolves the contract of marriage . . . For these reasons the court has decided on the dissolution of the contract of marriage of (the parties on trial) . . .[41]

During the second half of 1925 Shoghi Effendi must have been waiting to see what would happen as a result of this decision, but since it failed 'to perturb public sentiment', he commented in early January the following year that it was a step towards 'the eventual universal acceptance of the Baháʼí Faith, as one of the independent recognized religious systems of the world':

Among the disturbing factors that have intensified the difficulties of the present situation is the extraordinary judgment recently passed by the Supreme Religious Court of Egypt, declaring the Baháʼís of that land adherents of a Faith heretical in character, and at variance with the accepted doctrines of Islám, and hence utterly outside the sphere of its jurisdiction. What exactly the implication of this verdict will be, the effect its practical application will have on the relations of the Baháʼís with the followers of the Muslim Faith, what measure of publicity it will receive, what impression it will create in Muslim lands and particularly in hostile Persia, the future only can disclose. So far it has failed to perturb public sentiment or give rise to any official or public demonstration of a nature that would justify or necessitate any action on the part of the American Baháʼís . . . It is clear and evident that Western influence, the loosening of the bonds of religion, and the consequent waning vitality of the once powerful Muhammadan stronghold of Egypt are in a great measure to account for the indifference and apathy that now seem to characterize the attitude of the masses towards this important and vital issue. This decision, however locally embarrassing, in the present stage of our development, may be regarded as an initial step taken by our very opponents in the path of the eventual universal acceptance of the Bahá'í Faith, as one of the independent recognized religious systems of the world.[42]

This development was so dramatic that the Guardian addressed it again a year later:

Of all the diverse issues which today are gradually tending to consolidate and extend the bounds of the Revelation of Bahá'u'lláh, the decision of Egypt's religious Tribunal regarding the Bahá'ís under its jurisdiction appears at the present moment to be the most powerful in its challenge, the most startling in its character, and the most perplexing in the consequences it may entail. I have already alluded in my letter of January 10, 1926 . . . to a particular feature of this momentous verdict, which after mature deliberation has obtained the sanction of Egypt's highest ecclesiastical authorities, has been communicated and printed, and is regarded as final and binding. I have stressed in my last reference to this far-reaching pronouncement the negative aspect of this document which condemns in most unequivocal and emphatic language the followers of Bahá'u'lláh as the believers in heresy, offensive and injurious to Islám, and wholly incompatible with the accepted doctrines and practice of its orthodox adherents.

A closer study of the text of the decision will, however, reveal the fact that coupled with this strong denunciation is the positive assertion of a truth . . . that the Bahá'í Faith is a 'new religion', 'entirely independent' and, by reason of the magnitude of its claim and the character of its 'laws, principles and beliefs', worthy to be reckoned as one of the established religious systems of the world.[43]

As is common in precedence rulings, the issue did not die away with this ruling. Problems were renewed in 1929 in such wise that Shoghi Effendi sent the faithful Mountfort Mills to Cairo where he worked with 'Abdu'l-Jalíl Bey Sa'ad. The two men visited the Prime Minister and other high officials in an effort to improve the lives of the Egyptian Bahá'ís. When Mountfort left for other work, 'Abdu'l-Jalíl Bey Sa'ad pursued the negotiations alone. Later, in 1934, an Egyptian court refused to legalize for the Bahá'ís a Declaration of Trust, a document that states that one party holds property owned by others for certain objectives,. 'Abdu'l-Jalíl Bey Sa'ad, through his patience, persistence and tact, finally managed to have the document legalized. 'This historic act greatly facilitated future transactions with the Government.'[44] 'Abdu'l-Jalíl Bey Sa'ad was posthumously named a Hand of the Cause of God by Shoghi Effendi in 1942.[45]

Lorol Schopflocher

On 28 May, Lorol Schopflocher, the wife of future Hand of the Cause Fred Schopflocher, arrived in Haifa after a successful travel-teaching trip through Russia, Persia and Iraq.[46] Florence Evaline (Lorol) Schopflocher was a powerful teacher of the Faith who eventually circled the globe nine times and made teaching trips to eighty-six countries, including Russia, Burma, Japan, China, India, Iraq, Iran and Finland. In 1924 and 1925 she travelled in Iran and she had several audiences with King Feisal in Iraq.[47] Sent by the Guardian to speak with the King about the House of Bahá'u'lláh on her first visit, she apparently heard that the King was not receiving visitors.

> So one afternoon she simply drove to the palace and as she approached the gates she floored the accelerator, roared past the guards, and came to a screeching halt at the palace steps. The guards rushed shouting after the car, and a group of startled men came out of the palace to see what was happening. Among the latter was the king. Lorol descended from her chariot in full war gear and concern immediately focused on whether she was alright. The king took her in to take tea. And so one more success was achieved in what one might call the Indiana Jones technique of proclamation.[48]

Lorol was one of the first women to use air travel to aid her teaching. In 1926, she was the first woman to fly from England to India and flew twice on the Hindenburg. She had been scheduled to fly on the Hindenburg's catastrophic final flight, but her booking had been cancelled.[49]

Effie stays in Haifa

Effie Baker returned to Haifa from England shortly after Lorol, following an invitation from the ladies of the Holy Family. However, she found that Shoghi Effendi was away in Switzerland. She had initially planned to stay only two weeks, but discovering that Jináb-i-Fádil and Fujita were both ill she immediately set about caring for them and the ladies of the Holy Family until the Guardian returned. She wrote to Hyde and Clara Dunn in Australia about her change in plans:

> I have been a little help to them here in the Pilgrim House and am doing most of the work since Fujita was sick. He is what you might say resting on his oars a bit. The Holy Family said I've been such a help to them and Díyá'i'yyih Khánum (Shoghi Effendi's mother) says that at last she has found a Mother for the Pilgrim Home. They asked me if I could really be happy and content to stay here always and would it be possible for me to stay. I told them I am content to serve the cause wherever I am needed, that personally I could stay but my desire is to serve the cause and obey Shoghi Effendi and that he had told me to return to Australia so they have asked me to wait till he returns and then ask him if they can keep me here.[50]

Effie soon became good friends with the women in Shoghi Effendi's family and, not considering herself to be a good public speaker, she saw a great opportunity to serve the Faith and meet many interesting people by serving him in Haifa. When the Guardian returned on 15 October, she offered her services, but Shoghi Effendi told her it would be better to return to Australia. Then,

> a couple of days before the date of my departure, Shoghi Effendi took me with him for the last visit to Bahá'u'lláh's Holy Shrine. On the drive back he said to me 'You know Effie, a general always sends his good soldiers afar, he keeps the bad ones always under his eye'. Next afternoon I was walking up the terrace (the only one at that time) to visit the Holy Shrine for the last time. Shoghi Effendi was starting to come down with some Persian pilgrims. He told them to continue and stopped to speak to me. He said 'Effie I've reconsidered my decision. I'm going to keep you here'. I said 'Oh! Shoghi Effendi I am evidently one of the bad soldiers you told me about yesterday', and we had a hearty laugh together.[51]

That was the beginning of eleven years of service at the World Centre.

Shoghi Effendi quickly learned to appreciate her considerable talents as a model-maker and a photographer in addition to her superlative work as the Western Pilgrim House hostess. The value of her photography quickly became apparent. In February 1924, Horace Holley had written to the Guardian about an idea for a Bahá'í yearbook. Shoghi Effendi took the suggestion and called on Horace, a gifted writer and the Secretary of the National Spiritual Assembly of the United States and Canada, to publish in 1925 what was called the *Bahá'í Year Book*. Many of Effie's photographs were included. When Volume 2 came out the next year, the National Assembly suggested that the title be changed to *The Bahá'í World, A Biennial International Record*, which was approved by Shoghi Effendi.[52]

Because of her model and toy-making abilities, Effie also made landscape models to help Shoghi Effendi's planning of new sections of the gardens. In 1930, Shoghi Effendi used her photographic talents to document many of the Bábí Holy Places in Iran for publication in *The Dawn-Breakers*.[53] In 1936, Effie returned to her homeland, Australia, where she looked after the National Archives over a long period.[54]

The National Spiritual Assembly of the United States and Canada

The United States had had an administrative body acting, to some extent, at a national level since 1909 with the Executive Board of the Bahá'í Temple Unity. This group, however, was mostly concerned with the construction of the House of Worship in Wilmette. Shoghi Effendi, in *God Passes By*, indicated that the National Spiritual Assembly of the United States and Canada was not officially formed until July 1925. This was a little unusual given the fact that Shoghi Effendi had called for the Executive Board to be converted into an elected legislative body in April 1922 and addressed his first letter to the members of the National Spiritual Assembly of the United States on 23 December 1922.[55]

The 1922 election, however, bore no resemblance to what we know today as a National Convention. There were nominations, with different groups supporting different candidates, and even a 'straw vote' to reduce the number of possible candidates.[56] It took three years for Shoghi Effendi to gently guide the North Americans to the understanding of how a National Spiritual Assembly was to be elected. From March 1923 to July 1925, when the National Spiritual Assembly of the

United States and Canada was officially formed in the eyes of Shoghi Effendi, the Guardian sent at least nine letters that clarified some aspect of the electoral process or the duties of that body.[57]

Even so, when the National Spiritual Assembly of the United States and Canada was elected in July 1925, the result wasn't quite as Shoghi Effendi might have preferred. To the National Assembly, the Convention elected Horace Holley, Mountfort Mills, Florence Morton, Fred Schopflocher, Roy Wilhelm, Allen McDaniel, Carl Scheffler, Ali Kuli Khan and Amelia Collins. In addition, they also elected a group of alternate members who could take the place of regular members who were absent. This group included Alfred Lunt, William Randall, May Maxwell, George Latimer, Louis Gregory, Elizabeth Greenleaf, Mariam Haney and Keith Ransom-Kehler.[58]

The National Spiritual Assembly, however, would bear enormous responsibilities. In October, Shoghi Effendi faced another complication in his efforts to develop the World Centre on Mount Carmel. There was a possibility of Jewish developments near the Shrine of the Báb. In a letter to the newly elected National Spiritual Assembly, he wrote:

> Surely the Bahá'ís of the world, ever on the alert and with an eye to the future, will, no matter how pressed by financial obligations, arise while there is yet time to contribute each his share in securing for posterity such land as lies in close proximity to the Holy Shrine – an area the acquisition of which in time will prove indispensable if the sublime vision of 'Abdu'l-Baha is to be realized. I appeal to you, and through you to every earnest and conscientious believer, to safeguard in particular the land extending southward from these Shrines which now, alas! is gravely exposed to the assaults of covetous and speculating interests.[59]

The Americans quickly responded to this call.

The passing of Dr Esslemont

John Esslemont returned to Haifa near the end of September, but his health was still very delicate. Early in November, he suffered a relapse:

> The chronic disease from which he had suffered in the past had very

much undermined his weak constitution and his eagerness to serve the Cause he so dearly loved, despite all advice to the contrary, was a great tax upon his failing strength. His stay at the Black Forest in Germany all through the summer had improved his health, but upon his return to Haifa he felt rather weak and he was frequently in bed for a few days. Not until a fortnight ago was Dr. Esslemont seriously ill and even then the doctors thought that in spite of the fact that the trouble from which he had suffered in the past was now more active there was no reason for great anxiety. His health was slowly improving and everything was being done to give him the best medical advice obtainable here in Haifa, when suddenly and unexpectedly at about midnight of November 21st the doctor had a severe stroke of 'cerebral embolus'. The next day a second stroke followed and he at last succumbed to the third which he had at about seven o'clock of the next evening. The attending doctors were both European – one Italian and the other German. Our two Bahá'í doctors Yunis Khán and Mírzá Arastú . . . put themselves at his disposal . . .

The funeral service was both simple and touching. His body was washed by two of the friends, dressed and wrapped in white silk cloth and perfumed by attar of roses. On his finger Shoghi Effendi placed his own Bahá'í ring which he had worn for a good many years. Laid in a simple casket of walnut and placed in the hall of the Pilgrim House, the friends gathered together and said their funeral prayer over him. The casket was carried for a short distance by Shoghi Effendi and then placed in the Master's carriage and accompanied by the sons-in-law of the Master it slowly wound its way, followed by eleven other cabs carrying the friends, to the foot of Mt. Carmel. There it was laid to rest in that beautifully-situated cemetery, and flowers from the garden of the Master's home were scattered over his grave. Simple as he was in his life and character, equally simple was his funeral service. And yet just as in the simplicity of his character lay his many virtues, in like manner did the simplicity of that service sink into every heart and fill every eye with tears.[60]

John Esslemont had arrived in Haifa exactly one year earlier. In early 1926, Shoghi Effendi received a drawing from the family of Dr Esslemont for his gravestone. The design was obviously rather ornate, because on 23 January a reply written on behalf of Shoghi Effendi read:

With regard to the design of the grave of Dr. Esslemont, a picture of which you had sent enclosed, Shoghi Effendi wishes to inform you that although he himself liked the design and would have been glad to follow it altogether, up till the present the tombs of the Bahá'ís have been very simply built and the custom has been to have them as beautiful and at the same time as simple as possible. This general custom holds true even in the case of the tombs of the Master's mother and brother. The graves are built of white marble stones but the designs have in every case been simple, and he wishes you very much to make the family of Dr. Esslemont understand that although Shoghi Effendi will not be able to follow the design strictly he will try to make the tomb as near it as possible, while keeping within the range of the customary simplicity.[61]

The resulting tombstone, though more ornate than many in the Bahá'í cemetery, is clean and simple.

Another future Hand of the Cause

The day of Dr Esslemont's first stroke was the very day that a 17-year-old Persian youth arrived in Haifa. He knew little of the Faith at that time, even though others in his family were distinguished Bahá'ís and he had met Mírzá Maḥmúd-i-Zarqání, 'Abdu'l-Bahá's translator and secretary on his European and American journeys. At one point, he had read the book *Some Answered Questions* and had attempted to refute its arguments, but 'unable to find fault he was left frustrated although interested . . .' On 21 November, on his way to begin studying at the American University in Beirut, this youth, named Hasan Balyuzi, stopped in Haifa and had a single, short meeting with Shoghi Effendi. As he wrote later:

During my stay of one night (November 21st–22nd) on Mount Carmel two eminent Persian Bahá'í physicians who were there, Dr. Yúnis Khán Afrúkhtih and Dr. Arastú Khán Hakím, were called in the early hours of the morning to Dr. Esslemont's bedside. Shoghi Effendi sat up with him through the night.

The next day I left for Beirut in the company of Dr. Afrúkhtih and Dr. Hakím.

It was that bounty of meeting Shoghi Effendi and all that I saw in him, which confirmed me in the Faith of Bahá'u'lláh. The course of my life was changed.[62]

In Balyuzi's obituary in *The Bahá'í World*, Moojan Momen wrote:

He was taken to the house of the Master and put into a drawing-room all by himself. He did not know what was going to happen. Suddenly Shoghi Effendi entered the room. Balyuzi rose and wanted to kiss his hand [as was the Persian custom], but Shoghi Effendi would not allow this and instead embraced him. Then Shoghi Effendi sat him down and talked with him for more than an hour. What particularly impressed Hasan was the way in which Shoghi Effendi would answer a problem or a question by drawing the answer out of the questioner . . .

And so it was that his Faith was confirmed and when he went on to Beirut and the University he was asked his religion for the official forms, he said 'Bahá'í'.[63]

Years later, Hasan Balyuzi's wife noted that 'Hasan was so struck by the kindness and courtesy of the Guardian, at such an anxious time, to a boy of 17 that from that time he became confirmed in the Faith'.

The Guardian was encouraging Persian youth to study at the American University in Beirut, the same institution, then called the Syrian Protestant College, that he himself had attended. The college was becoming a 'centre of attraction' for Persian Bahá'í students and Hasan Balyuzi soon found himself in a leadership role as one of the most active supporters of the Faith. He arranged weekly programmes, encouraged the students to prepare talks in English on some aspect of the Faith and regularly reported on the activities to Shoghi Effendi. He also arranged visits to Haifa for the students at the Easter holiday. Hasan lived in Beirut until 1932, when he moved to London.[64]

1926

Looking for help

The passing of John Esslemont left Shoghi Effendi once again without qualified secretarial help. In January, he wrote a letter in which he told of the 'oppressive burden of responsibility and care which it is my lot and privilege to shoulder' and of 'my unceasing toil, my afflictions, and perplexities'. During the year, he wrote to various individuals, for example: 'There are most complex and delicate problems before me and I feel the need for competent, fearless and trusted collaborators'. In May, he wrote to Horace Holley saying, 'I have often felt the extreme desirability of having a collaborator like you working by my side here in Haifa. The loss of Dr Esslemont is keenly felt by me and my hope is that the conditions here and abroad will enable me to establish the work in Haifa upon a more systematic basis. I am waiting for a favourable time.' But in September, the Guardian again wrote to Horace saying, 'How much I feel the need for a similar worker by my side in Haifa, as competent, as thorough, as methodical, as alert as yourself. You cannot and should not leave your post for the present. Haifa will have to take care of itself for some time.'[1]

The first Alaskan pilgrims and others

During the first few months of 1926, several English and North American Bahá'ís visited Haifa on pilgrimage. These included Albert Joseph from Manchester in England, Orcella Rexford and Dr Gayne Gregory from Alaska, Canadian Elizabeth Greenleaf, and Victoria Bedekian and Keith Ransom-Kehler, who were travelling together.[2] Albert Joseph arrived on 4 January and was met by Rúḥí Effendi, whom he had known in England. He had the bounty of meeting the Guardian that first afternoon. On his return, Albert told others that the hours he had spent waiting for that meeting seemed like months. He had met Shoghi Effendi in Manchester, England, in 1921, but the man he met in Haifa was quite different from what he remembered. He noted that Shoghi Effendi had the 'same bright face; eyes that shone even more radiantly; but a spirit intensified.' Albert had questions he wanted to ask, but he never needed to because the Guardian answered them all in his talks. Over and over Shoghi Effendi told him that the Bahá'ís must meet often and be united.[3]

Orcella Rexford and her husband, Dr Gayne Gregory, also arrived in Haifa in January. Three years previously, in 1922, Orcella had gone on a six-month travel-teaching trip to Alaska with Emogene Hoagg and, while there, had met and brought Gayne into the Faith. The two married in November.[4] The couple left Alaska in 1925 to travel-teach in Honolulu, after which they criss-crossed America before travel-teaching through Europe. In January 1926, they received permission to visit Shoghi Effendi and went to Haifa.

Orcella wrote:

How overjoyed we were to think that at last the wish of our hearts was to be fulfilled, for I had long felt the need of consulting with our beloved Guardian about our work. We were with him eleven days, during which time there were no other pilgrims present. For this reason it was permissible for Dr. Gregory to have the supreme blessing of an audience with the Greatest Holy Leaf, one which was seldom granted. She expressed her joy at meeting the first Bahá'í pilgrim from Alaska to visit the Holy Land. She remarked, 'I hope as you have been a pioneer in Alaska in a material sense, in the future you will pioneer in the spiritual field. It is fine to have your wife to work with you; in this companionship you are like the two wings of a bird and can fly perfectly.' She gave him a vial of rose-water. How exalted he felt to be in the presence of the greatest living woman in the world! Those days seemed like days spent in heaven with Shoghi Effendi and the charming ladies of the household. We returned to America with greater inspiration to carry on our work which was crowned with greater success than ever.[5]

Elizabeth Greenleaf met Shoghi Effendi on 7 February, near the end of her pilgrimage. One of her questions was whether or not the Bahá'í Cause was a 'great spiritual democracy'. His answer was:

> Yes, in that the governing body is elected by a free and absolutely free ballot; that the delegates were elected by the people, and that in turn they elected the members of this body. However, after the body is elected, it is supreme. If there are any questions after the election, they should hold over in abeyance until the following year. But there must be absolute unity and loyalty to the body once elected. There must be the utmost loving kindness. That unless every one's heart was in the utmost loving state, we could not have the full expression of the Will of Baha'u'llah. That there was a unity existing that was not expressed. The test of loyalty is loyalty to the Assemblies.[6]

Hers was a fairly short pilgrimage. Shoghi Effendi said she could stay longer, but the sailing schedule was such that she had to leave then or stay another full month. The Guardian told her:

> The amount of spiritual blessing does not depend upon the length of time spent here. I am very pleased with you and have great hopes of your work in Canada. You and Mrs Maxwell must get together and plan how to reach people of capacity – people with culture, depth, influence and true education.

Shoghi Effendi concluded saying, 'It will please me if you devote all of your time in Canada with Mrs Maxwell. Your health is precious. You must guard it.'[7]

Victoria Bedekian

Next came a string of pilgrims, starting with Victoria Bedekian and Keith Ransom-Kehler, who arrived together on 29 January. They were followed by Dr and Mrs Guthrie, Edna McKinney and Berthalin Osgood. May Stebbins and her daughter Isabelle arrived on 19 March.

Victoria Bedekian, 'Auntie' to almost everyone, was on pilgrimage between 29 January and 3 April. She had become a Bahá'í in 1919 and this was her first visit to Haifa. She and Keith, with whom she was travelling, were met by Fujita who sent Auntie ahead in 'Abdu'l-Bahá's carriage to the Pilgrim House while he and Keith dealt with the luggage and Customs. Victoria was given a room with a view of the Shrine of the Báb which, at its first sighting, caused tears to cascade down her face. That surprised her:

> I stood at that window overlooking these much-longed for scenes and wept and wept. Why Haifa right from the beginning got all these tears is beyond my comprehension. I seldom if ever wept at home. I was a comfort to others there, I was resolute and brave. But here I was a babe, like a helpless child, needing comfort. Keith said that I sobbed so loudly at the Shrines that all heard me, so I tried to hide my sobs, and after some practice I learned to sob without a sound.[8]

Victoria had a difficult pilgrimage both physically and emotionally, suffering ailments and being overwhelmed by the whole experience. She was not young and physical exertion was painful. The ladies of the Holy Household took her under their collective wing. When she couldn't walk far, they took her in 'Abdu'l-Bahá's carriage for a ride around the area. When she could walk, they walked with her to make sure she arrived at the Shrines. Munavvar Khánum especially adopted Victoria and took care of her. She took her for walks, always arm in arm. Victoria thought this was pretty funny: she was tall and light complexioned while Munavvar was short and dark. Munavvar dressed in Persian fashion while Victoria wore Western clothes. Munavvar went with her to Bahjí, as well, where Victoria was so enthralled with the spiritual atmosphere that she wouldn't have eaten had her companion not kept putting food on her plate and insisting she eat.[9]

Victoria's first meeting with Shoghi Effendi was traumatic. It was at lunch and Shoghi Effendi was already there when Auntie arrived, but she didn't recognize him. She had been asked by a friend back home to especially greet Azíz'u'lláh Bahádur and somehow she thought that the Persian man across from her was Aziz, so she asked, 'Are you Aziz'u'llah Bahádur?' Keith Ransom-Kehler was also at the table and was horrified, quickly telling her, 'Why no, this is Shoghi Effendi!' The mistake bothered the Guardian not at all and he smiled and asked her about her travels.[10]

Victoria loved macaroni and Keith was amazed at how often she ate it while on the ship coming to Haifa. But it was a complete surprise to both when their first meal with Shoghi Effendi was a dish of macaroni. Shoghi Effendi handed her the dish and asked, 'Do you like this dish?' In surprise, Victoria replied, 'Well, how did these get here!' They all had a good laugh.[11]

On another day, however, a letter Victoria had written gave her a big reason to cry. She was a prolific letter writer and this one was to Alfred Lunt. Keith came by as she finished the letter, so Victoria showed it to her. Strangely, Keith asked her if she was going to send the letter. Baffled, she said yes. Keith then replied that she had better write a letter, too, since Victoria's needed an explanation. Confused and upset, Victoria took the letter to Shoghi Effendi to read. At lunch that day, Keith mentioned the letter and the Guardian suggested it needed a couple of changes. Victoria was devastated and ran from the room in tears. She wandered up Mount Carmel, got lost and then was caught in a downpour. As dusk fell, she found her way, dripping wet, to the Shrine of 'Abdu'l-Bahá and tearfully asked Him for guidance. Slowly she felt a calm come over her, as though angels had come to comfort her and take away her burdens. Then she descended to find the Guardian. She soon met him as he ascended looking for her. They sat together with her hands in his and he told her she must not feel sad. Then he gave her a small book and told her to read it and study it very carefully. The title was *Plan for Unified Action to Spread the Bahá'í Cause* and it was all about unity and how working together to build the Temple would also build unity. Shoghi Effendi told her, 'Read it, study it, and then write.' Reading the little book brought back Auntie's happiness and focused her on creating unity above all else.[12]

When Victoria returned to America, Shoghi Effendi wrote that she should put all her energies into the Plan for Unified Action:

> I have specially requested that indefatigable pioneer of the Cause of God, our well-beloved Bahá'í sister, Mrs. Victoria Bedekian, to concentrate for the present all the resources of her mind and heart upon this vast and vital undertaking. I have urged her to direct her energies to this lofty purpose, and by the aid of her most valuable letters arouse both the East and the West to a fresh consciousness of the significance and urgency of the object you have set yourselves to achieve.[13]

Victoria also enjoyed Fujita. She wrote that he had a parrot to which he fed oranges, candy and bread. Fujita said that the green and red bird had belonged to 'Abdu'l-Bahá in Akka and that it 'laughs and calls and shrieks'. She evidently had not been particularly enamoured of the 'screeching polly' until she learned that it had been a companion to the Master.[14]

One night while at Bahjí, Victoria was in the gardens enjoying the moonlight on the Shrine, when two men came toward her. One she recognized as Mírzá Muḥammad-'Alí, the Arch-breaker of Bahá'u'lláh's Covenant. For a moment they looked at each other, then Mírzá Muḥammad-'Alí asked, 'Who are you, and what do you want?' She replied that she was staying there that night and, after a silent pause, the men walked away.[15]

The next day, Victoria wrote about the 'Nakazeen Donkey'. The pilgrims were going to a Druse village, but there weren't enough donkeys to carry everyone. Munavvar Khánum said that they would have to borrow one from the Covenant-breakers, the 'Nakazeen'.

> All the pilgrims exclaimed that they would not ride a nacazin donkey, they would rather not go. Then I spoke up. 'I'll ride it, Monaver, I'll make a good Bahá'í out of it. A donkey at any rate has more sense than being a Nacazin, even if it is obliged to serve them.' Ho! 'Auntie' would ride the Nacazin donkey! And all was well, we could start. And strange to say, I never rode that donkey. Everybody wanted it. In the end, Berthaline Osgood took it. Poor little mule, so patient, so weary looking, so gentle. How aloof animals are from the sins of their owners! I rode a horse. It was the first time I had alighted one since my girlhood in the wild west of the Rockies in America.[16]

Victoria's husband, Mardiros, who was apparently not a Bahá'í, had purchased a black silk dress he wanted Victoria to give to the Greatest Holy Leaf. His request left his wife dumbfounded, since he had never even mentioned the name of that great lady before. But when she went into the presence of the Greatest Holy Leaf, she was too embarrassed to present Mardiros's gift. Just before she left, she asked May Stebbins to deliver the dress to her. Still embarrassed, she tried to avoid the Greatest Holy Leaf, but that lady would not let her leave without saying goodbye. She also gave Victoria two handkerchiefs for her husband, saying that they had been blessed by 'Abdu'l-Bahá Himself. Then she thanked her for the dress and said she would pray for Mardiros.[17]

While pressing Victoria and others to take care of their health, Shoghi Effendi's own health was suffering from the constant surge of problems. In March he noted: 'The overwhelming burden of pressing cares and responsibilities necessitated my departure at a time when . . . I was most anxious to receive my friends and coworkers from various parts of the world.'[18] At one point, Effie Baker wanted to see how late the Guardian worked each night. For several nights in a row, she attempted to stay up to learn when Shoghi Effendi turned out his office lights. She was never able to stay awake long enough to find out.[19]

Keith Ransom-Kehler

Keith Ransom-Kehler had arrived in Haifa with Victoria Bedekian on the steamer *Adriatic*. Five hundred passengers disembarked so she was surprised when Fujita, who had never seen her before, called up, 'Welcome, Mrs Ransom-Kehler. I am so glad to see you.' Isfandíyár and Effie Baker greeted her next. Keith wrote that they were

> greeted by Fujita, a child of Nippon, then by Isfendiar from the Cradle of the Faith, and next by Effie Baker, cameo-like, the first person in Australia to embrace this all inclusive message. On, on, the irresistible tide of fellowship and goodwill is carrying the soul of humanity to a new attitude of love, abnegation and service. Effie, with a self-effacement that only the love of God could give, reflects the spirit of the Holy Family in her work at the pilgrim house. She comes out to embrace me with an unaffected cordiality and to knit still closer those intangible bonds that will hold me to this sacred spot forever.[20]

For the next nine weeks, she basked in the serenity of the Bahá'í Holy Places and the presence of Shoghi Effendi. Though highly impressed with Shoghi Effendi's authority and bearing, she was overwhelmed by the load he carried. She said that he was 'nearly crushed' by a 'stupendous avalanche of personal correspondence', much of it from American Bahá'ís who wrote to air their dissatisfactions and complaints against individuals and Spiritual Assemblies. Keith wrote a long letter to the 1926 American National Convention in which she quoted the Guardian as saying, 'What we need is not so much devotion to the Cause . . . but . . . love . . . must be translated into love for one another. If this Cause cannot unite two individuals how can we expect it to unite the world?' He said that the 'greatest lesson' for the American Bahá'ís to learn was 'spontaneous, full and hearty support of the Spiritual Assemblies'. He emphasized that it was not because their decisions are 'sacrosanct' or 'infallible', but because such support is 'the only means by which the Cause can be safeguarded'.[21] Shoghi Effendi himself said that 'I am submerged in a sea of activities, anxieties and preoccupations. My mind is extremely tired and I feel I am becoming inefficient and slow due to this mental fatigue.'[22] In her letter, Keith wrote:

Is it generally known in America that our Beloved was forced, at an hour's notice, to leave Haifa, because he was threatened with what in the case of an ordinary person might be called a nervous breakdown from overwork? The state of his health, his chronic exhaustion is, I am convinced, a matter of as genuine concern to every true believer as it is to the members of the Holy Household. Eighty percent of his time is spent in reading and answering letters, ninety percent of which are purely personal. We see from his statistics that twenty percent of his time is left for the administrative work of the Cause, entertaining guests, meeting pilgrims, translating, thinking, reading, reflecting, meditation, planning, creating for direct and intimate contact with the detailed working of nine national assemblies and for these multifarious considerations connected with this unsettled and transitory phase of the Cause through which we are at present passing. The fact that under this ceaseless pressure there is not one moment left for recreation, exercise or personal expression of any description, clearly indicates that his power to go on functioning and enduring are entirely superhuman. Is it any wonder, beloved friends of God, that our Guardian was nearly crushed under this stupendous avalanche of personal correspondence?

It seemed very evident to the pilgrims who were there with me that we must take some vigorous measure to protect and relieve this most precious being from such a needless and unimportant burden. This is by way of explanation of his involuntary vacation.

He returned seeming fitter and more eager; but almost at once news so distressing and serious came to him from America that we sadly watched the little moment of reprieve that he had snatched from the treadmill of his daily life fade into anxiety and distress. Letters were reaching him from several scattered sources expressive of dissatisfaction with the 'Unified' plan to which he had given such hearty approval and expected so much. Some of the letters were written after the receipt of his cablegram sanctioning the soundness and nobility of the project. He sent for me at once and questioned me as to the cause of this attitude: I was quite as non-plussed as he and could offer no explanation. He said that one of the letters suggested that it was contrary to the desires of the Master; but he pointed out that such was not the case as the Master had never disapproved of the collection of funds provided it was entirely voluntary. 'I wish that it might be possible for you to attend the convention to take my message to them,' he said. 'I will arrive in time,' I answered, 'to send a letter with this news at any rate.' 'Do by all means,' he replied. 'Say that the present course, is fraught with the gravest danger to the Cause. It would lead rapidly to a division, which must at all cost be avoided. We must remove all demarcation by discussion sincere and full.'

On another occasion he said that the greatest lesson that we have to learn in America is the lesson that has already been learned in Persia – spontaneous, full and hearty support of the Spiritual Assemblies. 'But I have written this all many times in my letters,' he added sadly.

A few weeks before, the discussion had turned to those who feel that they must carry out special missions assigned them by the Master. 'Let them realize,' he said, 'that the voice of the Master is speaking to them through their Assemblies and of our subservience to them. This form of government is taken from the text of the Aqdas. The Master goes to the final extreme by saying that even if the decisions of the local Assemblies are contrary to fact they must be supported. People may think that this savors of absolutism and autocracy but it is the only means by which the Cause can be safe-guarded.' He then went on to say that though the decisions of the Assemblies must be obeyed they are neither sacrosanct nor infallible and must be always open to vision; the suggestions and criticisms of the friends must be gladly welcomed by the Assemblies, and seriously considered. 'If we are too precipitate and dictatorial on the one hand,' he said, 'or too aloof and independent on the other, the Bahá'í structure crumbles, the unity for which we are striving becomes a mere name and, – there is nothing left to organize. The most essential thing in all matters is for the friends to work in harmony, for if they do not work together,' he added with quick acumen, 'there is no need to teach – there is nothing to teach. What we need is not so much devotion to the Cause for this has been already abundantly proven and is being proved; but this love for God and for the Master and for the Cause, must be translated into love for one another. If this Cause cannot unite two individuals how can we expect it to unite the world?' . . .

Beloved brothers and sisters this is his message, this youth is under thirty, labouring day and night for us, sacrificing every human desire and tendency to further our efforts; deprived for our sake of all those natural satisfactions so significant to an alert and sensitive nature; with no more personal life than a graven image, no more thought of self than a breeze or a flower, just a hollow reed for the divine melody. Any one of us is ready to die for him, but can we conscientiously number ourselves among those who are willing to live for him?[23]

The 'Unified Plan' referred to above was one of two Unified Plans of Action developed by the National Spiritual Assembly of the United States and Canada. One plan involved the propagation of the Faith across the continent in response to the initial Tablets of the Divine Plan, and the other was to raise enough funds for the building of the first unit of the Mashriqu'l-Adhkár. Accomplishing these goals forced the new National Assembly to develop budgets. Prior to this, many people would contribute to specific projects and the idea of simply giving unreservedly to the Faith was a new concept. Not everyone approved of giving the National Assembly what they saw as carte blanche to spend their funds on whatever they thought to be most important, thus the opposition.[24]

Keith found it difficult to describe her pilgrimage to Bahjí so she described the setting instead:

Who could ever apply the word tomb to this spot where lies the dust that commemorates God's tabernacle among men? Right here in the midst of the desert is a garden perennially bright with flowers and fruits . . . The open court is now glass-enclosed and planted with luxuriant foliage, around which runs a narrow passage on four sides covered with beautiful Persian carpets of leaf-green background strewn with coral-colored butterflies. There is an awesome cheerfulness about this antechamber to Paradise. The realization that death is not somber or lugubrious mingles with holy veneration in this room where the mortal remains of Bahá'u'lláh will quicken and enrich the very fibre of our earth forever.

We kneel trembling before the very Threshold where 'Abdu'l-Bahá so often chanted His supplications . . . To whatever degree I shall be able to carry away with me the imprint of this divine visitation, here at least my naked heart has throbbed out its inmost aspirations before God . . .[25]

The pilgrim house at Bahjí is primitive and unforgettable. Opening on a small court-yard with a vivid patch of grass, one graceful lemon tree full of pale fruit, the stable door to one side, the kitchen to the other, the doors wide and deep, is the room where we sit at breakfast; and the birds seem to prefer this big room to high heaven, for they are incessantly darting in and out. Horses are evidently too valuable to be put in stables with outside openings. So Soheil Effendi must ride his Arabian stallion through the dining-room each morning to the grassy plain! 'Abdu'l-Bahá's white donkey and her foal continue the procession. Then breakfast: Yad'u'lláh, the care-taker of the house presiding at his shining samovar, every one having hot tea, olives cured in oil, goat's milk cheese, the flat cakes of bread split and toasted, Syrian honey, and for the Occidentals, oranges picked as needed in this vicinity . . .

I sit solitary on the steps of the quaint old pilgrim house, entranced . . . The minarets of 'Akká pierce a rose and saffron sky; the Mediterranean is still a precious blue. Twilight encroaches . . . Then, and as from the portal of paradise a mystical beautiful chant arises. It is the voice of a woman, broken with sobs, tragic with longing, rich in praise; . . . It is Laila, the cook, who in her humility has not even entered the Shrine, but is kneeling on the garden path outside . . . Laila passes me alert and smiling, restored completely by her abandonment to the Spirit.[26]

Keith's observations of the lives of those around her are revealing. Westerners, she says, are embarrassed to be seen praying, except at meetings, while the Arab stops and prays at the roadside. She notes a happy group of young boys passing by and comments that 'nothing could be more depressing than the part played by women in the public life of the Orient'. Women there wore the chador, which she said was 'gloomy and sinister to the last degree. Entirely of black with a tight-fitting black cap completely covering the head and ears and a thick black veil making any sight of the face impossible, it gives the impression of a victim just ready for the hangman; this is the costume tenaciously adhered to by millions of women.' 'In America,' Keith wrote, 'where women are so ubiquitous, men have to plan a good deal how to keep away from us; but here comes a troop of gay young boys for an afternoon of frolic – not a woman permitted to be in sight.'[27]

The arrival of the Jews in the Holy Land was having a dramatic impact for 'men and women (unveiled, naturally) are seen everywhere together'. For centuries, barter and bargaining had been the standard method for buying and selling. But suddenly one day, a Jewish merchant opened his shop and 'his astonished customers discovered that everything in his shop was marked with a fixed price'.[28]

Summing up her pilgrimage, Keith wrote:

It had seemed to me on leaving America that I came to Haifa as a blank page ready to be written upon with the language of the spirit. But one conversation with Shoghi Effendi, casual, impersonal, over the luncheon table, showed me that I was a mountain of dogmas, preconceptions, inflexibilities, and nonsense. In the nine weeks at Haifa, however, the predispositions of a lifetime vanished! . . . when I knelt in prayer before the Shrine of Bahá'u'lláh, I hadn't the smallest concern in this earth whether I ever knew anything or saw anything before the burning fact that God has kept His Covenant with us and that only as human beings grasp this conception and seize this unparalleled opportunity can we enter into the fullness of His Promise. For the first time in my life I was empty – and at peace.[29]

Upon her passing a few years later, Shoghi Effendi cabled:

> American believers grateful and proud of the memory of their first
> and distinguished martyr. Sorrow stricken, I lament my earthly sep-
> aration from an invaluable collaborator, an unfailing counsellor, an
> esteemed and faithful friend. I urge the Local Assemblies befittingly
> to organize memorial gatherings in memory of one whose interna-
> tional services entitled her to an eminent rank among the Hands of
> the Cause of Baha'u'llah.[30]

May and Isabelle Stebbins

Edna McKinney and Berthalin Osgood arrived some time in late
February or early March and were there when May Stebbins and her
fifteen-year-old daughter, Isabelle, arrived in Haifa on 19 March. As the
train pulled in, May and Isabelle saw a Persian man on the platform
eyeing them. Then they saw Fujita. The Persian turned out to be Rúḥí
Effendi, one of Shoghi Effendi's cousins. They were quickly taken to
the Pilgrim House where Effie Baker welcomed them. When May and
Isabelle went to breakfast the next morning, they found New Year's cards
with a photograph at each place, all made by Effie. The Holy Household sent over flowers and cookies. That afternoon, they all went up in
'Abdu'l-Bahá's carriage to the Eastern Pilgrim House for Naw-Rúz. After
cookies, tea, oranges and 'a Persian sweet with nuts inside', everyone
went to the Shrine of the Báb. The men went into the room on the west
while the women used the room on the east. After the men had chanted
prayers, everyone moved into the adjacent Shrine of 'Abdu'l-Bahá.

On 23 March, May and Isabelle went to Bahjí with Rúḥá Khánum,
Munavvar Khánum and Riḍváníyyih Khánum. After the two-hour trip,
they ate lunch under the trees and Victoria Bedekian joined them in the
afternoon. May described the inside the Shrine:

> The walls were white and nothing else in the room but the exqui-
> site Persian rugs on the floor. Two long green ones on either side
> of the rose ones at the ends. Of course we took off our shoes on
> entering the building. Another room opening off of the main one
> was covered with two long rose rugs which just covered the floor.
> A table with many beautiful lamps was in that room. The room

where the Tomb of Bahá'u'lláh was opened off of a corner of the main room. It had candelabras, lamps, large vases of flowers and two large crystal candelabras hanging from the ceiling. It was all brightly lighted as we went in, and the threshold, raised, was covered with jasmine flowers of the most exquisite perfume. I shall never forget the impression of that first visit. The beauty and the fragrance of it all, the quiet and solemnity. The bowing of the head in that soft bed of jasmine and breathing in the sweetness of it all.[31]

On 25 March, some of the women rode donkeys and horses up to the Druse village of Abú-Sinán, where 'Abdu'l-Bahá and the Bahá'ís had stayed at the beginning of World War I. They visited the house of Shaykh Sálih, where 'Abdu'l-Bahá had stayed. While there, May learned:

Their religion is a secret. One time a man stole one of their [holy] books and tried to sell it to a library. The Druse leaders appealed to 'Abdu'l-Bahá to get their book back or their religion would be violated. He saw the man and by sheer force of moral argument compelled him to return the book. They have been very grateful to him ever since . . . The women wear a head-dress which comes over their mouths, and think it very improper to show their teeth. The women were very pretty and the men very fine looking. They would not allow us to take their pictures, except one young man, the son of the sheik. The women brought one of their nice costumes and tried it on Isabelle, and she had her picture taken in it with the son of the sheik.[32]

On the way back, two of the horses they were riding began to rear up and bite each other. One of the women was thrown to the ground, but the other managed to slide off her animal.

When the pilgrims returned to Haifa, Shoghi Effendi, who had been ill for a week, came to see them and ask if they had read the Plan for Unified Action by the American National Assembly. The Guardian indicated that the plan was very good and that it was very important for all the believers to support it. If they didn't, the plan would fail. Edna McKinney and Berthalin Osgood left on 16 April, while May and Isabelle followed them four days later.

George Townshend

On 27 February, a remarkable literary partnership began. On that date, George Townshend, a Bahá'í who was also a cleric in the Church of Ireland, wrote to the Guardian:

> I have been told that you invited Miss Rosenberg to Haifa to help in translating work, though (as I believe) she knows little or no Persian. I am encouraged by this to offer now my services, such as they are, in this kind of work. Having myself no knowledge of Persian and being a clergyman resident in Ireland, my help can not be anything better than advice as to English idiom and grammatical structure . . .
>
> My thought is that the proposed English rendering of certain passages, when not judged quite satisfactory, might be sent to me for suggestions as to usage, etc.[33]

He continued by giving an example of how to improve the beauty and ease of understanding. In a letter written on Shoghi Effendi's behalf a month later, the Guardian added:

> I wish to add personally a few words and assure you of my deep and heartfelt admiration of your valuable help and suggestion. I am hoping that the enclosed rendering will meet with your approval. Please alter and revise it with all freedom, for I have a great appreciation of your literary taste and attainments.[34]

Over the next few months, the Guardian sent George his translations of the *Hidden Words* and George sent back his revised versions. How greatly Shoghi Effendi appreciated George's great talent with words was displayed when he wrote a personal letter to George in his own hand:

> I am deeply grateful to you for the very valuable, detailed and careful suggestions you have given me in connection with my recent translations of Bahá'í writings. As I have already intimated your excellent judgement, your literary ability and your deep sympathy and devoted care in revising and altering various passages which I have rendered into English are deeply appreciated by me and I shall make use of your suggestions in any future publication of these translations.[35]

With George's help, Shoghi Effendi's translations of the *Hidden Words* were converted from merely pretty to beautiful. A good example of the Shoghi Effendi/George Townshend collaboration is the Healing Prayer:

1923 *Version*	*Final Version*
O my God! Thy name is my healing. Thy remembrance is my remedy, Thy nearness is my hope, Thy love is my joyous companion, and Thy mercy is my healer in this world and in all the world. Thou art the Giver, the Knower, the Wise!	Thy name is my healing, O my God, and remembrance of Thee is my remedy. Nearness to Thee is my hope, and love for Thee is my companion. Thy mercy to me is my healing and my succour in both this world and the world to come. Thou, verily, art the All-Bountiful, the All-Knowing, the All-Wise.[36]

George worked on the *Hidden Words* until March 1927. For the next eighteen years, he was the Guardian's primary source of literary assistance; after the *Hidden Words*, he worked on the *Kitáb-i-Íqán, The Dawn-Breakers, Prayers and Meditations by Bahá'u'lláh, Epistle to the Son of the Wolf* and *God Passes By,* suggesting the titles for and writing the introductions to *The Dawn-Breakers* and *God Passes By*.[37]

George did all this work for Shoghi Effendi while doing his normal job as a clergyman of the Church of Ireland in Ahascragh, County Galway, Ireland. He had written to 'Abdu'l-Bahá in 1919 declaring his belief in Bahá'u'lláh and received two Tablets from Him. In the second, 'Abdu'l-Bahá wrote, 'It is my hope that thy church will come under the Heavenly Jerusalem.'[38] Because of that line, George spent the next twenty-eight years trying to bring the Church of Ireland to a belief in Bahá'u'lláh. But in 1947, he finally gave up, renounced his orders, left the Church and devoted all of his time to the Faith.[39] George's gifted ability to write resulted in *The Promise of All Ages*, in 1934; *The Heart of the Gospel*, in 1936; *The Old Churches and the New World Faith*, in 1949; and his crowning achievement, *Christ and Bahá'u'lláh*, in 1957. He was appointed a Hand of the Cause in 1951.

Persian martyrdoms

On 11 April, a cable from Shiraz arrived that read: 'Twelve friends in Jahrom martyred agitation may extend elsewhere.' The Guardian immediately cabled back instructions on dealing with the crisis, then sent another cable to Tehran directing the Bahá'ís to hold the election of the National Spiritual Assembly in spite of the problems, writing that 'No true Bahá'í can stand aside.' In combination with everything else he was dealing with, the Guardian was severely affected, even while he did everything that needed to be done. On 24 April he apologized that his tardiness in responding to letters was due to 'my unfortunate illness, amounting almost to a break-down, combined with the receipt of the most distressing news from Persia . . .'[40]

Queen Marie of Romania

Burdened as he was at that time, on 4 May a letter was published in the *Toronto Daily Star* newspaper that greatly raised the Guardian's spirits. It was written by the dowager Queen Marie of Romania. The Queen wrote in her diary on 30 January 1926 that she had 'received a kind modest little American a Miss Root' who told her about Bahá'u'lláh and gave her the book *Bahá'u'lláh and the New Era*. Within a month, the Queen was referring to 'my dear Baha'u'llah's teachings' and saying that it was the 'message in fact I have always been waiting for'. By 21 February, she was recommending the Faith to others.[41] She had been commissioned by a newspaper group to write articles and the one she sent to the *Toronto Star* was very surprising:

> A woman brought me a Book the other day. I spell it with a capital letter because it is a glorious Book of love and goodness, strength and beauty.
>
> . . . And when I opened the Book I saw it was the word of Abdu'l-Baha, prophet of love and kindness, and of his father, the great teacher of international good-will and understanding – of a religion which links all creeds.
>
> Their writings are a great cry toward peace, reaching beyond all limits of frontiers, above all dissension about rites and dogmas. It is a religion based upon the inner spirit of God, upon that

not-to-be-overcome variety that God is love, meaning just that. It teaches that all hatreds, intrigues, suspicion, evil words, all aggressive patriotism even, are outside the one essential law of God . . .

It is a wondrous Message that Baha'u'llah and his son Abdu'l-Baha have given us . . .

I commend it to you. If ever the name of Baha'u'llah or Abdu'l-Baha comes to your attention, do not put their writings from you. Search out their Books, and let their glorious, peace-bringing love-creating words and lessons sink into your hearts as they have into mine.[42]

In a letter written on 29 May, the Guardian wrote that this was a 'most astonishing and highly significant event in the progress of the Cause'.[43] On 28 July, He wrote to the Queen himself:

As one of the humble followers of the Faith of Bahá'u'lláh, upon whose youthful shoulders have fallen the responsibilities of His mighty Cause, may I venture to approach your Majesty and express in the name of the Bahá'ís of both the East and the West our feelings of joyous admiration and boundless gratitude for the queenly tribute which your Majesty has paid to the beauty and nobility of the Bahá'í teachings.[44]

A month later, the Queen responded:

I was deeply moved on reception of your letter.

Indeed a great light came to me with the message of Baha'u'llah and Abdu'l-Baha. It came as all great messages come at an hour of dire grief and inner conflict and distress, so the seed sank deeply . . .

We pass on the message from mouth to mouth and all those we give it to see a light suddenly lighting before them and much that was obscure and perplexing becomes simple, luminous and full of hope as never before . . .

With bowed head I recognize that I too am but an instrument in greater hands and rejoice in the knowledge.[45]

A second article by the Queen was published in the *Toronto Daily Star* on 28 September and yet another was printed on 27 September in the

Philadelphia Evening Bulletin. After receiving the first of the Queen's articles, Shoghi Effendi wrote to Martha Root that this was 'a well deserved and memorable testimony of your remarkable and exemplary endeavours for the spread of our beloved Cause. It has thrilled me and greatly reinforced my spirit and strength, yours is a memorable triumph, hardly surpassed in its significance in the annals of the Cause.'[46]

Juliet Thompson and other pilgrims

In May, Juliet Thompson and Daisy Smythe, two of May Maxwell's best friends, escorted fifteen-year-old Mary Maxwell to Haifa. Mary became greatly attached to the Greatest Holy Leaf during the pilgrimage and recognized her high spiritual station. She described 'Abdu'l-Bahá's sister as 'the essence of meekness and gentleness'.[47] She wrote home saying that

Shoghi Effendi said he wanted me to get a good general education first and then (if my health permitted, that's just what he said!) to take some lectures in some good college on either Economics or sociology or literature. Wouldn't it be wonderful if I could do all these? There are a great many unmentionable insects in this country and sleep is a very ticklish sensation! Yesterday we were with Mirza Badi (Bushrui) who used to live in Haifa but is now Governor of Tiberias and he was sweet enough to point out a bee that was walking up my leg! Did you ever?[48]

While the Westerners were there, a pilgrim couple came from India. Effie Baker wrote home that when they went to visit some relatives in the Bahá'í village of Adasíyyih on the shore of the Sea of Galilee, the wife came down with dysentery and became very ill. She was rushed back to Haifa and taken to the English Hospital, but it was too late and she passed away. A service was held in the House of the Master and all the Western ladies attended.[49]

Effie went to Bahjí on 28 May for the commemoration of the Ascension of Bahá'u'lláh:

With our beloved Guardian the men believers were sitting out in the beautiful little garden facing toward the Holy Tomb. At intervals they chanted singly and in chorus. The Ladies of the Holy Household & all of us visited the Holy Shrine silently praying and meditating until nearly the hour of the departure of Baha'u'llah. I went out into the garden at midnight and sitting behind a screen of green shrubs listened to our beloved Guardian chanting in sweet melodious tones, his face radiant with the light of love & devotion upon it. The Ladies during the early hours of the morning retired to an ante chamber off the inner garden. As the hour approached when the Spirit of Him whom God made manifest took its flight to the realms of the Abha Kingdom our beloved Guardian entered the inner garden, which was so full of light and luminosity from the many electric bulbs. Surely a fitting symbol of the Great [Sun] of Truth which had arisen and shed it vivifying rays in this New Age. Followed by the men believers, in great humility and reverence he approached and then placed his forehead upon the threshold of the Holy Shrine, then for a few moments prayed silently.

The men believers in turn followed his example. It was such a solemn, reverent & inspiring time. At the hour of His Passing our beloved Guardian stood & chanted the Tablet of Visitation, & the night's Holy Vigil ended. We then departed reaching Haifa at early dawn.[50]

In June, Effie thought that the Pilgrim House felt more like a hospital than a pilgrim house. She noted that almost every American pilgrim 'seemed to be a nervous wreck' and came on pilgrimage to recuperate. She noted that the last three pilgrims were sick for almost all of their time there and Shoghi Effendi wouldn't leave for Switzerland until they finished their pilgrimage.[51]

Shoghi Effendi keeps looking for help

Shoghi Effendi retreated to his calming Switzerland just after the commemoration of the Ascension of Bahá'u'lláh at the end of May.[52] On 30 June, while he was in Switzerland, he wrote to Hippolyte Dreyfus-Barney, again bringing up the subject of his need for help:

I stand in need of a capable, trustworthy, hard-working, methodical, experienced secretary who will combine the gift of literary expression with a recognized standing in the Bahá'í world. Dr. Esslemont was a most suitable companion, unhampered, painstaking, devoted, lowly and capable. I mourn his loss . . . A capable, painstaking secretary, wholeheartedly devoted to his work, and two chief advisers who would represent the Movement on specific occasions, with dignity and devotion, together with two Eastern associates, mentally awake and expert in knowledge, would I feel set me on my feet and release the forces that will carry the Cause to its destined liberation and triumph . . . I cannot express myself more adequately than I have for my memory has greatly suffered.[53]

It may be that Hippolyte was already suffering from the 'slow and painful illness' that would bring a premature end to his life two years later. To Shoghi Effendi that loss was great, as he described in his letter of 21 December 1928: 'To me, and particularly amid the storm and stress that have agitated my life after 'Abdu'l-Bahá's passing, he was a sustaining and comforting companion, a most valued counsellor, an intimate and trusted friend.'[54]

In October, the Guardian tried again, writing to North America:

The range and character of the problems confronting you . . . the steady increase in the number and effectiveness of vigorously functioning Centers in Central and Northern Europe, and the growing significance and complexity of the work that has to be necessarily conducted from the Holy Land, have all served to strengthen the feeling of absolute necessity for the formation in Haifa of some sort of an International Bahá'í Secretariat, which both in an advisory and executive capacity will have to aid and assist me in my vast and exacting labors. I have anxiously considered this important matter in all its bearings during the past few months, and have accordingly requested three well-informed, capable representatives from America, Europe and the East to visit the Holy Land this fall, that we may lay down the foundation of this vitally needed institution. We shall take counsel together and decide, not only upon the measures that have to be promptly undertaken to meet the pressing demands of the present hour, but upon the wider issues that on one hand will strengthen the ties that should bind the International Center of the Cause with the world at large, and on the other provide for the preliminary steps that will eventually lead to the proper establishment of the First International House of Justice.

It is my earnest hope and prayer that this exchange of thought and close cooperation in the work that has henceforth to be internationally and vigorously conducted, will enable me to participate more minutely and effectively in the labors of the various administrative departments of your Assembly, and thus reinforce the splendid efforts you are exerting for the extension of its influence and the widening of its scope.[55]

As in his previous attempts, no one could or would arise. Shoghi Effendi continued to try to establish an international secretariat, but it wasn't until the International Bahá'í Council was formed in 1951 that he achieved it.[56] Shoghi Effendi returned to Haifa on 15 October 'looking very well and happy'.[57]

Serving at the World Centre

The final touches were being made to the new Western Pilgrim House during the first part of the year and Effie shared the responsibility with Fujita for making it ready for pilgrims. Effie made fourteen pairs of curtains and dyed them 'art shades' 'in keeping with the calcimimed walls' and the new furniture. Effie and Fujita greatly enjoyed each other's company. She affectionately called him 'Fudge' and the two shared in many adventures. Fujita sometimes would go to the Garden of Riḍván and spend several days making pomegranate juice. He also brought back watermelons, sweet lemons and ripe dates from his trips there.[58]

Electric lighting was installed in the Pilgrim House in September, eliminating one of Effie's jobs, that of cleaning the kerosene lamps. The Australian Bahá'ís paid for a sewing machine which she used to mend the linen. Effie and Fujita weren't the only ones serving at the World Centre. Yad'u'lláh, a Persian from the village of Seysan, was the caretaker of both the Gardens of Riḍván and Bahjí. His two sons Isfandiar and Faroud were his assistants. When Abu'l-Qásim Khurásání, the gardener at the Shrine of the Báb, died in 1932, Isfandiar and Faroud took up his duties.

Effie noticed that Shoghi Effendi had a distinct sense of humour. One day a group of Persian women arrived on pilgrimage wearing the chador, completely veiled from head to toe. Shoghi Effendi noted that if they hadn't bowed in response to some of his comments, he would not have known which side was their face and which was their back. On another occasion when Effie was changing the bedding in a room where a pilgrim had stayed just a single night, he asked her what she was doing. Upon her response that she was changing the used sheets, he replied, 'He slept in the bed for one night, and do you think the Bahá'ís are dirty?'[59]

In late May, Effie added her voice to the call for the believers to write to the Guardian only when necessary and then to be brief and concise:

> In former letters I have mentioned that our Guardian desires to hear from you individually as well as collectively as he thinks it is (at the present time) essential for him to have that phase in the Cause, but when writing I personally ask you dear Friends to word your letters as concisely as possible, expressing in few words your love and apprecia-tion eliminating long details of personal troubles and ideas, etc.
>
> Such letters take so much of his valuable time in reading and you cannot imagine what an almost superhuman task the vital problems and perplexities of the Cause that he has to ponder over from day to day are.[60]

> . . . if they wish to send any [news]papers to Shoghi Effendi, to please mark the article they think he would like to see and if possi-ble underline the paragraph that has any bearing on the Movement etc. He spends so much of his valuable time searching over papers to see what the friends have sent them for. You have no idea what a stupendous task it is to cope with his mail. Personally I think it is better not to forward papers unless they have something vital per-taining to the Cause.[61]

Effie also passed on what she learned from the Guardian. Teaching without restraint was important, but 'overzealousness and eagerness . . . is sometimes more a retarding than a progressive factor . . . The only thing that is going to bring about the right working conditions is the true spirit of self sacrifice pervading the hearts of the believers which will cause self effacement, humbleness, sincerity and faithfulness to be the outstand-ing characteristics of our lives.'

September saw the return of Emogene Hoagg, who had been living in Florence, Italy. She arrived with Shoghi Effendi's cousin Maryam and his sister Mehrangíz, who had been studying in Paris. Jeanne Bolles, May Maxwell's sister-in-law, also arrived in March with her son. Her arrival was a surprise because she had not written for permission.[62]

Visiting students and others

On 10 November a young American student arrived with her mother. The student was from St Stephen, in Missouri, and, at the behest of the school, was investigating the various religions in Palestine, including the Bahá'í Faith. The school had been observing the students to see if they had spiritual susceptibilities. Finding that they had, Effie wrote that the school was

> working along the lines of a broad and sane interpretation of the Sermon on the Mount, and their endeavour has been to try and urge a student to go back to his community and put vitality into it. They certainly have received the rays of the Sun of Truth, not knowing from whence they come. Probably after her interview with Shoghi Effendi this morning, she may be able to recognise the source.[63]

Fifteen Bahá'í students from the American University in Beirut came to Haifa during their vacation, visiting Mount Carmel and meeting Shoghi Effendi. The Guardian had a great interest and confidence in these students. His encouraging and inspiring instructions 'thrilled them and they returned to the University with greatly refreshed minds, purified thoughts and a longing desire to serve in the Bahá'í Youth Movement.'[64]

Josephine Storey, an 'English woman of independent means' who ran a bookstore in Geneva, had encountered Jean Stannard, from whom she learned about the Faith. Miss Storey, accompanied by Elizabeth Nourse, came to Haifa to solidify her new Faith late in the year.[65]

The House of Bahá'u'lláh in Baghdad

The House of Bahá'u'lláh in Baghdad remained a source of anguish for Shoghi Effendi. On 6 November 1925 he wrote:

The sad and sudden crisis that has arisen in connection with the ownership of Bahá'u'lláh's sacred house in Baghdád has sent a thrill of indignation and dismay throughout the whole of the Bahá'í world. Houses that have been occupied by Baha'u'llah for well nigh the whole period of His exile in 'Iráq; ordained by Him as the chosen and sanctified object of Bahá'í pilgrimage in future; magnified and extolled in countless Tablets and Epistles as the sacred center 'round which shall circle all peoples and kindreds of the earth'- lie now, due to fierce intrigue and ceaseless fanatical opposition, at the mercy of the declared enemies of the Cause.

I have instantly communicated with every Bahá'í center in both East and West, and urgently requested the faithful followers of the Faith in every land to protest vehemently against this glaring perversion of justice, to assert firmly and courteously the spiritual rights of the Bahá'í Community to the ownership of this venerated house, to plead for British fairness and justice, and to pledge their unswerving determination to insure the security of this hallowed spot.

Conscious of the fact that this property has been occupied by Bahá'í authorized representatives for an uninterrupted period of not less than thirty years, and having successfully won their case at the Justice of Peace and the Court of First Instance, the Bahá'ís the world over cannot believe that the high sense of honor and fairness which inspires the British Administration of 'Iráq will ever tolerate such grave miscarriage of justice. They confidently appeal to the public opinion of the world for the defence and protection of their legitimate rights now sorely trampled under the feet of relentless enemies.

Widespread and effective publicity along these lines, in well-conceived and carefully worded terms, is strongly recommended for it will undoubtedly serve to facilitate the solution of this delicate and perplexing problem.[66]

Mountfort Mills had been continually engaged in the efforts to free the House of Bahá'u'lláh in Baghdad. The Guardian told him to go to London for consultations with various officials. Mountfort noted, in a letter to Horace Holley dated 26 March:

Nothing has gone wrong, but in the course of trying to put through the plan decided on by the authorities some unforeseen questions have come up that made it seem best to the Guardian to have me at this end. It's a difficult problem at best, enmeshed in Iraq politics and complicated by the wish of the Mandatory Power not to interfere more than absolutely necessary with the stumblings of its political babe in its efforts to stand up on its own two feet . . . The British are with us but hope to find a way to do without too much strong arm work . . . I am glad to say there has never been a suggestion that we are not right.[67]

On 6 April 1926, Mountfort Mills again wrote to Horace Holley at the time of the American National Convention, saying that the British Colonial Office had taken a 'stronger stand' than the Bahá'ís had expected and that the Convention

should be asked to adopt a resolution expressing its deep disappointment at the unexpected delay in the settlement of the Baghdad matter and urging the incoming National Spiritual Assembly to leave nothing within its power undone to induce the British and Iraq Governments to see that their property is restored to the Bahá'ís a the earliest date . . .

The difficulty has been in Baghdad where, on the firing line, it must be remembered what we want done is by no means easy, – further complicated, too, by these delicate and important negotiations with Turkey [Treaty of Friendship signed in 1926], which to them loom so much larger than our matter. I must confess, though, that here in London official attitude has been all we could ask and has gone too far in our direction to doubt its sincerity. But the plan is to get the Iraq Government to act against the largest and most influential group of its own citizens, the Shiahs, who also preside over the State Religion, a bad combination to antagonize & a most difficult task. We must be patient.[68]

On 16 October 1926, Effie Baker reported that great news had been received about the House of Bahá'u'lláh. The news had

really cheered him & the dear friends here. It is almost certain that the Government will appropriate the property, so it will be out of the hands of the Shi'ih sect who have made it a shrine to one of their heroes & thus it may be possible for the Bahais to acquire it though it may not be in a long time yet. It is gratifying to know that it will be out of the hand of fanatical Moslems.[69]

On 14 November 1926, Iraq's highest tribunal stunningly ruled against the Bahá'ís in the case of the ownership of the House of Bahá'u'lláh. Shoghi Effendi immediately sent a cable urging all American national and local spiritual assemblies to either write or cable the Iraq High Commissioner through the British Consular authorities to

protest vigorously against courts glaring injustice, appealing for redress in British sense of fairness, asserting spiritual claims of Bahá'ís to this sanctified abode and declaring their unfailing resolve to do their utmost to vindicate their legitimate and sacred rights. Similar appropriate communications to King of Iraq and British central authorities . . . America's action in present circumstances of unique significance and value.[70]

America responded, but it didn't change the decision and the battle continued.

1927–1928

Ethel Rosenberg returns

Near the end of 1926, Ethel Rosenberg and Isobel Slade had arrived in Haifa. Ethel had been invited by the Guardian earlier in the year to come and assist him with his translations. Being sixty-eight years old and not in the best of health, she invited Mrs Slade, another of the English Bahá'ís, to come with her on the journey to the Holy Land. When they arrived, they found Mountfort Mills and Laura Dreyfus-Barney already in residence, with Effie Baker and Fujita taking care of them all. No sooner had Ethel and Mrs Slade arrived than they went to the House of the Master and were taken into the presence of the Greatest Holy Leaf. Isobel Slade described her as

> a wonderful gracious figure with a white fleecy shawl and a white veil on her head. A beautiful face with dark blue eyes, a face lined with suffering that had been her lot in life. She might have been any nationality and though unable to speak English, one felt her understanding and knew that she was the rock on which the youthful Guardian depended so much in those early days.[1]

Unfortunately for Mrs Slade, her mother suddenly fell ill and she had to leave Haifa after just a short time.

Ethel greatly enjoyed reconnecting with friends from all around the world, but by late December she found herself in a blizzard of letters – writing letters of encouragement and letters about how the Administrative Order was supposed to work. Getting the Administrative Order functioning correctly formed a large part of her letter writing. In January 1927, a letter she wrote on behalf of Shoghi Effendi gently taught the English Bahá'ís how to elect their National Spiritual Assembly:

> He says that in one way we are not quite correct in the way we manage our elections for the National Assembly – Shoghi Effendi says that the intention is, that when once the 19 delegates have been elected by the friends of the respective centres in the proportions you mention, i.e. 12 delegates from among the London friends, five from the Manchester friends, and two from the Bournemouth group, that then, these 19 delegates assembled should choose by secret ballot from the whole body of the believers in Gt. Britain and Ireland, the nine friends they consider most suitable as members of the National Assembly. Heretofore, as I understand it, it has rather been our practice that the 12 London delegates elected six from the London friends – the Manchester five delegates elected two from Manchester and the Bournemouth delegates elected one from Bournemouth. But, Shoghi Effendi says, all the 19 delegates must clearly understand that they must select from the whole body of the believers in Gt. Britain and Ireland those 9 whom they consider the most fit and suitable members to constitute the National Assembly.[2]

Shoghi Effendi suggested that they follow the American-style National Convention. The British Bahá'í community, therefore, had its first National Convention at Riḍván 1927.[3]

As we have seen, the Guardian had recruited George Townshend in Ireland to help him with the translation of the *Hidden Words*. By early January, Ethel was competent enough in Persian to assist, so she and the Guardian sat together comparing the original Persian document with George's suggestions for wording. By early March, the translation was complete. Because of their help, Shoghi Effendi had placed on the title page beneath his own name, 'revised with the Assistance of G. Townshend and E. J. Rosenberg.' When he heard of the addition, George begged the Guardian to remove his name since he was still a member of the Church of Ireland clergy and didn't want to jeopardize his influence. Shoghi Effendi acquiesced and changed it to 'Translated by Shoghi Effendi with the assistance of some English friends.'[4]

Ethel greatly enjoyed the pilgrims. One pilgrim she found to be very interesting was Dr Habíb Kirmánsháh, who arrived from Iran in January and talked about the intensifying persecution happening in Iran at that time. He recounted the fanaticism of the mullas, who were telling the people that 'No matter what evil things you have done during your life, or what sins you have committed, if you kill a Bahá'í who is an enemy of Islam, or even if you take his property or severely injure him, all your owns sins will be wiped out and forgiven for the sake of this good deed of destroying an enemy of the Faith!!' But even though the ignorant would act on these exhortations, the Bahá'í teachings were still spreading rapidly in the country.[5]

Ethel returned to England on 7 May, but she took with her a gift from Shoghi Effendi to the English friends: one of Bahá'u'lláh's robes.[6]

* * *

Other pilgrims came and went. Mountfort Mills spent many weeks in Haifa early in the year, consulting with Shoghi Effendi about the House of Bahá'u'lláh in Baghdad, and the *Bahá'í News Letter* joyfully announced that he would finally be returning to America. The 1927 edition of *The Bahá'í World* included a note stating that the believers in Baghdad were taking photographs of the cave in the Sargul Mountain near Sulaymáníyyih where Bahá'u'lláh had spent two years in solitude.[7]

Sadie and Bertha Oglesby and Shoghi Effendi's advice on racial unity

Sadie and Bertha Oglesby, mother and daughter, arrived in Haifa on 11 March 1927, the first African-American women to go on pilgrimage. Sadie and her husband, Mabry, had joined the Bahá'í Faith in 1914 in Boston. From the beginning, they were concerned about the lack of true unity between many of the black and white Bahá'ís. When there were race riots in 1919 in both Washington and Chicago, the Oglesbys wrote to Harlan Ober offering two suggestions:

These hate campaigns are on in every group being fanned into flames so rapidly by the ignorant that it does not require one to be a prophet to see that society is sleeping on an active volcano which shows every sign of eruption at any moment . . . We believe that the Bahá'ís have a great opportunity as well as a great responsibility to bring this great life-giving information to the world . . . To this end we suggest the following for your consideration: 1st. United prayers over a continued period . . . 2nd. Conference initiated by Bahá'ís calling together leaders of races, churches, groups . . . We believe that the general unrest at this time properly handled can be used to stimulate great Bahá'í activities everywhere and will be the means of opening many doors for spreading the Cause never before opened. To sit, to talk, to listen – there is no virtue in that. To rise, to act, to help – that is a Bahá'í life. Deeds are the standard.[8]

By 1921, the Bahá'í community had begun a 'Program for Racial Amity', coordinated by Agnes Parsons and Louis Gregory, and the Oglesbys were involved.

A few hours after arriving in Haifa, the mother and daughter, along with other pilgrims, were greeted by Shoghi Effendi. The first thing he asked Sadie was how many African-American Bahá'ís there were in America. When she replied that there were only a few, he responded:

The believers should practice great kindness and show great love so that the colored people may be attracted to the Cause. Until the doors are opened and the colored people are attracted into the Cause the white people who are not believers will not have confidence in the sincerity of the friends and will not enter the Cause. The friends should practice all the teachings and not only a part, and this will draw the colored people to the Cause.[9]

It was a portent of things to come for Sadie throughout her pilgrimage. Shoghi Effendi later asked Sadie how forceful she had been in helping the Bahá'ís understand the true meaning of the oneness of humanity. He urged her to be more assertive. She wrote that he said

I should be insistent and urgent upon this matter. That I should be persistent and not quiet so that the believers may learn of this great need. He told me I had been negligent, indifferent and had not done my duty upon this subject.[10]

Sadie told the Guardian that her husband had 'been persistent' in speaking out to the Bahá'ís, but that she had, just as often, tried to keep him quiet. Shoghi Effendi said, 'Mr. Oglesby's way is the better way.'

The Guardian told her that it was important to speak out about racism, calling it 'the most vital and challenging issue'. He told her to make that her goal when she returned to America. This challenge intimidated Sadie and she replied that 'I have no strength or importance in America. I am so sorry.' But Shoghi Effendi insisted, saying, 'When you return to America do as I have told you. Be fearless and know that the invisible concourse will assist you and I will supplicate at the Holy Shrine on your behalf.' Other pilgrims were just as uncomfortable talking about the problems between the races:

One day at dinner with the pilgrims, both Eastern and Western, Shoghi Effendi, as he discoursed upon the matter of unity between the white and colored people, was interrupted several times and to each of those who sought information upon other matters he said, 'That is not important,' but urged the need of a center in America composed of the two races ... 'America's problem is the establishment of unity and harmony between the white and colored people.' He said, 'Racial prejudice and differences on the part of non-believers is a problem but there should be no racial problem on the part of the believers.'[11]

India has her problem, Germany has her problem, Persia has her problem, the other nations each has its problem, but America's problem is the establishment of unity and harmony between the white and the colored people.[12]

Shoghi Effendi asked Sadie why there were so few black Bahá'ís. Her answer was intriguing:

Having so long felt the force of unwelcome among the whites, the chasm is very deep and wide and is very difficult, and having acquired the habit of expecting unfriendliness from the whites, the colored people generally came among the Baha'is looking for shortcomings and flaws, and soon fell away. Were it possible to get them to read enough to cause them to stop looking at the creatures, and look for their guidance to the Teachings alone, they surely would become confirmed believers . . .[13]

She added that she and Mabry had only remained Bahá'ís because they could find 'no flaws' in their spiritual teachers, Harlan and Grace Ober. Sadie wrote that

> if it had been that I found them off duty once, we would have turned our faces in another direction; we were guilty of looking for shortcomings, but we have never seen them off duty with us, or with anybody else, at any time. If they had not remained in Boston until my husband and I were strong enough to turn our eyes toward God, I assure you . . . we still would have been looking in the dark.[14]

The Guardian repeated his prediction of what would happen if the black and white Bahá'ís became united:

> When the believers get their hearts free from prejudice the colored people will come into the Cause, and when the colored people come in and are made welcome, then the whites will come flocking in. The white people of America are watching to see what the Bahá'ís are going to do with the colored people; when they see the white Bahá'ís treating the colored Bahá'ís as themselves, then they will believe they are sincere. The people of the East are watching to see what the Bahá'ís of America are going to do with the colored people, and unless the Baha'is remove the prejudice and establish a center where brotherhood and justice is practiced toward colored people, there will be no center to which to turn when the world is in its great turmoil . . .[15]

Sadie still felt reluctant to take on the role that Shoghi Effendi proposed, but he didn't let up. On 27 March, he again brought his challenge to her: 'My charge to you is that when you go back to America, tell the friends to look within themselves and find <u>there</u> the reason of so few colored people are in the Cause, and remove this reason; until this is removed, the Cause cannot grow . . . This is vital.' He also suggested that she take her teaching efforts from Boston to the American South, the seat of the problem. Sadie realized that, if it was so important to the Guardian that he would repeatedly emphasize the part she should play, she should take up the challenge. Sadie and Bertha spent twenty days on pilgrimage and had a number of private talks with Shoghi Effendi.

Returning to America, Sadie wasted no time acting on the Guardian's request, taking an 'energetic' role at that year's National Bahá'í Convention. She spoke about her experiences on pilgrimage and racial unity and summed up, saying, 'We are not the same people we were before we went away . . . So I know what my work is now, as I never knew it before.'[16]

An American Bahá'í constitution

In May, the North American Bahá'í community made a major step forward with the writing of a document setting out its constitutional basis. Called by Shoghi Effendi a 'Declaration of Trust' in his letter of 27 May, it was to have far-reaching consequences:

> The Declaration of Trust, the provisions of which you have so splendidly conceived, and formulated with such assiduous care, marks yet another milestone on the road of progress along which you are patiently and determinedly advancing. Clear and concise in its wording, sound in principle, and complete in its affirmations of the fundamentals of Bahá'í administration, it stands in its final form as a worthy and faithful exposition of the constitutional basis of Bahá'í communities in every land, foreshadowing the final emergence of the world Bahá'í Commonwealth of the future. This document, when correlated and combined with the set of by-laws which I trust are soon forthcoming, will serve as a pattern to every National Bahá'í Assembly, be it in the East or in the West, which aspires to conform, pending the formation of the First Universal House of Justice, with the spirit and letter of the world-order ushered in by Bahá'u'lláh.[17]

The Declaration established a clear legal basis for the National Spiritual Assembly and became the model used by all other National Assemblies. Shoghi Effendi further emphasized this in *God Passes By*:

> The text of this national constitution comprises a Declaration of Trust, whose articles set forth the character and objects of the national Bahá'í community, establish the functions, designate the central office, and describe the official seal, of the body of its elected representatives, as well as a set of by-laws which define the status, the mode of election, the powers and duties of both local and

national Assemblies, describe the relation of the National Assembly to the International House of Justice as well as to local Assemblies and individual believers, outline the rights and obligations of the National Convention and its relation to the National Assembly, disclose the character of Bahá'í elections, and lay down the requirements of voting membership in all Bahá'í communities.

The framing of these constitutions, both local and national, identical to all intents and purposes in their provisions, provided the necessary foundation for the legal incorporation of these administrative institutions in accordance with civil statutes controlling religious or commercial bodies. Giving these Assemblies a legal standing, this incorporation greatly consolidated their power and enlarged their capacity, and in this regard the achievement of the National Spiritual Assembly of the Bahá'ís of the United States and Canada and the Spiritual Assembly of the Bahá'ís of New York again set an example worthy of emulation by their sister Assemblies in both the East and the West.[18]

During the following years, the National Assemblies of India and Burma, of Egypt, Iraq, Persia and the British Isles all adopted the American constitution almost without alteration.[19]

Another future Hand of the Cause

Sometime during 1927, another student arrived and enrolled at the American University, joining Hasan Balyuzi. This was Abu'l-Qásim Faizi, a 19-year-old who had attended the Tarbiyát School in Tehran. As soon as he could, Faizi went to Haifa to meet Shoghi Effendi. Arriving at the Master's House, he was brought inside and taken to the room across the hall from the entrance. Not knowing what to do, he sat in a convenient chair just inside the entrance, not realizing that this was the chair the Guardian always sat in. When Shoghi Effendi entered the room, Faizi was paralysed in that chair until the Guardian raised him to his feet, saying 'Come, let us meet each other as two brothers.' Through his tears, Faizi found his head resting on the Guardian's shoulder. Shoghi Effendi then sat his visitor back in the same chair and asked him about his plans, suggesting that he study English, Arabic and Persian.[20]

Like Hasan Balyuzi, after meeting Shoghi Effendi Faizi was immediately possessed of a great desire to serve him and the Faith. The two students went to Haifa as often as possible, sometimes taking another student, Gloria 'Alá'í, who would later become Faizi's wife. On one visit, Shoghi Effendi sent them a packet wrapped in silk, asking that they translate its contents from English into Persian. Opening the packet, they found a document written by Queen Marie of Romania praising the teachings of Bahá'u'lláh. The two young men spent two days making the translation. Shoghi Effendi praised their work, saying that it was correct, though not eloquent so he had made a few changes. At another time, the Guardian asked Faizi to chant a prayer. The Greatest Holy Leaf heard the chanting and asked if Faizi would chant for her, so the next morning he went to the House of the Master. Soon, he found himself standing before that august lady as well as the wife of the Master, Munírih Khánum, and a few other women. His chanting greatly moved all those present.[21]

When Faizi returned to Persia in 1933, Shoghi Effendi gave him a bouquet of flowers to be placed on the grave of the tireless teacher and martyr, Keith Ransom-Kehler, on his behalf.[22] Like Hasan Balyuzi, the Guardian named Faizi a Hand of the Cause in 1957.

Pilgrims, visitors and other happenings

Lorol Schopflocher arrived back in Haifa from another trip to India and Persia on 8 May 1927 and told many stories of her adventures. She stayed until 28 May when she departed for Cairo, Alexandria and Paris.[23] Another pilgrim asked the Guardian when he would come to America. His frank and very clear answer was, 'When you have learned to obey the National Spiritual Assembly.'[24] At about the same time, Mírzá Mohsen Afnán, a resident believer, passed away and his funeral was the first entirely Bahá'í funeral held in Palestine, showing the independence of the Faith.[25]

In July, an earthquake struck Palestine and caused a great deal of damage. A hundred houses in Akka collapsed while many were badly damaged in the Bahá'í village of Adasíyyih near the Sea of Galilee. The greatest damage was concentrated in Nablus, half way between Haifa and Jerusalem. The destruction there was so great that there was not a street left and most of the ancient buildings and churches were damaged. About 250 people were killed and twice that many injured.

Effie had been working at the Infant Welfare Centre when the quake hit. She said that

> there seemed a sudden rush of wind, then I felt myself swaying back and forth, I looked out of the window and the building in front seemed to be rocking also. It lasted about ten seconds. I was wondering what was going to happen to our room, and didn't realise it was an earthquake till Mrs Cotching, our medical officer said so. She really thought our building would collapse. Some of the Arab women waiting their turn, rushed into the room, they were so afraid.[26]

At the beginning of August, Dr Gertrude Brigham, director of the Art Department of Washington University in St Louis, Missouri, was touring Palestine with a group of thirty-six, and, having studied something of the Bahá'í Faith, determined to go on pilgrimage to Haifa and Akka. Arriving on a Sunday afternoon, she first had to find the Bahá'ís. Finding the House of 'Abdu'l-Bahá, she was met by Rúḥá Khánum, who served her iced lemonade. After an hour's conversation, Gertrude was invited to stay that night at the Pilgrim House where she met Fujita and Effie Baker. Since she was the only visitor that day, all the women from the Household came to enjoy her company. After tea at five o'clock, Effie and Rúḥá Khánum took Gertrude up to the Shrine of the Báb. Though she wasn't a Bahá'í, Gertrude prostrated herself at the threshold: 'I was deeply touched and immensely impressed by the quiet beauty of the spot, its atmosphere of peace, the richness of the numerous large Persian rugs, and the perfume of flowers, jasmine and tube roses.' That evening, since Shoghi Effendi was not in Haifa, Gertrude had dinner at the Pilgrim House with Effie, Suhayl Afnán, Muníb Jalál (both grandsons of 'Abdu'l-Bahá), and Fujita.[27]

The next morning, Gertrude was up at five to have tea with Effie and Fujita. Afterwards she saw Fujita's 'gardens, his canaries and other birds, his goldfish, and his immense Persian cat'. They also talked of their mutual friends since Fujita had lived in America for many years before coming to Haifa. Later in the morning, she joined Effie and two of 'Abdu'l-Bahá's granddaughters for a trip to Akka and Bahjí. After visiting the Most Great Prison and the houses in Akka where Bahá'u'lláh had lived, the group went to Bahjí and the Shrine of Bahá'u'lláh. Though having been recently at the tombs of Alexander the Great,

Saladin and Napoleon, she later wrote that 'they paled to insignificance in comparison with the beauty and simple grandeur' of the Shrine. On the way back to Haifa, they stopped at the Garden of Riḍván, returning to Haifa in time for lunch. Afterwards, Fujita took her to meet Munírih Khánum and the Greatest Holy Leaf who, after talking about the American friends they had in common, invited Gertrude to give her service to the Faith. Her final pilgrimage moments came when she viewed the portraits of the Báb, Baháʼuʼlláh and ʻAbduʼl-Bahá.[28]

Gertrude summed up her pilgrimage, writing: 'In retrospect my pilgrimage appeared altogether satisfying. I found myself deeply impressed by the dignity and sincerity and spirituality of the Bahaʼis in Haifa, and in entire sympathy with the meaning of the Movement which is creating a new world outlook.'[29] It was this pilgrimage, together with a year studying the Faith, that made her a believer.

Dr William Slater and his wife, Ida, made their pilgrimage in October. They spent nineteen days in Haifa with the Guardian and it was the high point of their lives. When they returned to America, Shoghi Effendi entrusted them with rugs he had selected from the Shrines of the Báb and ʻAbduʼl-Bahá and a letter to Albert Windust. The letter contained instructions on how to furnish the Foundation Hall of the House of Worship in Wilmette. It also instructed Albert to hang the rugs on the walls and to open the House of Worship for public meetings. The Slaters took great care of their sacred trust.[30]

By mid-October, Shoghi Effendi was forced to announce the official defection of the former Baháʼí teacher, ʻAbduʼl-Ḥusayn Ávárih. Once highly respected, he had rejected the Guardianʼs efforts to build the Baháʼí Administrative Order. His early teaching activities and the writing of a successful book on the history of the Faith had elevated his ego to breaking point which, Shoghi Effendi wrote, had 'emboldened him to launch a campaign of insinuation and fraud aiming at the eventual overthrow of the institutions expressly provided by Baháʼuʼlláh.' His efforts, however, backfired and the faithful followers of Baháʼuʼlláh in Iran denounced and shunned him. Even his wife abandoned him. 'Forsaken and bankrupt, and in desperate rage,' he connived with the most fanatical members of the Muslim clergy and anyone else who opposed the Faith. 'But', Shoghi Effendi wrote,

he has labored in vain, oblivious of the fact that all the pomp and powers of royalty, all the concerted efforts of the mightiest potentates of Islám, all the ingenious devices to which the cruellest torture-mongers of a cruel race have for well-nigh a century resorted, have proved one and all impotent to stem the tide of the beloved Faith or to extinguish its flame.[31]

As he had done in previous years, Shoghi Effendi again retired to the mountains of Switzerland to clear and rest his mind and to commune with his spiritual guides without distraction. By 1 November, he was back in Haifa.[32]

During the latter half of 1927, eight bedroom suites were added to the Western Pilgrim House. Effie Baker and Fujita carried up many of the bricks used in the construction and then did the cleaning up afterwards.[33]

Corinne True, her daughter Edna, and Ruth Moffett arrived in October, as did Julia Culver and Dr Sabine and her daughter.[34] Ruth Moffett quickly learned the theme of her visit when she told Shoghi Effendi how difficult it was to remember to say the obligatory prayer at the right hour. He began by telling her that obligatory prayer was a test from Bahá'u'lláh. We must, he emphasized, try harder to remember to do it at the right time, 'because Baha'u'llah asked us to do so'. During the time of the Báb, physical martyrdom was the test. Now, he stated, we 'must realise that we are being tested in ways that we have never been tested before. We must be wise. We must hold out our arms welcoming these tests knowing that they are for us, that we may become stronger, and able to meet the great ones and greater ones ahead of us.' Shoghi Effendi told Ruth the story of the 'Lightbearers':

God invited all humanity to a Feast, and when the time came for the guests to leave, He gave to each one a little lamp saying, it will guide your steps on the way home.

Some one said: It is bright moonlight, and threw the lamp aside.

Some held their lamp so close to themselves, that it did not light one step ahead.

A storm came up and many lights were blown out. Only a few held their lamps high above their heads to give light to all around who were stumbling. Many missed their way completely and were hopelessly lost in the wilderness.

Then God looking down in compassion sent his Messenger to

relight the lights that were blown out and guide the wandering ones.

And then another day, and again many threw away their lamps. So when the night was come, God sent another Messenger to save them.

But again they forgot, when it was day. This happened again and again.

At last God knowing there was to be a long dark night, sent his best beloved Messenger, Bahá'u'lláh.[35]

While Ruth was there, Shoghi Effendi asked the Greatest Holy Leaf for spiritual names for Ruth and her husband, Robert. She replied: 'For Ruth, Ruḥaníyyih, which means spiritual beauty, and the name of Robert is Ḥabíb, which means "beloved".' Shoghi Effendi emphasized that they should use their spiritual names as much as possible because 'it puts that spirit out into the others'.[36]

In November, after the last pilgrims had gone, Effie came down with dengue fever, an infectious disease carried by mosquitos and an illness that would plague her throughout the next year.[37]

1928: Pilgrims, enemies and Effie

On 4 January, Fred (Siegfried) Schopflocher reached Haifa. He brought Effie Baker a new and much better camera with which she was able to take even better photos. Some of the photos she coloured, using water-colours and brushes. When Fred left to return to America, he took with him the manuscript and Effie's photos for the next *Bahá'í World* which was to be printed there.[38]

Also in January of 1928, a Covenant-breaker tried to stir up trouble by attempting to implicate the Bahá'ís and the British with Saláru'd-Dawlih, an ambitious brother of Muḥammad-'Alí Sháh, who had been deposed by the Revolution of 1909 in Iran. On 17 January, the British Ambassador in Tehran, Sir Robert Clive, received the following tele-gram from the Foreign Office:

Most secret.

An absolutely reliable informant assures me that the Shah has been informed that through our help some Persian Bahais have been put in touch with Salar-ed-Dowleh and that he has been helped financially by us.

There is not a vestige of truth in these allegations which may do us harm by poisoning the Shah's mind against us and by prompting further outrages against the Bahais in Persia.

The source of this information is so confidential that there must be no risk whatever of it being compromised . . .[39]

The British High Commissioner in Palestine, Lord Plumer, became involved since the Bahá'í World Centre was in Haifa. After an investigation, he replied:

I reply to your letter of the 17th ultimo referring to stories about the Bahai Community at Haifa which were related to the Persian Minister at Cairo by one 'Mirza Jamil'. The man in question is almost certainly a certain Jamil Irani, a Persian formerly adherent to the Bahai sect and now turned Moslem and anti-Bahai. He is an excellent Railway Inspector, a clever man educated in America but nourishes a grievance against the Bahai sect to which his own father left all his money on his death. That Prince Salar-ed-Dowleh has conducted intrigue in Persia or through the Bahai Community at Haifa is most improbable and Jamil Irani's allegations to the contrary are, I suspect, trumped up to do the Bahais an injury.[40]

Allen McDaniel and his wife, and Mr Van Patten arrived from America and Josephine Storey came on her second pilgrimage from Geneva. The McDaniels arrived at the Haifa train station at 10 a.m. on 6 February after their overnight train ride from Egypt and were met by Fujita,

that remarkable 'major domo' of Baha'i life at the Persian Colony . . . Under his guidance we were piloted out of the clamouring throng of porters, dragomen, hotel representatives and vendors to a motor car. Seated amongst our nine varieties of luggage, we were soon whisked up a picturesque winding road along the hillside. A sudden turn in the road brought us our first view of Mt. Carmel, and in a moment we were descending from our petrol driven vehicle in front of the Pilgrim House. Here we were welcomed by [the] cheerful greeting of Effie Baker, whose cordial hospitality soon made us feel very much at home.[41]

Effie told them:

> 'Please feel that this is your home, that we are here to serve and make
> you happy, and while here you are the guests of Shoghi Effendi'.
> Such were the kindly words that greeted us on our arrival at the
> Bahá'í Pilgrim House. 'And perhaps you know that this building was
> designed by one American Bahá'í and built through the generosity
> of other American Bahá'ís'. After several weeks of continual journey-
> ing over sea and land, with its exactions and annoyances of drafty
> cabins, cold, cheerless hotel rooms, bills, tips, and fees, this home
> seemed a sanctuary of rest.[42]

The McDaniels met the Guardian at noon and he talked for almost an
hour. During that time, Shoghi Effendi showed an intimate knowledge
of what was going on in their home country. He had recently received
a telegram stating that the Chicago mid-year Convention had voted
for US$10,000 to be spent to complete the basement of the House
of Worship so that meetings could be held there. He was surprised
that they had decided to spend so much when their efforts to raise
$300,000 to complete the Temple had during the two years of the Plan
for Unified Action been unsuccessful. He questioned the wisdom of
the vote, giving them something to take back home and consult about.
Shoghi Effendi then stressed the relationship between the Chicago Spiritual Assembly and the National Spiritual Assembly, pointing out that
the local should in no way interfere with the authority of the national.
The local Spiritual Assembly was to supervise local activities only, while
the national did the same at the national level.[43]

During Riḍván, the first Bahá'í pilgrim from Tunis, 'Abdu'l-Hamid
Khemiri, reached Haifa. He was a 'representative of the Tunis Assembly
. . . a young man full of hopes and schemes for the future.'[44]

Effie Baker remained ill all through 1928. Josephine Storey sent her
a gramophone from Geneva, but finally Effie decided that she needed
some rest after three years without a break. On 6 July, she sailed to
Alexandria, then continued on to Switzerland, where she arrived 'very
worn, very thin, very eager to meet the friends but too fatigued to go
to them'. Josephine met her at Lausanne and decided that she was too
ill to continue to Geneva, so arranged for her to stay in a local 'rest
home' for three weeks before bringing her up to Geneva. Effie stayed in

Geneva with Josephine and described her cottage as 'a charming little home' and the view from the veranda windows as 'magnificent', with a 'view of the lake, the Rhone Valley with the river flowing down it and entering the lake and surrounding all the alps. Some of the peaks eternally snow-capped and glistening in the sunshine.' She wrote that 'the climate was telling on me a bit . . . and the heat in Haifa is so humid and enervating . . . I had that attack of fever just before Xmas. I am only six stone eight pounds now but hope to regain some of my lost weight during this rest.'[45]

Marion Yazdi from California was on pilgrimage in June. To her group, Shoghi Effendi strongly and repeatedly promoted the Plan of Unified Action for the construction of the Temple. The friends, he emphasized, must work closely with the National Spiritual Assembly and actively push ahead the Plan. Unity, as always, was the key. The Guardian said that he believed that the American Bahá'ís were capable of putting the plan into effect on their own and he said they were not to accept any funds from those who, however pure-hearted they might be, were not Bahá'ís. He also told Marion that the Persian Bahá'ís were eager to contribute to the construction of the House of Worship, but that he would not permit them to do so until the Americans had shown their willingness to sacrifice.[46]

Effie saw Martha Root and Julia Culver while she was in Switzerland. Grace Challis invited her to England where she spent two weeks before finally returning to Haifa on 31 October.[47]

Disruption in 'Ishqábád

In April 1928 Shoghi Effendi suddenly had another problem to deal with. The first Mashriqu'l-Adhkár of the Bahá'í Faith, in 'Ishqábád, in what is now known as Turkmenistan, was confiscated from the Bahá'ís. After the election of the Spiritual Assembly, the Marxist government of Russia suddenly decreed that the Assembly's constitution was invalid and substituted a new one of its own making. The government-defined constitution prohibited any social or religious activities and was obviously completely out of harmony with what the Spiritual Assembly was supposed to do. The constitution also banned all Bahá'í committees and organizations. But the emasculation of the Local Spiritual Assembly was just the first step. Soon afterwards, the Soviet government ordered that all churches, synagogues and other places of worship that existed in the country were to be the property of the Soviet Union. They did allow the Bahá'ís to rent their own House of Worship without charge for renewable periods of five years. The next step in the persecution of the 'Ishqábád Bahá'í community took place on 10 August when, with the permission of the government, the Bahá'ís were holding a meeting. Police broke into the meeting and wrote down the names of all present. Shortly thereafter, the chairman of the Assembly was called to police headquarters where he was told he must resign his position. They also asked him to spy on the Bahá'í community. Soon after, all those in a Bahá'í organization or committee were accused of being 'an English spy, a bourgeois in affiliation, a reactionary, or a helper of religious institutions' and their civil rights were removed.[48]

Ten years later, on 5 February 1938, the authorities increased their persecution and the members of the Local Spiritual Assembly of 'Ishqábád were arrested, the houses of the believers were searched and all Tablets and Bahá'í records were confiscated. Five hundred men from Turkistan were thrown into prison, where many died. Six hundred Bahá'í refugees, mostly women, children and the aged, fled to Iran. The Mashriqu'l-Adhkár was converted by the Soviets into an art gallery.[49] A large earthquake in 1948 badly damaged the structure and it was razed to the ground in 1963.[50]

1929

During 1929, Shoghi Effendi faced more Covenant-breaking, began construction of three additional rooms on the Shrine of the Báb, traversed Africa from south to north, directed Mountfort Mills to petition the League of Nations about the House of Bahá'u'lláh in Baghdad, and finally acquired possession of the Mansion at Bahjí. Pilgrims to the Bahá'í World Centre included Narayenrao Rangnath Shethji, known as Vakíl, and Martha Root.

More Covenant-breaking

Covenant-breaking, one thing that could make Shoghi Effendi physically ill, reappeared again between 1929 and 1932. This time it was Ruth White, who had met 'Abdu'l-Bahá in New York in 1912. Ella Cooper was there at the same meeting and had been quite taken with Mrs White. The Master noticed this and called her over to say, 'Be very careful.' Mrs White also went on pilgrimage in 1922, but she could never understand the concept of Bahá'í administration.[1]

Now Mrs White was attacking the Faith, claiming that the Will and Testament of 'Abdu'l-Bahá was a forgery. Shoghi Effendi wrote to Major Tudor-Pole that 'the most powerful and determined opponents of the Faith in the East, who have challenged the very basis of Bahá'u'lláh's Message . . . have not even hinted at the possibility of the Will being a forged document. They have vehemently attacked its provisions, but never questioned its authenticity.' Mrs White's efforts over the following years included writing to the United States Postmaster General demanding that the National Spiritual Assembly of the United States and Canada be stopped from using the mail to 'to spread the falsehood that Shoghi Effendi is the successor of 'Abdu'l-Bahá and Guardian of the Bahá'í Cause'. She also wrote to the authorities in Palestine requesting them to declare the Will to be a forgery, but was 'curtly' refused.[2]

On 31 December 1928, Ruth White wrote to the High Commissioner of Palestine with the charge that the Will and Testament of 'Abdu'l-Bahá was fraudulent. In January 1929, the National Spiritual Assembly forwarded a pamphlet published by Ruth White and on 27 February the Guardian responded, writing

> I have in a letter addressed to the National Assembly set forth my views regarding the contents of Mrs. White's pamphlet. I have thus far received no intimation from the Palestine authorities, and have no reason to believe that they will consider it worthy of their consideration. The friends, however, should avoid hurting her feelings and should abstain from provocation. Her case will suffer the fate which has met Dyar's opposition in 'Reality,' and should be totally disregarded by the believers.[3]

On 7 October 1930, Mrs White again wrote to the High Commissioner in Palestine saying that she had sent a photograph of 'Abdu'l-Bahá's Will to Dr Ainsworth Mitchell in England, who declared that no part of it had been written by the Master. After requesting that she send them copies of the photographed Will that she had supplied to Dr Mitchell, the Government of Palestine contacted the Governor of Haifa who requested that Shoghi Effendi allowed an expert to examine the Will and Testament. Rúḥí Afnán wrote that Shoghi Effendi

> sent me with the Will & the expert studied it before me and the governor in the office of the latter. The expert compared the original Will with the handwriting of the Master which Mrs. White had sent him as authentic samples. He said that they are both written by the same person & that person who had decided otherwise does not know what he is speaking about.[4]

On 10 July 1931, the Palestinian government wrote to Mrs White that they would take no further action on her claims and demands.[5] Though Mrs White's activities were very energetic, all they did, according to Amatu'l-Bahá Rúḥíyyih Khánum, 'was to stir up a temporary and insignificant cloud of dust'.[6] Other believers who had rendered important services to the Faith in the past, however, such as Wilhelm Herrigel in

Germany, were influenced and tragically didn't survive as Bahá'ís very long after the Master's passing, objecting to the Guardian's efforts to develop what they saw as an unneeded administrative order.[7]

In a letter written on behalf of the Guardian on 8 April 1931, Herrigel's rashness was noted:

> You mention in your letter that Mr. Herrigel is becoming conscious of the mistake he has made. He surely ought to have studied the true situation before taking sides and expressing his opinion. This is exactly what I wrote to him on behalf of Shoghi Effendi, but he was blinded by Mrs. White. Anyhow, Shoghi Effendi hopes that as time passes the truth that the Master's will encloses will more and more dawn upon him and make him repent for his past deeds.[8]

Interestingly, in 1941 Mrs White's husband cabled the Guardian that he was 'profoundly sorrowing and repentant pleading forgiveness'. Shoghi Effendi replied and offered him a path back into the Faith, but he never took it.[9]

The vision of Shoghi Effendi

On 27 February, Shoghi Effendi finished the first of what would become the extraordinary series of letters addressed to the north American Bahá'í community, 'general communications' that 'unfold a clear vision of the relation between the Bahá'í community and the entire process of social evolution under the Dispensation of Bahá'u'lláh' and establishing 'the Bahá'í Administrative Order as the nucleus and pattern of the world civilization emerging under divine inspiration at the focal point of human history'.[10] These letters would be collected and published in 1938 under the title *The World Order of Bahá'u'lláh*.

Pilgrim visits

Some time during the year, Narayenrao Rangnath Shethji, known as Vakíl, came on his second pilgrimage from India, the first having been in 1914. On his first trip, Vakíl had been unmarried, but engaged to a Hindu woman. This time he brought his wife, Jashodaben, who was still a Hindu, and his daughters Sushila, aged nine, and Kapila, aged seven. Jashodaben had supported her husband's Bahá'í activities, but remained staunch in her own faith. Shortly after arriving in Haifa, Shoghi Effendi sent them to spend the night in the Mansion at Bahjí. Before going to sleep Jashodaben said her prayers, then put the Bhagavad Gita and a picture of Krishna under her pillow. That night she had a dream in which a Holy Figure, whom she knew was Krishna, was standing by a cupboard. Krishna removed a series of beautiful crowns, one after another, and gave them to her to put in a new cupboard. The Figure said that the crowns now belonged to Bahá'u'lláh. Krishna and Bahá'u'lláh then appeared together and Krishna took off His crown and gave it to Bahá'u'lláh. Then He looked at Jashodaben and said, 'There is no difference between Us; We are the same.' When they woke up the next morning, Vakíl was overjoyed to learn that his wife was now a Bahá'í.[11]

Jashodaben was infatuated with the Greatest Holy Leaf and one night she thought she would like to cook some Indian food for her. The next day, before Jashodaben could mention it, the Greatest Holy Leaf asked, 'Would you like to cook some Indian food for me?' On another occasion, the Greatest Holy Leaf asked Jashodaben if there was a 'boon' she could do for her. Jashodaben said that she only wanted to have a faith that nothing could shake. When pressed, she added that she also wished that her children would remain faithful as well. The Greatest Holy Leaf was very happy with her and gave Jashodaben her own name, Bahíyyih.[12]

One day, Sushila was walking in the garden of the House of the Master, where they were staying, when suddenly she saw Shoghi Effendi. She was amazed because light was radiating from him. When he approached her, she gave him a rose, after which he walked away. For the moment, she forgot the whole world. Shoghi Effendi told her father that his two daughters would have a great future in the Faith, which they did. The family spent nineteen days in the Holy Land.[13]

When Isabel Rives arrived for her second pilgrimage during the first part of the year, she recalled a story of 'Abdu'l-Bahá to an early American pilgrim. 'Abdu'l-Bahá had said to the pilgrim:

'Come and see my garden.' He took her by the hand and almost ran over the roughest ground she had ever seen, worse than any ploughed field for it was covered with rocks as big as her head and body. That was many years ago. And now that rock bed has become a beautiful garden. A world-wide traveler who had seen many beautiful gardens declared this to be by far the most beautiful.[14]

Isabel decided one day to walk up the terraces from the German colony at the bottom to the Shrine of the Báb at the top. She wrote:

> There are nine terraces with steps leading from one to the other. All the walks and paths are red; that is, they are evidently constructed of tiling reduced to a fine gravel consistency. Each path or walk is bordered with small red plants; inside that another border of taller plants with green leaves; while within this enclosure there is beautiful green grass – a rare thing in the Holy Land; and then again more of the tiny red and green plants arranged in designs reminding one of an exquisite Persian rug. There are also many palms and curious trees . . . Then there are pomegranate and orange trees, and a very distinctive group belonging to the cedar variety. We have heard so often of how 'Abdu'l-Bahá used to sit under these trees and write many of his sacred Tablets.[15]

She was also surprised by the great activity taking place in the harbour area. She noted that when she had been on pilgrimage in 1922, there were no sewerage or water systems, or electricity. The only water at the House of the Master came from a deep well on the south side of the building from which water was raised by use of a pulley, a rope and a pail.[16] Now, all three existed.

When they arrived at the Shrine of Bahá'u'lláh, Isabel noted that the Mansion was very much in need of repair, but was reassured that it would be completely restored.[17]

Dr John Haynes Holmes, the well-known pastor of the Community Church in New York, travelled to Haifa specifically to see Shoghi Effendi and 'this great inclusive religion of our time'. Of Shoghi Effendi, however, his article in *Unity* magazine said almost nothing, but at the Tombs of the three Central Figures of the Faith he was enraptured:

> Our first view of Haifa was from Mt. Carmel, where Elijah in the ancient day confounded the prophets of Baal. What a place from which to summon the witness of Jehovah! On the left, the dazzling

blue of the Mediterranean; on the right, the wide curve of the beach sweeping to the walls of 'Akká; in the front the bay, with one great ship and numerous smaller craft peacefully at anchor; below, like a tumbling water-fall, the white stone houses of the town; and just in the center, like a lovely gem, the garden in which reposed the bodies of the honoured Bahá'í dead.

We visited this garden the next morning, after a special audience with the head of the Bahá'í Movement. In the center towered the cluster of noble cypresses, beneath whose grateful shade the venerable 'Abdu'l-Bahá sought quiet and refreshment. Around these trees, winding from terrace to terrace, and lined with giant hedges of geraniums, were paths, paved with broken fragments of red tile, which tempted the feet to meditative wanderings. Rose bushes, gorgeous with blossoms a few weeks hence, broke frequently the stretches of fresh, deep-rooted grass. On the lowest terrace, facing a straight avenue which shot down, and then on like an arrow, to the sea, was the granite mausoleum. We removed our shoes, in accordance with Arab custom, and stepped into the large room, dimly lighted, through stained windows, in which lay the body of 'Abdu'l-Bahá. I remembered him as the wise and gentle sage with whom I had talked on his last visit to America. Now his noble face was still in death beneath this richly inscribed drapery upon the floor! We stood shoeless upon rugs so soft and heavy as to be warm to the feet. We saw silver vases laden with flowers standing like candles about the grave. A great peace lay upon the place. I had never seen a tomb so beautiful! After long moments of reverent salutation, we moved away, and entered a second room where lay the body of the Báb . . .

Bahá'u'lláh, the third of the great trinity of Bahá'í leaders, was buried across the bay in 'Akká. In the afternoon, under the escort of a cousin of Shoghi Effendi, also grandson of 'Abdu'l-Bahá, we started for this ancient city. Our way led us first along the hard, clean beach of sand which stretched across the roadstead. It had been storming, and the waves were running high and breaking in wild cascades of foam. Fishermen were busy, as high winds and dark skies drove in the fish. Some were launching their huge boats through the breakers; others, far out upon the waves, were dragging their heavy nets along the deep; still others had landed and were laboriously hauling their catch to the shore. At intervals among the fishers walked long caravans of camels, each patient beast contrasting strangely with the background of sea and sky. Far ahead loomed the ancient city, its ridge of close-packed houses surmounted by the huge bulk of the mighty citadel and a minaret so graceful as to suggest a dream of paradise . . .

We went to the citadel, incidentally to see this relic of the Crusaders, primarily to visit the prison cell where Bahá'u'lláh had been held captive through so many awful years by his persecutors. As we mounted the huge walls, twenty feet thick, we heard the muezzin chant his call to prayer from the nearby mosque. The Moslem ruled this battleground today. Our escort was influential and tried hard, but we did not see Bahá'u'lláh's cell. For the citadel is still a prison – we saw the striped convicts in the yard! – and visitors could not be admitted . . .

Another fifteen minutes, and we were in the Bahá'í garden where lay the remains of Bahá'u'lláh. Huge cypresses and palms were close about; the same red-tiled walks threaded their way through luxurious grass and flowers. A strange peace again dropped down upon us from the encompassing atmosphere of beauty. With eager reverence we once more removed our shoes, and stepped into the sacred presence of the Prophet's tomb. Was it because this great man reposed alone that I was so deeply touched? Or was it because a sense of the man's greatness came sweeping suddenly upon me? Bahá'u'lláh was not only the supreme genius of the Bahá'í Movement; he was without question one of the supreme spiritual geniuses of history. There have been few in any age to compare with him in point of insight, vision, lofty thought and noble speech. I felt this as I stood within this quiet place. Were it possible to stand by the grave of Jesus, I felt I should be moved in this same way. Here, appropriately, was not darkness, but light; not gloom, but glory. Those Prophets' shrines are truly among the sacred spots on earth.[18]

Lorol Schopflocher was back in Haifa in March, again after a long trip through India. When she met Shoghi Effendi, he handed her a cable from her husband, Fred, who asked, 'Are you willing to contribute $50,000 to Temple which may mean you do not get a Cadillac this year?' Lorol laughed out loud and Shoghi Effendi grinned as he said, 'What do you think of this?' I laughed again and said 'Why not $100,000?' I scribbled a cable on a table napkin and sent Fugeta, the Master's old Japanese servant, off to the telegraph office . . . the reply came back, 'You win, love to Shoghi Effendi, love, Fred.'

Because of this, a further $110,000 was added to the Temple Fund on 16 March.[19]

Philip Sprague was on pilgrimage during the year and came away with memories of the 'exhilaration of the beautiful chants'. Shoghi Effendi also told him he should study the words of Bahá'u'lláh two hours each day, saying that the believers little realized their power.[20]

An Indian pilgrim wrote: 'We must understand Shoghi Effendi in order to be able to help him accomplish the stupendous task he has entrusted to us. He is so calm and yet so vibrant, so static and yet so dynamic.'[21]

Traversing Africa

As he normally did, Shoghi Effendi left Haifa for the summer. In September, he was in England. From there, he sailed to Cape Town, South Africa, and drove back the length of Africa to Cairo. Why he was in England and why he went to South Africa we do not know, but he did love to explore. He wanted to see the Congo, but was unable to get a visa for the country so had to bypass it.[22] He travelled up through East Africa, passing through Rhodesia, today's Zimbabwe, where he visited the grave of Cecil Rhodes, who founded both the diamond company De Beers and the country of Rhodesia. He also visited the Victoria Falls. At one point he rode as a passenger through part of East Africa with an English hunter, and at another he travelled on a train for five hundred miles. He also crossed the Nile River through a papyrus swamp on a ferry. We only know this much about his trip because of photographs he took on the way.[23] Shoghi Effendi was back in Haifa in October.

Expanding the Shrine of the Báb and the Bahá'í gardens

The Shrine of the Báb was intended to have nine rooms. In 1928, Shoghi Effendi began preparatory work, excavating the rock behind the building. During 1929, he added the final three rooms at the back of the building. Ḥájí Maḥmúd Qassábchí, who had carried out the renovations on the House of Baháʼuʼlláh in Baghdad, was put in charge of this work.[24] In addition to excavating deeper into the mountain, Shoghi Effendi also modified the interior of the Shrine. Originally, the centre-most room, which contained the remains of the Báb, was separated from the rooms to the east and west by a wall with wooden doors. Shoghi Effendi removed the doors in both walls and enlarged the openings so that they formed a wide arch through which it was possible to see completely through the building.[25] The rooms were completed during the year. The doors into the Shrine of ʻAbdu'l-Bahá, however, were left as the Master had built them.

Almost from the moment that Shoghi Effendi found himself to be the Guardian, he began to develop gardens at the Shrine of the Báb and the Shrine of Baháʼuʼlláh. Amatu'l Bahá Rúḥíyyih Khánum describes this:

> I doubt if Shoghi Effendi ever planted anything during his entire life, or ever had the desire to do so. He was not interested in gardening but in gardens, and never missed an opportunity to visit a beautiful or famous one; I cannot say how many gardens we visited together in twenty years . . .
>
> In the days of ʻAbdu'l-Bahá, when water was a major problem, He had created, both in Bahji and on Mt Carmel, small gardens next to the Holy Tombs, consisting mostly of citrus trees and flowers. Shoghi Effendi altered, extended and formalized these gardens. I remember in 1923 when I came with my mother on my first pilgrimage she remarked on the already formal layout of the small area of garden adjoining the Bab's Shrine and said it was a symbol of the Administrative Order the Guardian was building up all over the world. I am sure this idea had not occurred to Shoghi Effendi; but pattern and order were innate in him, there was no other way he could work.
>
> Professor Alaine Locke of Howard University in Washington, who was one of the Baháʼí pilgrims to visit Haifa during the first years of Shoghi Effendi's Guardianship, describes the impressions he received as he walked with Shoghi Effendi in the gardens of the Bab's Shrine: 'Shoghi Effendi is a master of detail as well as of

principle, of executive foresight as well as of projective vision. But I have never heard details so redeemed of their natural triviality as when talking to him of the plans for the beautifying and laying out of the terraces and gardens. They were important because they all were meant to dramatize the emotion of the place and quicken the soul even through the senses.'[26]

Shoghi Effendi laid out the gardens himself. Rúḥíyyih Khánum said that he

was practically an architect . . . a landscape gardener in his own right. It was something in him and if you analyse in him what that quality was that enabled him to build buildings, and staircases and entrances and make all of these beautiful gardens in Haifa that have become world famous, what the thing was in him that enabled him to do it so beautifully, it was a sense of proportion – he had a perfect eye . . .

[Shoghi Effendi] used to design these garden paths by going and standing there and looking at them and studying the situation and carrying out the work. He did it all himself . . . He wanted to make a retaining wall . . . that had a double curve in it. He said that a double curve was so much more beautiful than just one curve . . . He knew exactly what he wanted. He went up there and first he had pegs put in and then he had the gardeners come and take white soil and spill it out from their hand along the line of the pegs. Then he studied it from different angles and would go here and there, up and down, and have a look at it on the ground. He wouldn't like it and he would have his line rectified until he got it the way he wanted it. He would also go and see that the mason jolly well built it according to that line and not some other way out of his own head.[27]

According to Amatu'l-Bahá Rúḥíyyih Khánum, Shoghi Effendi never had an overall plan to develop the gardens around the Shrine. He did most of his planning by walking and looking:

. . . his method was to look, as he walked about the property, at the land he planned to develop; a pattern would suggest itself to his mind and he would study this, not only on the spot through observation of his area, but through drawings he made himself. Though many ideas in all fields of his work came to Shoghi Effendi in a flash, and although he may sometimes have seen at a glance the over-all design he planned to use for a garden, he worked out the dimensions and details painstakingly in his drawings which were not made to scale – as this would have taken a great deal of extra time – but on which all dimensions were calculated and indicated. For example: his main path was going to be, let us say, 25 metres long and 2 metres wide; beside this he allowed 25 centimetres for a border, a strip 1.20 metres wide for cypress trees, which were to be planted 1.50 metres apart, and so on. When he had it all planned he would go and stand and instruct the gardeners how to lay it out. Through string tied to pegs, giving long lines, a peg and string acting as a compass for circles, using the span (the space between thumb and little finger when fully stretched apart) as measurement of distance between trees, having light-coloured soil poured out to indicate a line, and other such simple methods he would, often in a single afternoon, have an entire section of garden laid out in full detail. Usually, knowing exactly what he intended to do, Shoghi Effendi would call other gardeners to follow along behind those that were laying out the design, so that as the plan was measured out on the ground, holes for cypress trees were dug, trees planted and flower beds set out and borders planted, all while Shoghi Effendi advanced with his measuring process in front of them! There is a proverb among the Arabs that whoever wears King Solomon's ring, when he turns it everything in the twinkling of an eye will be changed. Some of the Arab workers used to say Shoghi Effendi had found King Solomon's ring![28]

Developments in Haifa

When the British Mandate in Palestine was initially organized, most of the religious communities were recognized and given the right to administer their own affairs according to their own laws. The Bahá'ís, however, had not been granted this status, and consequently, had to use Muslim courts. Shoghi Effendi sent Mountfort Mills to speak with the Chief Secretary in Jerusalem, Mr Luke, about this problem. Mills later approached Mr Shuckburgh in the Colonial Office in London as well.[29]

Finally, on 4 May, the Bahá'í community in Palestine gained the legal right to administer their affairs through Bahá'í law. This affected things such as marriages and burials.[30]

Shoghi Effendi was constantly analysing the Bahá'í world with an eye to electing the Universal House of Justice. In August 1926, he had written that a competent secretariat was required in Haifa to strengthen 'the vital bonds that bind the Centre in Haifa with all the Assemblies in the Bahá'í world'. By 1929, Shoghi Effendi was thinking of forming an interim body, an International Secretariat or Council, as a prelude to the election of the Universal House of Justice. He, therefore, began to plan an international conference for the summer of 1930 at which a group of the Bahá'ís would discuss ways of more rapidly forming the National Spiritual Assemblies required before the Universal House of Justice could be elected. Unfortunately, some older Bahá'ís had a 'different concept' of what should happen at the conference. They wanted the interim body to be elected at the conference. Upon learning of this in December, Shoghi Effendi immediately cancelled the conference because it would only be 'a source of confusion, misunderstanding and even controversy'. The lurking danger he saw, as described by Amatu'l-Bahá Rúḥíyyih Khánum, was of 'immature people, not yet steeped in understanding of the Administrative Order he was unfolding and building, assuming a rank and power they were certainly incapable of safely holding'.[31] Things were held in abeyance until the formation of the International Bahá'í Council in 1951.

Petitioning the League of Nations about the House of Bahá'u'lláh

During the previous year, in 1928, Mountfort Mills had become pessimistic about progress in the case of the House of Bahá'u'lláh in Baghdad. In a letter to Horace Holley on 18 May 1928, he wrote:

> Many thanks for the copy of your epistle to the religious heads of Islam. Do let me know what results follow its receipt over there. It will be a most valuable lesson for us in Islamic psychology.
>
> What of this latter commodity I am running foul of just now, the Shiah branch of it more particularly, isn't very sympathetic. They don't seem to want the Iraq Government to take away from them those houses of ours in Baghdad at all and they are apparently able

to look so fierce about it that in spite of their handsome Sunni Mon-arch's [King Feisal] specific promises of last fall, which he readily admits making, he finds himself helpless to carry them out in the face of threatened Shiah Agitation. So it looks as if we may have to appeal to Geneva after all.[32]

By September 1928, Mountfort had drafted the appeal to the League of Nations in Geneva at the behest of Shoghi Effendi. On 3 September 1928 he wrote to Horace Holley about the petition:

Further negotiations in London in the Spring made it fairly clear that the Government of Iraq are not going to do any more than they have to . . . So we have gone ahead with the petition to Geneva, to be used as a final 'argument' with the Government first and then, if no results are obtained, presented to the Commission this Fall . . .

Preparing the original draft of the petition; submitting it to Shoghi Effendi and Baghdad for suggestions; getting it back and then making a final draft and sending that along to Baghdad in time for the last attempt there and yet be able to present it in Geneva for the Commission's meeting toward the end of this month has kept us pretty busy . . .[33]

On 19 January 1929, Mountfort again wrote to Horace saying that the Permanent Mandates Commission had favourably recommended the Bahá'í petition to the Council of the League of Nations, but stressed that it was strictly advisory. He wrote that

the petition bases its claims of Shiah interference with the religious practices of the Bahais upon the long history of Shiah persecution in Persia, and some rather uncomplimentary references to Persian Governments of the past are made. Well, since the petition was filed, Persia has been elected a member of the Council of the League and will sit as such when the matter comes up for decision in March. What attitude will she take?

Politically, she is hostile to Iraq; has refused so far to recognize the new State at all. Religiously, Shiah Islam is Persia's State religion. Which turning will she take?

For whatever value it may have as an indication, the Persian

Ministry of Foreign Affairs has responded to an appeal from the
Persian plaintiffs in the Baghdad action by an attempt to collect
the costs allowed them in Bagdad from Wahkil and the heirs of
Abdu'l Baha, the defendants, all now residing in Haifa and, of
course, outside the jurisdiction of the Bagdad courts. This attempt
was made through the Persian Consul in Haifa.

At best this could be only a form of intimidation; Persia would
have no power whatsoever to enforce any such claim . . .

I expect to be in Geneva for the meeting though, unfortunately,– and unfairly, I think, – the petitioners are not allowed to
be represented, either before the Council or the Mandates Commission . . .

Interesting, isn't it, that Baha'u'llah has taken a hand in the
matter and had the question brought up before almost the whole
world through their representatives in Geneva? There is more in
this, Old Man, than two or three little mud houses in Baghdad,
sacred though they be.[34]

Shoghi Effendi was able to announce a victory in April 1929: 'League
Council pronounced in favour Bahá'í Petition regarding Bahá'u'lláh's
House. Faith triumphant over deadliest enemy. Inform believers. Avoid
for present widespread publicity. Cause much indebted to Mountfort's
magnificent achievement. Shoghi'.[35] The next month, Shoghi Effendi
again gave credit to Mountfort Mills:

I must not fail in conclusion to refer once again to the decisive role
played by the distinguished and international champion of the Faith
of Bahá'u'lláh, our dearly-beloved Mountfort Mills, in the negotiations that have paved the way for the signal success already achieved.
The text of the Bahá'í petition, which he conceived and drafted, has
been recognized by the members of the Mandates Commission as 'a
document well-drafted, clear in its argument and moderate in tone.'
He has truly acquitted himself in this most sacred task with exemplary distinction and proved himself worthy of so noble a mission.[36]

When Martha Root visited King Feisal in January 1930 and praised him
for supporting the Bahá'ís, he said he had only done his duty and what
was right in order to maintain justice: 'Justice will always be followed.

We have formed a committee to study the whole problem and settle it in such a way as to satisfy all groups interested in this matter.'[37]

Unfortunately, it was a short-lived victory and the King's pious statement was ephemeral. His deeds did not match his words. The Guardian's request to avoid widespread publicity was prescient. The British thought the Bahá'ís had a just cause, but the country's Muslims did not. In 1930 a compromise was offered, to turn the house into a dispensary. The Bahá'ís accepted, but the Muslims refused and on it went. The League of Nations and the British were both supporting the Bahá'ís, but the Iraqi government was afraid to acquiesce for fear of what the general population might do. Later, a Session report of the Permanent Mandates Commission of the League of Nations, dated 13 November 1931, stated that 'Religious passion was at the bottom of this injustice and it was clear that the delays in righting the wrong were due to the same cause; the 'Iráqí Government was not strong enough to make a majority respect the right of a minority.'[38]

Shoghi Effendi kept trying and the League of Nations Council continued to press for a resolution of the problem, but the Iraqi government and King Feisal continued to make promises they never fulfilled. As late as the spring of 1934 they were still insisting that the problem would be resolved,[39] but it was not.

In a letter addressed to the Bahá'ís all around the world and dated 17 July 2013, the Universal House of Justice wrote that 'it was with utter shock and desolating grief that the Bahá'ís in Baghdad discovered on June 26th that the "Most Holy Habitation" of Bahá'u'lláh had been razed almost to the ground to make way for the construction of a mosque'. It was discovered that plans for doing this had been made for some time, and that the work had been carried out quickly, and without a legal permit. The Universal House of Justice encouraged the Bahá'ís to keep their focus on 'opening the hearts to the implications of the message of the Blessed Beauty', stating that 'events will only serve to heighten the sense of urgency with which this work is undertaken'.[40]

Martha Root

On 25 November Martha Root arrived on her second pilgrimage. Her first meeting was with Munírih Khánum and a few other women. When a teenage girl read her a message of welcome in English, a language many members of the Holy Household were trying to learn, she was almost speechless with emotion. When she met Shoghi Effendi, one of the first things he said to her was to take care of her health. About the Guardian, she later wrote that 'He is my great ideal of a Guardian. Oh, I see his great reality, – I just cannot describe how beautiful it was to meet him.' Shortly afterwards, Shoghi Effendi became ill and she was not able to see him for three weeks. When she arrived, she was only planning to stay for nine days, but the Guardian sent her a message, saying, 'Do not hurry on, stay a little with us.'[41]

Martha greatly enjoyed being with the Greatest Holy Leaf. 'Abdu'l-Bahá's sister was eighty-two years old, had pneumonia and had not walked for two months at that time, but Martha was still struck by her spiritual qualities. Entering her room, 'She received us sitting up in bed. Dressed so lovely . . . she is perfectly beautiful and very exquisite.' Before Martha left, the Greatest Holy Leaf gave her a 'beautiful little red ringstone'. It was well known that Martha commonly gave away things given to her as gifts and one of those present asked the Greatest Holy Leaf if Martha should be required to keep the ring. Bahíyyih Khánum responded, 'I could not say that. I know if she gives it away it will be a great sacrifice for it is very dear to her. But if she feels it would do a great service to the Cause somewhere and she gave it, it would do good.'[42]

Martha knew how hard the Guardian had to work, and now that he was ill she wanted to help. Shoghi Effendi, however, knowing how hard Martha worked on her travels, told those around him, 'Do not give her anything to do, she must rest.' Since she couldn't work, she decided to host a tea with the four gardeners at the Shrine of the Báb as the guests of honour. She also invited twenty eastern pilgrims. Later, she did the same thing for the Bahá'ís living near Bahjí, including guests from Akka and two other villages. She used tea that Roy Wilhelm had sent her and which he had intended for use in areas where good tea was difficult to find. She told Roy that his tea was very much appreciated.[43]

Dr Walter Guy joined Martha in November and was there for the commemoration of the Ascension of 'Abdu'l-Bahá. He was quite taken with the event:

All day long groups of women and children had been coming and going at the home of 'Abdu'l-Bahá.

At six p.m. I joined a group of men in the courtyard . . . They were dressed in various costumes, some in European clothes, others with fez of crimson hue, a few with the white cloth and double rings on their heads in the desert Bedouin style. Presently we passed into the large entry hall and here all shoes were removed before entering the Master's room from where He had ascended to the celestial world of the spirit.

In the corner of the large room was a tall narrow bed with high posts and white coverings. On a pillow rested the Master's white oriental headdress or fez. The group constantly grew larger until the room was filled, but still others came, forming a group in the large hall outside. Some wore beards, white or gray, others were young . . . These men were the exiles or prisoners of 'Akká and their descendants who had shared the imprisonment with the Master. As each one entered, he knelt at the side of the Master's bed . . . Sobs and moans filled the room, tears coursed down the cheeks of those greybearded men . . . how poignantly they realized the void in their hearts made by the passing of their loved Master . . . Rising from their knees, they kissed passionately the bed, its posts, and some the Master's fez.

Soon all who could get in the room had made their prayer. The sobs were stilled and at a word all sank to the floor. One of those present in the chamber raised a melodious chant, it was the sublime prayer of 'Abdu'l-Bahá, used always at His Shrine. Others chanted in and outside the room; one by one we again knelt at the side of the bed . . .

Carmel: It was the night on the Mountain of God . . . There were many men and boys, also a few women gathered there, to spend the hours of night in prayer and devotion, in commemoration of the Master of 'Akká . . . Soon all had gathered in the Holy Shrine. Shoeless, on rich carpets, two by two, each had knelt at the threshold of the sacred tomb – first in the Shrine of 'Abdu'l-Bahá; next in the tomb of the Báb. Sacred and holy prayers were chanted in each shrine. Here for the first time I heard the Guardian, Shoghi Effendi, in stately, measured cadences, chant the prayer of his Lord.

It was a deeply spiritual occasion, an experience that can never be effaced from memory's scroll. It was particularly Oriental in setting. All heads but mine were covered by the Oriental fez – the deep yellow of the Persian coats made a contrast with the dark suits of European design. The soft lights, the fragrant flowers, rich-hued rugs and carpets, the lamps and ornaments in the tomb chamber, and, to me, the strange chanting of the prayers – beautiful, appealing and intensely spiritual – made a scene of simple but holy splendor.

No preaching, no talking or praising; nothing but prayer. It was a promise of that New Day, its dawn already beaming on this mountain of ancient prophets . . .

Later all were gathered around the beautiful lawn and drank hot tea; more chanting was rendered, and finally in the large Eastern Pilgrim House, nearby, the Guardian said to me: 'Tomorrow you travel early and far; it is my wish that you go to the Shrines and pray alone. There I will bid you farewell.' Turning to his cousin . . . he said, 'Go with him.'

It was midnight when we together knelt at the holy thresholds, strewn with petals of white fragrant flowers, damp with the tears of the believers and followers of the Divine Friend and Teacher. The Shrines were empty and silent; the lamps, however, still illumined the beautiful adornments. I could but offer myself as an unworthy servant, one who, however, desired to become worthy . . .

The time of departure had come. The Guardian gave me the three-fold embrace and words for the friends. Faithful Fugeta holding my hand, we went together down the narrow way through the straight gate on Carmel's slope that leads to the Shrines which speak so eloquently of Life Eternal. We passed over barren rocks and through dark ways till we came to the Western Pilgrim House, a home of sacrifice and loving service; from thence early next day to travel homeward to service and work in the vineyard of human hearts. The Pilgrimage ended and work begun.[44]

Martha was very anxious to begin her next journey and she declined the Guardian's suggestion that she stay longer. He was finally able to meet her just three days before she left. Martha left to blaze a trail for Shoghi Effendi to Iran starting from Damascus. If successful, he would later send a commission over the same route. On 29 December, Martha left Haifa and travelled to Damascus with Mr Y. A. Rafaat. In Damascus, they were joined by a Persian lady from Shiraz and the trio joined a caravan of cars to cross the desert to Baghdad. It was an exhausting journey for most, but Martha said it was the 'easiest trip she ever took'.[45]

The Mansion at Bahjí back in Bahá'í hands

Back in November 1927, the Mansion at Bahjí had still been occupied by Mírzá Muḥammad-'Alí and the Covenant-breakers when Shoghi Effendi received a letter from them 'requesting us to repair the roof which may collapse at any time'. The Guardian flatly refused: 'He has been told emphatically that we shall not proceed with any repair unless and until they evacuate the entire building.' Two years later, on this day, the eighth anniversary of the Ascension of 'Abdu'l-Bahá, Shoghi Effendi sent a cable that read: 'Qasr [Mansion at Bahjí] evacuated. Restoration commenced.' A few days later, he wrote that

> the Mansion of Bahá'u'lláh, occupied for about forty years by Muḥammad 'Alí and his followers, has at last been evacuated and the enclosed photograph will indicate in what a state they have left it! Restorative work has commenced and the pilgrims are already visiting the room where Bahá'u'lláh passed away and where he passed the most peaceful and happiest days of his life.[46]

At some point before the Covenant-breakers left, Shoghi Effendi sent Abu'l-Qásim Faizí and Hasan Balyuzi to examine the Mansion. It was still in the hands of the Covenant-breakers at that time, so the Guardian cautioned the two not to enter into any discussions with them. But the conditions the two young men found in the Mansion left them aghast. The building was in dire need of repair, but was also filthy. The Covenant-breakers had even piled coal in the room of Bahá'u'lláh. Hasan was so shocked by what he saw that he asked their guide why it was in such a state. The man blamed Shoghi Effendi for not giving them money for repairs. Hasan countered by stating that it only required a broom to clean it.[47] Mírzá Muḥammad-'Alí and his companions similarly showed little respect for the Holy Shrine, building a blacksmith's shop near its entrance.[48] When the Covenant-breakers finally left, they removed everything portable with the exception of a single candlestick which was left in the room of Bahá'u'lláh.[49] It would be two more years before the restoration was completed.

1930

The year 1930 was notable for three things: the thwarted visit of the Dowager Queen Marie of Romania to Shoghi Effendi, the translation and editing of *The Dawn-Breakers*, and Effie Baker's monumental journey through Iran to photograph Bábí historical sites for the Guardian.

Queen Marie's attempted visit

In early 1930, Queen Marie of Romania intended to travel through the Middle East with her daughter, Ileana. The journey was to include a visit to Haifa to meet Shoghi Effendi. Somehow, word of this and the Queen's allegiance to the Bahá'í Faith suddenly became public. On 13 February, the *Palestine Bulletin* wrote to Shoghi Effendi saying that they had heard that the Queen was a Bahá'í and wanted information about the Faith. Shoghi Effendi replied by sending the paper a copy of the issue of *The Bahá'í World* containing Queen Marie's *Toronto Daily Star* newspaper article, which the *Palestine Bulletin* printed in full.[1] In honour of her visit, Shoghi Effendi had Bahá'u'lláh's Tablet to the Queen's grandmother, Queen Victoria, reproduced in beautiful calligraphy and illuminated in Tehran.[2]

Unfortunately, all this publicity became political. On 13 March, the Queen wrote, 'No Jerusalem and no Aka alas. This is a huge disappointment. But imagine they were turning my admiration for Abdu'l-Baha into a political complication.' The Guardian's repeated invitations were finally ended when, on 28 March, he received a cable, not from the Queen, but from the Romanian Minister in Cairo. Though the official reason for her not going to the Holy Land was the political unrest there, an angry queen suggested that political aversion to the Bahá'í Faith was at the core of it.[3]

The publicity surrounding her potential visit resulted in Shoghi

Effendi being inundated with requests for information which ended up being twisted for a variety of ends. In a letter to Martha Root, he wrote:

> Reporters who called on me representing the United Press of America telegraphed to their newspapers just the opposite I told them. They perverted the truth. I wish we could make sure that she would at least know the real situation! But how can we ensure that our letters to her Majesty will henceforth reach her. I feel that you should write to her, explain the whole situation, assure her of my great disappointment.[4]

For a long while, the Queen was not even allowed to write to Shoghi Effendi. Amatu'l-Bahá Rúḥíyyih Khánum recounts:

> Behind the scenes there must have taken place a real struggle between the courageous and independent Queen and her advisers for, after a long silence, she wrote to Martha Root, in her own hand, describing at least a little of what had taken place. In a letter dated 28 June 1931 she stated: 'Both Ileana and I were cruelly disappointed at having been prevented going to the holy shrines and of meeting Shoghi Effendi, but at that time were going through a cruel crisis and every movement I made was being turned against me and being politically exploited in an unkind way. It caused me a good deal of suffering and curtailed my liberty most unkindly. There are periods however when one must submit to persecution, nevertheless, however high-hearted one may be, it ever again fills one with pained astonishment when people are mean and spiteful . . . But the beauty of truth remains and I cling to it through all the vicissitudes of a life become rather sad . . .'[5]

Rúḥíyyih Khánum also remembered Shoghi Effendi talking about how

> the Greatest Holy Leaf had waited, hour after hour, in the Master's home to receive the Queen and her daughter – for Her Majesty had actually sailed for Haifa, and this news encouraged Shoghi Effendi to believe she was going to carry out the pilgrimage she had planned; time passed and no news came, even after the boat had docked. Later the Guardian learned that the Queen and her party had been

met at the boat, informed her visit was impolitic and not permissible, been put in a car and whisked out of Palestine to another Middle Eastern country. It is no wonder she wrote to Martha that people had been 'mean and spiteful'.[6]

Commemorating the Ascension of Bahá'u'lláh

Clara Weir attended the commemoration of the Ascension of Bahá'u'lláh over the night of 28 and 29 May. When she arrived with Ḍíyá'í'yyih Khánum and Rúḥá Khánum, the mother and aunt of Shoghi Effendi, she found a large group of men already in the garden before the Shrine. Since there were so many people, groups took turns entering the Shrine. When Clara's turn came:

The outer chamber was brilliant, the large cut-glass chandeliers scintillating with myriads of candles, and on a table a number of candle-lighted lamps threw their radiance upon delicate rug and velvet drapery. The outer Shrine is two stories high, with no windows on the ground floor, but having several above on each of the four sides. Through these windows one could see the blue sky, and beneath them, electric lights . . . brought into relief the color and waxen texture of the tropical plants, which form a miniature garden in the center.

Dark clad forms reverently sat along the walls or moved silently toward an open door through which flooded a radiance not only seen, but felt.

The inner Shrine, while dimly lighted by lamp and candelabra, yet revealed the soft green velvet draperies, and Persian rugs, and exquisite urns filled with flowers which shed their fragrance as rare incense in honor of a king. There was no somberness here, but rather a regenerating atmosphere, which, while bearing comfort to the weary heart, yet filled one with a heavy sense of loss and indefinable longing . . . Those who had gazed upon the splendour of His personality, silently wept . . .

After kneeling in silent reverence at the Threshold, each one, still facing the Shrine, entered an antechamber, to make room for the men. Shoghi Effendi entered first, and knelt before the inner Shrine, after a few moments retreating to the outer chamber. The room was rapidly filled, as men, old and young, reverently approached the Shrine. Shoghi Effendi then chanted a Tablet . . .

The chanting over, and homage offered at the Holy Threshold, the chamber was again emptied, and devotions were resumed in the garden. This rotation continued throughout the night . . .

Again the believers entered the Shrine until it was filled as before. At three o'clock, the hour of the Ascension of that Glorious One, Shoghi Effendi, Guardian of the Bahá'í Cause, again approached the Holy Shrine, and again chanted the sacred words which penetrated every heart and made it respond with gratitude, and renewed dedication to the service of the Most Glorious.

When we retired from the Shrine, the first streaks of dawn had already appeared in the eastern sky, while a sacred silence broken only by the song of a bird, seemed to permeate all nature.

It was four o'clock when we began our homeward journey.[7]

The Dawn-Breakers

By April, Shoghi Effendi had finished his translation of the *Kitáb-i-Íqán*, and had started the huge task of translating *The Dawn-Breakers*. On 17 April, the Guardian sent the first pages of Nabíl's momentous history to George Townshend, asking him to apply his literary talents to it:

> He is now working on the translation into English of Nabil's history. This is the most extensive, detailed and interesting history of the Cause still in M.S. form and as the author, a Bahá'í poet translated by E.G. Browne, was in close association with Mírzá Musa, Bahá'u'lláh's only true brother, it carries a good deal of authority also. Shoghi Effendi would be grateful if you would go over this translation of Nabil and make suggestions and alterations like the Íghan'. Of course in this case you need not be as literal as with sacred writings.[8]

Over the next five months, the Guardian mailed him several packages, each containing a hundred pages or more. By the end of September, George had read the whole manuscript and was floored:

The account of the early martyrdoms in the last manuscript you sent is the most terrible, pitiful, rousing thing. I knew little, almost nothing of it, and I find it stimulating to think this Faith has such antecedents, such splendid glorious heroes to keep on the tradition of. It all quickens in one a new desire, a new courage, a more grim determination . . .

. . . The whole thing is the most thrilling, pitiful, glorious and powerful picture. The action of the Cause, like its writings and the aura that is about it all, is lofty and majestic beyond anything one could imagine or reach to in mind, let alone in deed. Like the teachings themselves this courage and resolution seem to call one to a devotion such as one never knew. Its effect on me is immeasurable; the world here around me seems less real.[9]

On 4 November, Shoghi Effendi asked George to write the introduction to this momentous book, sending him a variety of materials to reference. *The Dawn-Breakers* was full of Persian names and places as well as Persian fanaticism, making it very challenging for Westerners. George built a bridge for Westerners by focusing the introduction on Dr Cormick, the Irish physician who attended the Báb on the eve of his martyrdom. Dr Cormick was the only Westerner to meet the Báb and he left a very sympathetic account of those moments. With the book and introduction basically completed, Shoghi Effendi again approached George for a title. The Guardian tentatively proposed *Idylls of the Immortals*, but was obviously not set on it. After a suggestion or two, George proposed *The Dawn-Breakers*, which Shoghi Effendi quickly adopted.[10]

Effie Baker photographs Bahá'í sites in Iran

Shoghi Effendi had requested the Persian Bahá'ís to photograph places associated with the Báb, but since there was insufficient response he sent Effie Baker to Iran with the mission to photograph as many of the sites as possible related to Bábí history.

The Iranian government had embarked on a programme of renovation and modernization and the Guardian feared that many places associated with the heroic events of the Faith would be either altered or destroyed entirely. He also wanted to illustrate his translation of

Dawn-Breakers with photographs of the original sites. Initially, the trip was expected to last for three months, but in the end, Effie spent six months carrying out Shoghi Effendi's bidding.

Effie's main camera was a No. 1A Kodak with a wide-angle lens perfect for landscapes. Shoghi Effendi sent her to the local Kodak shop where she found that they had a gross (144) of eight-exposure films. He told her to 'Take the lot'. Shortly thereafter, Shoghi Effendi asked Effie to also photograph as many relics of the Báb as she could. That required her to revisit the Kodak shop and buy a second camera, a 'half plate clamp camera with a triple extension for changing focal lengths'. This was a camera that used half-sized glass plates as film and were able to focus very close to an object. Effie found that the shop had seven dozen photographic plates and, again, Shoghi Effendi told her to buy them all. Though this gave her a lot of baggage, it proved the Guardian's prescience because when she arrived in Iran, she learned the government had banned all photographic supplies from being sold.[11]

This was a particularly difficult task, not just for the danger inherent in a Western Bahá'í visiting Bahá'í localities in Iran, but also for a woman who was fifty years old. Effie travelled from Haifa to Iran by car across Syria 'in territory where bandits were common'.[12] Much of her travel in Iran was done by train or car, but some sites required her to resort to 'bitterly cold night-riding on heavily laden mules across steep and stony terrain'. Commonly, she had to disguise herself with a black chador and usually had to keep her cameras hidden.[13] It was a great challenge for a photographer. Shoghi Effendi's orders were:

> to work under the supervision of the NSA and they were to advise the LSAs in the different villages I would have to go to. He gave me a list of names taken from the original manuscript which were of the utmost importance to obtain and said when dealing with the martyrs and places of martyrdoms I was to use my own discretion as to which were the most important to photograph. He said 'You know there were 20,000 martyrs and each respective family will consider their martyr the most important; in that case you will be taking such photos for years'.[14]

Effie left for Iran on Friday 18 July, taking the train to Damascus where she met Shaykh Abdul Rahman, a Bahá'í from Bombay, as well as three illuminators who were to accompany her. On Tuesday, Effie headed for Baghdad in a convoy of several cars because of the risk of bandit attacks. Mountfort Mills, who had returned from Baghdad just before she left, told her of his hair-raising passage. He had been given a front seat in his car, but moved when a French consul's wife refused the back seat and demanded a front seat. Mountfort had swapped seats with her. As they travelled, bandits attacked them and the woman who had taken Mountfort's seat was shot dead. When Effie's caravan passed the site of the attack, the remains of suitcases and luggage were still there.[15] They travelled until 5 p.m. when they stopped at a military post for 'a much needed wash and a refreshing cup of tea & something to eat'. After half an hour, they continued until midnight, when they stopped for a couple hours of sleep. Just after dawn they reached the first Customs post where they spent an hour drinking tea and filling out forms. They finally arrived in Baghdad at 10 a.m. on 24 July.[16]

In Baghdad, Effie spent three very hot days securing her Iranian visa. She spent time along the Tigris River, watching the many boats and photographing the 'Pontoon Bridges' showing 'a bridge, open for the water traffic to pass and again closed with the stream of human beings surging across after their long waiting at each river bank'.[17]

Effie left Baghdad by train at 9 p.m. on 27 July, passing through Customs at the Iraq border at seven the next morning. There was no problem because she was carrying a letter from the Chief Customs Inspector in Baghdad. The Iraqi side of the border was neat, clean and efficient, a far cry from what she then encountered on the Iranian side:

> The officials were not too clean & their officers watched them. The shed where we had to have our baggage taken for inspection was filthy, & the men whose duty it was to turn over our belongings hadn't seen water for some time. After a lot of fuss, & having our things strewn about the dirty earth floor, we were allowed to pack up and go.[18]

They were finally on their way by private car at 10:30, but were stopped several times along the way at police stations to show their passports and inoculation certificates. They arrived at one station just as the inspector took his lunch and afternoon siesta. It was four and a half hours before he deigned to stamp their passports. With passports stamped, they started to leave, but a gendarme stopped them and an argument ensued. The gendarme's supervisor was called and Effie's driver was hauled into the police station. Then the two men in her car went into the station leaving Effie with two Persian ladies sitting in the sweltering car that was rapidly surrounded by a crowd. Finally, an English-speaking man appeared and was able to tell Effie that the gendarme had demanded to be taken to a village twenty-five miles away, but refused to pay. Since the car was already full, the driver had refused to take him. Hence the excitement. Effie pulled out her passport and told the man to take it into the station and say that Effie would report to her

Consul about the matter as we had hired the car for our private use etc. Immediately he conveyed this threat a hurried consultation look place, & in a few minutes we got the command Burro! Burro! (Go!). We started but when we entered the street leading out of the town we found the officer who had caused all the trouble for us with the traffic pole (preventing cars from entering or leaving a city until police permits are produced) well pulled down across the road & he refused to lift it for our car to pass through. We showed him our permits. However, the other officer who had ordered us to the police station came along & whispered in his ear. Immediately up went the pole. He also gave the command Burro! Burro![19]

At 5:30 they were stopped in another village and told they could not proceed. Effie's group were preparing to spend the night in the car by a café when another car arrived with 'the source of our annoyance aboard it. He had a few words with his comrade in arms, & presently we got the command once more Burro!' After overnighting in the village of Krend, Effie's party reached Kermanshah at eight the next morning.[20]

Effie stayed in Kermanshah for two days, then continued to Hamadan across country that 'was an endless winding around barren rugged peaks, there at intervals crossing some fertile plains' then circling around peak after peak, ever climbing until they reached a plateau where Hamadan was situated. The city was at about 6,000 feet and surrounded by snow-capped peaks. They finally arrived in Tehran at 11:30 p.m. on 5 August.[21]

Effie spent two weeks in Tehran where she met Dr Susan Moody who, at 'Abdu'l-Bahá's request, had gone to Iran in 1909 to care for

women. Except for one year when the Bahá'ís were especially persecuted, she had been there ever since. On 18 August, Effie began her
photographic work. Her first stop was Sari, where the Local Spiritual
Assembly sent her to Takur, a three-day trip on horseback. Near the
end of the first day, Effie's horse stumbled and she was thrown to the
ground, landing on her shoulder, but they continued. After they arrived,
Effie stayed up all night putting on hot applications.[22] For a bed, she
had a stretcher, which the National Assembly thought would be more
comfortable than the usual mud divan and carpet. They left at 6 a.m.,
passing through Amul, then headed up a mountain on a trek lasting
until midnight. Effie wrote:

> We could not see a yard before us and the path was only wide enough
> for our horses to tread single-file. All we could do was to give our
> faithful steeds their heads and sit tight in our saddles, so with their
> noses nearly touching the ground and at times with their four feet
> together they would slide six or seven feet down the mountain-side.
> The stones loosened by their feet would go hurtling down to the
> valley below, warning us a false step meant certain death. It was an
> anxious time for all of us, including our drivers for the road was new
> to them.[23]

They reached Takur and the home of Mírzá Fazollah, a nephew of
Bahá'u'lláh, on 24 August. When they asked Effie what she wanted
after the long journey, she said a bath. After a while, she was called to
her bath to find a big brass tub with jugs of hot and cold water – surrounded by all the chador-clad women of the village who had come to
watch the Western lady bathe. Effie said, 'I wasn't sport enough,' she
would prefer no spectators. The next day, she photographed Takur and
Bahá'u'lláh's original house. On 27 August they continued, going to
Dhakala, where Bahá'u'lláh had been bastinadoed, then to Amul and
Barfurush, where she photographed the tomb of Quddús. They visited
Khafagarkolah and Fort Tabarsi and Mafroosak, before finally returning to Tehran on 6 September.[24]

In order to ensure that her photographs were good, she had to
develop the negatives each day, something distinctly difficult given the
circumstances. Instead of running water, she carried buckets of water
from a well. She made a darkroom of her tent by covering it with a

blanket and taping red paper over her torch. All this had to be done in complete secrecy for fear she would be thought a spy.

One thing Effie learned was that time had little meaning in Persia. If they planned to leave at 1 p.m., they rarely got away before 4 or 5 p.m. As a result, the photographic expedition took six months instead of the projected three. She also found the caravansarais to commonly be too dirty to sleep in, so she spent many nights sitting in the car.[25]

Her second photographic expedition took her to Tabriz, leaving on 10 September with Muḥammad Labíb as her guide and translator. He was an avid photographer himself and had taken many photographs of Bahá'í historical sites throughout Iran.[26] They stopped long enough in Qazvin to photograph where Ṭáhirih had lived, then proceeded to Zanjan, where they spent the night. The next day they reached Tabriz. The Chief of Police, who though not a Bahá'í was very sympathetic, helped her get photos of the Barrack Square where the Báb was martyred, and the prison beside it. Because of tribal warfare, Effie was unable to go to Mahku. After a quick trip to Meelan to photograph some Bahá'ís, she began her return to Tehran on 19 September, stopping in Zanjan on the way.[27]

On 22 September she headed for Mashhad, five hundred miles distant, where Mullá Ḥusayn had unfurled the Black Standard on his way to Fort Tabarsi. Once there, she took photos of various locations and was back in Tehran on 1 October. A week later, she was off to Isfahan where she photographed the homes of the 'Beloved of Martyrs' and the 'King of Martyrs', the prison where they were killed, and the square where their bodies were thrown. On 14 October, Effie and Muḥammad Labíb travelled to Shiraz. She photographed the House of the Báb, but gaining access to the relics of the Báb in the custodianship of the Afnán family, proved more difficult and required all Effie's tact. She solved the problem in a diplomatically compelling fashion:

> There were four brothers, three departed to their farms and villages outside Shiraz and they were gone and I could get only two or three relics, they guarded them very carefully, and I didn't know what to do about it, I thought there would be more. I got a piece of paper and wrote down the relics I knew about, and I went to the Afnan and said 'could you please write down any other relics that you know of that I could photograph, and please sign your name,

because I want to take this paper back to Shoghi Effendi and show
him that what I have photographed is authentic because he wants to
place these pictures in the archives at the Holy Tomb'. He evidently
sent for his other brothers because by the time I finished photographing in Shiraz I had about 19 pictures of different things, they
came one after the other. The Afnan family were the custodians of
the house of the Báb and lived in the next courtyard.[28]

More warfare kept her from Nayriz, but Muḥammad Labíb was able
to go there and secure the photos. On 3 November, they returned to
Isfahan. Their next destination was Yazd. Once there, Muḥammad
Labíb made a three-day trip into an area too dangerous for Effie, while
she stayed in Yazd and photographed Vahíd's house and other places.
On the return to Isfahan, their truck ran out of patches to fix the many
flat tires and the radiator ran dry. When they finally got there, Effie sent
a report to Shoghi Effendi:

Labeeb Effendi who is accompanying me has gone to some of the
villages on a donkey, it being impossible to go by car. He left Tuesday
morning from the village of Taft where we motored to and I did the
photographing there today. I am very anxious, for Persians time is
no object and I don't like him to get out of my sight. I continually
keep urging matters on, I really think he is heartily sick of me always
asking and asking to do things quickly but if I didn't I wouldn't be
in Haifa until next fall, I'm sure . . . The cities are built so badly,
twisty lanes and many of the places in my list are so hemmed in it
is very difficult to obtain a view, also the fanaticism and hostility of
the people has to be contended with. So far we have been able to
record nearly all the pictures desired. At Shiraz there are one or two
mentioned that it was not possible to take owing to the warfare that
has been taking place recently between the government and various
tribes in the surrounding districts . . . It was good foresight on your
part to send me with the necessary material. All photographic goods
are now banned in Persia and they are almost unprocurable. The
little stocks the dealers hold they are asking exorbitant prices for.
The plates for my camera are not to be procured, and the number of
my films . . . are not in stock very much.[29]

Effie and Muḥammad Labíb arrived back in Tehran on 29 November with the outlying work done. All that was left was Tehran itself. She spent the next two months photographing the city's gates, mosques, and the house where Ṭáhirih was held.

Effie took about a thousand photographs on her journey and reported to Shoghi Effendi what she had done. To safeguard them, she made three copies. One copy she left with the Persian National Spiritual Assembly, a second was posted to Shoghi Effendi and the third was posted to Fujita at the Pilgrim House. The originals she packed in her luggage.[30]

Shoghi Effendi's response to her report was that she should return as soon as possible because he wanted the photos for his translation of *The Dawn-Breakers*. Effie left Tehran at the end of January in the snow and travelled to Kermanshah. After leaving that city, a blizzard almost brought them to a halt. The car was frozen up and they were forced to push it for an hour to the top of the next ridge before they could coast down to a police outpost. The next morning the car was a solid block of ice and had to be chopped out with an axe. Then the driver had to boil water and pour it over the radiator to thaw it out before the car would start. They made only a short distance before the engine died. To reach the next village, Karind, the two male passengers had to push from behind while a boy cranked the engine every few minutes. Once in Karind, they found that the official at the post office was a Bahá'í who was very helpful. Effie photographed the village where Bahá'u'lláh had stayed on his exile journey to Baghdad. Finally arriving in Baghdad, she was delighted to find that the local Bahá'ís had photographed the House of Bahá'u'lláh, so she was able to leave the next day.

Effie had worried about all the negatives in her luggage and what the customs officials might do. Luckily, one of the first Iraqi customs officers she met was a Bahá'í and he made sure that he checked, sealed and paid duties in a legitimate fashion. Syria was another problem, however. Even though her luggage had been sealed and cleared all the way to Palestine, Syrian customs officials tore off the seals, confiscated the luggage and sent it to Damascus. When Effie reached that city, she went to the Customs House and found all her cases opened and three officers laughing at her. They presented her with a big duty charge. She refused to pay it, demanding to see the head officer. To that official, she said that she would pay the duty if she had to, but first she was going to talk with the British Consul as she was a British subject. That quickly changed his mind and he begged her not to do so, insisting that everything was in order and she was free to go. He had the formerly laughing officers repack her bags then, apparently, phoned ahead to make sure she had no difficulties at the Palestinian border.

Effie arrived at the Pilgrim House at 10:30 p.m. on 27 January 1931, after more than six months away. Fujita and Emogene Hoagg greeted her when she arrived, but there was little rest. The next morning Louise Drake Wright arrived for pilgrimage, followed one day later by Josephine Storey and two friends, then Frances Esty, her son, aunt and cousin. In less than two weeks, she was taking care of thirteen guests. The Guardian, however, was very happy with her work.[31]

Curtains and marble tablets

In October 1930, Loulie Mathews and Marion Little (who would assist Shoghi Effendi with the publication of *The Dawn-Breakers*)[32] arrived in Haifa on pilgrimage, bringing with them from America a curtain to be hung over the doorway of the room of Bahá'u'lláh at Bahjí. The curtain was the result of a request by the Guardian to Mason Remey. Mason wrote about the history of the curtain in a letter dated 23 October:

> About twenty-five years ago I made a design for a curtain to hang at the doorway of the Tomb of Bahá'u'lláh at Bahje. Madame d'Ange d'Astre, now of Paris, but who was then living in Washington, an expert with the needle, undertook the execution of this and it came out very well. The ground work was in shades of gold silk with white borders across the top and down the sides with a heavy fringe, while in the center panel was a sunburst of nineteen points with the *Greatest Name* in the center, and the ground was embroidered with ninety-five stars.
>
> A couple of years ago I had a letter from Shoghi Effendi saying that curtain had been so long in use that it was faded and the material was in shreds . . ., and he asked me if I would send another curtain to replace the former one . . . It ended up by Mrs. Barnitz and Miss Alma Knobloch doing the embroidery between them, while Miss Knobloch did the sewing of the curtain.
>
> The color was dark blue velvet with old gold embroidery but of

a somewhat more simple design than the original one. There was a large *Greatest Name* in the center of the curtain with a heavy gold band and fringe across the bottom and cords up the sides. It was lined with old gold damask brocade of a religious and formal character of fleurs de les and flowers.

Dr. [Walter] Guy took this curtain to Haifa when he made his recent pilgrimage.

Not many months ago Shoghi Effendi again requested me to arrange to send a similar curtain to be hung before the doorway of the room of Bahá'u'lláh at Bahje, and he also requested two marble plaques engraved with the *Greatest Name*, of the design such as is engraved on the ring-stone. For these he sent me a small design to be enlarged.

Mrs. Barnitz and Miss Knobloch again very kindly undertook to do the embroidery and the making of the curtain, I arranging as before for the material and the designing. The curtain was about the same size as the other curtain and the design similar, but we varied the color, using an old gold velvet with the embroidery and trimming of a little brighter shade of gold, lined with a damask brocade of the same color.

Some years ago I had a copy of the Greatest Name cut in marble and sent to Shoghi Effendi that I understand he placed above the doorway of the Tomb of the Master. This was made in Italy and I hear it came out successfully. Therefore I took up the matter of the two marble plaques with Mrs. Hoagg who is now living in Geneva, knowing that she was in touch with the reliable sculptor in Florence (where she formerly lived) who could do this work, he having made the former tablet.

These tablets were made and sent. I understand they are in white marble with the Greatest Name inlaid in marble of a different color, while around the name in an oval pattern is some leaf work decoration, also inlaid in color.[33]

Pilgrims

Some time during 1930, Siyyid 'Alí Riḍvání arrived from Iran on pilgrimage. It was a great bounty for him because he had once been attacked and left for dead. A conspiracy led by a hostile mulla caused a group of men to attack him, leaving him with twenty-three knife wounds. His body was thrown into an unused well. A Bahá'í had witnessed the assault and, thirty-six hours later when he felt it was safe, he and other Bahá'ís came under the cover of darkness and brought the body of Siyyid 'Alí Riḍvání out of the well. Amazingly, the Siyyid was still alive, but he took many months to recover. While on pilgrimage, the Guardian allowed Siyyid 'Alí Riḍvání to host a feast for the pilgrims in the Garden of Riḍván on the ninth day of Riḍván. Siyyid 'Alí Riḍvání made a second pilgrimage in 1953.[34]

At some point during the year, Jessie Macquarie and her daughter Netta, New Zealand Bahá'ís, visited Haifa. Jessie enjoyed her time at the Pilgrim House:

> Surrounded by lovely shrubs, trees, flowers – very refreshing to the eye after the sunless, foggy atmosphere of London, the Pilgrim House stands as a choice scintillating gem amidst a mosaic of the rainbow. It was built in circular fashion with central hall of beautiful white marble, with inviting and comfortable bedrooms leading off, complete in every detail that a guest could possibly require, showing the loving thought, care and service which Effie Baker has given so freely.[35]

Beatrice Irwin visited Shoghi Effendi sometime during the year. The visit galvanized and focused her many talents and seven years later, at the age of sixty, she set out for Mexico on the first of four pioneering adventures. Shoghi Effendi himself suggested she pioneer to Mexico and Tunis, both of which she did.[36]

Shoghi Effendi's efforts to find secretarial help continued and in November he apologized to one of his proofreaders:

> Unable to find a good typist, I have had to do the work myself, and I trust that the proofreaders will find it easy to go over and will not mind the type errors which I have tried to correct. I would especially urge you to adhere to the transliteration which I have adopted. The correct title is, I feel, 'The Kitáb-i-Íqán' the sub-title 'The Book of Certitude.' May it help the friends to approach a step further, and obtain a clearer idea of the fundamental teachings set forth by Bahá'u'lláh.[37]

Fortunately, two months later Emogene Hoagg arrived to help him type his manuscripts. Unfortunately, she was only able to stay for three months, then he was back on his own, again.

1931

When American Louise Drake Wright reached Haifa on 27 January, Thilde Deistelhorst from Berlin,was also there, as was Emogene Hoagg. On the 31st, Louise met the Greatest Holy Leaf, who said that Louise had 'the face of an angel'. Four days later, Louise walked up to the Shrine of the Báb, repeating 'Ya Alláh u'l Mustaghath' the whole way. While deep in prayer inside the Shrine, she suddenly saw a bright light above that began circling the room and changing colour to green and then blue. A great sense of peace and comfort came over her.[1]

The next day, Shoghi Effendi asked her to read some pages of 'Nabíl's Narrative' (*The Dawn-Breakers*) and tell him if she thought it would 'be of value to the believers'. A few days later, in her diary she wrote: 'Reading Nabil with amazement and wonder. Of all books this is the most inspiring.'[2]

Marion Jack and Alice Doolittle

Marion Jack from Canada and Alice Doolittle from Cleveland, Ohio, left America together and sailed to Haifa, arriving on 17 February. At the Western Pilgrim House, they met Emogene Hoagg, Effie Baker, Louise Wright, Thilde Deistelhorst, and Fujita. Emogene had been called to Haifa to type the hundreds of pages that Shoghi Effendi had produced for *The Dawn-Breakers* to that point.[3]

Marion enjoyed the Pilgrim House:

The Pilgrim House is a beautiful place for us all to be in. The six of us have our own bedrooms and there are two more for you girlies just opposite each other. There is a big hall in the middle. At either end there are smaller halls with a bedroom out of each. At the very end are sitting rooms with 2 bedrooms out of each. Then there is the library and a writing room all on this top floor. The front door is up here too, approached by marble steps (broad ones) from the street. Down stairs, on the ground floor, the entrance from the street is up a little stone passage. There is also a hall there in the middle – the dining room, and a little square sitting room to one end, and Fujita and Effie each have two bedrooms. The kitchen is not very big because not very much cooking is done in this house. The meals all come from Abdul Baha's house – except breakfast – which consists of eggs, toast, nice whole wheat bread, butter, tea and coffee. We have wonderful food I think, and I am always ready for it. Lunch is at one and dinner at half past seven. [4]

Alice Doolittle was a hairdresser and she had saved as much as she could from her earnings in order to go on pilgrimage. But when she learned that money was needed for the construction of the House of Worship in Wilmette, she promptly donated everything she had saved, $400. Alice's customers knew she had been saving for pilgrimage and were amazed that she gave up her hard-earned travel fund. Then one day, Alice later told her friends,

> My one wealthy customer gave me $400 but she said that I must use it on this trip only. When I talked to the others and asked 'What shall I do?,' they said, 'You must accept the gift, partly because of this generous soul. She will be hurt if you refuse. Also, you were meant to take this journey for the sake of God. Because of it, your services to the Cause will be increased.' So I went. [5]

On 23 February, Marion, Louise and Alice made a short trip to Jeru-salem. On their return, a larger group went to Bahjí. Shoghi Effendi had gained possession of the Mansion from the Covenant-breakers in 1929 and had restored it to its former glory, adding historical photo-graphs, paintings, Chinese vases, Persian carpets and books to illumine the history of the Faith. This work had just been finished and the group of pilgrims, that included Marion, Louise, Thilde, Alice, Effie and Olga Mills, were the first pilgrims to be allowed to sleep in the Mansion. Munavvar Khánum, Zahrá Shahíd, Thurayyá Afnán, Meh-rangíz Khánum and Díyá'i'yyih Khánum (Shoghi Effendi's mother) stayed there as well.

Marion wrote of being in the Mansion:

At present I am residing in a beautiful palace which has just been renovated, and re-decorated in the old style in which the first owner was pleased to have it. I know you would like.

The upper half is very lovely with arches & pillars – very big – 60 feet long & very wide. Eleven big rooms and two corridors empty out of, or into it. And the wide arched galley on the outside is all painted with quaint groups of figures, flowers, boats, etc. This runs around three sides of the building and is a beautiful place to sit for the view is superb all out over the valley of Achor and groves of olive trees and on the front a few hundred yards away an orange grove.

As you look past this delightful scene you see Acca all white or shrouded in mist & atmospheric effects at other times, and beyond is the bay of Acca & further on the slope of Mount Carmel with the port of Haifa nestling at its base . . .[6]

Emogene Hoagg, Corinne True, Mrs H.A. Harding and Miss Burton from Illinois, and Emma and Louise Thompson joined the pilgrims for the second overnight stay at the Mansion. Marion recounted that some slept downstairs while others had the privilege of sleeping upstairs.

Shoghi Effendi had spent two years bringing the Mansion back to its original state. He had brought in a man who had been at the Mansion many times in his youth to supervise the work. Amatu'l-Bahá Rúḥíyyih Khánum described what was done:

The roof, the woodwork, the frescoes on the balcony, the intricate stencilled decoration on the walls of all the rooms on the upper floor, the fine wooden-beam ceilings – all were restored to their original state. Having done this Shoghi Effendi proceeded to carpet it with valuable rugs sent by the Bahá'ís in Persia, to hang rare illuminations in the writing of the famous Bahá'í calligraphist, Mishkin Qalam, on its walls, to furnish it with bookcases filled with the translations of Bahá'í literature in many languages, to place innumerable photographs and documents of historic interest in its various rooms . . .[7]

Marion Jack was there to paint some pictures for Shoghi Effendi. One she did was a panorama of Akka and the Shrine of Bahá'u'lláh. On 5

March Louise Wright watched Marion paint a panorama of the Shrine of the Báb and Haifa:

> Miss Jack & I sat above the Shrines while she painted a landscape for Shoghi Effendi. Her picture is from the back of the Shrines on the . . . side. She gets half the Shrine, gardens, Haifa, sea, Acca, Mt. Hermon & hills. She is such a true dear! I hope that Shoghi Effendi will be pleased with what she is doing. He likes careful, detailed work & chose the view. She is going to Bahjí to paint what Baha'u'llah saw from the balcony there . . .[8]

For Alice Doolittle, the visit to the Shrine of Bahá'u'lláh was elevating. She was well aware that her big problem was her inferiority complex. She said: 'I was all wrapped up in myself. No one saw what was inside me. I thought of myself as an overlooked person . . . [In] Haifa, I told myself, "nobody will take notice of me there either".' But the Guardian treated Alice like a queen and showed her the greatest respect. 'I was in dreams!', she thought. But, she said later,

> I wasn't satisfied . . . In my folly I wanted Baha'u'llah Himself, to take notice of me. Well, on the last day of my pilgrimage I went alone into the Holy of Holies [Baha'u'llah's resting place at Bahji] and setting aside some flowers, I crossed over the Threshold to the inner room. How could I dare! I asked him for a sign . . .
>
> I can remember the shaking; the walls, the floor – and most of all, the atoms of my body. I felt thrown off my feet. Was it like wind, or waves, or an earthquake, or was it like all three? I was on my knees, with my forehead pressed to the beautiful Persian rug, crying my heart out in gratitude to Baha'u'llah. I stood up suddenly, quaking with the fear of God, It's Awe, they say. It is not that you are AFRAID of God, but something different. And I knew that I was a new person, born again. Inside I could hear myself shouting, 'Baha'u'llah HAS TAKEN NOTICE OF ME!'[9]

Before leaving Haifa, Alice asked the Guardian what she could do to serve the Cause, and he told her to 'Teach. Speak.' Alice protested that she wasn't a speaker, but he simply told her to use her notes and tell all the Bahá'ís about her pilgrimage.[10] Because Bahá'u'lláh had noticed her,

Alice returned to America and followed the Guardian's command.

Naw-Rúz was celebrated at the Shrine of the Báb on 21 March with Shoghi Effendi. The pilgrims who attended included Jenabi Motlagh and Dr Hakím from Persia, Mr Mushukati from Port Said, Louise Wright, Alice Doolittle, Corinne True, Mrs Harding, Miss Burton, Olga Mills, Emma and Louise Thompson, Marion Jack and Emogene Hoagg.[11]

Emma and Louise Thompson's visit was short and Shoghi Effendi spent one whole day with them in Bahjí. They and Marion Jack had dinner with him at the Pilgrim House,

> sitting in the dining room where Abdul Baha used to sit and looking into the great open court with a garden in the center, where stands a tree laden with yellow lemons each one worth their weight in gold, to us. They do not pick them only use them as they drop for Abdul Baha loved to look upon them. In a stable opening out of this court yard is where Naz the grey donkey lives, daughter of the first Naz, Abdul Baha's donkey who died about two years ago. In order to take Naz out doors she has to walk through the dining room. This arrangement holds through-out the East, that the animals may not be stolen – but it seemed strange to us. After lunch we rested and Shoghi Effendi went with Jackie to the porch of the Mansion where she was painting the view to be seen from there on a four foot canvas. Her picture is to be placed in the hall of the Mansion . . .[12]

On the evening of 24 March, the day before the Thompsons and Alice were to leave, Shoghi Effendi took Marion, Emma and Louise to the Shrine of the Báb for prayer, chanting for them himself. He then asked Emma to recite the Tablet of Aḥmad, after which he complimented her on doing so with 'fervor, sincerity & devotion'.

Marion described being with Shoghi Effendi at lunch one day where

> he stressed some points quite emphatically. The first was that in making friends with the Ahmad [Sohrab] group there should be no compromise for he said the Administration is as important as the spiritual – and we must be loyal to both, and he went on to point out that the Administration went further back even than Abdul Baha to Baha O'llah and the Aqdas.

He spoke quite at length on the question of mixing with the Colored friends socially, and even of intermarrying with them. He feels that we in America are not without prejudice and that we have carried on that inclination from our early days. He says we are very little different in our attitude from the non-Bahais in our conduct towards that race. He says it is not enough to meet them formally, but we must go out of our way to have them in our homes. He said that there is no difference whatever between the black & white race and we must realize that, but must if there is a choice give them the preference. He said that Green Acre was an excellent place to demonstrate this, that the Amity Conferences were good, but they were a little formal, too . . . He spoke of the Gregorys' marriage and said that Abdul Baha must have had great wisdom in joining these two, and that it would have been an excellent thing if more people would follow suit . . .[13]

One non-Bahá'í was with the group at some point. Both Louise Wright and Marion Jack mentioned a Mrs Halderman or a Mrs Aulderman. She was from northern Italy and was a pupil of the Theosophist Krishnamurti.[14]

Shoghi Effendi was still working on *The Dawn-Breakers* during Marion's pilgrimage and Marion wrote that Shoghi Effendi let the pilgrims help him to choose which photographs should be used in the book. She also noted that

Emogene Hoagg has been typing in the mornings and Muhrangies his sister has been working with him in the afternoons . . . Effie Baker went to Persia on a very extensive tour and photographed many many places where these terrible events had transpired . . . She has only been back a couple of weeks and has been developing them herself ever since.[15]

Near the end of her pilgrimage, Shoghi Effendi suggested to Marion that she go to Bulgaria to help the pioneer Louisa Gregory, wife of Louis Gregory (Mr Gregory would later be appointed a Hand of the Cause).[16] Marion, Olga, Emogene and Mehrangíz left Haifa on 1 April and sailed to Cyprus and then to Brindisi. From there, Marion and Olga continued to Trieste after which Marion continued alone to Sofia, Bulgaria,[17] the area of some of her greatest feats. She remained in Bulgaria for the next twenty-three years, including the period of the Second World War. Shoghi Effendi advised her to leave during the war for her own safety, but when she asked to be allowed to stay and teach the Faith, he agreed. When she passed away in Sofia in 1954, Shoghi Effendi said of her:

> You cannot be a hero without action. This is the touchstone. Not movement, coming and going, but in the evidences of your character. Jacky [Marion Jack] is a heroine because of her conduct, the heroic spirit reveals itself in her. Martha [Root] had the heroic action. She went 'til she dropped.[18]

Marion had long been a hero with action. She had served in the Holy Household in 1907 and 1908 and as a pioneer and teacher in the United Kingdom between 1911 and 1914. In 1919 and 1920, with Emogene Hoagg, she had adventured to Alaska and the Yukon, travelling 4,000 kilometres (2,500 miles) up the Yukon River and over the mountains to Juneau, Alaska's capital.[19]

Corinne True and Albert Windust

Corinne True arrived in Haifa with Mrs H. A. Harding in March. At that time, the dome of the Mother Temple of the West in Chicago was just being completed. They were greeted at the dock by Fujita, who had lived in the True household for seven years after the departure of the Master from America and had become like a son to Corinne. Fujita helped the ladies through Customs, then drove them up to the Pilgrim House in the Guardian's car. Effie Baker, too, was very happy to see Corinne because they had become good friends when together on pilgrimage in 1925.[20]

Later, Corinne wandered through the gardens around the Shrine of the Báb, noting that they were much more extensive than they had been on her previous visit. After spending some time in the Shrine, she emerged to find one of the gardeners with two guests, Mr and Mrs Browne. Corinne had met the Brownes on the way to Haifa and they had been impressed with her descriptions so they had come to see for themselves. Corinne took them through the gardens, which obviously had an effect on the visiting couple because they expressed the desire to visit the Shrine. The Brownes removed their shoes and reverently went inside. Corinne was quite surprised because Mr Browne was 'a leading Zionist who had studied to be a rabbi'.²¹

That evening at dinner, Corinne thought that the Guardian looked well enough, but that he also seemed overly busy. He seemed quite happy with the advances the Faith was making throughout the world and also with the progress on the Wilmette Temple. Then he shared a surprise with them. He told them that he had discovered 'Abdu'l-Bahá's safety-lock box and in that box were the Báb's original Tablets to the Letters of the Living and to Bahá'u'lláh. Shoghi Effendi planned to include reproductions of the Tablets in *The Dawn-Breakers* and was sending them to America with Albert Windust, who was there on pilgrimage, to be copied.²² The Guardian also told them that one of the new rooms added to the back of the Shrine of the Báb was going to be used as an international archive, with Effie Baker as the custodian. Since Effie was also the host at the Western Pilgrim House and did many other jobs, the Guardian joked about how many keys she would have to carry.²³

As always for Corinne, leaving the World Centre of the Bahá'í Faith was difficult, but her time there had obvious effects. When she arrived in Cairo

> a newspaper boy sold her a copy of the local English daily paper. When he disappeared she learned that what she had bought was more than a week old. She was disturbed, but had the same thing happened twenty years earlier she might have been furious. Undoubtedly daily study of the Creative Word had moderated some of her natural inclinations. The older she became, the calmer she grew . . . The Guardian had recognized her qualities in 1931 and on 'every visit you pay us', he wrote in his own hand soon after her return. 'Your staunch, unswerving faith, your boundless devotion, and assiduous care to preserve the integrity and extend the bounds of the Cause, are among the richly valued assets that the Faith of Bahá'u'lláh has in that land.²⁴

Albert Windust greatly enjoyed his pilgrimage. Louis Gregory wrote of his report to the National Convention that year:

The gardens on Mt. Carmel . . . were the most beautiful in Palestine. He described Shoghi Effendi's charming manners, insight and great abilities as a master of detail. He wants us to be ourselves, to worship God, but not to be imitators of others. During his visit he said that Shoghi Effendi never took the head of the table, but gave that honor to the oldest pilgrim. He pours forth a stream of divine eloquence and wisdom, both intellectual and spiritual. In his presence all imaginations flee as mists before the sun's rays . . .

The visit to Bahjí is a great event today. Its entire structure has been repaired by Shoghi Effendi. It is a great Baha'i Archives as well as a Holy Shrine. The room in which Bahá'u'lláh received Professor Brown in 1890, has been completely restored.[25]

On 1 May, the first National Spiritual Assembly of Iraq was elected[26] and, as he normally did during the summer, Shoghi Effendi left Haifa, returning in October. Late in the year, Effie Baker was able to host pilgrims from her part of the world when Amy Dewing and her daughter Vera arrived from Auckland, New Zealand. Amy's son, Bertram, had been in Haifa in April 1930. Effie accompanied the pilgrims to Bahjí and Akka.[27]

Nancy Bowditch

Nancy Bowditch arrived in Haifa from America, probably during the summer because she did not mention meeting Shoghi Effendi. She had met 'Abdu'l-Bahá in Dublin, New Hampshire, when she had participated in an outdoor play. Harlan Ober introduced her to the Faith after she had shaken the Master's hand at the end of the play and she soon enrolled. Her father, George DeForest Brush, was a well-known painter who initially laughed off the Faith, but who became a Bahá'í shortly before his death.[28]

Nancy was among the earliest pilgrims to spend the night at Bahjí. She described her arrival there:

After driving through the country outside of 'Akká, and passing under an old arch of a Roman Aqueduct and through a forest of eucalyptus trees, we at last arrive at the place where Bahá'u'lláh spent his last and happiest days. On the left as we approach is a walled-in area with cypress peering over the top, and a cluster of old farm houses; on the right a lovely sweep of cultivated fields and a distant range of mountains. At this point the old mansion at Bahjí looms into view . . . It is a big white house with an arched arcaded veranda around the second floor. All this is seen over the top of a high stone wall, vine covered at the base. Into this wall is set a small arch of plain white which frames the entrance door, a big green door, which seems to have been built to withstand any intrusion into this abode. But door and walls seem to cry 'welcome' as the smiling Turkish Bahá'í servant swings open the gate and greets one with the 'Greatest Name' . . .[29]

. . . Leaving the lovely yard filled with lemon trees we pass through another green door with a knocker, which the servant unlocks for us. We enter and mount a long closed-in marble staircase to the second floor and turn to the right through a small hall. Passing through gold and blue draped damask curtains we enter the central room of the house. This is about twenty feet wide and thirty-one feet long. The ceiling is supported by eight white marble columns, and roofed with deep blue. Around the central point is a skylight letting in a soft light on the white marble floor and the elaborately stencilled walls. In the very center of the hall is a table . . . draped with a Persian cloth and on it rests a large vase of plumelike sprays of coral flowers . . . There is an album placed among them all with pictures of the Bahá'í Temple in Chicago . . .

But who can describe this room [Bahá'u'lláh's room] or this house where Bahá'u'lláh lived in exile, and from where mighty Tablets from His pen went forth to a world in need. We visited this room the last. The shoes, the bed of Him who lived there were set out for us to see. We stood just where Professor Browne was standing when he received [his] wonderful impression. But it is the whole house that speaks of those souls who lived under its roof . . .

Shoghi Effendi has arranged a pleasant and convenient writing room for the friends. In it are two writing tables with every convenience, with the seal of the Mansion to stamp on the letter written there. Candles and flowers adorn the tables . . . On the right hand is a framed 'Greatest Name' in gold on white. Above this hangs a rug with a picture of the Temple woven into it, and on one wall is a large picture, a copy of one of Mr. Bourgeois' designs for a window in the Temple . . . There are various photographs of Bahá'í groups, and other objects concerning the Cause, among which is a hanging bookcase of Bahá'í literature in different languages . . .

Now we pass through the central hall, through a large corner bedroom . . . and out to the big veranda. Here is a marble fountain with gold fish and gently splashing water. The window sashes are of green, the blinds and doors of blue, the floor of white marble, and beyond all this the vistas of landscape through the pillars and arches . . . These are the lovely scenes which Bahá'u'lláh and His family must have gazed so often.[30]

That night Nancy and the other pilgrims slept in the Mansion. They arose early, then went to the adjacent Shrine of Bahá'u'lláh, passing through a closed garden, by 'gorgeous hedges of red geranium, over the red gravel paths to the white pebble path before the door that leads to the outer shrine'. She continued her description:

Here a lemon tree stood heavy with golden fruit, and a great cypress pointed heavenward. In the shrine the air was sweet with yellow jasmine that is thickly strewn on the threshold to the inner shrine. The outer room is a bower of green, reaching to the high sky-lighted ceiling, and the floor is completely covered with the finest silky Persian rugs, so fine that it seems wrong to tread them even without shoes. It is a place of indescribable sweetness and peace. But each pilgrim's heart knows best what sort of a place is the Shrine of Bahá'u'lláh.[31]

Mabel and Sylvia Paine

Mabel and Sylvia Paine arrived in Haifa on 9 November, ten years after their first pilgrimage. The first thing they noticed was the great activity in the harbour, which was being deepened and a long breakwater built. Rúḥí Afnán, Shoghi Effendi's cousin, met them at the dock and as they walked up to the Western Pilgrim House they noted that, contrary to the almost universal use of the veil by women in 1921, nearly all the women were now unveiled.[32]

The Pilgrim House garden, cultivated by Fujita, contained roses from California and from Frances Esty's garden. Mabel noted that Fujita was a good gardener and that Shoghi Effendi would commonly take some plant or bush and plant it in the gardens of the Shrines. Fujita also had a dog in a dog house, two cats, two parrots in a big cage in the kitchen, and canaries in another cage near the back door.[33]

At lunch on 10 November, Shoghi Effendi talked about the various problems faced by the Bahá'ís around the world. He said that 'in Germany it is the Semitic question; in Persia polygamy and opium; in France, alcohol; in England, class prejudice; in America, racial prejudice.' In the afternoon, they walked to the Shrine of the Báb. At the bottom of the terraces, they entered 'a gate and climb[ed] alternately by flights of stone steps and paths of red crushed stone. On either side are scarlet geraniums and palms. The approach to the shrine is steep. And this steepness I liked, thinking of it as a bit of symbolism.'[34]

Later that day Mabel and Sylvia visited the Greatest Holy Leaf, who 'although shadowed by age, was so full of love and a genuine interest in life and people that we did not think of her as old, but rather as ageless and eternal. The freshness of the beauty of love radiating from her captivated us.'[35] She looked very small and was bundled up to keep warm. Mabel wrote that her 'face is entirely beautiful, though old. It is full of love and a natural interest in people and life . . . She told me that she was grateful to me for coming so far to see her!!' Munírih Khánum, the Holy Mother, was 'more of a talker than Khánum' and that made it frustrating for her not to be able to speak with the pilgrims without a translator. Rúḥá Khánum, 'Abdu'l-Bahá's daughter, said she was surprised that pilgrims continued to come even though the Master was no longer there.[36]

A few days later, Rúḥá Khánum and the Paines were talking about children and Rúḥá Khánum said that her daughter had initially been refused admittance to the Catholic School in Haifa because the administrators thought she wouldn't go to the church to pray with the other children. Rúḥá Khánum had to explain that they believed in every religion, which surprised the Catholics, but they did admit her daughter. Later, they noticed that the girl prayed more devoutly in the church than did the Catholic children.[37]

The Paines went to Bahjí on 16 November. Again, Shoghi Effendi's garden work strongly moved them:

In these beautiful gardens and lawns around the shrine one sees a new and unique kind of place of worship, one which extends the atmosphere of the sanctuary to the surrounding out-of-doors. The spiritual charm of this arrangement at Bahji is that the brilliant and stately beauty of the surrounding gardens gently woos the soul away from earthly thought and prepares it for the yet more intense spirituality of the shrine itself. Just in front of the shrine are many interlacing paths where one may prolong the time of preparation before stepping from the kindly beauty of nature to the more lofty and searching worship which the shrine itself inspires.[38]

On 23 November Shoghi Effendi shared with the pilgrims parts of his most recent letter to the West, entitled 'The Goal of a New World Order'. In this letter the Guardian compared the unification of the states of North America into the United States to the formation of the future world state. He said the latter should be the easier, because:

It would indeed be no exaggeration to say that the absence of those facilities which modern scientific progress has placed at the service of humanity in our time made of the problem of welding the American states into a single federation, similar though they were in certain traditions, a task infinitely more complex than that which confronts a divided humanity in its efforts to achieve the unification of all mankind.[39]

'The Goal of a New World Order' later became part of the publication *The World Order of Bahá'u'lláh*.

On 27 November, the Paines joined the commemoration of the tenth anniversary of the passing of 'Abdu'l-Bahá. They had been on pilgrimage in September 1921, shortly before His ascension, so it was a powerful experience for them:

About six p.m. we went across the street to 'Abdu'l-Bahá's house. We were to enter His room, the room whence His spirit passed to the heavenly realm. A group of women were gathered outside the door, waiting to go in. They went in one by one and knelt with beautiful reverence at the bedside where the tired body of the great Servant of God and of mankind last lay. Little incidents of His last days came to my mind. How full of generous kindness and servitude, though the body was well nigh exhausted! His insisting on gathering the garden fruit with His own hand, though He ate it, seemingly, largely to please the gardener and asked, 'Do you desire anything more?' Then with a pathetic gesture of His hands touchingly, emphatically and deliberately said: – 'Now, it is finished, it is finished!' . . .

As 'Abdu'l-Bahá passed away at one-fifteen in the morning, the memorial service held each year occupies the evening and night up to about two. About eight-thirty we walked up the side of Mt. Carmel to the shrine. It was a night full of moonlight with many soft white clouds. Across the bay 'Akká looked like a diadem in the heavens. We found gathered around the shrine and on the broad south terrace a considerable group of Bahá'ís. This terrace, we were told, was a favourite walk of the Master's. Soon all went within the shrine and listened while different Bahá'ís, one at a time chanted prayers. One of the most beautiful prayers chanted was the one revealed by 'Abdu'l-Bahá to be chanted at His shrine beginning: 'He is the All-Glorious! O God, my God! Lowly and tearful, I raise my supplicant hands to Thee and cover my face in the dust of that Threshold of Thine, exalted above the knowledge of the learned, and the praise of all that Glorify Thee . . .'

After coming out of the shrine all sat on benches and chairs on the terrace and listened to the chanted recital of 'Abdu'l-Bahá's last days and His funeral, as related in the touching account written by Shoghi Effendi and Lady Blomfield. The funeral, we recalled, had drawn together an immense concourse of mourners from all over Palestine . . .

After this long and beautiful chant on the terrace, beautifully lighted both with electric lights and with the soft moonlight, all went again into the shrines and, during exquisite chanting of prayers, felt again the mighty power of 'Abdu'l-Bahá, the Servant of God.[40]

At one of the dinner talks, Shoghi Effendi examined the world and the place of the Bahá'í Faith within it:

There is to be another war. This will involve the whole world. This is necessary, because a new political structure is needed and cannot be erected until the old structure is destroyed. The nations are not yet ready to give up their sovereignty. England is not more ready than the United States to relinquish her sovereignty, in favor of the League of Nations . . .

President Wilson gained the ideas for his 14 points from the Bahai writings, but did not advance to the point of accepting the Bahai Cause. He was right in trying to lead the United States into the League. The United States must give up its policy of isolation. Wilson saw this but was hindered by politicians. Abdul-Baha said that Wilson's work was the dawn of peace and Baha U'llah's ascendency would prove to be the rising sun. Bahais must show their admiration for Wilson and his ideals though such ideals are unpopular in America. The Bahai teaching about a universal league of nations is now unpopular, but we should be loyal to it . . .

Bahai government is neither purely democratic nor autocratic. It is half way between. The House of Justice is not responsible to the electorate but to God. The two state elections diminishes the democratic element. The Guardian cannot legislate. He has only one vote in the House of Justice. He interprets the Sacred Books. The House of Justice is responsible to God and is inspired. How far this is applicable to national and local bodies is not so clear.

Some one said that some think that the N.S.A. is elected by those who vote by mail. The Guardian replied that the few days of the convention is too short a time for delegates to make acquaintance of the friends. They should seek all through the year to do this. He does not think the reading of all names voted for, an especially good procedure . . .

When someone asked about prayer he said; "Pour out your heart to God freely and fully. Then do something. God cannot work through you unless you act.'[41]

Other visitors

In 1930 a well-known Polish/American painter, Sigismond Ivanowski, was asked by Frances Esty of Buffalo, New York, to paint a portrait of 'Abdu'l-Bahá. Ivanowski had never seen the Master, but said that he thought he could do the painting if he 'could only come into the consciousness of 'Abdu'l-Bahá'.[42] He studied various Bahá'í materials, then one night had a dream of a picture. When he dreamed of the same picture the next night, an inner voice urged him to get up and paint it, which he did. One day, a friend who happened to be a Bahá'í, dropped by to visit and was startled to find Ivanowski painting a scene of 'Abdu'l-Bahá sitting on a bench under a tree at the top of Mount Carmel, looking out over the sea. When the Bahá'í asked what he was doing, Ivanowski replied, not wishing to lose the image in his mind, 'Do not interrupt me until I finish what I am doing.'[43] The portrait was completed in 1931, and when Frances Esty visited Shoghi Effendi in Haifa that year, she received his permission to send the portrait to the World Centre. Therefore, the next year, Mr Ivanowski and his wife personally delivered the portrait to the Guardian. Shoghi Effendi hung it in the Mansion at Bahjí. Ivanowski felt inspired to paint another portrait which was hung in Frances's home.[44]

Some time during 1931, Bahrám Kaykhusraw Vaṭankháh became a Bahá'í in India and immediately made his pilgrimage to Haifa. While there, he became very attached to the Guardian and was loath to leave. Shoghi Effendi said, however, that his service to the Cause would be the fulfilment of his wish and Bahrám, with exemplary obedience, set off to do the Guardian's bidding. For the rest of his life, he went wherever a Bahá'í teacher was needed, dedicating his life to serving his Faith. During the last years of his life, he visited more than three hundred villages and passed away in the last one. His final words, showing his true spirit of never-ending service, were, 'Which village will we visit tomorrow?' [45]

A pilgrim who had just returned to America from Haifa shared the story of how Shoghi Effendi, during a time of trouble between the Jews and the Arabs, had sent aid to both sides. Though each was helped, both were also upset that the others were receiving aid. Many of the Jews and Arabs thought it too dangerous to leave their homes, so it was the Bahá'ís who went and did their shopping for them in a spirit of service.[46]

* * *

Effie Baker took many photographs of the Bahá'í places in Haifa and Akka, but she rarely took photos of people. She did, however, manage to take the last photograph ever taken of the Greatest Holy Leaf in 1931:

I was photographing the picture of His Holiness the Báb in her room and Fujita was there to assist me. I had asked <u>Kh</u>ánum two or three times if she would let me take a snap of her and as she seemed determined I did not press her. As she was sitting on the side of her bed watching me take the copy of the Báb's picture with great interest I thought I would ask her again as I had a spare plate. She said yes! After I had quickly focused the camera Fujita spoke to me and just as I snapped the bulb she said 'what did you say Fujita?' and smiled, so that is how I got the photo. To me it is <u>Kh</u>ánum as I knew her. Some people say how thin and frail her hands showing the veins but I just love them for I knew the soft loving caressing touch of those lovely fingers.[47]

1932

Pilgrims

Many pilgrims came in 1932, including Clara Dunn from Australia, Keith Ransom-Kehler and Lorol Schopflocher. On 1 January, <u>Sh</u>áh Bahrám Mu'bidzádih arrived on pilgrimage from India. He wrote:

> To be with the Guardian was the rarest privilege and the happiest experience of my life. The Guardian was the personification of kindness, and those around him each felt that he was receiving more love and attention than the others. One night I said to my fellow pilgrim, Mr. Raḥmatu'lláh 'Alá'í, 'I feel that our Beloved is showing very special love and consideration towards me.' Mr. 'Alá'í smiled and said that he too felt exactly the same way about the love he received from the Guardian. We were both right, of course, because our Guardian loved all of us very much.
>
> To sit with Shoghi Effendi was like being in heaven. In his presence one understood the real importance and significance of the words 'Abdu'l-Bahá had used for him: 'the Sign of God on Earth'. To be with him was a real education. He was the quickener of the heart. He deepened the understanding of those around him and moulded their lives according to the teachings of Bahá'u'lláh. He once said that if people did not hearken to these teachings they would be exposing themselves to doom.[1]

Like many before him, Mr Mu'bidzádih was surprised that Shoghi Effendi could apparently read his mind. He said, 'I felt that the Guardian always knew what was passing through my mind. If I thought of a question, the answer came from him immediately.' He had been a

Zoroastrian priest before becoming a Bahá'í and one day Shoghi Effendi told him: 'There have been Zoroastrian priests who have accepted the Cause before you, but you are the first among them to proclaim your faith openly.'[2] Shoghi Effendi sent him to Jerusalem and then to Ada-síyyih to meet the Bahá'ís. He returned to India on 7 February.

Shoghi Effendi could always help people with their teaching efforts, even when they thought it wasn't possible. A group of pilgrims once arrived from Canada. They had been trying to offer the Faith to the Eskimos, but it was 'very difficult for them [the Eskimos] to understand the meaning in such similes as the nightingale and the rose because these things were entirely unknown to them.' The Guardian's solution was simple. As they left, he gave them a vial of attar of rose, saying that if they would anoint the Eskimos with it, they would get 'an inkling of what Bahá'u'lláh meant when he wrote of the rose'.[3]

Early in the year, Hájí Maḥmúd Qassábchí made a pilgrimage to the Holy Shrines. He had directed the renovation of the House of Bahá'u'lláh in Baghdad for 'Abdu'l-Bahá in 1920 and the construction of the three new rooms of the Shrine of the Báb in 1929. After his pilgrimage, Hájí Maḥmúd went to Damascus, where he was when he heard of the passing of the Greatest Holy Leaf. He immediately returned to Haifa for her funeral.[4]

Clara Dunn, future Hand of the Cause, arrived in Haifa in mid-April, much to the delight of her fellow Australian, Effie Baker. Clara and Hyde Dunn were Effie's spiritual parents. Shoghi Effendi, though, was keenly disappointed that Clara's husband had been unable to accompany her. Clara's stay was brief, but she was able to return home with the brilliant news that Shoghi Effendi said it was time to establish Australia's National Spiritual Assembly.[5] This Assembly, the National Spiritual Assembly of Australia and New Zealand, was elected in April 1934, at a National Convention held in Sydney and composed of three delegates from Sydney, three from Auckland, New Zealand, and three from Adelaide, Australia.[6]

The Dawn-Breakers

In early 1932 *The Dawn-Breakers* was published. Amatu'l-Bahá Rúḥíyyih Khánum later wrote of the book, 'Although ostensibly a translation from the original Persian, Shoghi Effendi may be said to have re-created it in English . . .'[7] The book had taken Shoghi Effendi two years to research, compile, translate and write. The writing itself had taken eight months, at the end of which Shoghi Effendi wrote:

> I have just completed, after eight months of continuous and hard labour, the translation of the history of the early days of the Cause and have sent the manuscript to the American National Assembly. The work comprises about 600 pages and 200 pages of additional notes that I have gleaned during the summer months from different books. I have been so absorbed in this work that I have been forced to delay my correspondence . . . I am now so tired and exhausted that I can hardly write . . . The record is an authentic one and deals chiefly with the Báb. Parts of it have been read to Bahá'u'lláh and been revised by 'Abdu'l-Bahá . . . I am so overcome with fatigue caused by the long and severe strain of the work I have undertaken that I must stop and lie down.[8]

As we have seen earlier in this book, Shoghi Effendi had sent photographer Effie Baker to Iran to 'painstakingly retrace the footsteps of the Báb in His native land, the scenes of His and His followers' martyrdoms and many historic sites. Had Shoghi Effendi not done this, all visual trace of many of these places in more or less their original state would have been lost forever.'[9]

Initially, 2,000 copies of the book were printed, together with another 300 numbered and signed copies. Shoghi Effendi strongly promoted the book as one all Bahá'ís should read. By early 1935, 1,302 copies of the first edition had been sold along with 127 of the numbered and signed copies.[10]

Abu'l-Qásim Khurásání

The custodian of the International Bahá'í Archives and the gardener for the Shrine of the Báb, Abu'l-Qásim Khurásání, died in April 1932. He had arrived in Haifa in about 1913 and was soon given responsibility for the gardens and the Shrine of Bahá'u'lláh. He was so diligent in his work that when 'Abdu'l-Bahá passed away in 1921, instead of rushing to Haifa he remained at Bahjí, knowing that the enemies of the Cause would undoubtedly make trouble. When they did, he was the victim from whom they forcibly stole the keys to the Shrine. A few years later, Shoghi Effendi transferred Abu'l-Qásim to be caretaker of the Shrine of the Báb, where he made the gardens the most beautiful in Palestine. When placed in charge of the International Bahá'í Archives, he took great care of them.[11]

The night before Abu'l-Qásim's death, Shoghi Effendi had a dream, twice. In the dream, the green verdure on the Shrine of the Báb withered away as if it had been burned. The dream greatly puzzled Shoghi Effendi until, a few hours later, word was brought to him of Abu'l-Qásim's passing. His funeral was led by Shoghi Effendi.[12]

After his passing, Shoghi Effendi put a photo of Abu'l-Qásim at the top of the stairs in the Mansion at Bahjí. Shortly before his death Abu'l-Qásim donated his relics and Tablets from 'Abdu'l-Bahá to the Archives he had so carefully watched over.[13]

Keith Ransom-Kehler

Keith Ransom-Kehler was in India in April of 1932, and Shoghi Effendi asked her to come to Haifa for a special assignment. When she arrived in Haifa in May,[14] Shoghi Effendi, asked her to go to Iran at his behest and as the representative of the National Spiritual Assembly of the Bahá'ís of the United States and Canada. Her special task was to petition Reza Shah Pahlavi to open Iran to the entry and distribution of Bahá'í literature and to remove the restrictions that had been placed on the Bahá'ís. Keith was 'thunderstruck' by the request, thinking of herself, after years of exhausting travel, as 'a poor, feeble, old woman' and not a 'standard-bearer'. Reza Shah had begun instituting social, educational and legal reforms upon his ascension to power in 1925, but the Iranian Bahá'í community had yet to benefit from them. Keith was a strong and audacious woman and Shoghi Effendi hoped she could do what the Iranian believers could not. He also asked her to help the Bahá'í community with the proper functioning of Bahá'í administration.[15]

Keith met Bahíyyih <u>Kh</u>ánum, the Greatest Holy Leaf, and wrote:

> From the Greatest Holy Leaf streamed an effulgence of beauty and heavenly love that I have never witnessed from an human being. To come into her presence was to hush and exalt the soul. She was like a bird at dawn, the coming of spring, a city on the far horizon;

everything that wakes our wonder and reveals the depths and not the tumults of the heart . . .

Her thoughtfulness, her loving kindness, her self-mastery, her complete dedication to the things of the spirit never ceased to the last hour that I saw her, just a month and a day before her ascension.

As I was making my farewells Ḍíyá assisted her to her feet in spite of my protests. She folded me oh, so tenderly in her precious arms and said: 'When you are come to Persia, I want you to give my love to every Bahá'í in all that land, to the men the same as to the women. And when you reach the holy city of Tihrán enter it in my name, and teach there in my name.'

How blind I was not to realize that she was sending her last message to Persia!

One morning [some time later] as I lay in my bed I suddenly burst into hysterical weeping. I could not control myself for half an hour. It seemed so unreasonable for I had not any idea what I was weeping for . . . When the telegram came the next day we realized that this occurred at the time of her passing.[16]

On 12 and 13 May, Keith Ransom-Kehler, Lorol Schopflocher and Lyle Loveday were asking Shoghi Effendi questions about various aspects of the Faith. It quickly became obvious that the American believers did not understand the stations of the Báb, Bahá'u'lláh, 'Abdu'l-Bahá and Shoghi Effendi or their true relationships. At one point, Shoghi Effendi said, 'To give Abdul Baha a station comparable to Bahá'u'lláh is absolute heresy,' and emphasized that Mírzá Muḥammad-'Alí had tried to insist that 'Abdu'l-Bahá had claimed the station of a Manifestation. He then concluded: 'Those who overestimate the station of Abdul Baha are quite as reprehensible and have done just as much harm as those who underestimate.' This shocked Lorol, who asked, 'Do you mean that those that have considered Abdul Baha a Manifestation are equally as bad as those who have opposed and denied him?' Shoghi Effendi replied, 'Yes, that is what I mean, for they continuously furnish the enemy with proof for false statements.' Lyle then said that he had always considered Bahá'u'lláh to be the Supreme Manifestation and that 'Abdu'l-Bahá was a teacher, but the Guardian corrected him saying,

Abdul Baha is not a teacher, an apostle or a chosen one, for there might be others. Abdul Baha is quite apart and different from anyone who has ever appeared on earth before. A perfect human being! Can you conceive a perfect human being? The phrase that best expresses Abdul Baha is the true exemplar, the Center of the Covenant. It is just as grave a mistake to over-estimate Abdul Baha as to under-estimate him. Abdul Baha never claimed to be a Manifestation, all his life he suffered from this assumption. But we must never go to the other extreme and confuse anybody else with Him or His station . . . His station is a mystery.

Lorol: Then if he is just a human being can we evolve to the same station in time?

Shoghi Effendi: No, no one can attain to the station of Abdul Baha.

Lorol: But surely humanity will sometime reach perfection.

Shoghi Effendi: No. Abdul Baha says that humanity will evolve and develop infinitely. To reach perfection means that advancement stops, there is nothing further to be obtained, mankind will ever continue his development towards perfection but no one will ever attain to or occupy the station of Abdul Baha. If you are asked to explain this you must say that this is a mystery. A mystery is not irrational, it does not run counter to reason, it transcends reason.[17]

The conversation then turned to the Shrines. Shoghi Effendi noted that 'Abdu'l-Bahá's body had been placed in the Shrine of the Báb by the Holy Household prior to his return from England, not at the Master's own request. Shoghi Effendi noted that the Master would someday be moved to another resting place and (in a note appended by one of those present), had drawn up a design for the World Centre that showed a shrine for 'Abdu'l-Bahá on the shore between Haifa and Bahjí.

Then Shoghi Effendi said:

Today the Americans are leading the Bahai world. The East has enthusiasm and devotion but no training. Unless the East takes on courage, directness and straightforwardness, which is what the West can teach the East, the center may shift from the East to the West . . .

America is the first country to formulate the declaration of trust and obtain legal recognition, which is a model for all the national spiritual assemblies in the future to follow. Even some of your local assemblies, like New York and Chicago, have been incorporated. It was an excellent thing for Horace Holley to have suggested [copyrighting] . . . the name Bahai . . .

[To Keith] While in Persia endeavour to impress upon the Persian believers the non-political character of the Bahai Faith.

Prominent Persians wish to occupy high political positions. The administrative offices which we may occupy are secondary, while the Persian craves position, power, prestige, glory. They must discipline themselves and restrain these ambitions. You must not be afraid to speak clearly on this subject. Courage, directness, and straight-forwardness is what the West must teach the East. While very tactful present these subjects with clearness, firmness and frankness. Do not mention this directly but intimate that unless the Orient can take on these characteristics the center may shift from the East to the West.[18]

Keith did not stay long in Haifa, but Shoghi Effendi personally helped her understand Islam and Iran. She was a very good student, and the Greatest Holy Leaf gave Keith the title of *Mu'allimih* (teacher). Keith spent more than a year in Iran and travelled extensively throughout the country, being constantly amazed by the loving welcomes she received.

Her primary mission, however, though initially very promising, was not very fruitful. Arriving in Tehrán, she was granted an audience with Abdul Hossein Khan Teymourtash, Reza Shah's first Minister of Court and closest political advisor, who told her the ban on Bahá'í books would be cancelled immediately. But when she had her books sent, they were stopped by customs officials. Keith sent seven long letters to the Shah, but unscrupulous officials probably ensured that they never reached him.

After her attempts at court, Shoghi Effendi directed her efforts to the villages and towns throughout Persia. Keith left Tehran on 22 September and visited Hasan-Abad, Qum, Kashan, and the village of Aran, where she met many officials including the police chief, then returned to Kashan. On 5 October, she journeyed to Isfahan and spent several days meeting with the Bahá'ís, the Governor, the head of the telegraph department, and the chief of the police.

On 10 October, Keith fell ill.[19] It had been an exhausting year and though she was full of plans for the future and only fifty-seven years

old, she was suffering from malnutrition and a variety of other ailments, including smallpox. She wrote:

> I have fallen, though I never faltered. Months of effort with nothing
> accomplished is the record that confronts me. If anyone in future
> should be interested in this thwarted adventure of mine, he alone
> can say whether near or far from the seemingly impregnable heights
> of complaisance and indifference, my tired old body fell. The smoke
> and din of battle are to-day too dense for me to ascertain whether I
> moved forward or was slain in my tracks.[20]

On 23 October, she passed from the physical realm. Keith was posthumously named by Shoghi Effendi as a Hand of the Cause and America's
'first and distinguished Bahá'í martyr'.[21]

In spite of Keith's efforts to ease the lives of the Persian Bahá'ís, the
year saw the introduction of new restrictions on the Bahá'ís of Iran,
thus giving Shoghi Effendi something else to worry about. No Bahá'í
literature was permitted to be imported and Bahá'í marriages were not
recognized.[22]

The Passing of the Greatest Holy Leaf

On 15 July, while Shoghi Effendi was away in Switzerland, Bahíyyih
Khánum, the Greatest Holy Leaf, the Guardian's greatest supporter,
passed from her earthly existence at the age of eighty-six. Her faculties
had been failing her for some time so her passing was not unexpected.
In March, Shoghi Effendi had written to the American believers about
completing the dome of the House of Worship:

> my voice is once more reinforced by the passionate, and perhaps,
> the last, entreaty, of the Greatest Holy Leaf, whose spirit, now hov-
> ering on the edge of the Great Beyond, longs to carry on its flight to
> the Abhá Kingdom . . . an assurance of the joyous consummation
> of an enterprise, the progress of which has so greatly brightened the
> closing days of her earthly life.[23]

But it was still a shock to Shoghi Effendi, who had depended on her
almost exclusively during the first years of his Guardianship. Something

of his feelings about her passing could be seen in the messages he sent to America, but which was addressed to her:

> Dearly-beloved Greatest Holy Leaf! Through the mist of tears that fill my eyes I can clearly see, as I pen these lines, thy noble figure before me, and can recognize the serenity of thy kindly face. I can still gaze, though the shadow of the grave separate us, into thy blue, love-deep eyes, and can feel, in its calm intensity, the immense love thou didst bear for the Cause of thine Almighty Father, the attachment that bound thee to the most lowly and insignificant among its followers, the warm affection thou didst cherish for me in thine heart. The memory of the ineffable beauty of thy smile shall ever continue to cheer and hearten me in the thorny path I am destined to pursue. The remembrance of the touch of thine hand shall spur me on to follow steadfastly in thy way. The sweet magic of thy voice shall remind me, when the hour of adversity is at its darkest, to hold fast to the rope thou didst seize so firmly all the days of thy life.
>
> Bear thou this my message to 'Abdu'l-Bahá, thine exalted and divinely-appointed Brother: If the Cause for which Bahá'u'lláh toiled and laboured, for which Thou didst suffer years of agonizing sorrow, for the sake of which streams of sacred blood have flowed, should, in the days to come, encounter storms more severe than those it has already weathered, do Thou continue to overshadow, with Thine all-encompassing care and wisdom, Thy frail, Thy unworthy appointed child.[24]

He also called her his 'sole earthly sustainer, the joy and solace of my life'. As she was the 'last remnant of Bahá'u'lláh', he wrote, 'So grievous a bereavement necessitates suspension for nine months throughout the Bahá'í world every manner religious festivity.'[25]

Shoghi Effendi's first act after her passing was to send to Italy for a suitable monument. He had it made from white Carrara marble and designed it as symbolic of the World Order of Bahá'u'lláh. The three steps at the base of the monument represent 'the three steps of the election of the Universal House: the first, the election of the delegates of the believers to the National Conventions; second, the election of the members of the National Spiritual Assemblies by the delegates; and third, the election of the Universal House of Justice by the members of the National Assemblies'.[26] The nine pillars that hold up the capping dome symbolize the National Assemblies. The dome itself symbolizes the Universal House of Justice. Shoghi Effendi also ensured that the head pillar precisely faced the Shrine of Bahá'u'lláh.

Shoghi Effendi reordered his surroundings so that he would never forget the Greatest Holy Leaf. He took an armchair from her room which he had always used and moved it to a place he used for rest from work. Photographs of her filled his room along with photos of her monument. In the Archives, he placed illuminated Tablets of 'Abdu'l-Bahá addressed to her. And, when he married Mary Maxwell five years later, the ring he put on her finger had been given to him by the Greatest Holy Leaf.[27]

On 25 August, a feast was held for the poor in the garden of the House of the Master to celebrate the life of the Greatest Holy Leaf. A thousand people were welcomed in her name 'without distinction of race, class, or creed'.[28]

1933–1936

In April 1933, a number of well-known Bahá'ís arrived at the Pilgrim House and were greeted by Effie Baker and Fujita. Americans Marzieh and Howard Carpenter, Marjorie Morten, Mark Tobey and Mountfort Mills were all there. Marzieh wrote in her diary for 17 April:

> Effie's three white cats with pink ears in the white marble halls. Canaries also – a swift, a salvaged bird's nest – makes doll's houses, knowledge of flowers. Takes exquisite care of pilgrim house. Floats roses in glass bowls. Puts a pink or yellow flower on Howard's tray. She and Marjorie seemed to get along very well.[1]

One day, Marjorie and Marzieh saw Shoghi Effendi get angry, something he did exceedingly rarely. The Guardian asked Marjorie to talk with Edith Sanderson in Paris about abstaining from partisan politics. 'But she is my old friend'. Marjorie protested. Marzieh wrote that the Guardian 'seemed to rise in his chair and suddenly to be much larger, towering, stern'. He then said, 'Politics is a filthy mess.'[2]

Of Shoghi Effendi, Marzieh later wrote:

> These details are few and incomplete. They say nothing of Shoghi Effendi's tenderness toward the believers: cables when they were ill, tributes when they died. All too often, every affliction from which they suffered made its way straight to him. They say nothing of the sums he disbursed for the poor, denying himself, traveling inexpensively when he was abroad for a brief rest, carrying little luggage along. They say nothing of how, when Howard fell mortally ill in Tehran, the Guardian, unasked, sent me money through the Tehran Assembly; or how, in California one year later, on the day and the very moment when I came home from Howard's burial to a

life that had collapsed, I was handed a cable from Shoghi Effendi.[3]

By 31 October, Haifa had a new shipping port protected by a 1.2-mile-long breakwater. Fourteen years earlier, on 23 November 1919, 'Abdu'l-Bahá had taken a group of pilgrims to the Shrine of the Báb; then, looking over the panorama of the bay, he told them that 'a great breakwater would be built to form a harbour, and ships from all over the world would come'.[4] This was the beginning of the Master's prophecy for the area:

> In the future the distance between 'Akká and Haifa will be built up, and the two cities will join and clasp hands, becoming the two terminal sections of one mighty metropolis. As I look now over this scene, I see so clearly that it will become one of the first emporiums of the world: this great semi-circular bay will be transformed into the fine harbour, wherein the ships from all nations will seek shelter and refuge. The great vessels of all peoples will come to this port, bringing on their decks thousands and thousands of men and women from every part of the globe. The mountain and the plain will be dotted with the most modern buildings and palaces. Industries will be established and various institutions of philanthropic nature will be founded . . . Wonderful gardens, orchards, groves and parks will be laid out on all sides. At night the great city will be lighted by electricity. The entire harbour from 'Akká to Haifa will be one path of illumination. Powerful searchlights will be placed on both sides of Mount Carmel to guide the steamers. Mount Carmel itself, from top to bottom, will be submerged in a sea of lights.[5]

Muhammad Mustafa and Sabrí Elias

Two Egyptian believers, Muhammad Mustafa and Sabrí Elias, were able to go on pilgrimage in 1933. Muhammad Mustafa had already had the privilege of going on pilgrimage several times before. On one of his visits, the Guardian called him into his office even though he himself was sick and in bed; he told him that even though he was ill, he still had to work. Mr Mustafa understood that the friends had to redouble their efforts immediately to help the Guardian. He became a translator of Shoghi Effendi's letters into Arabic. In postscripts to two letters written to Mr Mustafa, Shoghi Effendi wrote personal notes praising his translating and assuring him that he would never be forgotten.[6] He later became a Knight of Bahá'u'lláh to the Spanish Sahara.

Another future Knight of Bahá'u'lláh, Sabrí Elias, also came to visit Shoghi Effendi in the autumn of 1933. The Guardian had asked the National Assembly of Egypt and Sudan to send a pioneer to Ethiopia and Sabrí Elias offered to go. Before leaving for his post, he went on his first pilgrimage. When he arrived at the House of the Master, he was met by a man he thought, from his similarity to a photograph he had seen, was Shoghi Effendi. But this left him very confused because he did not find the 'spiritual acquiescence' he had expected. This person ordered a servant to bring tea, and then left. After a while, the servant asked when Sabrí Elias would like to meet the Guardian. The confused Egyptian responded, 'Right now, if possible, right now!' The servant left, then returned with the news that Shoghi Effendi would, indeed, meet him right then:

> A few minutes later, I felt the footsteps of someone entering the room. When I raised my eyes, I saw a person other than the individual who I met earlier, yet with some resemblance. But when my eyes met his, I could not control myself and fell down at those feet! He lifted me up by both arms and embraced me. There were many things that I felt at that moment that I cannot describe in words. Anyway, His Eminence bade me sit down with a gentle gesture, and said, 'Be comforted.'
>
> As I sat there spellbound, His Eminence surprised me by a question about the friends of Port Said, in spite of the fact that I presented myself upon arrival as a Bahá'í from Alexandria without mentioning that I have, indeed, spent a week in Port Said on the way.
>
> Wondering if I had met a certain Bahá'í of Port Said, His Eminence said: 'I hope that he is not busy with political matters, but rather occupied with the Cause of God. This time is the time for spreading and teaching the Cause. One should not busy himself with politics and [worldly] things.[7]

When it came time for Sabrí Elias to leave, Shoghi Effendi told all the resident believers and pilgrims to accompany him to the train station. He became a Knight of Bahá'u'lláh when he pioneered to Djibouti in 1954.

The visit of a sceptic

Most people who met Shoghi Effendi were highly impressed in some way or other, but a few were completely unable to see anything but a pleasant young man. Sometime about 1933, A. E. Suthers visited Shoghi Effendi. Suthers was very sceptical of anything non-Christian. Before visiting Haifa he had studied the Faith, though one of his primary sources of information was *Bahá'ísm: Its Origin, History, Teachings*, by William McElwee Miller, the heavily biased work of a missionary to Persia who was strongly against the Faith. Suthers followed Miller's example when in 1935 he published an article entitled 'A Baha'i Pontiff in the Making' in the journal *Moslem World*. In his article, Suthers introduced Shoghi Effendi by writing that 'According to the will of Bahá'u'lláh, a younger son Mohammed Ali was to succeed 'Abdu'l-Bahá, but the last-named disregarded this provision and appointed his own grandson . . .' Suthers was not impressed with the Guardian when he met him:

> There seemed to be nothing markedly spiritual in that handsome face, and when he spoke one was more conscious of his courtesy and reserve than of any profundity in his utterances. To play the role of prophet, and much more to pose as God, is a sobering undertaking. Claim infallibility, and the dictates of discretion will prescribe a mystifying silence, and if to infallibility is added impeccability, one can hardly afford to be original or enterprising.[8]

When Suthers learned that Shoghi Effendi had attended Oxford, he asked if he had studied psychology or philosophy. Shoghi Effendi said that he had not and wasn't interested in 'abstract thought'. This amazed Suthers, who wrote that it was 'an illuminating admission . . . explaining in part the paradox of his own person, that he could hold essentially abstract notions about divine effulgences to the extent of impersonating divinity without sensing either its futility or its humor.'[9]

Suthers' description of the Shrine of Bahá'u'lláh did a good job of conveying the physical appearance of the Shrine and the Riḍván Garden, which he admitted was 'not without its beauty', but mentioned nothing else. Bahá'u'lláh's station completely eluded him. His primary objection to the *Kitáb-i-Aqdas*, which he described as 'a small volume written by Bahá'u'lláh, a compendium of laws purporting to govern Bahá'ísm a

world-empire to be', was its 'dogmatic insistence on unreserved acceptance of Bahá'u'lláh as the sole hope of salvation'.

As he left, Suthers' conclusion was:

> What was the use of talk anyway? I was perplexed, depressed – at the
> seeming everlasting vitality of error; at the credulity of men. True,
> I reflected, it is a bubble religion, an evanescent phenomenon, but
> until it breaks, what a waste of ideals, of hope, of faith, of precious
> qualities of the human spirit! Moreover its fraudulent character, not
> to mention its ill-balanced dogmatism, and its attenuated ethics,
> covered o'er with the jargon of the social reformer, rasped my sense
> of decency and right.[10]

Shoghi Effendi probably also thought 'What was the use of talk
anyway?', but for a different reason.

1934

On 8 February 1934 Shoghi Effendi finished another of his 'general
letters' when he sent 'The Dispensation of Bahá'u'lláh' to the American
believers.

Mountfort Mills, who was acting as the Guardian's legal adviser in
the Middle East, at one point wrote to America and said that Shoghi
Effendi was 'thoroughly tired out'. Exhaustion was inevitable when

> all matters from the details of repairing a pump up to those of
> world importance are referred to him. The bulk of his work is cor-
> respondence, letters coming mostly from the United States and
> Canada. Advise friends not to send him letters during the summer
> months, thus giving him more time on his vacation for reflection
> and meditation.[11]

Then the Iranian government stepped up its persecution of the Bahá'ís.
Bahá'í schools were closed, meetings forbidden, centres shut, Bahá'í
government employees' jobs terminated and Bahá'ís in the military
stripped of their rank and imprisoned. There was no let-up in the troubles the Guardian had to deal with.[12]

On the positive side, however, Shoghi Effendi cabled the Bahá'í world on 10 May that the Bahá'í properties in Haifa and Akka had been granted tax-exempt status by the Palestinian authorities. This was the result of several years of effort by the Guardian to gain tax exemption for the lands surrounding the Bahá'í Holy Places as well as for the Holy Places themselves. The major benefit of this was that it secured 'indirect recognition' of the Faith.[13]

Músá Banání

Músá Banání and his wife, Samíḥíḥ, made their first pilgrimage in 1934. They were in the presence of Shoghi Effendi for twenty-six days and the experience 'created an intense flame of love and loyalty that melted and fused the essence of Músá Banání's being'. Many times, Samíḥíḥ was alone with the Guardian and, while he talked about the progress of the Cause and the future of the World Order of Bahá'u'lláh, she felt 'so low, so unworthy'.[14]

When it came time to leave, both of the Banánís were sad and Shoghi Effendi said, 'I assure you, you will come again to Haifa, and the next time you come to Haifa, after that you will go to the United States. And when you go there, you won't need a stranger to translate for you.' This prediction was fulfilled in 1953 when Hand of the Cause Músá Banání went to Chicago at Shoghi Effendi's direction for the Intercontinental Teaching Conference. Samíḥíḥ remembered the prophecy as they left Haifa. When they arrived, it wasn't a stranger who translated Músá's talks, it was his own son.[15]

Mr Banání's devotion to Shoghi Effendi 'remained the hallmark of his character to the end of his life'. In his turn, Shoghi Effendi saw the 'simplicity, directness, unbounded energy, and spiritual potential of Músá Banání and nurtured these qualities by showering a joyful love upon him'. The Guardian went so far as to tell a group of pilgrims that Músá Banání was 'one equal to a thousand'. Some of those pilgrims thought that it was an unusual thing to say about an 'unlettered' man,[16] but that man was appointed a Hand of the Cause in 1952.

Pilgrims from Germany

In March 1934, Anna Köstlin, Annemarie Schweizer and Karl Klitzing were in Haifa along with Inez and Max Greeven.[17] Annemarie

Schweizer had several times met 'Abdu'l-Bahá, who had honoured her by staying in her home during his visit to Stuttgart. After His passing 'she held fast to His Will and Testament; all doubts which arose in those years rebounded from her as from steel. She became one of the mothers of the German Bahá'í community.' She would later be arrested and sentenced by the Gestapo, but survived to become 'an immortal in German Bahá'í history'.[18]

Max Greeven, an American of German background, had married Inez Cook, an American who had visited 'Abdu'l-Bahá in 1920 and 1921. The couple pioneered to the Netherlands and then to Germany in the 1920s.

Anna Köstlin was a member of the National Spiritual Assembly, and the pilgrims took notes of this first ever meeting with the Guardian. What they consulted about is not certain, but decisions made soon after by the National Assembly may have been the result. These included renaming the 'National Assembly of the German Bahá'ís' to the 'National Spiritual Association of the Bahá'ís of Germany and Austria' in May 1934 and then to the 'National Spiritual Assembly of the Bahá'ís of Germany and Austria' two months later; the establishment of a Declaration of Trust and By-Laws for the National Spiritual Assembly; that new believers had to officially declare themselves as Bahá'ís, and that believers should be encouraged to contribute to the Bahá'í Fund.[19]

Max was amazed and overwhelmed at the great burden that Shoghi Effendi carried and greatly desired to be of some service to him. The Guardian, in return, recognized the purity of heart and the qualities possessed by Max. So he told the German friends that he would be 'pleased' if they were to elect Max to the Assembly. On 27 March he even wrote to a German believer that 'Mr. Greeven will greatly reinforce your efforts for the effective prosecution of your task. His attachment to the Cause and his realism combined with his remarkable capacity for appreciating spiritual values, all these are undoubtedly qualities which, if properly translated into action, can be of tremendous help to the general welfare and progress of the Faith.'[20]

As Shoghi Effendi hoped, Max was elected to the German National Spiritual Assembly at Riḍván that year[21] and, as conditions in Germany worsened, served as the Guardian's 'chief instrument in the "delicate and difficult mission" of having the Ministry of Church Affairs measures for curtailing Bahá'í activity rescinded'. Unfortunately, these efforts failed and in 1936, the German Bahá'í Summer School at Esslingen was closed, followed the next year by the termination of the National Spiritual Assembly of Germany and Austria and all other Bahá'í activities at the direction of Hitler's government.[22] The German National Spiritual Assembly was reformed in 1946.

Pilgrims from America

Another pilgrim who came shortly after Max was Helen Bishop, who wrote to Alfred Lunt that the experience had changed her point of view on many matters. The Guardian, she noted,

> is an example of how intellect can serve the spirit in a manner we of the West have never known. There is nothing emotional about the Guardian; he is a perfectly controlled and mature personality. I have never heard him recite an incident in which he was the major figure, or say anything which would in any way give him a chance to excel. This may sound naive but the point is that Shoghi Effendi simply refutes all those theories with which our academics are surfeited; that every ego is trying merely to maximate itself.
>
> Shoghi Effendi is very impersonal and he speaks only of the Word and our Faith. His speech is rapid and his English is stunning; when he speaks, the hours pass tirelessly. I should say that his most obvious characteristic is <u>Power</u>, but there is nothing arbitrary or even personal about it. Again and again he seems to convey to one that the Cause of Baha'u'llah will reach its aim and that we have only to be superlatively faithful and to be active and obedient. There is something about him that makes one believe that one can do anything if he requires it; for example, he told me to write, and somehow I simply must begin to do it.[23]

Corinne True arrived in Haifa sometime in the spring with her daughters, Edna and Katherine. For the first time, Corinne was able to land at a proper dock without having to take a small boat to shore. With the new breakwater, Haifa had become a real harbour. When they arrived, a battleship and a large steamer were also docked. Fujita was there to meet them and help them through Customs. Arriving at the Pilgrim

House, she called out to Effie Baker, who was an old friend. By this time Corinne was perfectly natural and at ease with Shoghi Effendi, even to the point of telling him that he wasn't eating enough. 'But Mrs True,' he protested, 'that's all I want.' 'You need to eat more, for eating only twice a day isn't enough,' she replied. Her daughters were aghast, but they soon saw that Shoghi Effendi was moved by her concern.[24]

The Administrative Order, and *Gleanings*

Sometime during 1934, the first National Spiritual Assembly of Iran was elected.[25] Tehran had had one of the first consultative bodies in the Bahá'í world, but the persecution they had faced forced the formation of the first National Assembly to be delayed until this year. The new Assembly was filled with notable Bahá'ís, including: 'Alí-Akbar Furútan, Valíyu'lláh Varqá, Dr Youness Khan Afroukhteh, Shu'á'u'lláh Ala'i and Faḍil-i-Mazandaráni.[26] Mr Furútan, Mr Varqá and General Ala'i would later became Hands of the Cause; Youness Khan had been 'Abdu'l-Bahá's secretary for nine years, and Faḍíl-i-Mazandaráni was an eminent scholar and writer.

On 21 April, Shoghi Effendi sent another of his 'general letters' to the Bahá'ís in North America. Entitled 'America and the Most Great Peace', this document was one of those published in *The World Order of Bahá'u'lláh*. During the summer, Shoghi Effendi finished his translation of *Gleanings from the Writings of Bahá'u'lláh*. He enlisted the help of George Townshend in December 1934 to give

> to the believers a befitting and authoritative rendering of the fundamental teachings of the Cause regarding God, soul, creation, the nature of Divine Manifestations and similar subjects. In addition he [Shoghi Effendi] is very keen to make of this work a means through which the non-Bahá'í public may be given the opportunity of acquiring an exact knowledge of, and a genuine interest in, the Message.[27]

1935: Pilgrims, properties, and a public presentation

Daoud Toeg of Iraq came to Haifa on his second pilgrimage in 1935. Shoghi Effendi had been away when he was there the first time, but he had had the bounty of meeting the Greatest Holy Leaf. On this pilgrimage, Mr Toeg was in Haifa for twenty days and was able to be in the presence of the Guardian many times. Nineteen years later, in 1954, he was one of those appointed to the first Auxiliary Board in Asia.[28]

Dr Khodadad M. Fozdar visited Haifa on his return from Europe to his home in India. While on the steamer crossing the Mediterranean, he explained the Bahá'í Faith to some German Jews who were travelling to see Palestine. They became so interested in the Cause that, when they landed in Haifa, they went to meet Shoghi Effendi. On Dr Fozdar's return to India he encouraged the Bahá'ís to visit the Guardian 'as he gives new spiritual sustenance'. Dr Fozdar later became a Knight of Bahá'u'lláh for the Andaman Islands.[29]

Two more German Bahá'ís made their pilgrimage that year: Edith Horn, a member of the National Spiritual Assembly of Germany and Austria, and Mr Nagel.[30]

Sabrí Elias returned for his second pilgrimage after an exhausting escape from his pioneering post in Ethiopia when Italy invaded the country. While pioneering in Addis Ababa, Mr Elias had, at Shoghi Effendi's request, managed to translate *Bahá'u'lláh and the New Era* into the Amharic language. When he arrived in Haifa, Shoghi Effendi greeted him with 'You have returned victorious and triumphant – because you were the cause of linking the north of Africa to the south!' Mr Elias brought 18 copies of the translation and a goriza (a rare black and white monkey of Ethiopia) skin as a gift. He thought the goriza was simply a personal gift to the Guardian, but Shoghi Effendi had him place it in the Bahá'í Archives in the presence of the resident Bahá'ís and pilgrims as a 'gift from the Land of Abyssinia'.[31]

Shoghi Effendi insisted that Sabrí Elias spend a month in Haifa, because of his exhaustion and illness. He was so ill that he couldn't keep food down, so he was sent to the al-Hamma hot springs, the same medicinal baths near the south end of the Sea of Galilee that 'Abdu'l-Bahá had visited in 1914. The baths cured him and he returned to Haifa for a last meeting with the Guardian before returning to Egypt.[32]

The Guardian was constantly developing the Bahá'í properties that stretched from the German colony at the base of Mount Carmel to the top. When Mountfort Mills returned to America in 1935, he brought back the Guardian's vision for developing a swathe of land 1,200 feet wide from the bottom to the top of Mount Carmel.[33] The Haifa Town

Planning Council, in support of Shoghi Effendi's ideas, were planning an access road to the Shrine of the Báb. There were, however, some objections to this vision. Two who objected were Dr Ameen Fareed and his sister. Fareed had been a thorn in 'Abdu'l-Bahá's side during his journey through Europe and America and had rebelled against the Master in 1914. Now, he and his sister were objecting to having their lands included with those of the Bahá'ís for planning purposes. In their letter, they wrote, '*we are not included* in this organization nor are we members thereof'.[34]

In late 1935, Shoghi Effendi was invited by Sir Francis Younghusband to make a presentation at the World Congress of Faiths in London in July 1936. Sir Francis really wanted Shoghi Effendi to attend: 'Now I wish to ask a great favour of you. Once more I want to try and persuade you to come to England to attend the Congress. Your presence here would carry great influence . . .'[35] Since the Guardian had long before decided not to personally participate in these types of events, and did not have the time even had he wished to do so, he asked George Townshend to write and make the presentation. George's paper was entitled 'Bahá'u'lláh's Ground-Plan of World Fellowship' and was presented on 16 July. Responses were all positive: it 'was received without a dissenting voice'; 'I think there is nothing to discuss in the paper as it expresses what is in the hearts of all of us'; and that 'everybody in the hall felt the unifying influence of the paper'.[36]

Implementing Bahá'í laws in the West

On 11 August 1935, Shoghi Effendi wrote to the National Spiritual Assembly of the United States and Canada about the enforcement of a number of Bahá'u'lláh's laws in the West. Prior to this time, the immaturity of the Bahá'í community had caused the Guardian to withhold the implementation of some of the laws laid out by Bahá'u'lláh. But now, with the national and local spiritual assemblies taking up their duties, he wrote:

> he feels it is his duty to explain that the Laws revealed by Bahá'u'lláh in the Aqdas are, whenever practical and not in direct conflict with the Civil laws of the land, absolutely binding on every believer or Baha'i institution whether in the East or in the West. Certain laws,

such as fasting, obligatory prayers, the consent of the parents before marriage, avoidance of alcoholic drinks, monogamy, should be regarded by all believers as universally and vitally applicable at the present time.[37]

1936: Effie Baker leaves the Holy Land

By 1936, Effie Baker had been in Haifa for more than ten years and, at the age of fifty-five, life at the Pilgrim House in Haifa was becoming stressful for her. Also, her mother back in Australia needed constant care, so Effie began cutting her ties to Haifa, resigning from the Social Service and the Infant Welfare Association.[38] Then on 3 January, Shoghi Effendi wrote to the National Spiritual Assembly of Australia and New Zealand that Effie had finished her time at the World Centre and was about to return home:

> Miss Effie Baker is leaving for Australia with the consent and full approval of the Guardian.
>
> As you know for over ten years she has been devotedly working for the Cause in Haifa, as keeper of the Western Pilgrim House and also as the custodian of the International Baha'i Archives. During this long period of service she has accomplished much for our beloved Cause, and she is now in need of some rest after so many years of strenuous labours. She is going to join her mother, and will, it is hoped, prove of great help to the friends throughout Australia and New-Zealand in both their teaching and administrative activities.
>
> The Guardian hopes, therefore, that the friends will give her all the opportunity she needs to help in the extension and consolidation of the Cause throughout Australia and New-Zealand.[39]

When Effie left, the Guardian entrusted her with what he called 'one of the finest photographs of the Master' to be placed in their National Baha'i Archives. He also sent a bottle of attar of rose extracted by the Baha'is of Persia.[40]

Lorol Schopflocher

Lorol Schopflocher was back in Haifa in May after a travel-teaching tour through Germany, Austria and the Balkans. Shoghi Effendi didn't even allow her a day there. He told her, 'I would like you to go to Egypt tomorrow and have telegraphed the secretary at Alexandria to meet you in the evening.' Lorol had been explaining the Administrative Order on her travels and took the Guardian's insistence to mean that Egypt needed the same message. In Egypt, she spoke mostly with the youth and encouraged them to arise. She helped them organize study classes focused on Shoghi Effendi's messages.[41]

The first stage in the implementation of the Tablets of the Divine Plan

Shoghi Effendi had understood from the beginning that his primary task was to implement the Tablets of the Divine Plan, 'Abdu'l-Bahá's plan for the spiritual conquest of the planet. But he also understood that without an administrative order to guide it, the Master's plan would not come to fruition. The Guardian had spent the first fifteen years of his stewardship raising up that divinely-ordained Order and preparing it for just this task. He had begun implementing the first Tablets of the Plan immediately upon being named Guardian: the spreading of the Faith into cities and towns across the United States and Canada where there were no Bahá'ís, but by 1936 he was ready for the next step.

With his eye on the world and understanding quite well where it was headed, Shoghi Effendi did something the Bahá'í world had not expected: he created a teaching plan for the National Spiritual Assembly of the United States and Canada that had distinct goals and a distinct time frame. The challenge was going to be that most of the plan would have to be carried out during an unprecedented world war. On 29 April, Shoghi Effendi cabled the 1936 American Bahá'í Convention:

> Convey to American believers abiding gratitude efforts unitedly exerted in teaching field. Inaugurated campaigns should be vigorously pursued, systematically extended. Appeal to assembled delegates ponder historic appeal voiced by 'Abdu'l-Bahá in Tablets of the Divine Plan. Urge earnest deliberation with incoming National

Assembly to insure its complete fulfilment. First Century of Bahá'í
era drawing to a close. Humanity entering outer fringes most peril-
ous stage its existence. Opportunities of present hour unimaginably
precious. Would to God every State within American Republic and
every Republic in American continent might ere termination of this
glorious century embrace the light of the Faith of Bahá'u'lláh and
establish structural basis of His World Order.[42]

After the years of preparation, Shoghi Effendi now began to implement
the tasks set out by 'Abdu'l-Bahá in His Tablets of the Divine Plan. For
the first time, the Guardian was giving a National Spiritual Assembly
goals to accomplish. Initially, it was just called the Divine Plan; not until
the following Riḍván did the plan gain a name: the Seven Year Plan. A
month after the first call, he gave the North American Bahá'ís specific
goals to accomplish by a specific date. They were to: 1) form at least
one Spiritual Assembly in every state and Alaska and in every Canadian
province; 2) establish a centre in every republic in South America and
the Caribbean; 3) gradually expand their efforts to Europe; and 4) complete the exterior of the House of Worship in Wilmette. This was all to
be done by the centenary of the Declaration of the Báb, the end of the
first Bahá'í century, on 23 May 1944. It was 'Abdu'l-Bahá's plan for the
spiritual conquest of the western hemisphere.

On 28 July, Shoghi Effendi set out the challenge in plain language:

I am eagerly awaiting the news of the progress of the activities initiated to promote the teaching work within, and beyond the confines
of, the American continent. The American believers, if they wish
to carry out, in the spirit and the letter, the parting wishes of their
beloved Master, must intensify their teaching work a thousandfold
and extend its ramifications beyond the confines of their native land
and as far as the most distant outposts of their far-flung Faith. The
Tablets of the Divine Plan invest your Assembly with unique and
grave responsibilities, and confer upon it privileges which your sister
Assemblies might well envy and admire. The present opportunity
is unutterably precious. It may not recur again. Undaunted by the
perils and the uncertainties of the present hour, the American believers must press on and prosecute in its entirety the task which now
confronts them. I pray for their success from the depths of my heart.[43]

On 29 October, he cabled his happiness at their response:

> Overjoyed unspeakably grateful American believers signal response my reiterated appeals. Inaugurated campaign fraught consequences involving immediate destinies American community. Shadows encircling sore-tried human society noticeably deepening. World crisis inexorably moving towards climax challenging torchbearers Baha'i civilization scale nobler heights individual heroism scatter more widely throughout length breadth American continents participate more strenuously concerted effort organized by national regional local agencies dedicated prosecution noble enterprise pour forth more abundantly resources in support fund created for its furtherance resolve more determinedly conquer whatever obstacles might retard its ultimate fruition. Dawn-breakers previous age have on Persian soil signalized by their acts birth Faith Baha'u'llah. Might not American believers their spiritual descendants prove themselves in turn capable ushering in on world scale civilization of which that faith is direct source and sole begetter?[44]

On 14 November 1936, the Guardian emphasized, again, what he was doing, why it was important, and America's part in the implementation of the Tablets of the Divine Plan:

> The promulgation of the Divine Plan, unveiled by our departed Master in the darkest days of one of the severest ordeals which humanity has ever experienced, is the key which Providence has placed in the hands of the American believers whereby to unlock the doors leading them to fulfil their unimaginably glorious Destiny. As the proclamation of the Message reverberates throughout the land, as its resistless march gathers momentum, as the field of its operation widens, and the numbers of its upholders and champions multiply, its potentialities will correspondingly unfold, exerting a most beneficent influence not only on every community throughout the Bahá'í world, but on the immediate fortunes of a travailing society. The repercussions of this campaign are already apparent in Europe, India, Egypt, 'Iráq and even among the sore-tried communities in Persia and Russia. The Faith of God is gaining in stature, effectiveness and power. Not until, however, the great enterprise

which you are now conducting runs its full course and attains its final objective, at its appointed time, can its world-encompassing benefits be fully apprehended or revealed. The perseverance of the American believers will, no doubt, insure the ultimate realization of these benefits.[45]

The succeeding teaching plans and the Ten Year Crusade were all part of the Guardian's efforts to implement the grand scheme described in the Tablets of the Divine Plan, a plan that would lead to the 'penetration' of the light of Bahá'u'lláh,

> in the course of numerous crusades and of successive epochs of both the Formative and Golden Ages of the Faith, into all the remaining territories of the globe through the erection of the entire machinery of Bahá'u'lláh's Administrative Order in all territories, both East and West, the stage at which the light of God's triumphant Faith shining in all its power and glory will have suffused and enveloped the entire planet.[46]

Shoghi Effendi completed his general letter 'The Unfoldment of World Civilization' on 11 March. Amatu'l-Bahá Rúhíyyih Khánum has written that it was an 'exposition of the state of the world, the rapid political, moral and spiritual decline evident in it; the weakening of both Christianity and Islam, the dangers humanity in its heedlessness was running, and the strong, divine, hopeful remedy the teachings of Bahá'u'lláh had to offer'.[47] This long letter now forms the final chapter of *The World Order of Bahá'u'lláh*.

Palestinian branches of National Spiritual Assemblies

Jeanne Bolles visited Shoghi Effendi in May 1936. She described the Guardian: 'He is so young, yet the white hair of age has already begun to show. His burden is so heavy, and yet he has the power to carry ten more of like weight. But . . . what inspired me was the potent energy of his speech and plans'.[48]

During her visit, Shoghi Effendi talked about the problems with land in Haifa and Akka. Shoghi Effendi wanted to have the Bahá'í properties owned by the various National Spiritual Assemblies of the world because it would both impress the authorities and protect the properties. The Palestinian Branch of the American National Spiritual Assembly had been recognized, after three years of difficult effort, and was now entitled to own property. The Indian National Assembly had also been recognized and several others were following its example. The American National Assembly at that time owned the Western Pilgrim House, 30,000 square metres of land in Haifa and a small tract between Haifa and Akka. Shoghi Effendi's plan was to have all National Spiritual Assemblies of the world owning pieces of the Bahá'í properties in the Holy Land.[49]

The only major complication for purchasing land was that every Bahá'í transaction had to be signed by Mustapha Bahá'í who worked in the Land Registry Office[50] and who was the son of the arch-breaker of the Covenant, Mírzá Muḥammad-'Alí. Even though Mustapha Bahá'í continually created problems, over thirty land transactions had been accomplished. By 1937, the Bahá'ís held a million dollars' worth of property on Mount Carmel, about a quarter officially owned by the National Spiritual Assembly of the United States and Canada.[51]

1937

By 1937, Shoghi Effendi had compiled and translated what was published as *Prayers and Meditations by Bahá'u'lláh*. His former professor, Bayard Dodge, to whom the Guardian had sent a copy, wrote back that 'The translation of deep and poetic thoughts, such as those in the *Prayers and Meditations*, requires an enormous amount of hard work . . . I have told you before how much I marvel when I see the quality of English that you use.'[1]

The Guardian is married

Since 1935 May Maxwell and her daughter Mary had been teaching in Europe, May in France and Belgium, and Mary in Germany. In a report to the Guardian in early 1936 May had expressed the hope that she might 'have the privilege of returning once again to the Holy Land'. On 21 January 1936, Shoghi Effendi wrote inviting her to come:

> I wish to assure you in person of a most hearty welcome. Your distinguished services, so loyally, courageously & devotedly rendered, in both the European & American continents, fully entitle you to visit the Holy Shrines & to draw fresh inspiration from the Source of His inexhaustible grace.[2]

A week later, he also invited her daughter Mary, who, following in the footsteps of her mother, was becoming a powerful Bahá'í teacher:

> The Guardian is very pleased, indeed, to learn that you are so much longing to visit the Holy shrines, after so many years. He wishes me, therefore, to hasten in extending to you a most hearty welcome . . .

Before coming to Haifa Shoghi Effendi would advise you to visit the centers in Germany and if possible to extend your trip to Austria and the Balkans . . . He would even suggest that you follow that route when you come to Haifa, as this would be of great interest to you, and of invaluable encouragement to the friends in these new and isolated centers.[3]

In his own hand, Shoghi Effendi added a postscript saying, 'I wish to assure you in person of a hearty welcome to visit the Holy Land and lay your head on the sacred Threshold after having rendered valuable services in the Faith in both America and Europe.' Mary did not hesitate; she leaped into the task the Guardian had given to her. Over the next eleven months she visited every Bahá'í community in Germany, going to great lengths to meet 'every isolated believer, group, or Assembly, from north to south and east to west of the country'. By the end of 1936, however, political unrest foreshadowing the upcoming war made travel though Austria and the Balkans untenable and Shoghi Effendi urged mother and daughter to come directly to Haifa from Germany.[4]

May and Mary Maxwell arrived in Haifa on 12 January 1937, completely unaware of the momentous event that was near at hand. Unknown to Mary, the Guardian had decided he wished to marry her. Later, he told her that his decision had been confirmed in a dream. In the dream, he was on a large ship going to North America and 'Abdu'l-Bahá was the Captain. Once ashore, they boarded a train which did not stop until it reached at a station called 'Montreal'. He then knew she was to be his bride.[5] And of her, he later wrote that she was 'destined to be my helpmate, my shield in warding off the darts of Covenant-breakers and my tireless collaborator in the arduous tasks I shoulder'.[6]

During his talks between January and March, Mary Maxwell recorded Shoghi Effendi's words. He told how the grandson of Násiri'd-Din Shah, the ruler of Persia when the Báb was martyred and Bahá'u'lláh imprisoned and exiled, came to Haifa and begged Shoghi Effendi to give him an introduction to the National Spiritual Assembly of Persia. The Guardian informed him of the Bahá'í law of non-involvement in politics and 'the Shah's grandson went away satisfied, but never came back'. The British authorities asked about his visit and Shoghi Effendi confirmed that it had happened. At another time, the grandson of Sultan Abdu'l-Aziz, the Ottoman emperor who had ordered the banishments of Bahá'u'lláh from Baghdad to Constantinople, then to Adrianople and finally to Akka, came begging for money. This he received from the Guardian, twice, as well as a copy of Esslemont's *Bahá'u'lláh and the New Era* in Turkish. 'It is astonishing that the grandson of Sultan Abdul-Aziz should come asking for financial help and the grandson of Nasiri'd-Din for political help. Abdul-Aziz was the greatest enemy the Cause ever had.'[7]

Near the end of the pilgrimage, Shoghi Effendi's mother took May aside and confided a special request from the Guardian. She told May that the Guardian wished to marry her daughter:

> One day his mother . . . mentioned the Will and Testament and its provision for a wife for the Guardian. I began to feel very cold and strange. She said simply: 'What would you think about your own daughter for such a position? What do you think of her qualifications?' Then she said, 'This must all seem very Oriental to you', and patted my knee. She said, 'It is a very difficult position – means great sacrifice, complete change of living.' May: 'I think an Oriental would seem much better fitted.' My daughter had had an easy, happy life, a comfortable life; I could not see her in that Holy Family. Negotiations moved forward very rapidly . . . During the third interview with Díyá'i'yyih Khánum, she said, 'The Guardian has given me the ring.' I was speechless . . .[8]

This desire, however, was not passed on to Mary for several weeks. Instead, Shoghi Effendi began teaching Mary calligraphy. Violette Nakhjavani writes,

> In reminiscing about those days, Rúḥíyyih Khánum used to say, with a twinkle in her eyes, that the beloved Guardian took her in hand and taught her Persian calligraphy after dinner in the course of those unforgettable evenings. He gave her a set of reed pens and ink and special mulberry papers and tutored her in the art of writing the Persian script. He also gave her a set of cards to copy from, on which the great calligrapher, Mishkin-Qalam, had written the Hidden Words of Bahá'u'lláh in three different styles of writing. In our early years in Haifa, she showed my husband and myself her copying note books in which Shoghi Effendi had himself written

a line in his exquisite handwriting for her to copy underneath. She told us, 'I could never copy his delicate script exactly, and the length of my sentence was always at least twice as long as his.' And then she would add, with a bewitching smile, 'I think Shoghi Effendi wanted an excuse to stay longer with me and to get to know me better!'[9]

Then one day, 'when the mimosa trees were in full bloom', Shoghi Effendi's younger sister told Mary that 'Shoghi Effendi wants to see you in his room'. Rúhíyyih Khánum never said what happened at that meeting, but she did say, 'I was alone with Shoghi Effendi for only 15 minutes before our marriage.'[10] May later said: 'Then my daughter had her interview with the Guardian and when she came back she had the ring in her hand. The Guardian told her to cable my husband – "Not for his permission, but his consent."'[11]

On 26 February, May sent Sutherland a mysterious cable that read: 'Your presence here by March twenty first essential in connection Marys future happiness great destiny complete secrecy absolutely essential mention to no one if necessary use pretext visit to Randolph [May's brother] . . .' The next day, Mary sent him another cable: 'My dearest Daddy – Ask your consent for my marriage confirm my great happiness absolute secrecy required until after wedding and official announcement longing for your arrival . . .'[12]

The marriage of Shoghi Effendi and Mary Maxwell took place on 24 March. Before then, only the parents, Shoghi Effendi's brother and two sisters knew that the wedding was to take place. On that afternoon, to the surprise of the local Bahá'ís, the chauffeur drove Shoghi Effendi and Mary Maxwell alone to the Shrine of Bahá'u'lláh. Rúhíyyih Khánum remembered that

> I was dressed, except for a white lace blouse, entirely in black for this unique occasion, and was a typical example of the way oriental women dressed to go out into the streets in those days, the custom being to wear black . . .
>
> When we arrived at Bahji and entered the Shrine he requested me to give him his ring, which I was still wearing concealed about my neck, and this he placed on the ring-finger of my right hand, the same finger that corresponded to the one of his own on which he himself had always worn it. This was the only gesture he made. He

entered the inner Shrine, beneath the floor of which Baháʼuʼlláh is interred, and gathered up in a handkerchief all the dried petals and flowers that the keeper of the Shrine used to take from the threshold and place in a silver receptacle at the feet of Baháʼuʼlláh.[13]

Violette Nakhjavani also described the moment:

> The ring, which was a simple Baháʼí ring in the shape of a heart, had been given to her the day Shoghi Effendi proposed. He had asked her then to wear it on a chain around her neck, and on the day of their marriage, in the Shrine of Baháʼuʼlláh, he took it from her and put it on her finger himself. It was a ring that had been given to Shoghi Effendi by the Greatest Holy Leaf, and Rúḥíyyih Khánum later had one made exactly like it for the beloved Guardian.[14]

The couple then returned to Haifa where, in the room of the Greatest Holy Leaf, Shoghi Effendi's mother placed Mary's hand in the hand of her son. Other than that, there was 'no celebration, no flowers, no elaborate ceremony, no wedding dress, no reception'. Shoghi Effendi's parents then signed the marriage certificate.[15]

With that, Shoghi Effendi went back to work and Mary, now titled Rúḥíyyih Khánum, went back to the Western Pilgrim House and joined her parents who had not been present during the momentous events. Shoghi Effendi joined them in the Pilgrim House for dinner,

> showering his love and congratulations on my mother and father. He took the handkerchief, full of such precious flowers, and with his inimitable smile gave them to my mother, saying he had brought them for her from the inner Shrine of Baháʼuʼlláh. My parents also signed the marriage certificate and after dinner and these events were over I walked home with Shoghi Effendi, my suitcases having been taken across the street by Fujita while we were at dinner. We sat for a while with the Guardian's family and then went up to his two rooms which the Greatest Holy Leaf had had built for him so long ago.[16]

The next morning, the gardener was told to take a cable announcing the marriage to the cable office. May said that he was so surprised and happy that 'they could not tell if he went first to the cable office or all over Haifa to spread the news'.[17]

The Bahá'í world, of course, reacted with great joy when the marriage was announced. The American Bahá'í community sent $19 from each of its seventy-one American Assemblies 'for immediate strengthening new tie binding American Bahá'ís to institution Guardianship' as a wedding gift.[18] Cables arrived from individual Bahá'ís and Bahá'í institutions around the world. When John and Louise Bosch wrote, 'Illustrious nuptial thrilled the universe', Shoghi Effendi responded with 'Inexpressibly appreciate thrilling message, deepest love'. Replying to a message from the Bahá'ís of Ishqabad, he wrote, 'greatly value message praying continually protection'. To another congratulatory message, he wrote, 'Assure loved ones Australia New Zealand profound abiding appreciation'. Shoghi Effendi even responded to a person he didn't particularly like or trust by saying 'praying for you Holy Shrines'.[19]

Though Rúḥíyyih Khánum had changed her name, her residence and her status, life went on much as it had before. Her parents stayed for two more months, dining almost every night with the young couple at the Pilgrim House. But though things appeared to be the same, the marriage of Shoghi Effendi and Rúḥíyyih Khánum bound the West and the East into a much closer embrace. When asked about announcing the marriage by the American National Assembly, the Guardian wrote: 'Emphasize significance institution Guardianship union East West and linking destinies Persia America. Allude honour conferred British peoples.'[20] In another cable to the Americans, he wrote:

> Institution Guardianship head cornerstone administrative order Cause Bahá'u'lláh already ennobled through its organic connection with persons of twin Founders Bahá'í Faith is now further reinforced through direct association with west and particularly with American believers whose spiritual destiny is to usher in world order Bahá'u'lláh. For my part desire congratulate community American believers on acquisition tie vitally binding them to so weighty an organ of their Faith.[21]

This uniting of East and West proved crucial after the passing of the Guardian. Hand of the Cause Mr Samandarí said that Rúḥíyyih Khánum was the 'bridge between cultures and languages, a Westerner imbued with Eastern understanding'. Shoghi Effendi had carefully trained her and given her a much greater understanding of his own culture, thus allowing her to see both sides of the issues and help everyone come to a fairer conclusion.[22]

May and Sutherland Maxwell

May felt keenly the implications of her daughter not only marrying into an Oriental household, but marrying the Guardian of her beloved Faith. Writing to a friend two years later, she said that Mary had been

> transported almost in a breath from the world of humanity to the very threshold of God, and often I have felt left behind in her flight. Her life was cut off as by a sword and only God can do these things, and only He can sustain us and recreate us for that higher rarified air she now breathes.[23]

May was amazed at how hard Shoghi Effendi worked. She wrote:

> Never have I seen anyone work as hard as Shoghi Effendi, and it must be very trying to him with his universal creative energy, his world horizon, his soaring ideals, to say nothing of the unfathomable depths of knowledge and wisdom which flow like undulated waves through his sacred entity at all times, it must be a cruel restraint that he has not a greater vehicle or channel through which to pour all this power throughout the world . . .
>
>   In this last visit to Haifa I came to understand as never before something of the agony our Guardian has endured. He spoke of it very simply one night and his uplifted gaze, the white purity and beauty of his face are forever graven on my heart. Nothing is too great to suffer for him, no daily discipline, effort or sacrifice, no surrender of all that is upon this earth can even touch the hem of his sacred suffering, the depths of the cup from which he has drunk. With all my heart and soul I thank the Beloved that He gave us such a daughter for him, who is, in the words of the Master, 'The apple of His eye and the jewel of His heart.'[24]

One day Sutherland Maxwell took a few informal photos of members of the Holy Family. Later, he learned that Munírih <u>Kh</u>ánum would like him to take her photograph. Sutherland took a number of photographs using a small camera belonging to Rúḥíyyih <u>Kh</u>ánum. These photos, taken when Munírih <u>Kh</u>ánum was ninety years old, were the last ones taken of her before she passed away.[25]

When it came time for the Maxwells to leave, May asked her daughter,

> 'Mary, do you think the Guardian will kiss me good-bye?' . . . I had never thought of this and I repeated her remark to Shoghi Effendi, but of course did not ask him to do anything about it! My parents were leaving in the afternoon and after lunch the Guardian went alone to my mother's room in the Pilgrim House to see her. When he had left I went to her room and she said, with her eyes shining like two stars, 'he kissed me'.[26]

Switzerland

Shortly after the Maxwells departed for their return to Canada in June, Shoghi Effendi and Rúḥíyyih <u>Kh</u>ánum themselves left for Switzerland.[27] Shoghi Effendi continued to retreat to the mountain fastnesses of Switzerland each summer, but now took his wife with him. Rúḥíyyih <u>Kh</u>ánum noted that on all of these trips, Shoghi Effendi kept mostly to himself, hardly ever making any close relationships and rarely speaking to people. One exception was Mr Hauser, from whom he had rented a room for many years in Interlaken. He had become very attached to Mr Hauser, who 'listened with so much interest to the enthusiastic account of his day's walk or climb, marvelling at the indefatigable energy and determination' of his young boarder. When Shoghi Effendi brought Rúḥíyyih <u>Kh</u>ánum to Interlaken in 1937, he wanted her to meet this man. Unfortunately, Mr Hauser had passed away, so they had to content themselves with a visit to his gravesite. Though Shoghi Effendi rarely spoke to strangers on his travels, his wife was the opposite. She would slip out of their compartment on the train looking for someone to talk to. 'He always knew (and never minded) when this happened,' she wrote.[28]

The challenge of being the Guardian's wife

The life of a Western woman in an Eastern household was quite a challenge during the first years of the marriage. Rúḥíyyih <u>Kh</u>ánum spoke little Persian and, though the members of the household could speak English, among themselves they naturally reverted to Persian, leaving Rúḥíyyih <u>Kh</u>ánum on the sidelines of many conversations. She was also required to cover her head and be accompanied by attendants when out in public.[29] Violette Nakhjavani describes the early difficulties of Rúḥíyyih <u>Kh</u>ánum's married life:

> But there were greater tests than mere loneliness and far greater trials than cultural isolation awaiting this young, naïve and open-hearted bride. Rúḥíyyih <u>Kh</u>ánum had a free and unsuspicious nature. She had entered this household with a sense of deep love, indeed almost veneration, for all who were related to Shoghi Effendi. What a blow it must have been so soon after her marriage to the Guardian, to first feel the winds of ill will blowing from the members of the household towards him, to recognize the signs of dissension harbouring within the bosom of his family towards the Centre of the Cause. She used to speak of those days with deep sorrow and pain. Many times we heard her say, 'When I saw those oak trees fall one after another, I wept and prayed for my own soul, a mere blade of grass' . . .
>
> She told us that during that first year of her marriage she suffered so much that one day she stood outside her room on the balcony and in deep distress said to herself, 'I have reached the end of my tether.' Her vivid imagination created a picture of her with a rope in her hand, herself at the bottom of the rope! Her sense of humour and her logical mind reminded her that, 'Well, you are at the end of your tether, you cannot go down any farther, but you can climb up it!' From then on, she said, she never reached the end of her rope, as she could always climb up again.[30]

Almost immediately after the marriage, Rúḥíyyih <u>Kh</u>ánum began acting as the Guardian's secretary. Within a few years, she was his principal secretary in English.[31] Her intimate description of him from the diaries she kept is interesting:

'Temperamentally Shoghi Effendi is a doer, a builder, an organizer, and loathes abstractions! . . . No one, observing Shoghi Effendi, could doubt for a moment that he was not perfectly equipped for this phase of the Cause and I believe he was created for it to do just what he is doing. He is the most extraordinarily unidirectional person I have ever seen. His whole nature and tastes and likes and dislikes are intense. He is like something travelling at high speed in one direction, which gives him almost infinite driving power. His persistence is irresistible; there is no dissipation of his forces. He only wants one thing, he wants it passionately, immediately, completely, perfectly. The Temple built – or a flight of steps here in the garden. He descends on it like a hurricane and never lets up until it is done. He drives ahead. It is extraordinary. He likes green lawns, red paths and white paths, red geraniums, cypress trees, and of course, a few other things – but I mean he does not like or want every tree and every flower. No, only just those few and in just such a place. The same is true of foods, the same of colours, of clothes – just a few things, he likes them passionately, he does not want anything else, he never tires of them! It is this almost narrow insistence on one or two themes that has enabled him to build in twenty years such a foundation in the Cause. A man of more catholic tastes and temperament could <u>never</u> have done it!'

'The Guardian is more sensitive than a seismograph, something in him, far deeper than intelligence or any outward information he may have, registers the <u>state</u> of the individual, registers things even the individual may not yet be aware of. I believe we should use him as our index and if he finds fault with some subtle attitude in us we should search ourselves till we find out what it is.' We might well ask ourselves if this should not always be our guide and whether, if we read his writings carefully we cannot find there the indications of our individual, our national and our racial shortcomings and be warned and guided accordingly. Shoghi Effendi, I wrote, 'rings true like the very tuning fork of the teachings . . .' 'He is the Guardian and the nature of his relation to God is naturally a mystery. He can grasp any mystery, he can interpret the most mystical passages of the Faith, he can write things that are of a profoundly mystical nature – he is <u>motivated</u> to do so' . . .

His one single personal hobby was photography; he took

superlatively artistic pictures of the scenery in Switzerland and other places during those early years . . .³²

On another occasion, Rúḥíyyih Khánum described the Guardian's physical appearance:

Shoghi Effendi was physically, as I understood from the members of his family, more like his Great Grandfather, Bahá'u'lláh, then he was like the Master. He was shorter in stature and consequently more like Bahá'u'lláh. His hands were so much like the hands of his Great Grandfather that Bahá'u'lláh's daughter used to take [Shoghi Effendi's] hands in hers and say 'these are exactly the hands of my Father. These are just like the hands of Bahá'u'lláh' . . .

In colouring, he had very elusive eyes. Sometimes the pilgrims would come to me and say, 'I didn't realise that the Guardian has blue eyes!' And I would say, 'He hasn't.' They said 'I'm sure his eyes are blue. I looked at them last night and I'm sure they are blue.' Well, they weren't blue. I suppose I looked in them more than anybody else. They were a very beautiful hazel colour. And sometimes they were brown and sometimes they were gray. He had dark brown hair and an olive complexion.

He had the most wonderful capacity for showing every single emotion that he had on his face. I have never in my life seen a face that could express so many shades of feeling as Shoghi Effendi's. I think he would have made the most marvellous actor in the whole world because they just passed over him like clouds in a pond. Every nuance showed up in his face with a rapidity that was extraordinary.

One of the things he used to show was intense eagerness and excitement over something. If he got very, very keen over a victory that had been won by the Bahá'ís some place in the world, he would open his eyes so wide that it would look as if the irises were two suns rising over the horizon . . . This intense eagerness and enthusiasm of Shoghi Effendi would suddenly splash out in his eyes when he opened them so wide that they just literally shone at you.

He had the most humble nature of any human being I have ever met. He attached absolutely no importance to himself, his personality, or his appearance. He would invariably brush away in an instant the slightest praise. Sometimes people would come and say 'Oh

Shoghi Effendi, it is so marvellous to be here, so wonderful to have this privilege of meeting you and hearing what you have to say.' In one second, he would interrupt and say, 'The great privilege here is to be able to visit the Holy Shrines and to pray in the Tombs of the Báb and Bahá'u'lláh.' I used to beg him to go and have his picture taken so the Bahá'ís would have a record of what he looked like. He said, 'No, I don't attach any importance to this.' and then I said 'If you won't do it for the Bahá'ís, won't you please do it for me? Can't I at least have a picture of you in this world.' He said no. I said, 'But you are so beautiful.' And that would irritate him because he didn't think he was beautiful . . .

He also had a marvellous bubbling quality, something I have never seen in anybody in my whole life. You felt that inside of him, there was a spring, and crystal-clear and pure, this thing just jumped in his heart.

And this is the thing that the Master knew so well in him. He said to take care of him that 'no dust of despondency should stain his pure and radiant heart'. . . He understood how essential it was that the radiant heart of Shoghi Effendi should never be clouded. I'm sorry to say that I think it was clouded from the very first days of his ministry to the very end of his life. And he used to say something to me which saddened me terribly every time he said it – and he often said it – he said, 'If I were happy, you would see what I would do for this Cause.' We all know what he did when he was unhappy, then think of what he would have done if he had been radiantly happy.[33]

Rúḥíyyih Khánum soon learned how divine inspiration worked. She also had to become accustomed to Shoghi Effendi's ability to know the answers to questions before they were even asked:

Shoghi Effendi used to think about things, worry over them often and be very concerned over things, for days and days and days and weeks. Then suddenly, the flash would come and he would know exactly what he wanted to do. At other times, you would barely get a chance to open your mouth and you'd get the answer. I can remember coming upstairs and saying that there was a man downstairs who has come from Baghdad and he says he wants to see you. [Shoghi

Effendi] said. 'This instant tell 'Alí Asgar to put him out. Tell him to leave this instant.' Afterwards we found out that the man had been associated with the Covenant-breakers in Iraq, but [Shoghi Effendi] had no conceivable way of knowing.

He had sometimes these violent reactions to things. And of course he was always right, but it was very baffling because you couldn't understand why you couldn't even finish delivering the message and you got the answer.[34]

Hermann and Anna Grossmann

Hermann and Anna Grossmann, along with their daughter Susanne and Dr Grossmann's sister Elsa Maria, began their pilgrimage on 29 March, just days after Shoghi Effendi's wedding. When the Guardian came to lunch the first time they were the only pilgrims, and Elsa Maria wrote:

Our hearts started pounding, since it was the fulfilment of our longing when he suddenly stood before us. I think we were very quiet for a long time. So many impressions rushed upon us and we were deeply moved, so that it took us a while to compose ourselves. But our Guardian was very understanding and demonstrated his love and kindness. The longer one is permitted to remain in the presence of Shoghi Effendi, the more intensely one senses the calm with which he fills his surroundings, the spiritual power that emanates from him. To sit opposite him at the table, to see his clear-cut features and feel the penetrating depth of his eyes is – I felt – to step into another world, a world in which we realize that it alone is spiritual reality and everything else is insignificant. It is a world in which matter is not eliminated but in which spirit has overcome matter. And in this world one remains in his presence, whether in conversation, through which he is teaching us, is concerned with the most difficult and most spiritual problems or is about the down-to-earth questions and issues of everyday life . . .[35]

Anna, too, felt the power of Shoghi Effendi:

The Guardian's clear, superior wisdom, his answers to many a question, his encouragement and ideas, served to reinforce and expand the future activities of the pilgrims, inspiring them for the coming years in the service of this great Revelation. The deep reverence and appreciation that the pilgrims felt towards Shoghi Effendi was even more strongly rooted when they left Haifa. For Hermann Grossmann, Shoghi Effendi as the leading figure of the Bahá'í Faith became the focal point of his being . . .[36]

Shoghi Effendi spent much of his time with the Grossmanns talking about the Bahá'í Administrative Order. Dr Grossmann had brought an original Tablet he had received from 'Abdu'l-Bahá to give to the Guardian. The next day, Shoghi Effendi asked if he realized how significant the Tablet was. When Dr Grossmann mentioned a particular passage, the Guardian directed him to another in which the Master wrote that Hermann Grossmann had 'been enabled to rend the veils asunder, to gaze on the beauty of the Sun of Reality, and to walk in the path of the Kingdom'. These things were most significant. Dr Grossmann was appointed a Hand of the Cause in 1951.[37]

When they went to the Shrine of Bahá'u'lláh, Elsa Maria was strongly affected:

> Whereas in the resting place of the Báb the impression of loveliness and tenderness dominated all other feelings, in the Shrine of Bahá'u'lláh there was a sense of unwavering power, unspeakable glory and majesty, and then – like a victory call permeating everything and drowning out all other sound – the consciousness of a Faith that no power on earth could possibly destroy. To kneel at the threshold of the inner Shrine in Bahjí and to immerse one's face in the flowers is like sensing the proximity of the countenance of the Lord of the Universe, and our prayers will continue to be but stammers until in the storm of our innermost feelings we find rest in being close to Him.[38]

One day, Shoghi Effendi asked Hermann Grossmann if he had any desire to return to South America, the land of his birth. He replied that he was happy in Germany, where he had moved when he was ten years old. The Guardian suggested that one day he might be glad to return to South America. As a Hand of the Cause years later during the last years of the Ten Year Crusade, Dr Grossmann did, indeed, return happily to

South America 'helping the Bahá'ís to create the conditions necessary for the election of their National Spiritual Assemblies' which would be essential for worldwide participation in the election of the Universal House of Justice.[39]

In the middle of their pilgrimage, the Grossmanns went to Jerusalem, Tiberias and Nazareth. The Church of the Holy Sepulchre in Jerusalem struck them, but not in a positive way. They saw guides angrily competing for customers and not stopping even as they stood before what was called the grave of Jesus. The dome over the Tomb of Christ was in danger of collapsing, but the unchristian attitude of one Christian sect for another meant that workmen could not pass from one part of the church, controlled by one sect, into another part controlled by a different sect who refused them access.[40]

When it came time to depart Haifa on 20 April, they were accompanied to their ship by May and Sutherland Maxwell, Rúhíyyih Khánum, Husayn Rabbani and Fujita. They carried with them, as a gift from Shoghi Effendi, a carpet for the National Spiritual Assembly of Germany and Austria.

Agnes Alexander

Agnes Alexander, who would be appointed a Hand of the Cause in 1957, arrived the very day the Grossmann party left. She was pioneering in Japan at that time, so became the first pilgrim to come from that country. Agnes's journey from Japan became interesting when she reached Port Said at midnight. Her impending arrival had been cabled to the local Bahá'ís and they found her on board the next morning. One of them, Ahmad Yazdi, she immediately recognized because she knew his brother, Ali Yazdi, in California. Ahmad's first words to her were, 'The Guardian is married and you will never guess to whom.' But Agnes immediately knew that it had to be Mary Maxwell. After Agnes met some of the Bahá'í women that afternoon, one of the Bahá'ís drove her to the train station in Kantara. But when she showed her passport in the Customs office, the man noted that it had expired that day. Luckily, there was a Bahá'í working in the Customs office so arrangements were made for her to continue to Haifa, but with the admonition that she would have to renew her passport before she could leave.[41]

There were two English women in her compartment who were

going to Jerusalem and they became very curious about all the Bahá'ís who kept coming in about her passport. That gave her the opportunity to tell them about the Faith. Shortly before dawn, there was a 'terrific crash'. All the lights went out and all the baggage in the racks over their heads was hurled to the floor. It turned out that a projecting load from a passing freight train had smashed into their car. No one was hurt, but there was a half-hour delay before they were under way again. Too excited to try to sleep, Agnes went to the dining car for a cup of coffee and met an Irish policeman from Jerusalem. When he asked where she was going, she said Haifa, to which he replied, 'It is very beautiful there, it is Muhammadan.' Agnes, of course, took the opportunity to 'explain to him the reality of the Bahá'í Cause'.[42]

Agnes was met at the train station by Fujita, who took her to the Western Pilgrim House where she was enthusiastically welcomed by May Maxwell. She wrote: 'What a bounty God granted me that after waiting thirty-six years to visit the Holy Land, when at last I reached there my spiritual mother greeted me!' But May didn't waste time talking about ancient history. They'd no sooner sat down then she was telling her all about her daughter's marriage, even pointing across the street to Shoghi Effendi's rooms at the top of the House of the Master, saying, 'That is where she is.' They were interrupted when Agnes was told that the Guardian would see her in half an hour, so she hurried away to get cleaned up.

Soon, escorted by Fujita, Agnes was presented to Shoghi Effendi. She wrote:

> The meeting with the Guardian seemed very natural. He spoke of the room we were in, that it was the room in which the Master received His guests, and pointed out the chair in which He sat. The Guardian spoke of the Cause throughout the world and then of Japan and said that the Japanese should establish the Cause in Japan, that the next books to translate into Japanese were the *Hidden Words*, then the *Gleanings*, and afterwards the *Íqán* and *Some Answered Questions*. Then he said I should not return to Japan alone, that I should have help, and that someone might go with me from America. It was a great surprise to me when he said he wanted me to go to Germany, for I had never dreamed of it, but I had hoped I could go to Paris where thirty-six years before I had received the confirmation

to go forth and teach His Cause. The Guardian added that I might spend a week or so in Paris and in London.[43]

That evening at dinner she sat opposite Shoghi Effendi, who was seated between his new wife and his mother-in-law. 'His conversation was inspiring. Addressing Mr Maxwell, he spoke of the Plan of Bahá'u'lláh, that the Báb had declared and referred to it and 'Abdu'l-Bahá had embodied it in a blueprint, as it were, and we were the champion builders to carry out the Plan.'[44]

Because of her stalwart services to the Faith in Hawaii and Japan, the Guardian treated her as an honoured guest and she, in turn, gave him the same love and respect she had given to his Grandfather, though she had never met 'Abdu'l-Bahá. At dinner that first night, Shoghi Effendi asked her to write the history of the Bahá'í Faith in Japan and the Hawaiian Islands, where she had also taught the Faith.[45] Agnes, like others before her, learned that the Guardian spent 80 per cent of his time on correspondence and that 80 per cent of his correspondence was from individuals, leaving him little time and energy for the world-wide work of the Cause.[46]

The next day, Agnes accompanied the women of the Holy Family to a meeting at the Tomb of the Greatest Holy Leaf, where prayers and Tablets were chanted. She was intrigued that the women did not close their eyes or bow their heads, as was common in the West. When she asked about it, they said, 'We were listening to the words.'[47]

Agnes wanted to bring Shoghi Effendi's words of wisdom to others and was happy when May told her that the Guardian allowed pilgrims to take notes at the dinner table. But when she brought her notebook and tried to write what he said, she initially found it very difficult:

After that every evening before dinner I supplicated the Beloved for His assistance that I might be able to write the words of knowledge which flowed from the Guardian, and only through His help was I enabled to write. I realized afterwards that it was a spiritual matter which depended on one's spiritual condition and not the outward ability to write. When I left Haifa I felt great regret that I had not done better.[48]

On 23 April, Agnes went to the Shrine of the Báb alone and came away with a bouquet of flowers, courtesy of the 'radiant gardener'. That afternoon Adelaide Sharp arrived from Tehran and they were able to meet Munírih Khánum.

Agnes had brought with her a Japanese scroll to give to Shoghi Effendi. She had originally planned to give him a scroll on which she had placed a Greatest Name made by Mason Remey, but it had been stolen the year before. She replaced the stolen scroll with a typical Japanese one showing a beautiful rising sun. At first, she hesitated:

> Knowing that he received many presents . . . The evening after I gave it to him, he spoke of it at the table and said he was going to hang it in the hall in Bahjí. I was deeply touched and said, 'It is a great honor to the nation of Japan!' Another evening when he came to dinner he said he had been to Bahjí that afternoon and had hung the scroll in the hall there, on either side of which he had placed paintings of Dr. Hermann Grossmann's, and he asked me when I would meet him to tell him about it. It then became clear to me why the thief had taken the Greatest Name scroll from my home in Tokyo, for otherwise the Japanese scroll would not have hung in Bahjí. At the top of the scroll, the rising sun appeared casting a glow beneath which was the ocean, and between it and in the sky three storks were in flight. Such a scroll would be displayed by the Japanese at times of congratulation, as the New Year season.[49]

On 7 May, Ḥusayn Effendi, Shoghi Effendi's brother, took Agnes and Adelaide Sharp to Akka and Bahjí. They paused briefly at the cemetery outside Akka where 'Abdu'l-Bahá's sons and Nabíl, author of *The Dawn-Breakers*, are buried, then visited the Most Great Prison and the Garden of Riḍván. Then they continued to Bahjí where they were to spend the night. Agnes recorded her stay:

> When we reached Bahjí we were each assigned a room for the night. There the surrounding country seemed pervaded with an atmosphere of peace. It reminded me of Makawao, Maui, on the slope of the mountain Haleakala. In the Esslemont room, in the Mansion, I saw the Japanese edition of Esslemont's book which had been sent from Tokyo, and also the clippings from Japanese newspapers carefully placed in a drawer. In the hall of the Mansion, I burned

the incense which blind Mr. Watanabe had sent by me from Kyoto which Shoghi Effendi had told me I might do. From that blessed place we wrote letters to friends. I had started a letter to George Beatty in Japan, but could not finish it, as the auto arrived to take us back to Haifa. That evening at dinner I spoke to the Guardian again of George, and asked if I should write him that he must give up drink. A laughter started which went around the table, the beloved Guardian joining in it. He answered me, 'Wait until he is a Baha'i.'[50]

Agnes had arrived in Haifa with many questions, but found that it was not easy to speak. Even so, she still received her answers:

When I reached Haifa my heart was full of many things which I wished to speak to the Guardian about concerning Japan. In his presence I felt self-conscious when I spoke, and as Adelaide Sharp spoke only of Persia, I found it difficult to speak. God did not deprive me, though, and when I left Haifa there remained nothing in my heart which had not been answered. All I could say then was, 'It is all-satisfying!'

Whenever I was able to speak, the Guardian would immediately answer with soul-satisfying replies. I spoke of George Beatty, that he said he could not be a Bahá'í because he drank . . . Shoghi Effendi said: 'Any person considering to become a believer must make up his mind to give up drink. Bahá'u'lláh says, 'Do not approach it,' that is, you must not drink it. A believer is expected to accept the law of Bahá'u'lláh without questioning. We have no perfect Bahá'ís. Only the Master was perfect. A Bahá'í is a person who accepts the law with entirety.'

I spoke of the brother, Mr. Daiun Inouye, that he was a Buddhist priest. Shoghi Effendi said that he could not be a Bahá'í and remain a priest, that he should make every effort to find other means of livelihood even though it were less money, and that it should be explained to him . . .: 'Bahá'u'lláh is the Bearer of a New Revelation which abrogates the old, the Founder of a New Dispensation. We have our own laws. We must not be members of any organizations but we must cooperate with all provided cooperation does not imply acceptance. We must do just what others do who enter our meetings, reciprocate like people who address Bahá'í meetings. We must make distinction between association and affiliation. Our Faith abrogates the laws of previous revelations, therefore we cannot be members of other organizations.'

One day as I was writing to the blind friends in Japan, I spoke of the spread of the Cause among them and asked the Guardian what he would suggest for me to write them. He said: 'The effect of 'Abdu'l-Bahá's Tablets to the blind in Japan we are now beginning to witness. The Braille Committee has been internationally extended. The blind should be told that the Cause will be the greatest comfort and the words of Helen Keller should be quoted, and they should be told what the Bahá'ís are doing for the blind in particular that it is international in scope. There will be many more blind after the war' . . .

He said: 'The immediate future in Japan is very dark. Japan is going to suffer. The time is not now for great headway. The Pacific will become a great storm center in the coming war – great suffering.'[51]

On her last afternoon in Haifa, the Guardian sent for Agnes and gave her a beautiful photograph of 'Abdu'l-Bahá which he had wrapped in a white silk handkerchief. The photo was to be given to the Japanese Bahá'í Archives when they were established. He also gave her a large copy of the Greatest Name to replace the one that had been stolen. He spoke once more of Japan's future:

Japan has a very great future. It is very much like Germany, full of vitality and in the future it will be devoted to the Cause. Now it is the transition time. They need a rude awakening. They must be shaken before they awaken. Nationalism and militarism are all instruments which God is utilizing for the use of His purpose. This turmoil is a preparation . . . If you are able to, encourage friends not only to visit Japan but to settle there. Travelers have not been able to achieve what was wanted . . . Come again with Japanese Bahá'ís, not only interested but Bahá'ís, for I do want the Japanese Bahá'ís to take an active share in the international affairs here in the future when the International House of Justice is formed. Its seat will be here in Palestine. I hope we will have pilgrims from Japan.[52]

Before she left, Agnes asked Shoghi Effendi what message she should take back to America. He said that the American friends

> have a twofold task of promoting: first teaching and second the completion of the Temple ornamentation, the seven year plan to the end of the first century. If they cooperate and persevere they will succeed. Mr. Schopflocher has offered $100,000 and the remaining amount would be $30,000 per year (for seven years). It is very easy to achieve this if the friends persevere and cooperate . . . If cooperation is sustained to the end – and the teaching work must not suffer and must be established . . . at least a group in every state, and if a group is not possible, then one resident believer not only in every state and province in America, but in every republic in the American continent, and the eight islands of Hawaii . . .[53]

Just before her ship sailed, Shoghi Effendi sent for Agnes again and reiterated what he had said the day before to stress its absolute importance: the Americans had a twofold task and only seven years remained to get them done. They 'must make a tremendous effort in teaching and a tremendous effort to finish the second and third units of the temple by the end of the first century . . . it was 25 years since the Master laid the corner stone' and that it would be thirty-two years before it was completed. He said that 'by the end of the first century they must be through with the ornamentation and particularly as this will enable the friends in Persia to start the third Temple . . . He quoted the Master's words that another Temple could not be built until the one in Wilmette was completed.'[54]

Just as Agnes was leaving, Shoghi Effendi's mother Ḍíyá'í'yyih Khánum gave her a small Persian rug showing the Greatest Name.

Dhikru'lláh Khádem

Dhikru'lláh Khádem made his fourth pilgrimage in April 1937 after having been in Haifa the year before. His first pilgrimage had been in 1925 and he was so eager to be on pilgrimage with the Guardian that Shoghi Effendi said, 'I give you a permanent visa. Any time you can come. You are welcome.' After he returned in 1926, 1937, 1938, 1939 and 1940, Shoghi Effendi told him, 'I'll call you.' He did not visit

Shoghi Effendi again until March 1952, a few days after he had been designated a Hand of the Cause.[55]

Mr Khádem was one of Shoghi Effendi's important Iranian contacts whom he strongly encouraged to translate letters and articles from English to Persian. Starting in 1932 with articles from *The Bahá'í World* (Volumes 5 and 6), he translated a number of the Guardian's important letters, such as sections of *The Advent of Divine Justice* and *The Promised Day is Come*.[56]

On 3 April, Mr Khádem and other pilgrims heard Shoghi Effendi talk about the Tablet of Carmel. Bahá'u'lláh had revealed it, he said, while standing very close to where the obelisk now marks the future site of the Mashriqu'l-Adhkár and the 'power and melody of His voice deeply impressed the monks of the monastery who were standing in reverence and listening.' 'Have you read the Tablet of Carmel?' Shoghi Effendi asked:

> The Tablet is there in the Pilgrim House. The Blessed Beauty revealed this Tablet when His tent was first raised on Mount Carmel near the Deyr (Carmelite Monastery). The Tablet was not completed. It contains the divine mysteries of God. Bahá'u'lláh said, 'Call out to Zion, O Carmel,' which means, O Carmel, address Jerusalem, 'and announce the joyful tidings: He that was hidden from mortal eyes is come! . . . Hasten forth and circumambulate the City of God . . .' The City of God refers to the establishment of the Shrine of the Báb on Mount Carmel. The City of God in this Tablet is Bahá'u'lláh's promise to entomb the sacred body of the Báb. A 'celestial Kaaba' is a mystery [which he did not disclose, nor did I dare to ask]. These are mysteries. Bahá'u'lláh proceeds in this Tablet, 'Ere long will God sail His Ark on thee,' a further mystery which means that the Universal House of Justice will be established here on Mount Carmel under the shadow of the Shrine of the Báb. The Ark, in this Tablet, is the Ark of God's civilization. And 'the people of Bahá,' the occupants of the Ark, are members of the House.'[57]

After each of Mr Khádem's pilgrimages, Shoghi Effendi sent him on a special mission. On one of the earlier pilgrimages, Shoghi Effendi gave him a mission saying, 'Go to Egypt, and tell the friends the glad tidings.' But the Guardian didn't tell him what the 'glad tidings' were and he was too afraid to ask. Years later Mr <u>Kh</u>ádem remembered:

So we went to Egypt and met the friends. In a packed hall in Cairo, I stood before the Bahá'ís, desperately wanting to tell them the glad tidings. But I couldn't think of anything. I prayed, 'O God! *Yá Bahá'u'l-Abhá*! [O Thou the Glory of the most Glorious!] What to tell them?'

A voice within me said that I should tell them about the sufferings of the Bahá'ís of Iran, although this did not seem to be glad tidings. But I started to tell them that I had been to the prison in Tehrán and met the entire membership of the Assembly of Yazd, including two Afnáns (relatives of the Báb), while an officer stood guard. Two tall fences, about two meters apart, had separated us. The old Ḥájí Muḥammad Ṭáhir Malmírí [the father of former Universal House of Justice member Adib Taherzadeh and of the well-known translator of Bahá'í texts, Habíb Taherzadeh], the great historian, then in his eighties, was in chains amidst the other prisoners. His vision and hearing were both impaired. You can just imagine the state of our emotions.

I said to the prisoners, 'I came from the beloved. He sends his bounties, blessings, and greetings to you all.' Upon hearing this they started to dance!

But the aged Ḥájí Ṭáhir could not hear, nor could he see me. He asked his companions, 'What does he say?'

So I said louder, 'I came from on high and brought the good pleasure of the beloved for you.' This phrase, *'az fawq ámadam*,' is one that the Bahá'ís understand.

Finally comprehending, Ḥájí Muḥammad Ṭáhir cried and raised his hands in thanksgiving to Bahá'u'lláh. He said, 'This only shows the generosity of the beloved Guardian! Who are we to deserve such a bounty?'

These are the stories that came to mind when I met the Bahá'ís of Egypt.

After our meetings, we prepared to go back to the Holy Land, but I was so unhappy. I kept blaming myself for not asking the Guardian what were the glad tidings that I was to deliver to the friends in Egypt. I felt that I had failed to accomplish my assignment. When we arrived in the Holy Land, while I was still silently agonizing over this, the beloved Guardian said to me, 'The great glad tidings were the stories of the sufferings of the Bahá'ís of Iran that you have already told the believers in Egypt.'[58]

Amelia Collins

Between 4 November and 1 December 1937, Amelia Collins was in Haifa on pilgrimage. One of her first diary comments was: 'In Haifa one becomes lost in the spiritual atmosphere that pervades everything surrounding us . . . Rarely did any outside matter enter the conversation and this talking constantly of heavenly things causes delight and satisfaction.' One of the dominating topics of the Guardian was the Administrative Order. Shoghi Effendi emphasized that the assemblies must

> be outstanding in their ideals of justice and ability to solve diffi-cult problems according to divine techniques . . . the Gov't will ask Assemblies advice and even their association in government. This may really happen in America and it will be refused, for the Gov't will want only their help, and will not be willing to accept the source of their knowledge.[59]

Shoghi Effendi was also very conscious of the position of the Faith in the increasingly Jewish country, and of the dangers of proselytizing. He told Milly, 'We do not teach them if they ask but give them literature . . . Moslems will resent us, they do not feel kindly toward the Jews. If the Jews become interested the Moslems will be still more antagonistic and make it more difficult. Not the time to teach.'[60]

The Mashriqu'l-Adhkár was another topic Shoghi Effendi men-tioned. They were to be open to everyone, but for worship only, using the Holy Scriptures of all religions. He also talked about what he expected to be the first four Houses of Worship:

1st temple Ishkabad on a plane [plain]
2 " Chicago Lake
3 " Teheran Slope Mt.
4 " Carmel Promintory overlooking the sea
Perhaps best place on Mt Carmel would be that now occupied by

Carmelite Monastery. Baha'u'llah visited this mon. and it is sacred ground. The Temple to be built on Mt Carmel must be on a lower slope than the Shrines for it must be under the shadow of the Shrine of the Bab.[61]

Shoghi Effendi said that the principal reason for his pushing for the completion of the Chicago House of Worship was so that the Bahá'ís could concentrate on teaching. He mentioned 'Abdu'l-Bahá's prophecy that the Temple would be a great, silent teacher. The Guardian also mentioned that completion of the Temple would 'infuriate the missionaries . . .'[62]

Shoghi Effendi stated that American President Woodrow Wilson was greater than President Lincoln, but that he could not succeed with his Fourteen Points and the League of Nations because he was a generation too early.[63]

Margery McCormick and Emeric Sala

Margery McCormick's pilgrimage, from 3 to 16 November 1937, resulted in a surprise for her. She wrote that

> I wasn't sure then what would happen on pilgrimage; I just knew that I wanted to visit the Shrines and to meet the beloved Guardian. But no one had told me that I would be expected to find my role in the Faith. Each day, at the dinner table, the beloved Guardian would encourage me to prepare a public talk. When I explained to him that I was not able to speak in public and had all my life been shy, he listened carefully and then continued speaking of the talk – I knew I must make an effort.[64]

Margery McCormick had always been very shy, but by the end of her pilgrimage she had, with the Guardian's help, prepared a talk. Shoghi Effendi urged her to memorize it. Even so, she left as a 'frightened, raw recruit'. When she returned to New York, she was met at the dock by a number of Bahá'ís and whisked away to the local Bahá'í centre and asked to speak. Thanks to Shoghi Effendi, she was prepared and her career as a platform speaker began.[65]

Late in December, Emeric Sala arrived in Haifa on pilgrimage from

Canada, having been persuaded by May Maxwell to extend a European business trip. He was the only Western pilgrim at that time. Emeric had arrived thinking that his primary purpose was to meet Shoghi Effendi, but after he arrived, he wrote:

> I did not meet him. I met, instead, the Guardian. Shoghi Effendi, the man, sacrificed himself long ago to the Faith, which is to unite all humanity. There is, perhaps, no man living who has given so much of self. He has given everything to God. Therefore, whatever we receive from him, is not from him but through him from God. He has no will of his own. Yet, as soon as he expresses a wish, followers of the Faith fulfil it.[66]

Initially, Emeric asked how could he know when Shoghi Effendi spoke as the Guardian and when as Shoghi Effendi. When Emeric asked this question, Rúḥíyyih Khánum, the Guardian's wife of less than a year and who was sitting next to him, asked: 'I would like to know too; which is which?' The Guardian did not answer the question.[67]

One day, Shoghi Effendi asked Emeric a question: 'Since after the martyrdom of the Báb the authority of the Faith was passed on to Bahá'u'lláh, and after his passing to 'Abdu'l-Bahá, to whom was it transferred after the ascension of 'Abdu'l-Bahá?'

> I answered, of course, to Shoghi Effendi. He said no. I then said the Guardian. He again shook his head. I then ventured the Universal House of Justice. He again said no, and I could see from his expression that he was disappointed with my inability to answer his question. Then he asked, are the friends not reading my letters? The answer, he said, is clearly stated in *The Dispensation of Bahá'u'lláh*. It is divided into four parts: Bahá'u'lláh, the Báb, 'Abdu'l-Bahá, and the fourth part entitled 'World Order of Bahá'u'lláh', which is the answer to his question.[68]

Emeric realized that what Shoghi Effendi 'wanted to impress upon me' was

> that the authority of the Faith did not rest upon him but on the World Order of Bahá'u'lláh, which was based on two pillars: the

Guardianship and the Universal House of Justice. His vision of the future went far beyond the Guardianship . . .[69]

and in recounting this story years later he referred to the Guardian's words in one of his earliest 'general letters' to the American Bahá'í community, in 1929:

> To dissociate the administrative principles of the Cause from the purely spiritual and humanitarian teachings would be tantamount to a mutilation of the body of the Cause, a separation that can only result in the disintegration of its component parts, and the extinction of the Faith itself.[70]

On Emeric's last night, Shoghi Effendi brought him two huge grapefruit and asked him to take them back as a gift to the American friends. Emeric first wondered where he could put them in his luggage, then worried about them being confiscated when he arrived in America. Shoghi Effendi simply said, 'Just try, take them if you can.' Because of the heat and the long passage back to America, the grapefruit had shrunk considerably in size by the time Emeric reached Montreal. The grapefruit went through Customs without a problem. When Emeric took the fruit to the next Bahá'í meeting, the problem arose of how to share two grapefruit among twenty people. That was solved by making grapefruit juice. Everyone had a spoonful of juice from Shoghi Effendi's gift.[71]

Emeric and his wife Rosemary pioneered to Zululand, part of South Africa, in July 1954.[72]

1938–1939

In 1938, seven of Shoghi Effendi's long 'general letters' he had written to the American believers between 1929 and 1936 were combined into one book with the title *The World Order of Bahá'u'lláh*. In his introduction Horace Holley wrote that it unfolded 'a clear vision of the relation between the Bahá'í community and the entire process of social evolution under the Dispensation of Bahá'u'lláh' and disclosed 'the full degree to which Bahá'u'lláh's Message applies to the world of humanity and not merely to those who are believers at this time'.[1] It defined the 'visible Order', the institutions and administration of the future world government and is a guide for creating the future Bahá'í world. Shoghi Effendi offered this explanation:

> this priceless gem of Divine Revelation, now still in its embryonic state, shall evolve within the shell of His law, and shall forge ahead, undivided and unimpaired, till it embraces the whole of mankind. Only those who have already recognized the supreme station of Bahá'u'lláh, only those whose hearts have been touched by His love, and have become familiar with the potency of His spirit, can adequately appreciate the value of this Divine Economy – His inestimable gift to mankind.
>
> Leaders of religion, exponents of political theories, governors of human institutions, who at present are witnessing with perplexity and dismay the bankruptcy of their ideas, and the disintegration of their handiwork, would do well to turn their gaze to the Revelation of Bahá'u'lláh, and to meditate upon the World Order which, lying enshrined in His teachings, is slowly and imperceptibly rising amid the welter and chaos of present-day civilization.[2]

Ethel Dawe

Australian Ethel Dawe arrived in Haifa aboard the steamship *Stratheden* on 6 January and stayed for ten days. She was highly impressed with Shoghi Effendi's power and love and Rúḥíyyih Khánum's inspiration. But meeting the Holy Mother, Munírih Khánum, 'Abdu'l-Bahá's wife, is what impressed her the most. At their first meeting Munírih Khánum embraced her and said 'Read the Words of Bahá'u'lláh, dear, read the Words of Bahá'u'lláh. They are creative Words. Blessed are the hours spent with the Words of God.' When she departed, Ethel Dawe carried a gift from the Guardian for Australia – a lock of Bahá'u'lláh's hair.[3]

Rom Landau, impressed and depressed

Rom Landau, a Polish/British sculptor, author, educator and Arabist, came to Haifa on 17 March. He was searching for truth and unity – and having a difficult time finding it. He interviewed the Greek Orthodox Patriarch in Jerusalem who summed up the various attempts at unity, saying, 'Heads of other Churches come and visit me and speak of unity and fellowship. But after they have left they go to their missionaries and make them proselytize among the Greek Catholics even more than before. Their one concern is how to increase their own flock. Universal fellowship interests them only for reasons of propaganda. They don't really have it at heart.'[4]

Landau was 'anxious to ascertain Shoghi Effendi's views on several subjects and to meet the guardian of a faith which, in its Christian tolerance and its supernational and super-denominational appeal, contains some very attractive features,' and he had made arrangements for this visit before leaving England. However, the meeting both surprised and depressed him:

> Rarely has my imagination deceived me more blatantly than it did in the case of Shoghi Effendi. I imagined him a rather impressive-looking man, attractive by reason of some quality of gentleness or of a mixture of humanity and force. I expected dignity and should not have been surprised if I had met with unctuousness.
>
> When Shoghi Effendi entered the room with a buoyant step I could hardly believe that the dapper little man, so sprightly and neat

in his European clothes with a black tarboosh, was connected with a movement of the spiritual significance of the Baha'is. He greeted me with a very charming smile, repeating several times: 'You are welcome, you are welcome, I am so glad you came.' His eyes and mouth did not cease smiling . . .

His answers were brisk and self-assured as his gestures and smiles. He spoke quickly, not nervously, but with a youthful alacrity, as if apprehensive lest the time at his disposal might not be fully utilised for the spreading of Baha'i doctrine. His English was excellent – he had been up at Oxford – and only rarely did too florid a turn of phrase betray him.

When I asked Shoghi Effendi about the future there was no hesitation about his answer. 'There is a wonderfully bright future in store for humanity' – his words overflowed in a torrent – 'but before it can come about terrible suffering will be inflicted by a world war. It will be far worse than the last war. Only through war and suffering can humanity learn the bitter lessons without which the new revival is impossible.' . . .

At the end of our conversation he presented me with several Bahá'í books, and, thus encouraged, I asked him whether I might take his photograph. 'No,' he said, 'all the Baha'is would like my photograph, but I don't believe in the worship of personalities. It can easily overshadow the essential adherence to a principle.' His refusal was the most personal and attractive statement of the afternoon, and I was glad that he would not let me photograph him.[5]

Landau wrote that he was both impressed and irritated by Shoghi Effendi, but he did not understand what the Guardian told him about developing a new world order. With the rapid approach of war, Landau expected the Bahá'ís to be attempting to avert the conflict, to be dashing here and there dousing the fires of the arsonists, not understanding that Shoghi Effendi was trying to change the heart of the arsonist so that they would build rather than destroy.[6]

Habíb Taherzadeh

Sometime during 1938, a Persian student in his late twenties was returning from England to Persia. His boat made an unexpected three-hour stop in Haifa and as a Bahá'í, though a very inactive one, he hiked up to the Shrine of the Báb where he met a Persian man. This visitor was Habíb Taherzadeh. He bluntly asked the man, in English in order to show off, 'I am a Bahá'í; I want to see Shoghi Effendi.' The man turned out to be Ḥusayn Rabbani, Shoghi Effendi's brother, who welcomed him and said that since it was the 9th Day of Riḍván, the Guardian would soon be at the Pilgrim House. When they reached the Pilgrim House, Habíb sat in the farthest section. Suddenly, everything went quiet and Shoghi Effendi entered with 'majesty' and sat under the great portrait of the Master, just opposite from Habíb.

After being introduced to Habíb, Shoghi Effendi said, 'Do you know what has happened today? I have received a telegram that the first group of pioneers have arrived in Buenos Aires, Argentina. This is the beginning of a great movement of pioneers to the Western Hemisphere.' The Guardian was referring to the Kevorkians, Armenians from Lebanon who were among the first pioneers to that area.

After the commemoration of the 9th Day of Riḍván, Shoghi Effendi led the believers to the Shrine of the Báb, where he chanted the Tablet of Visitation in a voice, Habíb recalled, that shook the building. When he finished, the Guardian left. After only a few minutes, a man came in and took Habíb's arm, saying that Shoghi Effendi wanted to see him. Habíb then walked down the mountain with the Guardian to the House of the Master, a walk that was rough and rocky. On the way, Shoghi Effendi said that he was satisfied with the English Bahá'ís and asked if Habib had met any. Habíb, who had spent his time in London on material things only, had to say no, but that he had corresponded with a Bahá'í lady. When Shoghi Effendi asked him who she was, Habíb couldn't remember – so the Guardian told him who it was. Suddenly, Habíb's material world began to change. Habíb remembered that 'this was his power. He could read your heart; what you were thinking. He would talk to you and give you the answer to what you were thinking.'

When they arrived at the House of the Master, Shoghi Effendi walked directly inside, leaving Habíb standing confusedly in the street. Then Shoghi Effendi reappeared and invited Habíb in. For the next fifteen minutes, the Guardian talked to the young man, speaking initially about the great work Habíb's father was doing and the importance of teaching. By then, Habíb said, 'I was so uplifted I was in another world'. Tears flowed down his face and he didn't remember much else of what Shoghi Effendi said. Finally, the Guardian arose, embraced Habíb and said that the next time he came, he would have to stay longer.

When Habíb left, he didn't really know where he was going, though he did manage to find the way back to his ship. When he entered his cabin, he sat sobbing with tears rolling down his face. Arriving back in Persia, the first thing he did was order books from England.[7]

This meeting was the springboard for Habíb's own pioneering to South America a few years later. And in the 1970s, he went to Haifa, where he lived very simply, to be the chief translator into English of *Tablets of Bahá'u'lláh Revealed after the Kitáb-i-Aqdas* and *Selections from the Writings of the Báb*, with the assistance of a committee at the World Centre.

The Passing of Munírih Khánum

Munírih Khánum, the wife of 'Abdu'l-Bahá and known as the Holy Mother, passed into the Abhá Kingdom on 30 April. She was ninety-one years old and she died in Haifa while the American National Bahá'í Convention was in session in Chicago. Shoghi Effendi immediately cabled the Convention saying that all Riḍván festivities were to be suspended and that the delegates should devote a special session to remember her.[8]

Next to Bahíyyih Khánum, the Greatest Holy Leaf, Munírih Khánum was Shoghi Effendi's strongest and ablest supporter. But within three years, her children, the children of 'Abdu'l-Bahá, would break the Covenant of Bahá'u'lláh. Though she did not see that happen in the physical world, she was well aware of what was occurring, as Baharieh Rouhani Ma'ani describes:

> Munírih Khánum . . . was a mother who had spent a good part of her life bearing and raising children. They were 'Abdu'l-Bahá's daughters. They were referred to as Holy Leaves. She was emotionally very attached to them and they were to her. They were all married by the time of 'Abdu'l-Bahá's ascension and, except for one, all had children. When Bahá'íyyih Khánum passed away, the grandchildren had come of age and at least one was already married to a man whose family had sided with 'Abdu'l-Bahá's opponents. In the succeeding years more of her grandchildren married into families

who had a chequered history when it came to upholding the provisions of the Covenant. The situation with the grandchildren gradually worsened, threatening the spiritual health of the immediate members of 'Abdu'l-Bahá's family. Although none of them was declared a Covenant-breaker during Munírih Khánum's life, the signs of defiance were there. Instead of being role models supporting Shoghi Effendi in word and deed, they expected to be treated differently and to be allowed to do as they pleased. The consequences were clear. Unless they drastically changed their attitude and obeyed the Guardian of the Faith, their spiritual well-being was in jeopardy. Munírih Khánum could see this but hoped that such a catastrophic outcome would be averted . . .

Munírih Khánum faced the saddest and most grievous challenge of her life after the Greatest Holy Leaf passed away. By then she was in her mid-eighties. During the remaining years of her life she witnessed the worsening of problems besetting the people she most loved, problems arising from their failure to understand and appreciate the implications of 'Abdu'l-Bahá's Will and Testament regarding Shoghi Effendi's guardianship.[9]

Shoghi Effendi's writing

Rúḥíyyih Khánum, as the Guardian's secretary, was almost always with him when he translated or wrote his books and letters in English. She said that he liked to have someone in the room while he worked. The way he wrote was quite different from anything his wife had experienced before: he 'wrote out loud',

> speaking the words as he put them down. I think this habit in English was carried over from Persian; good Persian and Arabic composition not only can be, but should be chanted. One remembers the Bab revealing the *Qayyumú'l-Asmá* out loud, and Bahá'u'lláh revealing His Tablets in the same way. This was the Guardian's custom in English as well as in Persian and I believe it is because of this that even his long and involved sentences sound even more flowing and intelligible when read aloud. The length of some of these sentences was at times a cause of comment on my part; Shoghi Effendi would raise his head and look at me, with those wonderful eyes whose

colour and expression changed so frequently, with a hint of defiance and rebelliousness in them – but did not shorten his sentence! I can recall only one occasion when he admitted, ruefully, that it <u>was</u> a long sentence; but he still did not change it. It said what he wanted it to; it was too bad it was so long. On the other hand he liked to use a structure sometimes of very short sentences that followed each other one after the other like the cracks of a whip. He would call my attention to this variation in style, pointing out how each method was effective, how the combination of the two enriched the whole and achieved different ends. He was very fond of the device of alliteration, much used in oriental languages but now no longer so common in English. An excellent example of his use of this is provided by this sentence reiterating words beginning with 'p' from one of his cables: 'Time pressing opportunity priceless potent aid providentially promised unfailing.'

Shoghi Effendi's method of composition was like that of a mosaic artist at work, who creates his picture with clearly defined and separate pieces; each word had its own place and if he struck a difficult sentence he would not change it around so as to accommodate a thought that grammatically could not fit into the sentence structure but would stick to it, sometimes literally for hours, until I at least was worn out by his verbal repetition of the phrase as he battled to subjugate it and fit it in the way he wished to, typing one piece of his mosaic after another, until he had solved his problem. I seldom remember his ever abandoning a sentence and starting over in a new form. Another characteristic in his choice of words was that because of popular misuse or abuse of a thought which a word conveyed he saw no reason to abandon or shun it, but used it in its proper and exact meaning. He was not afraid to speak of 'conversion' of people to the Faith, or to call them 'converts'; he lauded the 'missionary zeal' of pioneers in 'foreign mission fields', at the same time making it plain we have no priests, no missionaries and do not proselytize.[10]

Shoghi Effendi always wrote on small, lined pads and always by hand. Whenever his editing resulted in too many notations, he would patiently rewrite the whole letter or document by hand. Once a letter or manuscript was complete, Shoghi Effendi would then type it up himself on a small portable typewriter using the 'two-finger method', making any changes he thought necessary as he pecked away.[11] It was in this way that between 1938 and 1940 he wrote not only his voluminous correspondence, but also *The Advent of Divine Justice* and *The Promised Day Is Come*, as well as the translation of *Epistle to the Son of the Wolf*, completed sometime between the two in the winter of 1939–1940 as the world descended into war.[12]

Bahá'ís and the coming war

Starting in 1936, the Palestinian Arabs began to resist the British author-ities, at first only with labour strikes and political protests. By late 1937, this had escalated to widespread violence. The British authorities, aided by Jewish police groups, suppressed the rebellion with brutality.[13] To escape this epidemic of violence, Shoghi Effendi left Haifa in the late spring of 1938 and spent most of the rest of the year in Europe. On 25 December, he sent a long 'general letter' to the North American believers, entitled *The Advent of Divine Justice*, written while he was in Europe. In addition to warning them of the coming war and admonish-ing them to stand fast, he 'with a kind but firm hand . . . held up before the face of the North American Community the mirror of the civiliza-tion by which they were surrounded and warned them, in terms that riveted the eye and chilled the heart, against its evils . . .'[14]

Sachiro Fujita had faithfully served the Guardian from the time of the passing of 'Abdu'l-Bahá. In 1936 he had made his first visit back to Japan since leaving there in 1903, staying for three months. In 1938, Shoghi Effendi told him that war was coming and that he should return to Japan. So, after nineteen years in the Holy Land, Fujita returned to his native land. Though he hoped not to be gone for too long, the separation lasted until 1955, due to great difficulties getting a visa and passport after the war and then finding passage.[15] But once back, he remained serving in Haifa until his death in 1976.

With the fast approach of world war and many more Bahá'ís in the world, what part the Bahá'ís should play became a point of intense concern. Bahá'u'lláh taught that Bahá'ís should not kill, but that was what war was all about. In 1938, Shoghi Effendi addressed this conundrum:

> With reference to the absolute pacifists or conscientious objectors to war: their attitude, judged from a Bahá'í standpoint, is quite

anti-social and due to its exaltation of the individual conscience leads inevitably to disorder and chaos in society . . . The Bahá'í concept of social life is essentially based on the subordination of the individual to that of society . . .

The other main objection to the conscientious objectors is that their method of establishing peace is too negative. Non-cooperation is too passive a philosophy to become an effective way for social reconstruction. Their refusal to bear arms can never establish peace. There should first be a spiritual revitalization which nothing, except the Cause of God, can effectively bring to every man's heart.[16]

While the believers, he feels, should exert every effort to obtain from the authorities a permit exempting them from active military service in a combatant capacity, it is their duty at the same time, as loyal and devoted citizens, to offer their services to their country in any field of national service which is not specifically aggressive or directly military. Such forms of national work as air raid precaution service, ambulance corps, and other humanitarian work or activity of a non-combatant nature, are the most suitable types of service the friends can render, and which they should gladly volunteer for, since in addition to the fact that they do not involve any violation of the spirit or principle of the Teachings, they constitute a form of social and humanitarian service which the Cause holds sacred and emphatically enjoins.[17]

The Guardian returned to this topic in June of the next year:

It is still his firm conviction that the believers, while expressing their readiness to unreservedly obey any directions that the authorities may issue concerning national service in time of war, should also, and while there is yet no outbreak of hostilities, appeal to the government for exemption from active military service in a combatant capacity, stressing the fact that in doing so they are not prompted by any selfish considerations but by the sole and supreme motive of upholding the Teachings of their Faith, which make it a moral obligation for them to desist from any act that would involve them in direct warfare with their fellow-humans of any other race or nation. The Baha'i Teachings, indeed, condemn, emphatically and

unequivocally, any form of physical violence, and warfare in the bat-
tlefield is obviously a form, and perhaps the worst form which such
violence can assume.

There are many other avenues through which the believers can
assist in times of war by enlisting in services of a non-combatant
nature – services that do not involve the direct shedding of blood –
such as ambulance work, anti-air raid precaution service, office and
administrative works, and it is for such types of national service that
they should volunteer.

It is immaterial whether such activities would still expose them
to dangers, either at home or in the front, since their desire is not
to protect their lives, but to desist from any acts of wilful murder.

The friends should consider it their conscientious duty, as loyal
members of the Faith, to apply for such exemption, even though
there may be slight prospect of their obtaining the consent and
approval of the authorities to their petition. It is most essential
that in times of such national excitement and emergency as those
through which so many countries in the world are now passing that
the believers should not allow themselves to be carried away by the
passions agitating the masses, and act in a manner that would make
them deviate from the path of wisdom and moderation, and lead
them to violate, however reluctantly and indirectly, the spirit as well
as the letter of the Teachings.[18]

In England, Philip Hainsworth, who became a Bahá'í in 1938, was the
first person to apply to the British government and be granted non-
combatant status as a Bahá'í. David Hofman helped him prepare his
application and in November 1939 Philip went before a tribunal which
would decide on the validity of his request. His judge was known to
be very hard on conscientious objectors; he spoke very little to Philip,
but questioned David, who was there representing the National Spiritual Assembly. Later, stories in two local newspapers were headlined:
'Persian Faith modifies man's pacifism'.[19]

During the upcoming war, Philip served as a stretcher-bearer. *The
Daily Telegraph*, an English newspaper, in its obituary of Philip in 2001,
wrote that 'During the North Africa campaign he was accorded the
unusual – for a pacifist – accolade of being granted a commission; he
left the RAMC in the rank of captain.'[20]

Some Bahá'ís were not able to avoid combat postings, but sincere belief and divine assistance helped them uphold their principles. During the First World War, for example, Curtis Kelsey had been drafted into the army as an infantryman and sent to France. With a rifle in his hands but Bahá'u'lláh's teachings in his heart, Curtis was headed for his first battle when an electrician was suddenly needed. Curtis had worked in his father's electrical business so soon found himself in the Signal Corps. Though the job was commonly as dangerous as being an infantryman, it solved Curtis's dilemma of how to do his duty and not kill anyone.[21]

Not all Bahá'ís who served in the military were as lucky as Curtis. Seven German Bahá'ís were forced to enlist in the German army during the Second World War, and all lost their lives. One, Fritz Macco, played a notable part before his death in an attempt to rescue Lidia Zamenhof. Lidia was the first Polish Bahá'í and the daughter of the creator of the Esperanto language. Because she was of Jewish ancestry, Lidia was arrested and confined to the Warsaw ghetto. The German Bahá'ís were very concerned about her and asked Fritz, who as an ambulance driver had considerable freedom of movement, to find her. Fritz succeeded at huge risk to himself; he managed to find Lidia and offered to help her escape. But she preferred to share the fate of her friends, so Fritz was the last German Bahá'í to see her alive. Fritz was killed soon after.[22] Compulsory military service has been a problem suffered by other European, American and Iranian Bahá'í youth during more recent conflicts.

The German Bahá'í community was heavily persecuted during the Nazi era. In 1937, all Bahá'í institutions were dissolved by order of Heinrich Himmler. The homes of Bahá'ís were searched and all Bahá'í literature was confiscated. Hermann Grossmann managed to save a part of his extensive Bahá'í library by donating it to the University of Heidelberg, but he and his family were targeted. The German Bahá'ís were continually harassed and many were fined or imprisoned simply because they were Bahá'ís. In one case, 20-year-old Ruth Espenlaub-Schnizler was prosecuted for 'an offence against the "Decree for the Protection of the People and the State".' Bahá'ís were prohibited from publically sharing their faith, so it was quite a surprise when the prosecutor, in an unusual twist to prove her guilt, 'gave a detailed explanation of the history and doctrines of the Faith and clearly set out the claim of Bahá'u'lláh.' The persecutions ended with the war in 1945.[23]

A local tragedy

An unfortunate tragedy struck the Haifa Bahá'í community in 1939. Habíb Miskar, one of the oldest Bahá'ís in the community, was inadvertently killed because of the political strife between the British authorities, impatient Jewish activists and discontented Arabs. One day when Habíb was walking near the gate to the House of 'Abdu'l-Bahá, a group of militia came running up the street chasing a terrorist. Habíb was old and infirm so he chose to run to the gate of 'Abdu'l-Bahá's house to get out of the way. The militia saw only two running men dressed in robes so, not knowing which was the terrorist, shot and killed both. Habíb 'died at the entrance to the home he had entered so many times as a faithful and welcome believer'.[24]

Shoghi Effendi and Rúḥíyyih Khánum were in Switzerland in August as the clouds of war were about to burst. On 8 August, Rúḥíyyih Khánum wrote in her diary: 'Got up at six today and went to get us the necessary visas (always providing we can get out of Switzerland) and have been on the road just 18 hours! And this is not the first day of rushing . . . and this is typical of my life. No time for anything . . .' They arrived back in Haifa about 6 September, just days after Germany invaded Poland and started a six-year conflagration. The journey from Switzerland had been difficult and Rúḥíyyih Khánum wrote:

> Back in the Middle East . . . an utterly exhausting trip, most of the time without sleepers. One night we slept an hour and a half! It does not seem real at all that war has come to the world. Passing through blackened towns – seeing troop trains moving up – waiting to hear the radio news . . . Shoghi Effendi's way has been opened as it always will be – the scene seemed to crash behind us, but we were safely through.[25]

The Divine Plan

The American Seven Year Plan would begin its third year at Riḍván 1939, and early that year Shoghi Effendi felt the need to remind the Bahá'ís of their duty to the Divine Plan. The Americans, he later told a pilgrim, were 'enthusiastic but not sustained in their effort, easy to start but need frequent reminders'. He much preferred what he called the

English 'steady drizzle' which, though slower to start, was much more steady and persistent than the American efforts, 'which were unsteady and spasmodic'.[26] So, in a letter written on 28 January 1939, Shoghi Effendi gave the Americans a push:

> The period ahead is short, strenuous, fraught with mortal perils for human society, yet pregnant with possibilities of unsurpassed triumphs for the power of Bahá'u'lláh's redemptive Cause. The occasion is propitious for a display, by the American Bahá'í Community, in its corporate capacity, of an effort which in its magnitude, character, and purpose must outshine its past endeavors. Failure to exploit these present, these golden opportunities would blast the hopes which the prosecution of the Plan has thus far aroused, and would signify the loss of the rarest privilege ever conferred by Providence upon the American Bahá'í Community. It is in view of the criticalness of the situation that I was led to place at the disposal of any pioneer willing to dedicate himself to the task of the present hour such modest resources as would facilitate the discharge of so enviable a duty.
>
> The Bahá'í World, increasingly subjected to the rigors of suppression, in both the East and the West, watches with unconcealed astonishment, and derives hope and comfort from the rapid unfoldment of the successive stages of God's Plan for so blest a community. Its eyes are fixed upon this community, eager to behold the manner in which its gallant members will break down, one after another, the barriers that obstruct their progress towards a divinely-appointed goal. On every daring adventurer in the service of the Cause of Bahá'u'lláh the Concourse on high shall descend, 'each bearing aloft a chalice of pure light.' Every one of these adventurers God Himself will sustain and inspire, and will 'cause the pure waters of wisdom and utterance to gush out and flow copiously from his heart.' . . . Audacious must be the army of life if the confirming aid of that Kingdom is to be repeatedly vouchsafed unto it . . . Now is the time to reveal the force of one's strength, the stoutness of one's heart and the might of one's soul.'
>
> Dearly-beloved friends! What better field than the vast virgin territories, so near at hand, and waiting to receive, at this very hour, their full share of the onrushing tide of Bahá'u'lláh's redeeming

grace? What theatre more befitting than these long-neglected nine remaining states and provinces in which the true heroism of the intrepid pioneers of His World Order can be displayed? There is no time to lose. There is no room left for vacillation. Multitudes hunger for the Bread of Life. The stage is set. The firm and irrevocable Promise is given. God's own Plan has been set in motion. It is gathering momentum with every passing day. The powers of heaven and earth mysteriously assist in its execution. Such an opportunity is irreplaceable. Let the doubter arise and himself verify the truth of such assertions. To try, to persevere, is to insure ultimate and complete victory.[27]

A not too gentle reminder was apparently what the North American Bahá'í community needed. A year later, as war raged elsewhere, their home-front goals had been accomplished, as had most of their Latin American goals.

The passing of Martha Root

Shoghi Effendi had carried out a voluminous correspondence with Martha Root as she traversed the world spreading the message of Bahá'u'lláh to queen and peasant alike. But on 28 September, her road came to an abrupt end when she ascended to the Abhá Realm while in Hawaii. Shoghi Effendi himself was ill with a temperature of 104° F when the cable arrived, but, as Rúḥíyyih Khánum wrote, 'He was the Guardian, it was Martha Root who had died.' Over the objections of those around him, Shoghi Effendi sat up and dictated a cable to America, which read in part: 'Martha's unnumbered admirers throughout Bahá'í world lament with me earthly extinction her heroic life. Concourse on High acclaim her elevation rightful position galaxy Baha'i immortals. Posterity will establish her as foremost Hand which 'Abdu'l-Bahá's will raised up first Baha'i century. Present generation her fellow-believers recognize her finest fruit formative age Faith Baha'u'llah has as yet produced.'[28]

Monuments for the Purest Branch and Navváb

Rúḥíyyih Khánum said that Shoghi Effendi was 'very tenacious of his purposes, very determined, but never unreasonable'. Once his objective was set, he never deviated. He did, however, sometimes change his plan for accomplishing that objective. When he initially decided to move the remains of the Purest Branch and Navváb to the Monument Gardens, he immediately ordered two monuments similar to that of the Greatest Holy Leaf and early on planned to put one on either side of her tomb. When he actually looked at the ground, he decided that they would be more beautiful if set together by themselves. Rúḥíyyih Khánum wrote:

> All through the Guardian's ministry we see the light of Divine Guidance shining on his path, confirming his decisions, inspiring his choice. But there are always unforeseeable factors in every plan. Acts of God, and the sum of human endeavour, constantly change plans, little or big. This has always happened to the greatest as well as the smallest human beings, and the words of the Prophets themselves attest it. Shoghi Effendi was subject to such forces, but he also frequently modified his own plans. Examples of this are many and interesting: at one time he conceived the idea of placing the Mausoleum of Bahá'u'lláh on Mt Carmel, but later gave this up entirely and fixed its permanent place in Bahjí . . .[29]

Shoghi Effendi wanted to move the remains of Mírzá Mihdí, the Purest Branch and son of Bahá'u'lláh, and of Navváb, Bahá'u'lláh's wife and the mother of 'Abdu'l-Bahá, from the cemetery outside Akka to the Monument Gardens near the Shrine of the Báb. At the beginning of December 1939, he selected a location, then began excavating burial sites in the solid limestone of Mount Carmel. When the Covenant-breakers learned of this, they immediately protested to the British authorities. Badí'u'lláh, claiming that he, as the son of Bahá'u'lláh and half-brother of Mírzá Mihdí, should control where they were buried. When Shoghi Effendi explained to the authorities that Badí'u'lláh and his group were enemies and had been strongly denounced in the Will and Testament of 'Abdu'l-Bahá, they quickly ruled in the Guardian's favour. On 15 December, the Haifa District Commissioner wrote in his report that:

An application was made at the beginning of the month by the representatives of the Bahai community to remove the remains of Mirza Mihdi and of his mother, Assiyeh [Navváb], from the cemetery in Acre, where they were interred, to the Bahai Garden at Haifa. The removal was opposed by a dissenting faction led by Badia'u'llah. The original request had been made over a year ago and authority given by the Health Department but exhumation had not, for some reason, been carried out. The dissenting faction claimed that, as he stood nearer than Shoghi Effendi in relationship to Mirza Mihdi, whose exhumation it was proposed, he, not Shoghi Effendi, was entitled under Moslem law to decide as to the disposal of the remains. Badia'u'llah and his faction, it may be explained, have identified themselves with the Moslem religion.

As I was satisfied that the request was made by the recognised heads of the Bahai community and had the approval of the greater part of the community, I authorised the reinterment to take place, and informed Badia'u'llah that I could only recognise a request from the recognised head of the community and that he must obtain satisfaction of any legal rights he claimed in the Courts. The reinterment was carried out without incident and, so far as I am aware, no court proceedings have yet been taken.[30]

Shoghi Effendi immediately went to Akka and removed the remains of the Purest Branch and his mother to Mount Carmel himself. In late December, the caskets of the two holy souls were taken to the Shrine of the Báb, then interred in their monuments the next evening. Rúḥíyyih Khánum described the reinterment of those holy remains:

The garden is dark. Twilight has fallen on Mount Carmel and the veils of dusk have deepened over the bay of 'Akká. A group of men stand waiting by the gate, beneath the steps. Suddenly there is a stir, the gardener runs to illumine the entrance and amidst the white shafts of light a procession appears. A man clothed in black rests the weight of a coffin on his shoulder. It is the Guardian of the Cause and he bears the mortal remains of the Purest Branch, Bahá'u'lláh's beloved son. Slowly he and his fellow bearers mount the narrow path and in silence approach the house adjacent to the resting place of the Greatest Holy Leaf. A devoted servant speeds ahead with rug and candelabra from the Holy Shrines and swiftly prepares the room. The gentle, strong face of the Guardian appears as he enters the door, that precious weight always on his shoulder, and the coffin is laid temporarily to rest in an humble room, facing Bahjí, the Qiblih of the Faith. Again those devoted servants, led by their Guardian, return to the gate and again remount the path with another sacred burden, this time the body of the wife of Bahá'u'lláh, the mother of the Master . . .

As we meditate beside those two eloquent coffins, covered with woven cloths, strewn with jasmine from the Threshold of the Báb's Tomb, so all pervading is the presence of their spirits – or maybe it is their memory, as perfume lingers when the flower is withered – that the very room they rest in for so short awhile becomes itself filled with the sweet peace of a shrine . . .

The last stone is laid in the two vaults, the floors are paved in marble, the name plates fixed to mark their heads, the earth smoothed out, the path that leads to their resting place built, but storm and rain sweep unceasingly over the crest of the mountain postponing the final arrangements until the day before Christmas dawns, bright and clear, as if a sign that this is the appointed time. At sunset we all gather in that humble, twice blessed house. We hear the voice of one of the oldest and most devoted believers of the Near East raised, at the command of his Guardian, in prayer. Tremulous, faint, yet filled with a poignant faith and love hard to describe but never to be forgotten, he prays. As voice follows voice, one of them that of the Guardian himself, it seems as if one could almost hear the refrain of those prayers sung in triumphant joy by an invisible concourse on high.

And now, again on the shoulder of the Guardian, they are borne forth to lie in state in the Holy Tomb of the Báb. Side by side, far greater than the great of this world, they lie by that sacred threshold, facing Bahjí, with candles burning at their heads and flowers before their feet. It is the eve of the birth of Christ. She who was foretold of Isaiah, he who was the son of Him of Whom Jesus said: 'Howbeit when he, the Spirit of truth, is come, he will guide you into all truth,' rest quietly here their last night before the earth hides them forever more from the eyes of men.

The following sunset we gather once again in that Holy Shrine.

The Guardian chants the Tablet of Visitation, first in the Tomb of the Báb, then in the Tomb of the Master. The privileged friends who have been able to make the pilgrimage to Haifa for this sacred occasion enter with the Guardian a second time the Báb's Shrine. Slowly, held aloft on the hands of the faithful, led by Shoghi Effendi, who never relinquishes his precious burden, first the mother of 'Abdu'l-Bahá and then the Purest Branch are ushered from that Holy Spot. Once they circumambulate the Shrines, the coffin of beloved Mihdí, supported by the Guardian, followed by that of the Master's mother, passes us slowly by. Around the Shrine, onward through the lighted garden, down the white path, out onto the moonlit road, that solemn procession passes. High, seeming to move of themselves, above the heads of those following, the coffins wend their way. They mount the steps and once again enter that gate leading to Bahíyyih Khánum's resting place. They pass before us, outlined against the night sky, across whose face fitful clouds make sport of the full moon. They approach, the face of the Guardian close to that burden he bears. They pass on toward the waiting vaults.

Now they lay the Purest Branch to rest. Shoghi Effendi himself enters the carpeted vault and gently eases the coffin to its preordained place. He himself strews it with flowers, his hands the last to caress it. The mother of the Master is then placed in the same manner by the Guardian in the neighboring vault. Not six feet apart they rest. The silent faces of the believers in the brilliant light of the lamps, form a waiting circle. Masons are called to seal the tombs. Respectfully and deftly they fulfil their task. Flowers are heaped upon the vaults and the Guardian sprinkles a vial of attar of rose upon them. The pungent scent is caught up on the breezes and bathes our faces. And now the voice of Shoghi Effendi is raised as he chants those tablets revealed by Bahá'u'lláh and destined by Him to be read at their graves.[31]

Shoghi Effendi immediately described this event as 'of such capital significance as only future happenings, steadily and mysteriously unfolding at the world centre of our Faith, can adequately demonstrate'.[32] The Purest Branch, 'the martyred son, the companion, and amanuensis of Bahá'u'lláh', and the 'saintly mother of 'Abdu'l-Bahá', were 'at long last reunited with the Greatest Holy Leaf with whom they had so abundantly shared the tribulations of one of the most distressing episodes of the Heroic Age of the Faith of Bahá'u'lláh':

> Avenged, eternally safeguarded, befittingly glorified, they repose embosomed in the heart of Carmel, hidden beneath its sacred soil, interred in one single spot, lying beneath the shadow of the twin holy Tombs, and facing across the bay, on an eminence of unequalled loveliness and beauty, the silver-city of 'Akká, the Point of Adoration of the entire Bahá'í world, and the Door of Hope for all mankind.[33]

1940

By 1940, ten National Spiritual Assemblies had been formed. These included the Assemblies of Australia and New Zealand, British Isles, Caucasus, Egypt, Germany and Austria, India and Burma, Iraq, Iran, Turkistan and the United States and Canada. With the beginning of the World War, however, the National Assemblies of Germany and Austria, Caucasus and Turkistan were forced to disband by their respective governments.[1]

A dedication and a commemoration

In February, Dhikru'lláh Khádem and his wife Javidukht returned to Haifa on another pilgrimage. They had the bounty of being present at the dedication of the monuments to Mírzá Mihdí and Navváb, the son and wife of Bahá'u'lláh, on 9 February. The event began with a large gathering at the Pilgrim House followed by a visit to the Shrines of the Báb and 'Abdu'l-Bahá. The Guardian asked Mr Khádem to chant two prayers, which he later said were for reducing the persecution of the Bahá'ís in Iran and for opening the doors of pilgrimage to the Iranian believers. The Guardian then gathered the rose petals from the Shrines of the Báb and 'Abdu'l-Bahá and spread them on two white sheets which were taken to the burial monuments and laid over them. Shoghi Effendi then placed a rose on each 'with such care that it seemed as if he were searching for the exact spot to adorn their holy and blessed hearts, an act, the tenderness of which deeply moved all who were present at the dedication'. The Guardian then led the procession to the Monument of the Greatest Holy Leaf where he chanted the Tablet revealed for her by Bahá'u'lláh.[2]

Shoghi Effendi then turned toward the Monument of Navváb and recited passages from the book of Isaiah 54:2-7, saying that 'Abdu'l-Bahá had explained that this chapter in the Old Testament was addressed to her:

> Enlarge the place of thy tent, and let them stretch forth the curtains of thine habitations: spare not, lengthen thy cords, and strengthen thy stakes; For thou shalt break forth on the right hand and on the left; and thy seed shall inherit the Gentiles, and make the desolate cities to be inhabited. Fear not; for thou shalt not be ashamed: neither be thou confounded; for thou shalt not be put to shame . . . For thy Maker is thine husband; the Lord of hosts is his name; and thy Redeemer the Holy One of Israel; The God of the whole earth shall he be called . . . For a small moment have I forsaken thee; but with great mercies will I gather thee.[3]

The Guardian concluded by saying, 'Thanks to God, now their holy, blessed remains have been placed in pure, shining marble, and the promises of God have been fulfilled. The result of these prophecies will become manifest in the second Bahá'í century.'[4]

The next day, 10 February, the anniversary of the birth of Bahá'u'lláh by the lunar calendar, Shoghi Effendi sent all the pilgrims in two cars to Bahjí. In the afternoon, the pilgrims and resident Bahá'ís gathered on the ground floor of the Mansion to await the Guardian. When he arrived, the group moved to the garden facing the Shrine of Bahá'u'lláh. Some sat on the ground and some in wicker chairs. Shoghi Effendi saw each person to a seat then sat in a wicker chair himself. After talking about Bahá'u'lláh, Shoghi Effendi asked one of the group to chant the Tablet of the Feast, then he led the friends into the Shrine. He anointed each person with attar of roses then went to the threshold and placed his head upon it. Dhikru'lláh Khádem then chanted two prayers, after which the Guardian chanted the Tablet of Visitation. After a moment of silence, the Guardian backed away from the threshold, keeping his eyes fixed on the entrance.[5]

Before the Khadems returned home, Shoghi Effendi gave Dhikru'lláh Khádem two missions: to arrange for Iranian pilgrims to receive permission to go on pilgrimage and to encourage Iranian Bahá'ís to pioneer. In the latter, he was particularly successful.[6]

The passing of May Maxwell

On 24 January, May Maxwell sailed from New York for Buenos Aires, Argentina, with her niece, Jeanne Bolles. May had arisen to answer a call from the Guardian for Bahá'ís from the American community to pioneer and travel teach in South America and she was excited by the opportunity. They arrived on 27 February. Salvador Tormo, a member of the local Bahá'í community, had gone to the dock to meet them, but unfortunately was unable to find them. But May was radiant, 'like a girl of sixteen in her joyous enthusiasm'. This enthusiasm was tempered by May losing her purse with $250 and spending the first night in a very noisy hotel. The next day, they moved to the much quieter City Hotel where May had a very refreshing sleep. The next evening, 29 February, May and Jeanne dined together, then received their first phone call from Haig Kevorkian, a Bahá'í originally from Armenia. But the next morning, 1 March, May had a terrible pain in her breast and by that afternoon she had departed the physical plane.[7]

Four cables arrived for Shoghi Effendi, and Rúḥíyyih Khánum took them up to him. He opened and read each one then, as she recounted the moment, then he looked up at her

with a mixture of shock, love and compassion on his face. She said the look frightened her, and she began backing away until she reached the wall. She said she wanted to sink into the wall so deep was the fear engendered in her by that look. Shoghi Effendi went over to her, held her in his arms and broke the news to her with great tenderness. He told her 'Now I will be your mother'. Then he spoke of the high station of May Maxwell in the Abhá Kingdom, of her joy in at long last having reached her heart's desire, of her nearness to her beloved Lord and Master, 'Abdu'l-Bahá. Then gently, in order to dispel her shaking grief, he began to talk to Amatu'l-Bahá in a lighter mood, to describe her mother's activities in the next world, where she was going and what she was doing in that sublime company. She would have been ushered immediately into the presence of Bahá'u'lláh first, of course, he assured her. And no sooner had she come there than she naturally asked permission to tell Him about her precious daughter. But she talked so much that Bahá'u'lláh had finally become tired and had passed her on to

'Abdu'l-Bahá. Here again she did nothing but talk about her beautiful daughter, until at length, exhausted, 'Abdu'l-Bahá passed her on to the Greatest Holy Leaf. And there she is still talking about her beloved daughter, stopping every passing member of the Concourse with her opening lines, 'Do let me tell you about my daughter . . .!' By the time he reached this point in his narrative, Rúḥíyyih Khánum was laughing through her tears.[8]

The day after May Maxwell's death, Shoghi Effendi sent to the National Spiritual Assembly of the United States and Canada a cable calling for memorial gatherings to be held in 'both Americas' in her name, summarizing 'the life, the death, and enduring legacy of this immortal apostle of 'Abdu'l-Bahá', and confirming 'her rank as a martyr of the Cause'.[9]

Three Iraqis on pilgrimage

On 24 February, three Iraqi pilgrims arrived in Haifa after travelling through Mosul, Aleppo, Hama, Homs, Tripoli and Beirut. These were Adíb Baghdadi and Salmán Bloomi, secretary and treasurer, respectively, of the National Spiritual Assembly of Iraq, and 25-year-old Azíz Sabour, a teacher from Kurdistan. When they first met the Guardian, the overwhelming reverence of the Eastern Bahá'ís asserted itself and Azíz tried to bow down before him, but Shoghi Effendi said, 'God forbids, it is not permitted, but we may embrace.' He made the three men aware that they were not to treat him as many had done to 'Abdu'l-Bahá. Later, when one of the pilgrims tried to pull another back so that he was not walking next to the Guardian, but behind him, Shoghi Effendi plainly stated, 'No, no. I don't agree. Don't stay behind.'[10]

During their pilgrimage, they were able to visit Bahjí three times and the Archives twice. They also listened to him talk on many subjects. One of the first was how Bahá'í holy places were open to everyone. Mentioning that the British Commissioner and his wife had both visited the Shrine of the Báb and had taken off their shoes and entered, he compared that with the reception of Keith Ransom-Kehler when she tried to visit the Shrine of Imam Husayn in Iraq. The Shi'a clergy had refused her entry because she was a Christian and a woman. When Keith told them that she was grieved to not be allowed to visit the Shrine, 'they were surprised . . . that an American lady becomes grieved because of her being not allowed to visit the Shrine of the Commander of the Martyrs'.[11] Shoghi Effendi emphasized that the Bahá'ís believed in the station of the Imáms:

> The Bahá'ís are the only people who can prove the right of the Pure Imáms. Bahá'u'lláh proved their right in 'The Book of Certitude'. The friends of the West will prove their right and will promulgate Islam. This is an essential belief in our Faith. We acknowledge the validity of the Imámate Institute and the invalidity of the Caliphate. The greatest proof is the collapse of the Caliphate after thirteen centuries.[12]

When Azíz said that they tried to teach, but nobody would listen, the Guardian said,

> 'The people of the world shall suffer a great calamity. Unless they suffer, they do not wake up. The believers should also be ready. Trials, opposition and upheavals will take place in all human society, but that will lead to the establishment of the Most Great Peace. The belief of the Shi'ah in dissimulation (i.e. recanting the belief under duress and danger) is not acceptable in the Bahá'í Faith . . . It brings shame to the Cause and makes the enemies more daring. The Islamic court in Egypt, in Babbá, had issued its verdict saying, '*Bahá'ísm is an independent religion*'. So what do we Bahá'ís say?' He smiled and said, 'Do we say we are Muslims?' . . .
>
> For the sake of this point, teaching the Faith to the Shi'ah is easier than to the Sunnîs . . . But, this is the belief of the people of Bahá . . . So don't admit anyone into the Community, unless he has professed the truth of the Pure Imáms.[13]

The Guardian also talked about the Mansion of Bahjí. After their first visit, he asked if they had gone to the room of Bahá'u'lláh. He then noted that he had specifically not put electric lights in the room, but had kept the original lighting. He also said that he had placed 5,000 books in 40 languages, both Eastern and Western, in the various other rooms. Recounting some of the history of the Mansion, He told his visitors that when Mírzá Muḥammad-'Alí and the Covenant-breakers forcibly took the keys to the Shrine of Bahá'u'lláh after the passing of the Master, the British Governor intervened and took the keys himself, denying both the Bahá'ís and the Covenant-breakers access to the Holy Shrine while he determined the true ownership. The Governor was then astonished when he received cables from the 600 Bahá'í centres in Iran protesting the actions of the Covenant-breakers. Within a year, the keys were back in the hands of the Bahá'ís. Shoghi Effendi said that when the Mansion came back into the hands of the Bahá'ís in 1929, the Sham'ah family of Damascus still had a one-third interest in it. The Covenant-breakers tried to acquire that interest through bribery and blackmail, using a son of Mírzá Muḥammad-'Alí, Músá Bahá'í, who worked as an official in the Estate Registry. They succeeded in acquiring a one-sixth interest (which would later cause problems, in 1952).[14] Though Músá Bahá'í tried to slow land purchases by the Bahá'ís, by 1940 he had officially registered 32 land transactions from the name of Shoghi Effendi into the names of the local branches of the National Spiritual Assemblies of America and India.[15]

Mr Baghdadi asked if the number of members of the Universal House of Justice could be more than nine. The Guardian responded by saying, 'Not only can that be, but the number of all the Houses of Justice, local and national, will increase afterwards, but not now.'[16]

Shoghi Effendi asked the pilgrims about the House of Bahá'u'lláh in Baghdad. They told him that the Shi'a had designated the house as 'Huseiniyyah' (place for ceremonies). The Guardian responded, saying that, 'Yes, it is "Huseiniyyah" after the Name of Bahá'u'lláh: Ḥusayn 'Alí'.

On 1 March, Shoghi Effendi was 'pale with sorrow' and told the Iraqi pilgrims of the passing of May Maxwell:

> She taught the Faith to Mrs Keith Ransom Kehler, to Mr Dreyfus, to Mrs Barney. Keith is her spiritual daughter . . . Forty years ago the Americans established the Faith in Europe and now they are establishing it in America! Men and women, young and old are serving the Faith in the South. The lights are shining from America. The Friends should be waiting for the glad tidings from America in order that they increase their own courage and follow the model of their services. All these are the fulfilment of the promises of 'Abdu'l-Bahá . . . Doctors told Mrs Maxwell that she was ill and should rest, but she did not heed to this advice. She travelled to Argentina and

crossed twelve thousand miles. This is something hard. She had the hope of visiting the Blessed House of the Báb in Shiraz.[17]

When the Fast started on 2 March, the three Iraqi pilgrims tried to fast. On the first day, Shoghi Effendi sent them breakfast at dawn, but also indicated that fasting was not required for pilgrims.[18]

One day, Mr Baghdadi commented on the savagery of those opposed to the Faith in Iraq. This led the Guardian to talk about the future divine civilization, after which Mr Baghdadi asked if the divine civilization would be established in 1963. The Guardian responded:

'Calamities and trials are necessary for spreading the Cause and unless they happen the Cause will not spread. The material upheavals must precede the establishment of the Divine Civilization. Iran is the Cradle of the Cause. America is the Cradle of the Divine Civilization . . .

'This date is its beginning. The Americans spread the Cause everywhere.' I [Azíz] asked, 'Is this the effect of the visit of 'Abdu'l-Bahá to America?' He said, 'This is one of its effects and the effects of the "Tablets of The Divine Plan". Have you read "The Divine Plan"? The Americans opened North America, South America, South Africa, Australia, France, Germany, Sweden and [the] Balkans. They are energetic and attracted. The German Friends are meticulous. The present political condition shall change and they will open their neighbouring countries . . .

'This [present day] civilization can never meet with the Divine Civilization, as water can't mix with oil. They always remain separate. The Friends and especially the Spiritual Assemblies should not imitate the politicians. They should serve the Faith bravely and with sublimity, with exaltation and with cleverness. Their criterion is to behave in an opposite way to the behaviour of the politicians, who can tell lies and make false promises. The Friends and the Spiritual Assemblies should maintain justice even with the enemies of the Faith.'[19]

Shoghi Effendi had just received the first six parts of Volume VIII of *The Bahá'í World* for review. He noted that the post office didn't open the packages because they trusted the Bahá'ís. The Guardian's worldwide communications did cause some problems for the telegraph office, however. When 'Alí-Aṣghar, the Guardian's messenger, took Shoghi Effendi's cables for transmission, the officials were often surprised and confused, saying that they did not know where Guatemala and Puerto Rico were. After searching their books, they would have to ask 'Alí-Aṣghar for help. The cost of sending international telegrams was high, about £30.[20]

Shoghi Effendi also gave the pilgrims instructions. One day he noted that there were 100 Bahá'í centres in America and 600 in Iran, but only 9 in Iraq. He told them that they should raise the number of centres in Iraq to 19. He emphasized the need to establish Bahá'í centres in the north and south of the country, including Ahsa, the birthplace of Shaykh Ahmad. The Guardian also told them that he wanted pioneers to settle in Sulaymaniyyih and Kirkuk. After their pilgrimage, the Kirkuk goal was quickly fulfilled by Azíz Sabour because of a passport problem he had while in the Holy Land. The problem forced him to be a week late returning to work at his school, for which he was dismissed from his job. Azíz took advantage of his dismissal to pioneer to Kirkuk.[21]

When the three pilgrims from Iraq left on 7 March, Shoghi Effendi gave them copies of Esslemont's *Bahá'u'lláh and the New Era* in 24 languages, a photograph of the inside of the Shrine of Bahá'u'lláh for their Archives, and a photograph of the Mashriqu'l-Adhkár in Chicago for the National Assembly. Individually, he gave them each two photographs of the Chicago Mashriqu'l-Adhkár. To Azíz, he said to show the photos to the Kurds.[22]

A wartime journey to England and Africa

After the passing of May Maxwell, her husband Sutherland was left alone in Montreal, so Shoghi Effendi quickly invited him to live in Haifa. Sutherland accepted and sailed to Rome on the S.S. *Rex*. Meanwhile, Shoghi Effendi had decided that he needed to travel to England. War was already raging in Europe, so getting permission and visas for this journey was extremely difficult. The British Palestinian authorities couldn't issue the necessary visas, so the Guardian appealed to Lord Lamington, his old friend from the beginning of the British occupation of Haifa, but correspondence was much delayed:

Impelled by the forces which so mysteriously animated all his decisions, the Guardian decided to proceed to Italy, for which country
we had obtained a visa, and we therefore left Haifa on 15 May in a
small and smelly Italian aquaplane, with the water sloshing around
under the boards our feet rested on as if we were in an old row-boat.
A few days later we arrived in Rome and I went to Genoa to meet
my father who arrived on the last sailing the S.S. *Rex* ever made
as a passenger ship. As soon as we returned the Guardian sent my
father and me to the British Consul to inquire if our visa had by any
chance been transferred from Palestine, but there was no news and
the Consul said he was absolutely powerless to give us a visa as all
authorizations had to come from London and he was no longer in
a position to contact his government! We returned with this heart-
breaking news to the Guardian. He sent us back again. Of course we
obeyed him implicitly because he <u>was</u> the Guardian but neither my
father nor I could see what more there was we could possibly do than
we had already done. Nevertheless we found ourselves again seated
opposite the Consul and saying very much the same things all over
again, with the exception that I happened to mention that Shoghi
Effendi was the successor and grandson of Sir 'Abdu'l-Bahá 'Abbás.
I had already, of course, said that he was the Head of the Bahá'í
Faith and so on. The Consul looked at me and said 'I remember
'Abdu'l-Bahá . . .' and went on to recount some contact he had had
with the Master; he was obviously deeply touched by this memory.
He took our passport, stamped a visa for England in it and said
he had no right whatsoever to do so and that it was not worth the
paper it was stamped on, but it was all he could do; if we wished to
try to enter England with it, that must be our own decision and we
risked being refused. With this we immediately left Italy for France,
passing through Menton on 25 May and proceeding to Marseilles.
Within days, Italy entered the war against the Allies.[23]

Barely having escaped, the trio took the train to Paris where they found
'every station . . . crowded with thousands of refugees fleeing before the
rapidly crumbling Allied front in the North.' There they discovered that
all ports to England were closed – except one at St Malo in Brittany. St
Malo, like Paris, was swarming with refugees and British trying to get
home. Twice a day for a week, Rúhíyyih Khánum and her father went

to the boat company to see if a ship was available. All the while, Shoghi Effendi, from morning to night 'would mostly sit quite still, immobile as a stone image, and I had the impression he was being consumed with suffering, like a candle burning itself away.' Rúḥíyyih Khánum wrote:

> It may seem strange to others that he should have been terribly concerned, but a mind like his was so infinitely better equipped to understand the danger to the Cause of our situation than we were – and God knows I was ill with worry too. Both my father and I were still feeling the great shock of my mother's sudden death from a heart attack and this, combined with everything else, made him, at least, almost numb. Not so the Guardian, who realized that if he fell into the hands of the Nazis, who had already banned the Cause in their own country and were closely associated with the Grand Mufti of Jerusalem – who was actively engaged in Arab politics and the avowed enemy of the Guardian – he would very likely be imprisoned, if not worse, and the Cause itself be left with no leader and no one to encourage and guide the Bahá'í world at such a time of world chaos. It seems to me the situation was very similar to those days in Akka when the Master had been in danger of being taken off to a new place of exile and when He too had waited for news of a ship.[24]

Finally, during the night of 2 June, two boats reached St Malo. Shoghi Effendi, Rúḥíyyih Khánum and Mr Maxwell boarded the first, and reached Southampton the following morning. The Germans arrived at St Malo the next day.

Why Shoghi Effendi needed to go to Britain isn't certain. He did send a few cables during this time. In one, sent to America on 20 July, he noted that the 'long-predicted world-encircling conflagration, essential pre-requisite to world unification, is inexorably moving to its appointed climax.' The Guardian wasn't interested in an old world order that was consuming itself, because the cable focused on what needed to be done regardless of the world condition: 'The Divinely-appointed plan must and will likewise pursue undeflected its predestined course. Time is pressing. The settlement of the two remaining Latin Republics, the sounder consolidation through formation of firmly-knit groups in newly-opened territories, the provision of adequate means for the ornamentation . . . of first story of Temple, stand out as vital . . .'[25]

Shoghi Effendi's party had almost as much trouble getting out of England as they had getting in and it was only due to his station as Guardian and Sutherland Maxwell's friendship with the Canadian High Commissioner that they were able to leave. But the only ship they could travel on was going to South Africa. On 28 July, the trio sailed on the S.S. *Cape Town Castle*. Rúḥíyyih Khánum wrote that it was a

> fast ship and once we had left the shores of England in a large convoy we were on our own; I remember how I used to watch the strange zigzag wake of the ship on the sea as she pursued an erratic course in order to make her a less vulnerable target for submarines. As Italy's entry into the war had closed the Mediterranean to Allied ships the route through Africa was the only way open to us to get back to Palestine.[26]

Once in South Africa, it was decided that Sutherland's health was too poor for such a long overland journey, so he was left in Durban to find air passage in the face of a long waiting list and the low priority of non-government and non-military travellers. While waiting for a flight, Sutherland filled his time by designing a tombstone for his wife's grave.

Shoghi Effendi had made a similar journey across Africa from Cape Town to Cairo by car in late 1929. Now, he and Rúḥíyyih Khánum travelled through Rhodesia (now Zimbabwe) where they visited Cecil Rhodes' grave at Bulawayo and went to Victoria Falls,[27] and then into the adjacent jungle to experience the rainforest.[28]

Shoghi Effendi had long been fascinated by the Belgian Congo and had tried to obtain a visa on that first trip in 1929, but was unable to do so.

> His venturesome spirit, his love of scenic beauty, attracted him to the high mountains and deep jungles of the world and had led him to make his previous trip. Now, by some strange miracle, in the very middle of the war, we were able to get a visa for the Congo. When we reached Stanleyville and made an excursion into the deep virgin jungle, I realized that it was Shoghi Effendi's love of natural beauty that had been one of the reasons which had led him there; he wanted to see the flowering jungle. Alas, it was neither the place nor the season for this and we went on our way disappointed.[29]

Shoghi Effendi and Rúḥíyyih Khánum entered the Congo at Lubum-bashi, a major copper mining centre, where the Guardian admired beautiful green malachite carved into various objects.[30] While in the Congo, their car broke down on an isolated jungle track. While it was being repaired, Rúḥíyyih Khánum asked Shoghi Effendi if she could stretch her legs a bit. With his assent and a caution about lions, she walked off down the lonesome road, 'drinking in the beauty of untouched nature', and completely oblivious of the passing time. All of a sudden, a man on a bicycle appeared and told her that 'the gentleman in the car was very worried over her'. That is when she realized that she had been gone for almost two hours. She borrowed the man's bicycle and raced back to her worried husband.[31]

From Stanleyville in the Congo (now called Kisangani), they made a three-day journey to Juba, Sudan, after which they travelled down the Nile by boat to Khartoum, which Rúḥíyyih Khánum said she considered to be 'the hottest place on earth'. Relaxing at their hotel in Khartoum after dinner one evening, they were amazed when

> up out of the dark came a group of air passengers to spend the night, and with them Mr W. S. Maxwell! It was a strange fluke indeed that brought us together in the heart of Africa and it was also very reassuring as neither of us had the faintest idea where the other was and no way whatsoever of getting in touch. In Durban Shoghi Effendi had simply instructed my father to go to Palestine, to a hotel in Nazareth and wait for us there, when we could all three return to Haifa together.[32]

In a second surprise, the Governor-General Sir Stewart Symes was an old acquaintance and invited them to lunch at the Palace on 1 October. The epochal journey was finally completed six months after it began. Rúḥíyyih Khánum noted: 'Although Shoghi Effendi never visited the Western Hemisphere and never went farther east than Damascus it is interesting to note he twice traversed Africa from south to north.'[33]

The secretary of the National Spiritual Assembly of the Bahá'ís of Egypt, Muhammad Mustafa, was working in the clearing section of the State Railways, Telegraphs and Telephones office in Cairo. Part of his job was to file copies of all cables and telegrams into the archives. One day, he encountered a cable saying that Shoghi Effendi would be passing through Cairo on his way to Haifa. Mr Mustafa was completely bewildered by this mysterious telegram because he had heard nothing about the Guardian's unexpected visit. The telegram specifically mentioned 'Shoghi Rabbani', but was not addressed to any of the Bahá'ís or the National Assembly. Mr Mustafa quickly checked all possible sources that could have had information about the Guardian's visit. He checked the post office box, the post office near the Ḥaziratu'l-Quds and the other believers, asking whether anyone had received any letters or cables for the National Assembly. There was nothing. He finally decided that if the Guardian had wanted to meet the community he would have contacted them. If he hadn't contacted the Bahá'ís, it probably meant that they should not try to find him when he passed through.

Mr Mustafa realized that he couldn't spread the news that the Guardian would be passing through Cairo because the cable had not been addressed to him. Trying to keep such information secret was extremely difficult, though, and the next day he contacted the chairman of the National Assembly, Judge 'Abdu'l-Jalíl Bey Saʿad. The thought of Shoghi Effendi coming to Cairo was electrifying. The two men, however, understood that they could only have the pleasure of the sweet hope that they would encounter Shoghi Effendi. Their wishes unfortunately went unfulfilled and the Guardian passed through unseen on his way to Haifa.[34]

Finally back in Haifa on 27 December, Rúḥíyyih Khánum wrote:

> It seems unbelievable that in the midst of so many anxieties and after half-a-year's absence during which we seemed to be racing all the time on the tip of a tidal wave (first to get away from Haifa in time and then to get back to Haifa in time) the Guardian should have had the mental power and physical strength upon his return to the Holy Land to sit down and write such a book as *The Promised Day Is Come* – a book in which he made it quite clear that the 'retributory calamity' which had overtaken mankind, whatever its political and economic causes might be, was primarily due to its having ignored for a hundred years the Message of God for this day.[35]

Though the Second World War ultimately didn't reach Haifa directly, the threat was always there. Rúḥíyyih Khánum noted, however, that though he remained outwardly calm, the Guardian had a constant burden of responsibility that he could not abandon even for a short time:

> he could never lay it down for a single moment. I remember on one occasion, when I was frantic because he always had to have everything referred to him for decision, even when he was ill, he said that other leaders, even Prime Ministers, could delegate their powers for at least a short time if they were forced to, but that he could not delegate his for a single moment as long as he was alive. No one else was divinely guided to fulfil his function and he could not delegate his guidance to someone else.[36]

1941–1944

1941 was a time of intense anxiety for Shoghi Effendi. It was in this year that the Covenant-breaking activities of his own family came to a head, as well as those of Ahmad Sohrab, with whom in earlier years he had shared the task of translating the Master's correspondence. And this was taking place against the backdrop of the Second World War. Although the region was not under direct attack, the repercussions included an abortive revolution in Iraq and continued with the German General Rommel pushing the British nearly to Alexandria, the occupation of Crete (which the Nazis saw as a springboard for the conquest of the Middle East), and the continued enmity of the Grand Mufti of Jerusalem, who had aligned himself with the Nazis. Haifa was a strategic port oil refinery for the British and was defended by anti-aircraft guns scattered around the city, two within a mile of the House of the Master. They often had air raids and a few bombs fell on the city, but the biggest concern for Shoghi Effendi was shrapnel from the guns, which fell indiscriminately when they were fired. Large chunks of metal not uncommonly fell near the Monuments of the Greatest Holy Leaf, the Purest Branch and Navváb, but none were ever damaged. The authorities required residents to build an air raid shelter, but neither Shoghi Effendi nor Rúḥíyyih Khánum ever went into it. When the British invaded Lebanon, residents of Haifa could hear the heavy firing and on occasion French Vichy planes dive-bombed the port in Haifa. Unlike the First World War, communication continued to the Bahá'í communities in North America and Persia. Only in Japan, Europe, Burma and, briefly, Iraq were the Bahá'í communities cut off.[1]

The war forced everyone to be as economical as possible and the Guardian was very aware of financial matters:

He more than once refused to permit an individual to make the pilgrimage who he knew was in debt, saying he must first pay his debts. I never saw the Guardian settle a bill he had not first carefully added up, whether it was for a meal or a payment of thousands of dollars! If there was an overcharge he pointed it out – and also if there was an undercharge. Many times I went to astonished people and called to their attention that their addition was wrong and they should do it again or they would be the losers. He also was a determined bargainer, never paying what he felt was too much for a thing. More than once, when a beautiful ornament for the Shrines, Archives, or gardens was too expensive, and the seller could not or would not meet the Guardian's price, he would not buy it even though he wanted it and had the money. He just considered it wrong and would not do it. Although Shoghi Effendi for many years had had a private automobile and chauffeur (like 'Abdu'l-Bahá before him), because spare parts were not procurable for it during the worst years of the war he had it sold and used taxis. I have no doubt that as with sufficient money one can usually buy anything he could have procured another car, but it never entered his mind. He was against extravagance, ostentation and luxury as such, denying himself and others many things because he felt they were either not justified or not appropriate.[2]

The Promised Day Is Come

Since his return from Africa and war-torn Europe, Shoghi Effendi had been working on the book-length letter entitled *The Promised Day Is Come*, whose title recalled the words of Bahá'u'lláh: 'The promised day is come, the day when tormenting trials will have surged above your heads, and beneath your feet.' In just three months the letter was finished and on 28 March he sent it to the Bahá'ís whom he addressed as 'Friends and fellow-heirs of the Kingdom of Bahá'u'lláh'. As Amatu'l-Bahá Rúḥíyyih Khánum has written, the letter 'thunders his denunciations of the perversity and sinfulness of this generation, using as his missiles quotations from the lips of Bahá'u'lláh Himself . . . The Guardian paints a terrible, terrifying and majestic picture of the plight to which the human race has been reduced through its steadfast rejection of Bahá'u'lláh.'[3]

Shoghi Effendi's command of language

By 1941, Rúḥíyyih Khánum was Shoghi Effendi's principal secretary, writing thousands of letters on his behalf. She was the first to admit that her handwriting and spelling were not always perfect. 'If you look at some of those letters, you will see that Shoghi Effendi, on reading them, has put a cross over the t's, a loop over the l's, a dot over the i's, and made the a's look like a's and the o's look like o's!' She also made fun of her own spelling which was sometimes ingenious and occasionally outrageous. Since she was never sure of it, she would ask Shoghi Effendi for the correct spelling of words and one day, in humorous exasperation, he turned to her and said, 'Before you came into my life, I could spell; now you have confused me!'⁴ Shoghi Effendi, on the other hand, was a master of both Persian and English. Rúḥíyyih Khánum comments:

> The language in which Shoghi Effendi wrote, whether for the Bahá'ís of the West or of the East, set a standard which should effectively prevent them from descending to the level of illiterate literates which often so sadly characterizes the present generation as far as the use and appreciation of words are concerned. He never compromised with the ignorance of his readers but expected them, in their thirst for knowledge, to overcome their ignorance. Shoghi Effendi chose, to the best of his great ability, the right vehicle for his thought and it made no difference to him whether the average person was going to know the word he used or not. After all, what one does not know one can find out. Although he had such a brilliant command of language, he frequently reinforced his knowledge by certainty through looking up the word he planned to use in Webster's big dictionary. Often one of my functions was to hand it to him and it was a weighty tome indeed! Not infrequently his choice would be the third or fourth usage of the word, sometimes bordering on the archaic, but it was the exact word that conveyed his meaning and so he used it. I remember my mother once saying that to become a Bahá'í was like entering a university, only one never finished learning, never graduated. In his translations of the Bahá'í writings, and above all in his own compositions, Shoghi Effendi set a standard that educates and raises the cultural level of the reader at the same time that it feeds his mind and soul with thoughts and truth.⁵

'Alí-Akbar Furútan

Early in 1941, 'Alí-Akbar Furútan was able to go on pilgrimage from Iran with his wife, 'Atá'íyyih, his mother, Ṣughrá, his eight-year-old daughter and several others. They travelled overland and at the border of Palestine were asked about two 'very expensive silk rugs' they carried. Explaining to the Customs official that they were for the House of 'Abdu'l-Bahá, the rugs were released without charge. The Customs official then travelled to Haifa with the pilgrims on the same bus. The man was very taken with the rugs and offered to give 'Alí-Akbar the money if he would buy two similar rugs and send them to him, saying he would trust him only because he was a Bahá'í.[6]

The Furútans arrived in Haifa on 16 February. 'Atá'íyyih, her daughter and Sughrá were taken immediately to meet the women in the House of the Master while the men were taken to the basement. Soon, however, they were escorted into the presence of Shoghi Effendi. At first, the pilgrims tried to prostrate themselves at the feet of the Guardian as they would have done with 'Abdu'l-Bahá, but Shoghi Effendi quickly prevented the action and brought them into a room. After asking about the Bahá'í community in Iran, Shoghi Effendi turned to Mr Furútan and said, 'You are the secretary of both the National and Local Spiritual Assemblies. The affairs of the National Spiritual Assembly are conducted in a very organized manner, and I testify to your work. Your services are now local and national, and they will be international in the future.'[7]

Most days during the pilgrimage, the Furútans went from the Pilgrim House to the House of the Master at 4 p.m. The women would go to meet Rúḥíyyih Khánum while the men met with Shoghi Effendi. One of the Guardian's topics was that the Bahá'í community in Iran had to become distinguished from other communities and that the believers must 'strive that their individual actions, in all aspects of their personal lives, contribute to the emancipation of the Cause. Nor must they conceal their faith . . .' He also said that since women had achieved a new level of freedom in Iran, including the right to go without the veil, they should take advantage of this freedom to engage in more activities.[8]

The pilgrims spent three days in Akka and Bahjí, including two nights in the Mansion. They also visited the House of 'Abbúd, the

Mosque of al-Jazzár where 'Abdu'l-Bahá had met Badí, the youth who had suffered martyrdom after carrying the Tablet from Bahá'u'lláh to the Shah of Persia, and the Khán-i-'Avámíd, the caravanserai where some of the early Bahá'ís had stayed. Shoghi Effendi had written them a note which they took to Mazra'ih, where Bahá'u'lláh had lived. The house at that time was occupied by an English couple, retired General McNeill and his wife Lilian, who was a Bahá'í, and the Guardian's note gained them access to the room of Bahá'u'lláh. The same note, when presented to the barracks guard at the Most Great Prison, allowed them to visit the cell of Bahá'u'lláh.[9]

On 24 February, Shoghi Effendi rented a car and took the Furútans on a drive up to the top of Mount Carmel, stopping at the site of the future Mashriqu'l-Adhkár. The Guardian noted: 'The first Bahá'í Mashriqu'l-Adhkár was built on the plain of 'Ishqábád. The second Mashriqu'l-Adhkár was built on the banks of Lake Michigan. The Mashriqu'l-Adhkár of Tehran will be built on the slope of a mountain. When the Mashriqu'l-Adhkár of Haifa is erected on Mount Carmel, its view will include all the three views: sea, mountain and plain.' Later, back at the House of the Master, Shoghi Effendi talked about the development of the terraces around the Shrine of the Báb. The nine terraces below the Shrine were already partially developed and the Guardian spoke of the nine additional terraces that would lead to the top of Mount Carmel. Each terrace, he said, would be illuminated by electricity.[10]

After twenty-three days, the Furútans returned to Iran. Ten years later, in 1951, Mr Furútan was named a Hand of the Cause of God.

Failure of Ahmad Sohrab's rebellion

In 1941, Ahmad Sohrab's attempted rebellion peaked and failed. Shoghi Effendi addressed his activities in a message to America on 12 August:

> The extinction of the influence precariously exerted by some of these enemies, the decline that has set in in the fortunes of others, the sincere repentance expressed by still others, and their subsequent reinstatement and effectual participation in the teaching and administrative activities of the Faith, constitute in themselves sufficient evidence of the unconquerable power and invincible spirit

which animates those who stand identified with and loyally carry out the provisions and injunctions of the Will and Testament of 'Abdu'l-Bahá.

And now more particularly concerning the prime mover of this latest agitation [Ahmad Sohrab], which, whatever its immediate consequences, will sooner or later come to be regarded as merely one more of those ugly and abortive attempts designed to undermine the foundation, and obscure the purpose, of the Administrative Order of the Faith of Bahá'u'lláh. Obscure in his origin, ambitious of leadership, untaught by the lesson of such as have erred before him, odious in the hopes he nurses, contemptible in the methods he pursues, shameless in his deliberate distortions of truths he has long since ceased to believe in, ludicrous in his present isolation and helplessness, wounded and exasperated by the downfall which his own folly has precipitated, he, the latest protagonist of a spurious cause, cannot but in the end be subjected, as remorselessly as his infamous predecessors, to the fate which they invariably have suffered.

Generated by the propelling and purifying forces of a mysterious Faith, born of delusion or malice, winning a fleeting notoriety derived from the precarious advantages of wealth, fame or fortune, these movements sponsored by deluded, self-seeking adventurers find themselves, sooner or later, enmeshed in the machinations of their authors, are buried in shame, and sink eventually into complete oblivion.

The schism which their foolish leaders had contrived so sedulously to produce within the Faith, will soon, to their utter amazement, come to be regarded as a process of purification, a cleansing agency, which, far from decimating the ranks of its followers, reinforces its indestructible unity, and proclaims anew to a world, skeptical or indifferent, the cohesive strength of the institutions of that Faith, the incorruptibility of its purposes and principles, and the recuperative powers inherent in its community life.[11]

The family of the Master breaks the Covenant

This year, 1941, was also a year of reckoning within the family of 'Abdu'l-Bahá. After the death of Mírzá Muḥammad-'Alí in 1937, Bahá'u'lláh's youngest son Badí'u'lláh had taken his place as Shoghi Effendi's arch foe and, working with Siyyid 'Alí Afnán, another supporter of Mírzá Muhammad-'Alí, took aim at the family of 'Abdu'l-Bahá. Siyyid 'Alí Afnán had joined forces with Mírzá Muhammad-'Alí immediately after the ascension of Bahá'u'lláh. At one point during the time of 'Abdu'l-Bahá, the Siyyid had repented, but that repentance had been short-lived.[12]

The members of 'Abdu'l-Bahá's family enjoyed their high status, their association with the Guardian and the adulation they received from the pilgrims. The Covenant-breakers took advantage of that. All of 'Abdu'l-Bahá's family knew that Covenant-breakers were to be shunned and at first they did so, but the whisperings of those opposed to Shoghi Effendi began to have an effect on the elevated egos in the family. Between 1941 and 1945, two of Shoghi Effendi's sisters and five of his cousins married Covenant-breakers, and the families of 'Abdu'l-Bahá's daughters Túbá Khánum and Rúhá Khánum moved in with Covenant-breakers. Years of behind-the-scenes contact came out into the open in 1941. First, Shoghi Effendi's oldest sister, Rúhangíz, married Nayyir Afnán, a son of Siyyid 'Alí Afnán. He was to become the Guardian's greatest enemy, though his enmity had begun much earlier. A pilgrim who had arrived shortly after Shoghi Effendi was named the Guardian remembered going to Bahjí and encountering Nayyir, who lived in a house between the Shrine of Bahá'u'lláh and the Pilgrim House. Nayyir was not happy and said that Shoghi Effendi was impatient and difficult to work with, but since he had been appointed in 'Abdu'l-Bahá's Will and Testament, he had to obey him. The remarks upset the pilgrim. When the pilgrim returned to Haifa, the Guardian asked if he had met anyone. He responded that he had met Nayyir. Shoghi Effendi then asked if Nayyir had said anything. The pilgrim couldn't repeat the dismaying conversation so said, 'Oh, nothing in particular.' By the next morning, however, realizing what he had done, the pilgrim went to Shoghi Effendi and told the true story. The Guardian's response was, 'We must be grateful that he accepts the Will and Testament. What he said about me doesn't matter.'[13]

Then his youngest sister, Mehrangíz, married another son of Siyyid 'Alí Afnán. One of Shoghi Effendi's cousins married yet another son. Then another cousin, at the instigation of Shoghi Effendi's sister Rúhangíz, married a granddaughter of the Siyyid. In October and

November, Shoghi Effendi was forced to send cables announcing the defection of his sisters and cousins. Túbá Khánum, a daughter of 'Abdu'l-Bahá, and her family were also expelled at the same time for living with their Covenant-breaking children. And by 1951, both of Shoghi Effendi's brothers, Ḥusayn and Riáz, had actively joined them as well.[14]

Rúḥíyyih Khánum became the Guardian's shield during these extremely difficult years. Violette Nakhjavani recounts:

> There was a time when Shoghi Effendi could not trust any member of his family to be alone with the Persian pilgrims for fear of the negative impact of their poisonous innuendoes and inferences. He would ask Rúḥíyyih Khánum to go down and sit with them. She told us that she had once been ill with jaundice, had had a fever and was as yellow as a canary, but despite this Shoghi Effendi sent her down to sit with the Persian women pilgrims. She could not go back up to bed until the last one had finally left . . . It was also in this turbulent period that Shoghi Effendi pulled her up short one day, and gesturing to her hand, said, 'Your destiny is in the palm of your own hand.' This was a great shock for her and made her realize that she was not immune to her own tests of faith. 'When Shoghi Effendi married me', she used to say, 'I felt safe and smug and thought I had nothing more to worry about, my destiny was in his hand.' She would always make us laugh when she finished this very serious tale.[15]

Shoghi Effendi once sent Rúḥíyyih Khánum to meet with Shoghi Effendi's cousin Rúḥí in an attempt to bring him back to the Covenant. He listened to her plea, but then closed the conversation by saying, 'I'll pray to Bahá'u'lláh that He will forgive Shoghi Effendi.'[16] Rúḥíyyih Khánum was very concerned. She wrote in her diary that the Master's family

> have gone a long way to crushing every ounce of spirit out of the Guardian. By nature he is cheerful and energetic and has a unique and marvellous brightness of nature that is capable of making him fairly scintillate when he is happy or enthused over something. But the perpetual strife of life with the Master's family, the blows he has

sustained in the course of being Guardian, (from various crises in the Cause) . . . have all clouded over . . . him. Whenever, (during the last 5 years I have been able to observe him), he has begun to brighten, someone would come along and plump down some weight of care or misery on him and that would be that! It is criminal! How many times I have heard him say: 'If I were only happy, if they would only make me happy, you would see what I would do for this Cause!' He is like a spring. Every time it begins to bubble and flow, something comes along and plugs it up again! When one realizes that all the work he has done for the Cause has been in spite of his sufferings and persecutions, and never because he was free and happy and at rest within himself, one realizes how great the accomplishment is and also one wonders what it might have been if he had been happy. Shoghi Effendi has been abused. That is the only word for it, abused, abused, abused. By now he has reached the point of a man fighting with his back to the wall. He says he will fight it out to the last round . . .'[17]

Rúḥíyyih Khánum was the only person on whom Shoghi Effendi could absolutely rely. She wrote, 'I was all alone: a wife, a companion, a secretary and the housekeeper.'

A rare pilgrim

There were very few pilgrims during the war, but a few did manage to find their way to Haifa. At Christmas 1941, Australian James Heggie managed to reach Haifa and the presence of Shoghi Effendi. He had joined the army specifically to get posted to the Middle East:

We couldn't get leave for a full month so it wasn't until just before Christmas 1941 that I got to Haifa on three days leave. After some difficulty I was able to contact the Bahá'ís, finding the Guardian just before dark inspecting the terracing of the Bahá'í gardens on Mt. Carmel and arranging to meet him the next morning. But that evening I was taken to the Archives by the Guardian's brother. Rúḥíyyih Khánum welcomed me the next morning at the house of 'Abdu'l-Bahá and sat in at the interview with the Guardian. The first of many. I was the first westerner to visit Haifa for over two years, and

as I'd just recently been to Wilmette the Guardian asked of many of
the friends, especially of Hyde Dunn, who'd died early in the year. I
was able on that occasion to visit 'Akká and Bahjí and the Garden of
Riḍván. I asked if it was possible to get a Bahá'í ring-stone as well as
some photos of recent date of Haifa and the offer of any Bahá'í book I
desired; as the only one I hadn't read was the recently published *Epistle
to the Son of the Wolf* I chose that book. Also I had an invitation to stay
at the Western Pilgrim House on my next visit – which was a month
later. This time I made the acquaintance of Sutherland Maxwell who
was staying in Haifa at the time, had a number of interviews with
the Guardian, one of which was of over an hour, and again visited
'Akká and Bahjí. This time I met the father of Shoghi Effendi who
had rooms at Bahjí. The Guardian liked to meet the young Bahá'ís
and to talk to them – they certainly felt the impact, and for a life
time. I couldn't tell anyone what the feelings were that I went through
during those visits to the Guardian but they established a direction
and planted a seed that has never ceased to grow. I was the first male
believer from Australia that the Guardian had met, before that he's
only met three others – Effie Baker in 1925, Clara Dunn about 1933,
and Ethel Dawe in 1938 on her return from England.[18]

1942

During these years, Shoghi Effendi was deeply immersed in preparing
and writing his seminal book *God Passes By*. Rúḥíyyih Khánum was his
proofreader, as Violette Nakhjavání describes:

> They would sit side by side, each holding several copies of pages typed
> by Shoghi Effendi, and for hours on end, they proof-read and trans-
> literated those endless Persian names together. She said from the time
> she married until the Guardian's passing, she was always in the room
> with him when he composed messages, both in English and Persian.
> He composed out loud, and always chanted the Persian in his heav-
> enly voice. For years after she treasured the pile of finished as well as
> unfinished embroidery which she used to sew during those hours.[19]

On 20 March 1942, Shoghi Effendi was busy working on *God Passes
By* while two army fighter planes buzzed around in the sky overhead.

Suddenly, the planes' wings touched and the pilots lost control. One plane came roaring down, barely missing Shoghi Effendi's room at the top of the House of the Master, and crashed in a ball of flame less than a hundred metres away.[20]

Sutherland Maxwell and the Shrine of the Báb

Sutherland Maxwell was now a Haifa resident, living in the Western Pilgrim House and having his meals with Shoghi Effendi and his daughter Rúḥíyyih Khánum. Though he was an internationally known architect and an eloquent Bahá'í, he was known in Haifa as May Maxwell's husband.[21] To illustrate Sutherland's relationship with the Guardian, Rúḥíyyih Khánum told the story of the attar of rose. Shoghi Effendi like to sprinkle himself with the aromatic fragrance, including his cheeks and moustache. One day, in an affectionate gesture, he similarly anointed Sutherland. Rúḥíyyih Khánum said that

> she would never forget the look of mingled horror and delight on her father's face! To be daubed with perfume was hardly in keeping with the habits of a Scotsman, but to have his cheeks caressed by his beloved Guardian was more than he felt he deserved. Caught between deference and distaste, he was overwhelmed by confusion.[22]

On another occasion, when Shoghi Effendi was away from Haifa during the summer, he left Sutherland in charge of 'all practical affairs in Haifa' and for 'the payment of all the workers and gardeners'. Sutherland was so worried about making mistakes that he divided the money he paid them into separate envelopes. Then, when Shoghi Effendi returned, he presented him with – instead of a list of accounts – a box full of empty envelopes covered with scribbles, leaving the Guardian in the dual states of delight and despair at the same time.[23]

Shoghi Effendi soon learned that Sutherland could be a great partner in his vision for the World Centre. Shoghi Effendi had, according to Rúḥíyyih Khánum, a 'perfect sense of taste and proportion' but 'he had to see it in a drawing or a model'. One day shortly after Sutherland came to live in Haifa, Shoghi Effendi asked his wife to make some drawings of some item. She looked at the Guardian and replied,

'But Shoghi Effendi, you have one of Canada's best architects across the street! Let him do it for you.' He had looked up at her surprised, and asked, 'Can your father do it?', to which she rejoined, 'Can he do it? He has built churches, hotels, parliament buildings, and numerous houses. This is child's play for him.'

This was the beginning of what Rúḥíyyih Khánum liked to call a 'partnership between the Guardian and my father.' [24]

It was to be a unique partnership. Over the next decade, Sutherland designed stairs, walls, pillars, lights, and garden entrances for the Guardian. He drew, painted and made models. When Shoghi Effendi asked him to design a main entrance to the Shrine of the Báb, Sutherland did so. When Rúḥíyyih Khánum brought her husband the completed colour drawing, Shoghi Effendi, sitting up in bed, looked long at the drawing then finally said, 'It's not fair!' When a shocked Rúḥíyyih Khánum asked what he meant, the Guardian replied, 'Why, no one can resist anything when it looks as beautiful as this!' The gate was built as designed and the original drawing ended up framed and mounted on the wall by the Guardian's bed. [25]

Late in 1942, Shoghi Effendi asked Sutherland to make a design for the superstructure of the Shrine of the Báb. Shoghi Effendi was by then deeply immersed in writing *God Passes By*, so he gave Sutherland only 'a few brief indications' of what he wanted. He said it 'must have a dome and an arcade, must be neither purely western nor purely eastern in style and not look like a mosque or a church'. Beyond that, he left Sutherland free to use his imagination. The first design Shoghi Effendi did not like, so he mentioned that he considered the dome of St Peter's Cathedral in Rome to be the most beautiful in the world. Sutherland returned to work. Rúḥíyyih Khánum describes the process used by the architect and his guide to reach the final design:

The second drawing my father made Shoghi Effendi considered too European in emphasis – though he was satisfied with its proportions – and asked my father to change it. My father was delighted by this suggestion and reverted to the style of dome he had used in his design for the American Bahá'í Temple which he had entered in the original competition for that building, and which showed a marked Indian influence in some of its details. This last design greatly pleased the Guardian with the exception of the treatment of the upper part of the clerestory which he felt needed some height at the eight corners.[26]

Shoghi Effendi didn't like the corners of the building. He said, 'You have to pull it up a little more.' If there are any architects in this room that it isn't very easy once you have designed the whole building . . . to just 'pull it up a little more'. . . So, Daddy went home, home being across the street, and he began to pull up the corners. He would send one design back after another and show it to the Guardian and Shoghi Effendi would say no, it still has to be pulled up more in the corners. And he worked on it and he got those corners . . . higher. Then he had that the way he liked it, but he didn't like the clerestory section, the intermediary section between the arcade and the dome. Originally, it was flat and Shoghi Effendi said it was bare. It's got to have something in those eight corners.

Daddy went back and started working on that and that was the hardest thing in the whole Shrine. It took him weeks and weeks and weeks. He must have made hundreds of studies and every two or three days, he'd bring a new drawing to Shoghi Effendi and Shoghi Effendi would say 'No, I don't like it. It should be a little higher, it should be a little thinner, it should be a little longer, it should be a little rounder, it should be a little flatter.' He knew exactly what he wanted, but he couldn't design it himself . . . but he knew exactly the impression he wanted to get. And he got it out of my father . . .[27]

For weeks and weeks Sutherland submitted to him sketch after sketch until the present highly original minarets were approved by him on 25 December 1943 . . . Although Shoghi Effendi liked very much the design in its final form, as shown in the coloured elevation my father had drawn, he said he wished to have a scale model made before reaching a final decision on a subject of such tremendous importance as in that way he could better visualize the structure as it would appear when built; should this meet with his approval he planned to officially unveil it on the occasion of the one hundredth anniversary of the Declaration of the Báb during the Centenary festivities that were to be held in Haifa.

It was extremely difficult in those days to find anyone capable of executing such a model and though nominally someone undertook to do the work, in practice most of it devolved on my father himself, who was extremely pressed for time to get it completed. In May the model was delivered.[28]

On 23 May 1944, Shoghi Effendi unveiled a model of Sutherland's design for the Shrine of the Báb before a group of Bahá'ís in the Pilgrim House and then cabled the world with the news that the design for the Shrine of the Báb had been chosen. But there was a war going on and the American Bahá'ís were expending all their resources on meeting the objectives of the first Seven Year Plan, so the start of construction was delayed until 1947.[29]

Ten years later, Shoghi Effendi received some diary pages recorded by Badí Bushrui, one of 'Abdu'l-Bahá's secretaries. In those pages, Shoghi Effendi discovered notes from a talk by the Master in which He explained how the Shrine should be 'embellished and beautified'. After reading the diaries, the Guardian said, 'And there it is on Mt Carmel, just as the Master described it.'[30]

Hearing the Guardian's announcement, Milly Collins immediately sent in a contribution for its construction. Soon afterwards, she received a letter that read, 'I am enclosing a receipt, at the instruction of our beloved Guardian, for the sum you so spontaneously and generously sent to him . . . He wants you to know that this is the first contribution he has received for this glorious undertaking, and he is not surprised that it should come from you!'[31]

1943: Pilgrims and plans

On 17 June 1943, Mr Yool, a Bahá'í from Manchester, England, was able to get leave from his unit and go to visit Shoghi Effendi, who greatly enjoyed his visit.[32]

Two non-military pilgrims also received permission, Sabrí Elias and his new wife, Raissa, from Egypt. Sabrí had opened Addis Ababa, Abyssinia (now Ethiopia) to the Faith in 1933 and, after being forced to leave by the Italian invasion, was about to return to his post now that the British had expelled the invaders. When the Eliases requested pilgrimage, another Egyptian had also asked for the privilege. Shoghi Effendi agreed, but added that he could only come if he also pioneered to Ethiopia. The man didn't want to pioneer so he had to stay home while Sabrí and Raissa Elias went to Haifa.³³

It was Sabrí Elias's third pilgrimage, but Raissa's first. She only had one specific meeting with the Guardian and she noted that

> he was a person of great perception – of course he was a human being, yet . . . was undoubtedly distinguished above other humans . . . The moment he came into the [Master's] house, when I would be in the presence of Rúḥíyyih Khánum, everything in the house would seem to vibrate! I would even feel the very furniture of the house shaking. An overwhelming sense of veneration would then possess me. Even Rúḥíyyih Khánum herself would stand up with her arms around her bosom in reverence, as he would be passing. He would pass by the door of the room where we sat on his way to the room where he granted us the honour of an audience. Then I would enter the room, greeting him with 'Alláh-u-Abhá, my Master!' and he would then talk to me. Sometimes, I would be able to reply to His questions and sometimes I would not be able to. Once, I felt the need to talk to His Eminence and I tried to look into his eyes but I could not!³⁴

Shoghi Effendi told Raissa that she and her husband would establish many assemblies in Abyssinia, including a National Spiritual Assembly. He cautioned them not to teach hastily and that he would send more pioneers from Egypt, Iran and the United States. Raissa spent a lot of time with Rúḥíyyih Khánum because she was the only woman on pilgrimage. Every afternoon she had tea with the Guardian's wife. One day, when they were eating delicious cakes, Rúḥíyyih Khánum asked if she could make cakes that were as good. Raissa replied, 'No, but my mother does,' whereupon Khánum laughed, 'Oh, but your mother will not be with you in Ethiopia!'³⁵

There was only one other pilgrim in Haifa at that time, Nadím Bashád, who was an old man from Iraq. Each day, Sabrí Elias and Nadím would wait for the arrival of Shoghi Effendi and then circumambulate the Shrine of the Báb before entering. The two pilgrims entered first and prostrated themselves at the threshold. Then Shoghi Effendi came forward and did the same. When the Guardian stood up, he chanted the Tablet of Visitation. Sabrí remembered that 'many times he would sprinkle attar of roses in our palms, to refresh our souls and minds'. When they were finished, Shoghi Effendi returned to his house. At the end of their pilgrimage, Sabrí and Raissa emotionally said goodbye. Shoghi Effendi's last words to them were, 'Mussolini did not conquer Abyssinia! You are the [spiritual] conqueror of Abyssinia!' When the couple left for the train station, the Guardian had all the resident believers go with them, just as he had done at the end of Sabrí Elias's pilgrimage in 1933 when he was pioneering to Abyssinia for the first time.[36] In 1954, they became Knights of Bahá'u'lláh for French Somaliland (now called Djibouti).

Akka and Haifa

Shoghi Effendi was very aware of the world around him, not just the Bahá'í world, and when there were needs he could help with, he responded quickly. The Akka District Commissioner wrote to the Guardian that he could find no place for a children's school and asked if some of the rooms in the House of 'Abbúd could possibly be used. Shoghi Effendi immediately made several rooms available and would not accept any payment for their use.[37]

At another time, the Municipality of Haifa decided to change the name of the street that ran in front of the House of the Master to 'Baha Street'. The Guardian immediately dispatched his secretary to the Mayor to tell him that as 'Baha' was the name of the Founder of the Bahá'í Faith, the plan was 'not only inappropriate but insulting'. The city authorities then changed the name to 'Iran Street'. This further incensed Shoghi Effendi, who threatened to tear the sign down with his own hands, even if it resulted in him being put in jail. The idea of the Guardian in jail greatly worried Rúḥíyyih Khánum. She said, 'I was very upset by this prospect, as I did not want him to go to jail without me and did not see what I could do to get in jail with him.'[38] Apparently, the Municipality backed down because the street became known as Persian Street.

At one point during 1943, a member of the family died and his widow came to ask Shoghi Effendi to accept the terms of his will. The will stipulated that an amount of money was to be given to the Guardian along with some of Bahá'u'lláh's seals that had been entrusted to her by 'Abdu'l-Bahá when He left on His journey to the West. Shoghi Effendi, however, refused even to meet her since she was associating with other members of the family who were Covenant-breakers. He sent Rúḥíyyih Khánum instead, and when she told the Guardian about the will and the seals, he

> said to tell her he did not want a million seals or the whole of Mt. Carmel, he wanted sincerity and loyalty and that unless she cut herself entirely from _____'s family . . . in her heart, he could do nothing for her, and to keep the seals and the Will . . . the Guardian would have liked very much to have had the seals – so precious – for the Archives, but, as he told me, he could not very well take the seals and put her out of the house! The thing that puzzles me is that it is now 23 years since the Master died, couldn't she once during those 23 years, many of which she was very close to the Guardian, give him those precious relics which she says were never given her but only <u>entrusted</u> to her!³⁹

1944: Centenary of the Faith

God Passes By

Shoghi Effendi's great desire was to have his seminal work, *God Passes By*, completed during the centenary year of the Faith in 1944. It was an immense task. Rúḥíyyih Khánum wrote about the tremendous effort Shoghi Effendi had put into the book:

> He read 200 reference books; all the books written by Baháʼís, by enemies, all the Tablets, everything. He typed the manuscript twice himself. He used to work 16 hours a day.⁴⁰

The method of Shoghi Effendi in writing *God Passes By* was to sit down for a year and read every book of the Baháʼí Writings in Persian and English, and every book written about the Faith by Baháʼís, whether in manuscript form or published, and everything written by non-Baháʼís that contained significant references to it. I think, in all, this must have covered the equivalent of at least two hundred books. As he read he made notes and compiled and marshalled his facts. Anyone who has ever tackled a work of an historical nature knows how much research is involved, how often one has to decide, in light of relevant material, between this date given in one place and that date given in another, how back-breaking the whole work is. How much more so then was such a work for the Guardian who had, at the same time, to prepare for the forthcoming Centenary of the Faith and make decisions regarding the superstructure of the Báb's Shrine. When all the ingredients of his book had been assembled, Shoghi Effendi commenced weaving them into the fabric of his picture of the significance of the first century of the Bahá'í Dispensation. It was not his purpose, he said, to write a detailed history of those hundred years, but rather to review the salient features of the birth and rise of the Faith, the establishment of its administrative institutions, and the series of crises which had propelled it forward in a mysterious manner, through the release of the Divine power within it, from victory to victory . . .

How many hundreds of hours Shoghi Effendi spent on reading his sources and compiling his notes, how many days and months in painstakingly writing out in longhand – and often rewriting – the majestic procession of his chapters, how many more wearisome days he sat at his small portable typewriter, hammering away with a few fingers, sometimes ten hours on end, as he typed the final copy of his work! And how many more hours we spent late into the night, when the daily typing was over, seated side by side at his big table in his bedroom, each with three copies of the typescript before us, proof-reading, making corrections, putting in by hand the thousands of accents on transliterated words which Shoghi Effendi would read aloud, until his eyes were bloodshot and blurred, his back and arms stiff with exhaustion, as we worked to finish the entire chapter or part of a chapter he had typed that day. It had to be done. There was no possibility of working at a slower pace. He was racing against time to present the Bahá'ís of the West with this inimitable gift on the occasion of the one hundredth anniversary of the inception of their Faith. In spite of the fact that he mailed off to America the corrected manuscript in instalments, conditions in the United States delayed the publication and the book was not off the press until the middle of November 1944.[41]

Rúḥíyyih Khánum continued to worry about how hard the Guardian was working. At the end of 1943 she had written in her dairy:

I am really worried over Shoghi Effendi. When he used to get so very distressed and upset in the past it affected him, but not as it does now. Sometimes I think it will lead to his premature death . . . he breathes so hard, almost like one who has been running, and he has such huge shadows under his eyes. He forces himself to go on and finish the letters he has had piled for days on his desk – but he reads a thing sometimes ten minutes over and over because he can't concentrate! I think no suffering is worse than seeing someone you love suffer. And I can't remedy it. All I wonder is how God can stand to see him suffer so.

Although the summer was peaceful in the sense there were no horrible crises . . . I don't think the Guardian ever worked so hard during his 'vacation' before, and I am sure I didn't! He often says 'this book is killing me' to which I invariably answer 'me too'. In other words the way he has worked on this Centennial Review [*God Passes By*] is really cruel; for two years he has literally slaved over it – along with all his other work and cares . . .[42]

With such a powerful book, Shoghi Effendi again turned to George Townshend for help. George, strongly affected by this new book, 'having read every line of the Guardian's monumental work, having gloried in it, wept over it, lived with it from February 1943 to February 1944, offered his editorial "suggestions and corrections" as he deemed necessary . . .'[43] He wrote to Shoghi Effendi:

My chief trouble was to prevent my tears spoiling your manuscript as I read your account of 'Abdu'l-Bahá's activities in the west . . .

I return the last instalment of the Survey that has reached me, and am sorry to think it must be nearly the very last, and that my work on these is almost over. I shall miss it, and the thrill and the illumination and the detachment of it.[44]

Shoghi Effendi, as he had for *The Dawn-Breakers*, asked George for a title and an introduction. He, again, supplied both. Unlike with the introduction to *The Dawn-Breakers*, written when he worried about having his name associated with the Bahá'í Faith while still an active clergyman for the Church of Ireland, this time George had no reluctance in placing his name at the end of his masterpiece of an introduction. The choosing of the title, however, 'taxed George's imaginative invention. Only after letters and two cables urging the point had been received did inspiration come to him. He cabled "God Passes By" and received the instant reply "Delighted title eagerly awaiting letter".'[45]

But *God Passes By* had been written in English and published in the West. No sooner had he finished the book than Shoghi Effendi began a comparable volume written in Persian for those long-suffering believers in Iran. This book was similar to, though shorter than, *God Passes By*. Rúḥíyyih Khánum, though conversant in Persian, could be of little help with this project:

> Whereas I had sat through most of his writing of *God Passes By* in English there was no point in my doing so for this epistle. The difference between the style of Shoghi Effendi's letters and discourse in Persian – liberally sprinkled with Arabic – and every-day Persian is comparable to the difference between Shakespearian English and modern journalese! My command of Persian and ignorance of Arabic were such that I could not catch more than three or four words out of ten. Nevertheless he would read to me, or rather chant to me, some of its passages and the majestic flow of his words, their perfection and power, were evident to me even though I could not fully follow their meaning. I remember how, as I approached his room, I would hear his voice chanting his composition to himself as he wrote, infinitely plaintive, infinitely beautiful. It was also fascinating: he would chant the sentence he was writing until he struck a bump, a word that would not fit smoothly, the lovely voice, unconscious of itself, would stop, then go back to the beginning of the sentence and start off again up to the same point; if he did not get over it that time this would be repeated until he did! It was like some wonderful bird trying out its melodies to itself, lost in its own world. This epistle ran to a hundred pages in fine handwriting and is another of Shoghi Effendi's masterpieces. These two reviews of a hundred years were the Guardian's priceless Centenary gifts to the Bahá'ís, wrought with great cost to his strength and health, and devised during years when the world was rocked by its greatest war.[46]

God Passes By and its Persian version were the last books Shoghi Effendi either wrote or translated until he began working on the codification of the Kitáb-i-Aqdas in 1954.

The British Six Year Plan

Shoghi Effendi had given the North American Bahá'ís their first teaching plan. The British, however, didn't wait to be asked. At their National Convention in April 1944, they cabled the Guardian asking for their own plan and goals. Shoghi Effendi delightedly complied, asking them to form nineteen spiritual assemblies in England, Wales, Scotland, Northern Ireland and Eire.[47] Although the small British community was severely challenged, the next six years saw a majority of their number arise to pioneer, and their final victory in 1950 would delight the heart of the Guardian and lead to his bestowal on them of their own 'spiritual mission', as described later in this book.

Completion of the first Seven Year Plan

The North American Bahá'ís successfully completed all the goals for their Seven Year Plan on time to end the first Bahá'í century at the commemoration of the Declaration of the Báb. Among other things, the Plan had called for the establishment of the 'machinery' of the Administrative Order as a means of furthering the teaching work. Rúḥíyyih Khánum wrote:

> It was the Guardian who had 'so laboriously erected' this 'machinery', with the help of willing and eager tools he found amongst the North American believers, who grasped his thought, obeyed his command and hastened to put into action his instructions. It was the Guardian alone who possessed the divine and indefeasible right to direct the battle of Bahá'u'lláh's forces of light against the forces of darkness.[48]

In spite of a world war and its attendant chaos, the victory was won:

> In looking back on those glorious and terrible years of the last war the success of the first Seven Year Plan seems truly miraculous. While humanity was being decimated in Europe and Asia, while the World

Centre of the Faith was being threatened with unprecedented danger on four sides, while the United States and Canada were engaged in a world conflict, with its attendant anxieties, restrictions and furor, a handful of people, lacking in resources but rich in faith, lacking in prestige but rich in determination, succeeded in not only doubling the number of Bahá'í Assemblies in North America and ensuring the existence of at least one in every state of the Union and every province of Canada, but in completing the extremely costly exterior ornamentation of their Mother Temple sixteen months ahead of the scheduled time, and establishing not only a strong Bahá'í group in each of the twenty Latin Republics, but in addition fifteen Spiritual Assemblies throughout the entire area. In the last months of the Plan Shoghi Effendi fairly stormed the remaining unfinished tasks, with his valiant little army, too excited to feel the exhaustion of seven years' constant struggle, hard at his heels. When the sun of the second Bahá'í Century rose, it rose on triumph.[49]

Shoghi Effendi put the great effort into perspective:

1944, a year memorable for the sharp contrast between the rising tide of spiritual victories culminating in the Centenary celebrations of a world-embracing Faith and the swiftly ebbing fortunes of a war-ravaged, disillusioned and bankrupt society, is drawing to a close. In every continent of the globe . . . the communities laboring for the promotion of the Faith of Bahá'u'lláh have, throughout five tumultuous years, been providentially spared to hold aloft its banner, to preserve its integrity, to maintain the continuity of its institutions, to enrich its annals, to consolidate its structure, to further disseminate its literature and to befittingly celebrate its Centenary. Preponderant indeed has been the share of that privileged community, which has been invested by the Pen of the Center of the Covenant with a world-wide mission, in the prosecution of a task which, ever since the onset of this world upheaval and despite its mounting horrors, the builders of the Administrative Order of the Faith of Bahá'u'lláh have so unflaggingly pursued. Neither the participation of the Great Republic of the West in this fierce contest, nor the sorrows, burdens and restrictions which such direct association with the agonies of a travailing age has entailed, have thus far been capable of dimming the splendor of the exploits that have immortalized the record of the services of this community since the ascension of 'Abdu'l-Bahá. Indeed, coincident with the period of America's direct participation in this world struggle and in direct proportion to the turmoil and the tribulations which such a participation has engendered, the members of this community have evinced a heroism and proved themselves capable of a concerted effort that have eclipsed the notable achievements that have heralded the establishment of the Administrative Order of the Faith as well as the first stage in the development of the Seven Year Plan.[50]

The first Seven Year Plan, ushered in on the eve of the greatest conflict that has ever shaken the human race, has, despite six years of chaos and tribulation, been crowned with a success far exceeding the most sanguine hopes of its ardent promoters.[51]

The splendid and unique success that has attended the Centenary celebrations so admirably conducted by the American Bahá'í community, has befittingly crowned not only the fifty year record of services rendered by its valiant members but the labors associated with the entire body of their fellow-workers in East and West in the course of an entire century . . . The consummation of the Seven Year Plan . . . set the seal of complete spiritual triumph on these historic celebrations. A memorable chapter in the history of the Faith of Bahá'u'lláh in the West has been closed. A new chapter is now opening . . .[52]

1945–1946

At 3:30 p.m. on 5 January 1945, two WACs (Women's Army Corps), Dorothy Clark and another Bahá'í from Washington DC – so far unidentified – decided to see if they could make a spur of the moment pilgrimage from Cairo, where they were stationed. At first, they simply asked whether it might be possible to get a plane to Haifa. The answer, initially, was no, but 'a little bit of flirting' got them a free trip on a Headquarters flight that left at 8 a.m. the next morning. All they had to do was get their bosses' permissions and the appropriate visas. It was a rush, but their bosses cooperated and, by convincing the Egyptian officer in charge to return to his office at 7:30 p.m., they obtained their visas. Their flight took them to Tel Aviv, from where they travelled to Haifa by bus.

When they arrived, they called Rúḥíyyih Khánum, who invited them to the House of the Master, then took them to the Pilgrim House. When she was called that evening to meet Shoghi Effendi, the Washington Bahá'í was

> scared to death. Over to the big house again and I was left in the living room waiting to see Shoghi Effendi. Well, I did not know what to say or do when I saw Him, but somehow He knew this and he took my hand and welcomed me warmly. He told me to sit in the big chair which is so much like a princess chair in order that he could talk with me. Then he started discussing our Faith . . . My heart was so happy and I loved Shoghi Effendi with all my heart. He is so kind, stern, sincere and so completely balanced in every way, dress, manner, approach, ideas, etc.
>
> He stayed and talked with me about fifteen minutes and then He left. Rúḥíyyih Khánum walked back with us and no longer was I afraid.[1]

That night the two WACs had dinner with Rúḥíyyih <u>Kh</u>ánum and her father Sutherland Maxwell. The next day, Sutherland took the women. into the Baháʼí gardens, which enchanted them. When they entered the Shrine of the Báb, the Washington WAC wrote that 'sadness at once touched me, and at that time I wished that I had been alone. Never have I see a more beautiful, peaceful place.' After touring the Monument Gardens, she wondered why the Baháʼís troubled Shoghi Effendi with their 'petty personal troubles'.

The next morning, the Washington WAC was taken to the Archives where she saw the pictures of the Báb, Baháʼuʼlláh and ʻAbduʼl-Bahá. She noted that 'the Báb was so delicate and I loved his frailness, but Baháʼuʼlláh is so different. He appeared to me to be fearless, firm, and his eyes were like someone who could read your very soul.' Afterwards, she returned to the Shrine of the Báb: 'All I could do in the Shrine of the Báb was to sob and sob and Riaz chanted the prayer of the Tablet of Ahmad.' That afternoon, Shoghi Effendi arranged a trip to Nazareth for the two WACs, Rúḥíyyih Khánum and Sutherland.

The next day, 9 January, the two women went to Bahjí. After touring the gardens, they entered a 'place which appeared to be a flower house and there was the Shrine of Baháʼuʼlláh'. The Washington WAC wrote that 'the beauty of the place is breathtaking. The Shrine so suited His personality. So powerful. There I did not feel sad but only childish and so very happy and secure.' From the Shrine, they visited the Mansion, then returned to Haifa. That evening, the Washington WAC met with Shoghi Effendi who advised her on many things about the Faith. Unfortunately, Dorothy never had a chance to meet the Guardian. The next day at 9:30 a.m. the two WACs travelled to Jerusalem and then back to Cairo.[2]

The second stage in the implementation of the Tablets of the Divine Plan

Almost immediately following the end of the Seven Year Plan in 1944, Shoghi Effendi had been alluding in his messages to the 'next stage' in the evolution of the Divine Plan. But, he wrote, this 'cannot, however, be embarked upon, until the external causes . . . are removed through the cessation of hostilities, and the signal victories already won through its initial development are sufficiently consolidated throughout the

Western Hemisphere.'³ The war was not yet over, and throughout the time of preparation in 1945 the Guardian encouraged the believers to proclaim and teach the Faith, to consolidate what they had already achieved, and that:

> Above all, the healing Message of Bahá'u'lláh must during the opening years of the second Bahá'í century, and through the instrumentality of an already properly functioning Administrative Order . . . be vividly, systematically brought to the attention of the masses, in their hour of grief, misery and confusion.⁴

Soon after the war ended and beginning in 1946, Shoghi Effendi activated even more of the administrative machinery he had built and began the second stage in his development of 'Abdu'l-Bahá's Tablets of the Divine Plan, which he said began the Second Epoch of the Formative Age. To the North Americans, he introduced the Second Seven Year Plan at Riḍván, which was to be completed by the centenary of the birth of Bahá'u'lláh's mission in the Síyáh-Chál. The goals of this plan were to: 1) consolidate the victories won throughout the Americas; 2) complete the interior ornamentation of the Mashriqu'l-Adhkár in Wilmette; 3) form three National Spiritual Assemblies in Canada, Central America and South America; and 4) spiritually revitalize wartorn Europe. The final goal was the most important and Shoghi Effendi wrote that nine pioneers should be sent immediately. He emphasized the importance of Europe:

> Particularly in the heart of the European continent, where the present turmoil, suffering and destitution are mysteriously paving the way for the revival of a Faith which the Beloved Himself has unequivocally prophesied, where a once flourishing community is struggling to fulfil the high hopes entertained for it by Him, and where the prosecutors of the Divine Plan, are to lend their direct and systematic assistance when launching the second stage of their world mission, must the American believers contribute the major share in the work of rehabilitation which the followers of Bahá'u'lláh must arise to perform.⁵

The Second Seven Year Plan, Shoghi Effendi wrote,

set in motion on the morrow of that universal and cataclysmic upheaval, must, despite the great confusion that still prevails, the spiritual torpor, the disillusionment, the embitterment, the political and social restlessness that still afflict the human race, meet, as it gathers momentum and multiplies its agencies across the ocean, in lands and amidst races that have borne, for the most part, the brunt of this dire and bloody contest, with a success no less startling and complete than that which rewarded the self-sacrifice, the vigilance and the strenuous labors of those who inaugurated the initial phase of this glorious Mission. Might not this second and still greater adventure, undertaken by the trustees of a God-Given Mandate, demonstrate in both hemispheres, despite the prodigious scale on which it is launched, such prodigies of service as will carry its prosecutors far beyond their avowed objectives, and eclipse, through the wisdom, the valor and the exploits of those pioneers and administrators immediately responsible for its planning and execution, the splendor of every previous collective enterprise undertaken by the followers of Bahá'u'lláh in the West?[6]

The British Bahá'ís were already embarked on their Six Year Plan, to run until 1950. The National Spiritual Assembly of India and Burma was now given a Four and a Half Year Plan to run from early 1946 to July 1950. Its goals were to 'reconstitute dissolved Assemblies, the extension of relief to the needy, the promotion of the teaching work, the dissemination of Bahá'í literature, the construction of the Hazíratu'l-Quds, the re-establishment of schools and committees . . .'[7]

Persia was given two plans. The National Spiritual Assembly was given a Forty-Five Month Plan, also designed to be completed by July 1950, and there was a separate Women's Four Year Plan. Shoghi Effendi didn't give the National Assembly a specific plan; he asked them to create a plan similar to the North American plans. The goals they came up with were to: consolidate all local communities; re-establish 62 dissolved assemblies; form 22 new groups and 13 new centres; establish Local Spiritual Assemblies in Afghanistan, Arabia and Bahrain; and to send pioneers to India and Iraq. When they sent the list of goals to him, Shoghi Effendi praised it as a 'magnificent plan'. The women's plan was designed to emancipate women and increase literacy. Its goals were to hold literacy classes for girls and women; hold semi-annual conventions; to hold a national convention for women; and to issue a periodical.[8]

Relationship of National Spiritual Assemblies and the Guardian

With new National Spiritual Assemblies being created, Shoghi Effendi was faced with 'new and inexperienced believers who had not yet grasped [the] true significance and implications' of the World Order of Bahá'u'lláh. In one case, Shoghi Effendi was forced to overturn a decision of a National Assembly and a member of that assembly was not happy with his action. The Guardian replied:

> Just as the National Assembly has full jurisdiction over all its local Assemblies, the Guardian has full jurisdiction over all National Assemblies; he is not required to consult them, if he believes a certain decision is advisable in the interests of the Cause. He is the judge of the wisdom and advisability of the decisions made by these bodies, and not they of the wisdom and advisability of his decisions. A perusal of the Will and Testament makes this principle quite clear. He is the Guardian of the Cause in the very fullness of that term, and the appointed interpreter of its teachings, and is guided in his decisions to do that which protects it and fosters its growth and highest interests.
>
> He always has the right to step in and countermand the decisions of a national assembly; if he did not possess this right he would be absolutely impotent to protect the Faith, just as the N.S.A., if it were divested of the right to countermand the decisions of a local assembly, would be incapable of watching over and guiding the national welfare of the Baha'i Community.
>
> It very seldom happens – but it nevertheless <u>does</u> happen – that he feels impelled to change a major (as you put it) decision of an N.S.A.; but he always unhesitatingly does so when necessary, and the N.S.A. in question should gladly and unhesitatingly accept this as a measure designed for the good of the Faith which its elected representatives are so devotedly seeking to serve.[9]

Philip Hainsworth

With the war over in 1945, millions of men who had been under arms were being released to go home. On Thursday 25 April 1946 – the same day as the American Bahá'ís were hearing the Guardian's Message to their Convention inaugurating the second Seven Year Plan – a British Captain, Philip Hainsworth, boarded a train for Haifa along with Yusuf Jarrah and Yusuf's new bride, Hyatt. Yusuf Jarrah was the great-grandson of the former Governor of Akka who had accepted the Faith during the time of Bahá'u'lláh. They arrived in Haifa the next afternoon. On Saturday, Philip met Yusuf and asked to be taken to tell Shoghi Effendi that he was there. Yusuf said that people didn't just drop in on Shoghi Effendi, but with Philip insisting, they went to the House of the Master. It was the first of several *faux pas* the brash Philip was to make over the next few weeks, as he himself would recount decades later.[10]

Yusuf took Philip into a small downstairs room to the left of the main stairs. Rúḥíyyih Khánum soon came down and told him that Shoghi Effendi had just received two full bags of mail and was sorry that he could not see Philip. When mail arrived, the Guardian poured all of it onto his desk, then sorted it into piles with one for each continent. Apparently, Shoghi Effendi, to his surprise, was reading a letter Philip had sent announcing that he was coming to Haifa just when Philip was announced. That was Philip's second *faux pas* – Bahá'ís were normally expected to ask Shoghi Effendi for permission to visit and did not just show up. When Philip met Shoghi Effendi the next day, the Guardian said, 'If you had written to me asking permission to come to Haifa, I do not think I would have given it, but because you wanted so much to come, God has granted your wish.'[11]

To prepare to meet Shoghi Effendi, Philip put on his best tropical uniform, which consisted of shorts and a short-sleeved shirt, then went to the bus stop at the top of Mount Carmel with plenty of time. But no buses came. When he asked a passing Jewish girl about the buses, she said that 'because some of the drivers were Arab Muslim and had Friday off, some were Jewish and had Saturday off and some were Arab Christian who took Sunday off, there was only bus service . . . four days of the week!' Suddenly worried about time, Philip ran down the mountain to the Western Pilgrim House, arriving very hot and sweaty, his shirt very wet. Suddenly, a young Persian girl came in and said that Shoghi

Effendi was ready to see him. Philip met a 'smallish, dapper man in a dark grey suit, a black fez and brown boots'. Philip later said that he felt very comfortable with the Guardian.[12]

That evening at dinner with Rúḥíyyih Khánum and Sutherland Maxwell, Philip said that he would attend the Holy Day celebration for the Ninth Day of Riḍván. Sutherland said that he would ask Shoghi Effendi for permission, which shocked Philip, who hadn't expected to need permission. A note was, however, sent to the Guardian. A couple of days later, Rúḥíyyih Khánum took Philip into the Archives. While there, they found a small box containing wood fragments and dust that had fallen on the floor. As they very carefully gathered up the fragments and dust, Rúḥíyyih Khánum explained that when the casket containing the remains of the Báb had been transferred into the marble sarcophagus from the Bahá'ís of Rangoon, one section had to be shaved so that it would fit. What they were cleaning up were those shavings.[13]

On 29 April, Philip and Sutherland were taken to the Eastern Pilgrim House for the start of the Holy Day. Philip was wearing his tropical uniform of shorts and short-sleeved shirt. The two Westerners walked in between rows of Persian believers sitting on the floor, to the end of the room where Shoghi Effendi sat along the right wall in the position 'Abdu'l-Bahá had used to sit. Philip sat down, crossed his legs and folded his arms – something the Persians thought was unforgivable. Another *faux pas*, though he didn't know it until later. After much chanting, Shoghi Effendi led the way to the Shrine of the Báb with Philip at his side. Later, the Guardian talked about recent events in the Bahá'í world. He was delighted with the fact that the Americans had elected, with the highest vote count, not only a woman to their National Assembly, but a black woman, Elsie Austin. Then he told how in the future the kings and rulers would walk up the steps to the Shrine of the Báb, lay their crowns at the door, and pray. They would then go to meet the Universal House of Justice to 'receive their instructions'. As he said this, he pointed to a place on the hill above. Thirty years later, Philip, along with others attending an International Convention, visited the site selected by the Universal House of Justice for its seat. It was the same exact place.[14]

Shoghi Effendi had put Sutherland Maxwell in charge of the Guardian's mail, visitors, government contracts and general errands. Sutherland was 72 years old and, though he did a very good job, the stress caused a blood vessel in his ear to burst, which resulted in him becoming deaf in that ear and 'shaken and dizzy for weeks on end'.[15]

On 4 May, Sutherland and Philip were driven to Bahjí for the commemoration of the Twelfth Day of Riḍván. Philip remembered:

Overlooking the Mansion was the large, forbidding-looking building owned by the Covenant-breakers. We had to enter the Mansion very discreetly as the Covenant-breakers were said to watch most jealously what happened in the Mansion and the appearance of a British Army officer entering may have caused difficulties.[16]

While there, Philip heard a story that when 'Abdu'l-Bahá was in prison, his half-brother, Mírzá Muḥammad-'Alí, the Arch-breaker of the Covenant, gave Bahá'u'lláh's robe and prayer beads to a Bedouin. When 'Abdu'l-Bahá was released, the Bedouin visited him wearing that robe and 'dangling the precious prayer beads under His eyes'.[17]

On 18 May, Yusuf took Philip to the Most Great Prison, then in the hands of the British army. They were initially unable to enter, but Philip, after an hour and a half of pleading, basically pulled rank on the subordinates and spoke with the prison superintendent. He was quickly allowed to enter the cell of Bahá'u'lláh. Afterwards, they went to the Riḍván Gardens. A few days later, Shoghi Effendi told him that the Bahá'ís did not have to pay rent, taxes or rates to either the government or the municipality, a privilege denied all other religious groups in Haifa. The Guardian said the reason was that all Bahá'í lands were open to the public and all produce from those lands was donated to the poor. When the Catholics had tried to get the same privileges, they were told that they could have them if they did as the Bahá'ís did. The Catholics refused and, consequently, so did the government.[18]

On 29 May, Sutherland and Philip were taken to Bahjí in the afternoon for the commemoration of the Ascension of Bahá'u'lláh. Shoghi Effendi had arranged for them to get a few hours sleep, since they were not used to the all-night vigils of the Persians. Philip was put in Shoghi Effendi's room in the Mansion. At 2:25 a.m., the two Westerners joined the Persian and Arabic friends. There were chants, punctuated by short talks by Shoghi Effendi. At one point, the Guardian turned to Philip, pointing to his posture of feet tucked under the chair, head bowed and hands in lap, and said, 'You are getting more like a Persian every day!' Following the prayers, Shoghi Effendi led them into the Mansion. Going into Bahá'u'lláh's room, the Guardian knelt to pray and was so overcome with emotion that others had to help him to his feet. They then returned to the Shrine. After Philip had gone to the threshold, Shoghi Effendi went to the same spot, collected two handfuls of rose petals, and gave them to him.[19]

That was Philip's last day in the Holy Land. On his return to England, he became one of the prime movers of the British Six Year Plan. Later, in 1951, he pioneered to Uganda, where he and his family served for many years; after returning to the British Isles he served with distinction on the National Spiritual Assembly, often as its Secretary.

A new Hand of the Cause

Amelia (Milly) Collins had become a Bahá'í in 1919 and was told that she must write a letter to the Master asking for confirmation and strength. One sleepless night she pondered this and finally scribbled a quick note. With the dawn, however, she decided that she did not need to bother 'Abdu'l-Bahá with a letter because she was certain that He would know of her devotion. Some time later, Milly received a Tablet from the Master that addressed her as 'lady of the Kingdom' and stated His hope that she would be confirmed to 'erect a structure that shall eternally remain firm and unshakeable.'[20] Her 1923 pilgrimage has been described earlier.

On 22 November 1946, Milly received a cable from Shoghi Effendi that read:

> Your magnificent international services exemplary devotion and now this signal service impel me inform you your elevation rank Hand of the Cause Bahá'u'lláh. You are first be told this honour in lifetime. As to time announcement leave it my discretion.[21]

Not since the time of Bahá'u'lláh had a Hand been appointed while the person was living. Both 'Abdu'l-Bahá and Shoghi Effendi declared certain believers to be Hands of the Cause after their passing, but the last living Hand had died in 1928 and there had been no living Hands until Milly was appointed. The next year, the Guardian sent her a letter confirming this:

The high rank you now occupy and which no Bahá'í since the Master's passing has ever held in his own lifetime has been conferred solely in recognition of the manifold services you have *already* rendered . . .[22]

This high station was not announced to the world until December 1951, just after Shoghi Effendi appointed Milly Collins to the first International Bahá'í Council.

The Guardian in Scotland

Shortly after the War, in 1946 or 1947, Shoghi Effendi took Rúḥíyyih Khánum to Scotland to acquaint her with her Maxwell roots. They made a second trip later. On the first trip they travelled by train, while on the second they had a car. During these travels they visited Loch Lomond, Gleneagles, Stirling, Edinburgh, Glasgow and Aberdeen. One evening after dinner in Gleneagles, people were dancing Scottish reels in their kilts and Shoghi Effendi greatly enjoyed watching. Rúḥíyyih Khánum loved the bagpipes. She noted that 'there's something about the bagpipes that makes our blood tingle, and it goes right straight through us'. She added that 'I can't truthfully say that it went through Shoghi Effendi . . . but he didn't particularly object to the bagpipes, let's put it that way, and he knew that I liked them very much.'[23]

1947–1949

The years 1947 and 1948 were extremely turbulent in Palestine. The British were to end their Mandate for governing the country in 1948, and the Jews and Arabs fought for control of the new nation. Civil war wracked the country and the Bahá'ís were in the middle of it all. But Shoghi Effendi finally had some extra help with the arrival from the United States of Gladys Anderson in 1947 and her fiancé Ben Weeden in 1948. Their marriage would be the first Bahá'í wedding to be registered in the new State of Israel.

Gladys Anderson comes to help

On 30 March 1947, Gladys Anderson arrived in Haifa to serve as a secretary for both Shoghi Effendi and Sutherland Maxwell. Rúḥíyyih Khánum had been extremely anxious at Shoghi Effendi's heavy workload and knew her friend Gladys was available so, with the Guardian's permission, she invited Gladys to come. Gladys responded: 'Had a fairy godmother given me a wish that was dearest to the heart, the news in your cable fulfilled it!'

When the day came that she sat across from Shoghi Effendi at the dining table, she was impressed by 'the beauty of his face', his 'resonant voice', and that it 'was just like a bubbling stream to hear him laugh'.[1]

> My first impression was of his warm, loving smile and handclasp, making me feel instantly at ease . . . In the course of these interviews, I was to become increasingly conscious of his many great qualities, – his nobility, dignity, fire and enthusiasm, – his ability to run the scale from sparkling humor to deep outrage, but always, always putting the Bahá'í Faith ahead of everything . . . In his practical, logical manner, Shoghi Effendi made me feel both a welcome

guest and a needed helper, he outlined some of my duties which started the very next day! His advice, given me on that initial visit, was to overshadow all my efforts on his behalf; he said he wanted me to follow his instructions explicitly, if I was unsuccessful, or ran into difficulties, to report to him precisely and he would give me a new plan of action . . . For the Bahá'ís working at the International Center, during this period at least, there was no special day of rest. It was then that one learned that each moment belonged to the Faith . . .[2]

She also wrote about listening to the plans of Shoghi Effendi at the dinner table:

Sparkling with excitement and new plans, he would produce messages and letters from his pockets, oftentimes pushing his dinner plate away untouched, calling for paper and pencil and thrill us all with his new ideas and hopes for the Bahá'ís to carry out . . . The beloved Guardian disliked very much to have his picture taken, therefore any photographs extant do not reflect his true 'image'. In the first place, the emotions flowed so rapidly over his features that one would need a series to catch his many moods. It was a delight to see and hear him laugh . . . he seemed to twinkle like a star when some plan had been successfully brought to a conclusion. His sense of humor was a joy! He was like a high mountain, strong, always there, but never conquered, filled with unexpected heights and depths . . . he was extremely thorough and taught us all a new sense of perfection and attention to detail . . . he was in close touch with the expenditure of all funds . . . He was enthusiastically concerned with Bahá'í statistics . . . We could never appreciate his grasp of all affairs connected with activities at the 'grass roots' right up to the World Center . . .[3]

Gladys quickly learned that working for the Guardian commonly meant doing the impossible. The morning after her arrival, Sutherland took her downtown and introduced her to important people, including their law firm, bankers, various businessmen, local city and government officials in Haifa and high-ranging people from Jerusalem. Gladys had a 'gift for friendship' which helped in her work.[4] Her arrival allowed

Sutherland to take a six-week vacation in Cyprus, where he visited Nicosia and Kyrenia. When he returned, he began working on drawings of the Shrine of the Báb.[5]

Gladys was given her first big task in May. She received a call informing her that a very important person wanted to visit Bahjí – for security reasons, no name was given. Gladys reported the call to Rúḥíyyih Khánum who passed the message to Shoghi Effendi. The Guardian said that it would be the High Commissioner of Palestine, General Sir Allan Cunningham. Shoghi Effendi said that it was Gladys's job to meet and escort him to Bahjí. Gladys was aghast, but when Shoghi Effendi asked you to do something, you just did it. On the day of the visit, Rúḥíyyih Khánum made sure Gladys was dressed appropriately and the Guardian carefully explained what she and Salah Jarrah, the caretaker at Bahjí, were to do.[6]

The first to arrive was the District Commissioner of Akka. He was soon followed, just as Shoghi Effendi had predicted, by General Cunningham. Gladys presented the High Commissioner with a bouquet of flowers, then led him and his entourage to the Shrine of Bahá'u'lláh. Upon reaching the Shrine the High Commissioner removed his shoes, then only he and Gladys went inside. Gladys went to the Sacred Threshold, knelt down and said a short prayer, then backed away. General Cunningham followed her example and said his own prayers. Once back outside, he confided to her that that was 'as near to heaven on earth as one could possibly get'.[7]

From the Shrine, Gladys escorted the High Commissioner into the Mansion. They first visited the room of Bahá'u'lláh, then she gave him a tour. He noted the displays of Bahá'í books, commenting on the various languages in which they were written. At the end of the tour, Sir Allan signed the guest register and they moved to the balcony. Salah brought tea and soon the rest of the entourage joined them on the balcony, having their tea. Salah had taken them on their own tour of the Shrine and the Mansion. When the High Commissioner departed, the District Commissioner of Akka remained a while and invited Gladys to have dinner at his home two weeks hence. Shoghi Effendi was delighted with the results of the visit and happy that the District Commissioner of Akka had invited Gladys to his home.[8]

Life in Haifa

With the number of people living in the Western Pilgrim House and the House of the Master, several Persian women took responsibility for keeping the houses clean. Gladys wrote:

> on quiet sunny days it was a quaint picture to see them on the patio adjacent to the kitchen working over huge trays of dried foods such as grains, peas and especially rice, all had to be picked over carefully for bits of debris. The only girl who could speak some Engllsh was Khorshid so she took care of Mr. Maxwell and me over at the Pilgrim House. She would bring our food over and clean up after each meal. It was very refreshing to me to come home from my morning's work and find a nice cool drink waiting for me and every afternoon about four she would bring us tea . . .
>
> When Shoghi Effendi's work-room needed a thorough cleaning, they would wait until he had left to go to the Shrine Garden, then they would all work together, being very careful to put things back where the Guardian had left them. On one day they needed an extra pair of hands, so I went to help them. Of course, Rúḥíyyih Khánum was always present when this cleaning was done, she also helped. I noted that this room was most orderly, spartan, a single electric bulb hung from the ceiling, a small bed near his work table.[9]

Gladys was very taken with the everyday activities in Haifa:

> There were horse-drawn carts delivering cooking and heating oils to the housewives, the carts had a large sunflower painted on the rear, the driver calling a long-drawn out ' gaaaassss', the Arab lady who went by each morning calling 'leban, leban', we call it yogurt, if you wished to buy you came to the gate with a container, she would lower the can from the top of her head and ladle out the amount you required. A man with a huge tray on his head would sell fresh poppy seed buns which were delicious.
>
> The coffee vendors had beautiful urns, carried on their backs, if they found a customer, they would swing the urn around, very deftly, rinse out the little cup and pour out a fresh coffee for you, they would put cardamom in it which added a delicious aroma and

flavor. Due to the fact that they burned charcoal you could smell them before you could see them and this tickled your taste buds! I never purchased street coffee, I wasn't sure how sanitary the cups would be.

The nut vendors were usually Sudanese boys, wearing light blue tunics over their white pantaloons, a red fez on their head and a red sash around their waist, they were most colorful and very fine looking. They would set up their business on a tripod of three sticks, place a wooden tray on it with a small charcoal burner at one side over which they roasted the nuts. They were usually inexpensive varieties including sunflower and watermelon seeds . . . If you purchased any nuts, the vendor made a small cone of newspaper for you to carry them in. You could also buy lunches on some street corners, the stands made me think of our pop-corn stands, more often than not, they would be selling Arab bread which had been cut in half, making a pocket, these would be filled with minced meat, vegetables or small balls of grain fried in deep fat. In season, fruits were piled up at the edge of the sidewalk and I have seen push-carts filled with cactus fruit, called sabres, on a bed of cracked ice. In this case, the man selling them had a very sharp knife, hooked at the end, with gloves on his hands, he would slit the fruit skin and you would remove it yourself. I have seen people on their lunch hour buying five or six of these eating them right on the spot.

It was not unusual to see strings of camels on the city streets, most often there would be a donkey and rider, leading a string of three camels roped together. The camels have such a snooty expression and very long eyelashes, when they were shedding their coats they looked like bags of rags. I saw some on the empty lot across from where I was living, with their legs folded under them and chewing their food, the lower jaw swings from side to side.

There were many sidewalk cafes in the lower town, mostly near the Arab quarter, small stools were out during the day and usually filled with Arab men playing backgammon and sipping coffee . . .

Bread was delivered to our house by motorcycle, it was carried in the sidecar with no wrapping. The driver would stack up the loaves on his arm, sometimes he would drop a loaf, it would roll in the gutter, he would calmly pick it up and deliver it with the rest! He kept a weekly tally in pencil on the wall by the gate, at the end of the week he would add it up and after being paid, erase it and start over again the next time he came to deliver. This bread was from a Jewish bakery made in round loaves, we also bought bread from the Arab bakery, this was made from white flour and was round and flat. I noted that this bread was often used to mop up food by tearing off a small portion, running it around the plate until one had a nice mouthful then popping it in the mouth. Also, I have seen it used as a sort of napkin, they would wipe their fingers on it and eat that portion too! This kind of bread was delicious when toasted.

The milkman would have a neighborhood distribution point where large cans would be left, he then would take small containers around to the different houses, siphoning it off from the larger cans. You just had to stop thinking of sanitary precautions.

There was a man with a tiny monkey who would come and sit by the Gate. He had a drum that was very ingenious, it was made of a Kraft cheese can with sheepskin over each end, he even used the tin curl you get when opening one of these cans, attaching it with a thong so that it would hit the drum head with each turn of the handle. It was more like a rattle than a drum, the monkey would perform all kinds of antics to the beat and after the performance was over the man held out his hand for a contribution. If business wasn't profitable he just moved on to another location. He had extra drums to sell if you wished to buy.

As the disturbances deepened most of these colorful people disappeared and I missed seeing them. The streets had become so dangerous, you never knew what was going to happen, bombs exploded, there was sniping and once I saw a man kill himself with a hand grenade. These hand grenades were sold in the Arab quarter, they were in piles on the sidewalk and the price was about the equal of our fifty cents. Very few knew how to handle them. In the case of the man who killed himself, he had it in his home and was examining it, came out on his balcony with it then because he didn't know any better, he pulled the pin.[10]

Gladys was fascinated by Shoghi Effendi's gardens. She noted that

It was the custom of the Guardian to visit the Shrines on Mount Carmel most every day . . . His plans for beautifying the gardens surrounding the Shrines, both in Haifa and Bahji, were very dear to his heart, being a relaxation as well as an accomplishment. How his eyes shone when some difficult transplanting, or new effect turned out as he had anticipated. Though he did not claim to be a 'landscaper', he transformed the rough mountain area on every side, he dared attempt what others said would be impossible! Everything was utilized to the best advantage, he often pointed out that while the gardens had a lovely formal appearance, they were also a nursery, young trees and plants being skillfully placed in readiness to be moved where and when they were needed. When a new area was readied for expansion, so also were the plant-ings ready, each new development creating more and more beauty. The dear Guardian always lamented the fact that due to the climate, and the lack of sufficient water, it was not possible to have green lawns when all the exquisite flowering trees were in bloom. To compensate for this, he created lovely effects by special plantings under the trees, such as a huge bed of coral plants under the flame tree, (Royal Poinciana) each in the height of its season. He seemed to derive keen enjoyment in experi-menting with various grass seeds, always hoping for the most velvety green species to be found . . . At one time he became intrigued with cactus plants and proceeded to lay out a plan for a cactus garden. Later this garden was playfully nicknamed 'Arizona' in honor of that state being the home of so many species. This garden became a focal point of interest due to the fact that it was built in a section of the main garden where there had been a huge depression. The usual refuse from the existing gardens would have taken a long period of time to build it up to the proper level. As an aftermath of the street battles that took place in the city of Haifa in 1948, many old build-ings were being demolished. The Bahá'ís received permission to remove as much rubble as was needed to fill this large hole. In a matter of days, the cactus garden began to unfold. It was found that many Haifa resi-dents were growing cactus plants organically on their terraces and balconies! Some were purchased but many were donated by friends and strangers, later they would stroll through the gardens to see how their offerings were progressing. Shoghi Effendi had earth of various colors brought to this garden, some clear golden yellow, some warm pink, providing a striding contrast to the walks filled with small rounded white pebbles or coral colored crushed roof tile. In a com-paratively short time this garden was completed and Shoghi Effendi would be driven to Panorama Road, at the top of Mount Carmel, where he could look down on his handiwork. It truly resembled a large mosiac from this vantage point.[11]

Commemoration of the Ascension of Baha'u'llah

Shortly before the Commemoration of the Ascension of Bahá'u'lláh, Shoghi Effendi sent Gladys to get passes so that the Bahá'ís could go from Haifa to Bahjí and back by taxi. The British had set a curfew stating that no one was to be out between 6 p.m. and 6 a.m. Gladys described the adventure:

> Upon inquiry I found that the office that issued passes was in a secret place. I had to contact a special man who would escort me to this place, he left me at a street corner and I did not see which building he entered, and in a short while he returned with the necessary documents. The Bahá'ís in the general area, some from Trans-Jordan, came for the Holy Day observances whenever possible, this time our party was comprised of six taxis and we passed through all the road-blocks on the way to Acre without incident.
>
> The ladies and children gathered in the Pilgrim House and the men were with Shoghi Effendi in the Mansion. Just before the sunset hour, chairs were placed around the edge of the garden adjacent to Bahá'u'lláh's Shrine. Lights in the garden and around the eaves of building were turned on and shed a luminous glow on the greenery.
>
> Inside the Pilgrim House, Rúḥíyyih Khánum was talking to the ladies in Persian, at times she would turn to me and tell me in English that she was sharing news of the Bahá'í World with them. A large Persian rug had been placed in the center of the room for the small children, they sat very straight with their arms folded over their chests, sometimes their little backs would get tired and they would slump down, then they would catch their mother's eye and straighten up quickly. The children chanted prayers as their part in the observance. We could hear the voice of the beloved Guardian from the garden where he was speaking to the men, telling them the latest Bahá'í news and of his plans for the progress of the Faith.
>
> At midnight, word came for the ladies to enter the Shrine, we went around the rear of the building so that we would not disturb

Shoghi Effendi and left our shoes outside. As we entered, each lady held out her hands, palm upward, and Rúḥíyyih Khánum drew the glass stopper of a vial of Attar of Rose across each palm, then the lady would raise her palms to her forehead anointing herself with this precious fragrance, soon the beautiful aroma permeated the whole interior. Each one knelt in reverence at the Holy Threshold and then retired to a small room to the left of the Holy Tomb. A chair was placed in the doorway of this room for Rúḥíyyih Khánum. I was standing directly behind her so I could see the men as they came in and paid their respects, then they stepped back and knelt on the floor around the gem-like garden in the covered courtyard of the Shrine.

When all was quiet, Shoghi Effendi entered, approached the Holy Threshold, knelt in reverence, backed away a few steps and knelt. There was absolute silence, then he raised his beautiful resonant voice and chanted the Tablet of Visitation. It was my impression that his chanting was in two parts, the first I would describe as in the tenor range, the second part in a much deeper voice. Then, he again approached the Threshold, knelt there for a moment, then backed away step by step, leaving the Shrine, each man did the same, the only sound was the whisper of their stockinged feet, then the ladies did the same thing until the Shrine was empty.

Oh, how lovely it was, all the lights were on, the glowing colors of the Persian rugs, the dainty garden, the *objets d'art* placed here and there, the perfume, but above all the privilege of being there. Outside the night birds were singing, the air was soft and balmy, the moon was shedding its light, truly a taste of paradise. At this point everyone retired for a rest until called again to enter the Shrine to be there at three o'clock in the morning, the hour of Baha'u'lláh's Ascension. The earlier scene was repeated.

Had it not been for the curfew, we would have returned to Haifa immediately, as it was, we got what rest we could, then, at dawn, we left Bahjí. It was hard to leave this peaceful place, the sun was rising, the birds were singing and etched on the sky-line was a line of Arab women with containers on their heads going to the well for water. As we drove toward Haifa, there was a thick ground fog covering the road which slowed our progress. Suddenly, as we neared the outskirts of the city, our caravan was challenged and halted by a road-block, armed men thrust their guns through the windows of the taxis and we were advised that our passes had been cancelled and that we would not be allowed to enter Haifa. There had been a serious disturbance during the night! A conference was held with Shoghi Effendi, with the result that he sent Mr. Maxwell and myself to the nearby police station where we explained our position and why we were there. Due to the excellent relations that Shoghi Effendi had with the British authorities, some phone calls were made and we were allowed to continue to our homes. The streets of the city were deserted and there was an eerie, foreboding atmosphere as we passed through the silent streets.[12]

When the American journalist Marion Weinstein had visited 'Abdu'l-Bahá in 1919 shortly after the Balfour Declaration that allowed 'the establishment in Palestine of a National Home for the Jewish people', she had asked Him about the future of Palestine. He replied:

For Palestine Abdul-Baha has the brightest hopes. 'It will develop day by day now,' he declared, 'in industry, in commerce, in agriculture, under an enlightened government. Up to the present the people of this country were like lost sheep. Now they have found their shepherd.

'If the Zionists will mingle with the other races and live in unity with them, they will succeed. If not, they will meet certain resistance. For the present I think a neutral government like the British administration would be best. A Jewish government might come later.

'There is too much talk today of what the Zionists are going to do here. There is no need of it. Let them come and do more and say less.

'The Zionists should make it clear that their principle is to elevate all the people here and to develop the country for all its inhabitants. This land must be developed, according to the promises of the prophets Isaiah, Jeremiah and Zachariah. If they come in such a spirit they will not fail.

'They must not work to separate the Jews from the other Palestinians. Schools should be open to all nationalities here, business companies, etc. . . .

'This is the path to universal peace here as elsewhere – unity. We must prevent strife by all means. For 6,000 years man has been at war. It is time to try peace a little while. If it fails, we can always go back to war.'[13]

Few appeared to be paying attention to 'Abdu'l-Bahá's words as the battle for Israel began. On 29 November 1947, the United Nations passed a plan to partition Palestine into a Jewish section and an Arab section. Almost immediately, Jews and Arabs were in conflict. On 30 December, a fanatical Jewish group drove by the Haifa oil refinery and threw bombs into a crowd of Arabs by the main gate. Six were killed and forty-two wounded. The enraged Arabs then stormed into the refinery compound and attacked Jewish workers. British soldiers and police needed an hour to subdue the riot. Forty-one Jews were killed and forty-nine were wounded. Jewish radicals responded by attacking an Arab village near Haifa. These murderous riots set the stage for the Battle of Haifa the following April, with the Bahá'í community caught in the middle.[14] Shoghi Effendi, however, as the Master had done before him, continued with his own plans regardless of what the rest of the world was doing.

The Guardian's Plans

The Guardian initiated teaching plans for two more National Assemblies in 1947: Australia and New Zealand, and Iraq. The National Assembly of Australia and New Zealand was given a Six Year Plan to end in 1953, with the goals of establishing two new local assemblies in Australia and nineteen new groups in Australasia. The goals for Iraq's Three Year Plan were to build a National Bahá'í Hall, reinforce the national fund, increase the number of local assemblies, consolidate the Faith and translate Bahá'í literature into Arabic.[15]

On 7 December 1947, he wrote to the Haifa Local Building and Town Planning Commission about the Shrine of the Báb:

In connection with the accompanying drawings and application for permission to build, I wish to add a word of explanation.

The Tomb of the Báb, and of 'Abdu'l-Bahá, so well known to the people of Haifa as 'Abbás Effendi, is already in existence on

338

Mt. Carmel in an incomplete form. In its present state, in spite of the extensive gardens surrounding it, it is a homely building with a fortress-like appearance.

It is my intention to now begin the completion of this building by preserving the original structure and at the same time embellishing it as a monumental building of great beauty, thus adding to the general improvement in the appearance of the slopes of Mt. Carmel.

The purpose of this building will, when completed, remain the same as at present. In other words it will be used exclusively as a Shrine entombing the remains of the Báb.

As you will see from the accompanying drawings the completed structure will comprise an arcade of twenty-four marble or other monolith columns surmounted by an ornamental balustrade, on the first floor or ground floor of the building. It is part of the building that we wish to begin work on at once, leaving the intermediary section and the dome, which will surmount the whole edifice when completed, to be carried on in the future, if possible at an early date after the completion of the ground floor arcade.

The Architect of this monumental building is Mr. W.S. Maxwell, F.R.I.B.A., F.R.A.I.C., R.C.A., the well-known Canadian architect, whose firm built the Chateau Frontenac Hotel in Quebec, the House of Parliament in Regina, the Art Gallery, Church of the Messiah, various Bank buildings, etc., in Montreal. I feel the beauty of his design for the completion of the Báb's Tomb will add greatly to the appearance of our city and be an added attraction for visitors.[16]

1948

Living in Haifa in 1948 was interesting. Just going for the mail meant being frisked and having all packages searched. On 12 January, Gladys was in a Jewish shopping centre running errands when there was an explosion. Soon, 'the center began to buzz like a bee hive [and] everyone started making for home and I started down one street and the bullets were zinging around so I went in another direction as quickly as possible, but had to go way out of my way to get home. There has hardly been fifteen minutes go by since then without shots flying about.' Gladys said that most businesses closed by 3:30 so that people could get home before dark, when it was too dangerous to be out. A Christian

Arab told her that their children were old at fifteen and 'conditions are making us two-faced hypocrites!' She also met a Jewish girl who said that her husband's guards, who had worked for him for four years, had recently shot and killed him. Gladys noted that their outside social life was nil because they had to protect the Faith and stay completely neutral. If they associated with Jews, the Arabs hated them, and vice versa.[17]

The British Mandate was to end on 14 May 1948 and the Jews and Arabs began to really fight for position, for who would be in charge when that date arrived. In February Rúḥíyyih Khánum wrote:

> We know Bahá'u'lláh will watch over us. But being human we have our moments of anxiety, such as when shooting flares up all over town and the beloved Guardian has not yet come down from the Shrines, and the road is closed, and he has to come home on foot – then we just know it's up to Bahá'u'lláh . . . it is no exaggeration to say a night without shooting just isn't any more. Sometimes it goes on, off and on, all night. But you soon sleep through it except for a bomb . . .[18]

> Rage is my primary emotion these days. The senseless wanton murder infuriates me. Most people want nothing more than to be left alone . . .[19]

And in March:

> Arms are sold openly in Arab quarters . . . Hassan said he and his cousin Muhammad were sitting in a cafe in Tiberius; they heard a boy hawking, he was crying 'Grenade, grenade!' Hassan could not believe his ears so he called him over and asked him what he was selling? He said bombs. He had a sack on his back. This he obligingly dumped on the ground and unloaded a pile of hand grenades! . . . I saw a man from my own bedroom window a few days ago with a revolver in his hand and a crowd of Arabs around him. He wanted to make sure it was working so he came over to our garden wall, fired two shots at it, and headed off for the town, probably to do his bit of murder.[20]

Ben and Gladys Weeden: First wedding of western Bahá'ís by eastern Bahá'ís

During all the violence, Gladys Anderson's fiancé Ben Weeden arrived on 19 March, blissfully unaware of what was happening. The two were married next day.[21] Gladys drove to Jerusalem two days before the wedding with two Bahá'í men in a private taxi hired by Shoghi Effendi. They were stopped about twenty times and had their luggage searched twice before reaching Jerusalem. Gladys settled into the Swiss Pension and waited for her future husband to arrive, jumping every time the phone rang or the door opened. Finally, at 1:15 a.m., Ben arrived. Gladys said that 'I did manage to maintain my dignity and greet Ben as if we had only parted a short while before!' Gladys described the wedding:

> We were married by the Amman L.S.A. and never was a wedding more suited to our hearts' desire. The soft chanting of a Prayer in Persian, then one of the Bahá'ís anointed our hands and foreheads with rose-water. Our marriage certificate was very impressive; it had been made by a Bahá'í in calligraphy in Persian with the Greatest Name at the top. It was a mighty precious moment when we clasped hands and declared 'Verily, we are content with the Will of God!' Only one man in the group spoke English so after shaking hands all around Ben and I gathered our little pink cloud around us and strolled arm in arm to the center of Jerusalem. We asked directions to a jewelry shop, Ben wanted to buy me a gift, and were led into a building to a shop right out of the Arabian nights, it was full of all the beautiful arts and crafts the East is capable of producing. When the owner found out we had just been married he ordered Turkish coffee for us and we browsed around sipping our coffee feeling ourselves to be in a 'technicolor' dream world.[22]

The newlyweds then went to Jericho and had a short honeymoon at a small hotel called the Winter Palace. When it came time to go to Haifa, they hired a private taxi, hoping not to get involved in what the newspapers were calling 'the battle of the roads'. Their only battle, however, was with mud when, because of recent rain and a passing lorry, the taxi suddenly skidded off the road and rolled into a field. Gladys hit her head, but Ben ended up with a broken rib. The car's doors were jammed shut and the top was crushed. A British army lorry stopped to help and pried the doors open. As Gladys stepped out of the car, one of the soldiers said, 'Why, Miss Anderson, what has happened to you!' The soldier had been with the High Commissioner on his Bahjí visit.[23] The rest of the trip, until they reached Haifa, was fairly normal except that their Arab driver drove the whole way with an automatic pistol in his hand. Finally arriving in Haifa, Ben was introduced to his new home when a machine gun opened fire nearby, forcing them to hide for about twenty minutes.[24]

Ben wrote about the importance of the wedding:

> Due to the shifting and changes going on at that time at the American Consulate and other government offices of the British Mandate, we could not get our marriage recognized at that time. This worried us quite a bit as it was the first marriage of western Bahá'ís by eastern Bahá'ís.
>
> After the British Mandate ended we took the matter up with the new State of Israel here in Haifa. It was surprising how smoothly the whole thing went. They registered and endorsed the records of our marriage as entered in the Bahá'í book used here at the World Center to record such Bahá'í marriages and filed their copy, giving full recognition to the Faith and its right to perform marriages . . . When we presented the records to the American Consulate there was no hesitation as to registering Gladys as Mrs. Weeden, and so, it would seem now that through one of the consulates, the U.S. has recognized the Bahá'í marriage of two Americans.[25]

Of Shoghi Effendi, Ben wrote:

> From what little I have seen I would say there are not a great many Easterners that could stand the pace Shoghi Effendi sets. One can only marvel at the scope of his mind and the strength of him. Yet, tho' he is fire and steel, he is the most loveable, understanding, compassionate and considerate person I have ever known. He is without peer. There is no one like him. How I wish other Bahá'ís could know him as Gladys and I have been privileged to know him. In writing as I have, I am not writing of his station as Guardian, that is quite

beyond my pen. How all Bahá'ís should work for this great figure! His burden is great.[26]

I wish it were possible to give you some idea of the tremendous amount of work Shoghi Effendi is putting into the gardens. They literally change and grow from day to day. This year there has been a lot of rain in Palestine and every tree and flower has grown and bloomed in a riot of glory . . . I would also like to tell you of the many metal peacocks and vases, of metal and marble used throughout the gardens. Many of them came from England and the old estates that have been broken up.[27]

Shoghi Effendi wanted Ben and Sutherland to go to Italy to find and purchase materials for the construction of the superstructure of the Shrine of the Báb, but he told Ben that first he should visit the Shrine of Bahá'u'lláh. The road to Akka had been subject to 'much trouble and shooting', so Ben and Gladys went by boat:

We taxied to the shore where an Arab picked up Gladys and waded out to a little rowboat. Another, about half my size grabbed me above the knees and with me waving like a tall pole, stuck me in the boat. We were rowed to a fishing boat . . . There were probably 75 Arabs on board with their guns, goods and chattels. You can't imagine the picture it made. The trip took about an hour and a half and was interesting all the way . . . We had to again get into a rowboat and it was a scramble as everyone was in a hurry to get ashore. We had to land on a little narrow shelf but for a wonder no one fell into the water . . . Acca is dirty, hot and crowded with Arabs. We got a taxi to Bahjí and there found that peace beyond understanding . . . Pilgrimaging is not easy these days. It looked as tho we would have to stay all night but about five, Bardi, one of the house boys, turned up with a taxi and yelled in Persian 'Get going! Get going!' We did and on the ¾ hour drive back saw plenty of evidence of the fighting along that road. Bardi and the Armenian driver of that taxi certainly had their nerve making that trip. It was funny to see them and hear them yell to the Arabs and then when we met Jews they would yell 'Shalom Shalom.'[28]

Ben commonly went to the Shrines of the Báb and 'Abdu'l-Bahá and he noticed a difference between them. In the Shrine of the Báb, 'it is the spiritual side of you . . . that matters at most times. To me it seems as tho my soul was bared, questioned, instructed and given strength . . . In 'Abdu'l-Bahá's Shrine I have always found the utmost happiness, understanding and comfort.'[29]

The contrast between the atmosphere in the Shrines and the violence elsewhere could not have been greater. The battle for Haifa grew worse in April as the Jews and Arabs fought for control of the city. Rúḥíyyih Khánum wrote:

> There was often shooting all around the home of the Master, amounting sometimes to minor battles; no one ever shot at us or attacked us, but the danger of being hit was not to be underestimated. As the terrorism increased, certain areas, including our own, were voluntarily blacked out at night with no street lights at all; there were often day-time curfews imposed, when pitched battles or major acts of terrorism took place and only the British forces moved about, their great tanks howling down the abandoned streets, often firing random bursts from their machine guns as they rolled by. The wailing noise of their sirens was a most eerie, unpleasant sound, but at night it was really terrifying to an already nerve-racked population living on the edge of a volcano which might explode any time.[30]

Marble from Italy for the Shrine of the Báb

In mid-April, in the midst of the fighting, chaos and confusion, Ben and Sutherland left Haifa in an armoured taxi in order to catch a plane from Lydda airport (now Ben Gurion) to Rome. Shoghi Effendi was sending them to place orders for columns and ornamental stone for the construction of the Shrine of the Báb because he had been unable to find suitable stone more locally. In a letter to Ugo Giachery on 6 April, the Guardian wrote that Ben was unable to obtain a visa in Palestine and asked Ugo to try and get him one on his arrival.[31]

A few days later, Shoghi Effendi wrote a second letter, this time to Horace Holley in America, saying that his funds in Palestine had been blocked and asking if it would be possible to obtain a loan from the

American believers ('those in a position financially to do so') in order to make the expected contracts. He wrote that

> he himself wishes to be considered the guarantor in this matter and will repay the loan at the earliest possible moment. He is very anxious to have no misunderstanding on this point. He is financing this work from the international funds of the Cause and will only consider an arrangement by which he will repay this temporary loan . . .[32]

Ben and Sutherland left Tel Aviv on 13 April and, according to Sutherland, 'encountered no villains and have not heard any gunshots except for a few in Tel Aviv at night time'. Their first flight to Rome was cancelled, but Sutherland wrote to Shoghi Effendi that

> we were rewarded by a very interesting night trip in a splendid four-engined Norwegian plane, American made and capably staffed by capable Norwegians. There is nothing in particular to dwell upon, other than to say it was quite interesting to be one of forty or more passengers in an up to date plane.[33]

They were met at the airport in Rome by Ugo Giachery, who with his wife Angeline had pioneered to Rome from the United States in 1947 under the Second Seven Year Plan. Ben was very impressed with Dr Giachery, noting that 'he has given us no end of help. In fact, I do not know what we would have done without him. He was able to get me off the plane at Rome without a visa, had rooms for us and has opened every door that might help us.' Ben and Sutherland were there when the Bahá'ís of Rome elected their first Local Spiritual Assembly at Riḍván 1948. Ben wrote to a friend in America, Carl Krug: 'They have a truly top-notch group of fourteen Bahá'ís.'[34] In fact, Ben was very impressed by both Sutherland Maxwell and Ugo Giachery, writing after his return from Italy:

> The huge task Sutherland has performed in designing and creating these additions to the Shrine is truly heroic, and one cannot help but stand in awe of the terrific strength and vitality he puts into his work. In the future many will see this and find it hard to remember

the sum of his years when he gave himself to this great undertaking. Few will understand the problems he has mastered and the toll the burning fires of creation have taken. Fewer still will know of the strength and encouragement, care and loving kindness with which Shoghi Effendi has ever given and showered on those who are close to him.

There is another humble worker of whom few will ever hear, and that is Ugo R. Giachery in Rome. He has had the difficult task of arranging contracts regarding the cutting of six hundred and fifty odd tons of stone, inspecting the work, and will care for the shipping and in general has been acting as Shoghi Effendi's agent in Italy. All this has been a great task in itself but in addition he has carried on pioneer work of the highest value and acted as the N.S.A.'s representative at teaching conferences and at UN meetings.[35]

Prior to this time, Ugo had received only a few letters and cablegrams from the Guardian; in fact, he was 'practically unknown' to him,[36] but he had been given the huge undertaking, with Sutherland and Ben, of finding the marble and other materials needed for the work. It wasn't an easy task in a country 'whose economy had been shattered by a disastrous war'. Shoghi Effendi was an exacting taskmaster and Ugo wrote that

My efforts therefore had to be multiplied if I wanted to keep pace with Shoghi Effendi's eagerness. As I redoubled my efforts, my recompense became greater. Never before in long years of business activity had I received such a recompense! A flow of appreciation, of tender and abiding love, of undeserved praise and gratitude came my way almost every day, for well over nine years. My life was transformed; the greatest joy and elevation came to me from a gentle and noble hand that penned letters and cables in words loomed with the indestructible threads of superhuman love . . .[37]

For some time, no one in Haifa knew if Ben and Sutherland had made it or not because there was no communication.[38] But getting to Italy was just the first part of the problem. Sutherland wanted to match the stone in Haifa with similar Italian marble. His search was simplified by the Italian Geological Office in Rome, which had samples of every description. When Sutherland found the perfect match, an Italian contractor for the Shrine construction was immediately dispatched to examine the site. Find it he did, but all the approaches had been destroyed during the war and repairs would require much time and money, so Sutherland returned to the Geological Office. He found a second marble quarry near the village of Chiampo, northwest of Venice. Then he located a source for rose-coloured granite near Lake Maggiore. On 29 April, the first contract was signed for marble from Chiampo, followed on 5 May by a second contract for all the necessary machinery. Soon architects, draftsmen, quarriers, stonecutters, sculptors and artists were at work converting masses of rock into massive columns, delicately-carved capitals and sculptured panels.[39]

The end of the British Mandate

While Sutherland and Ben were in Italy, the battle was raging in Haifa. On 27 April, Rúḥíyyih Khánum wrote of the latest excitement:

> Yesterday we had a moment of mad excitement as suddenly the maid rushed up and knocked and said the Haganah [a Jewish paramilitary organization] wanted to get in. Fortunately I was dressed . . . and went down quickly as I could for it seemed first our dumb bunny . . . went to the door, when she saw a gang of Jews with tommy guns and revolvers she nearly had a fit and went to call Banu, Banu came and the Jews said 'Open the door', she said she had to call the house and meantime was rushing looking for B___ who was not there and then to call me and they said 'If you don't open it we'll break it in!' At this juncture I arrived and immediately let them in. They were five, all young men. I asked if they spoke English and one said he spoke a little. I asked him if he knew whose house this was, the Head of the Bahá'í Community, and he said yes, but somehow I think they did not know and were attracted here for one of two reasons, either because shortly before a truck load of Arabs stopped for a while in front of our door and they thought we had Arabs here or because of our car, for one of their first questions was 'Whose car is that in the garage?' When I told them they were satisfied. It turned out one of them spoke Persian as he said his mother was a Persian though he was from 'Yerushalim' so I talked to him in Persian all the time.

They did not seem keen on searching the house, were very decent and polite and told me, at first, not to be afraid to which I replied I certainly was not! After a very brief look about, and refusing to go downstairs or into the kitchen etc., they left . . .[40]

Rúḥíyyih Khánum and Gladys Weeden made a point of going about their normal business, but less often. There were snipers and road blocks, but they felt it was important to show that the Baháʼís were staying in spite of the problems. Their car was searched every time they went out, and if the guards did not know them they would have to show their passports.

Shoghi Effendi, too, continued to go up the Shrine of the Báb each day, visiting the Shrines and working on the gardens, coming home before dark. Only rarely was he not able to do so because of the curfew. But that did not mean that it was safe. One day, Gladys drove the Guardian to the Shrine (the usual Arab driver had left the area) when suddenly the occupants of a car up ahead opened fire on the occupants of another car. The second car sped past Shoghi Effendi, putting him and Gladys between the blazing guns and their frantic target. Rúḥíyyih Khánum wrote:

The other car soon overtook his and went on with its private war, but one can imagine our feelings when we heard of this incident later on! Yet there was nothing we could do. Everyone who has lived through such experiences knows that there are only two things in such circumstances one can do – go away, or carry on as usual. We just carried on.[41]

One thing that struck the authorities of the new State of Israel was that Shoghi Effendi was the only 'oriental notable of any standing' not to run away during the fighting. This and an awareness of the basic tenets of the Faith resulted in the emerging leaders of Israel being very cooperative with the Guardian. One of the first things the new government did was to place signs reading 'Holy Place' at the Shrine of Baháʼuʼlláh, which was in a more isolated place than the Shrines in Haifa.[42] Virtually all the Covenant-breakers fled Haifa and Akka, joining forces with the Arab community in Lebanon against the Jews and eventually becoming integrated into Islamic society.[43]

What Shoghi Effendi did was the key for many as to whether they should flee or stay. The House of the Master was in the Arab section of Haifa and those living around Shoghi Effendi kept a very watchful eye on its inhabitants. Every day the neighbours would ask, 'Is Shoghi Effendi leaving?' Rúḥíyyih Khánum wrote:

> They say when he does they will . . . the Palestine policeman now living in K_____'s house asked him when he should go and K_____ told him: 'When you see Shoghi Effendi leave, grab your coat, lock the door and follow him!' The man also said . . . 'If you don't tell me Shoghi Effendi is planning to go, if he does, you are responsible for my life.' The sudden esteem in which our neighbours hold us is rather funny after 25 years ignoring the Cause and the Guardian![44]

One of the Covenant-breakers, when he fled, told a relative: 'Watch what Shoghi Effendi does. If he stays, you stay; if he leaves, you leave.' A girl from a Covenant-breaking family met Rúḥíyyih Khánum on the street and said that she had been instructed that if threatened with danger, she was to go to Shoghi Effendi's house because she would be safe there.[45]

Shoghi Effendi's greatest concerns were the Twin Holy Shrines. The War of Independence was swirling around both, and he worried about possible damage. There was another worry – in trying to divide Palestine into a Jewish State and a Palestinian/Arab region, the authorities at one time considered splitting the country so that Haifa would be in the Jewish part with Akka and Bahjí in the Palestinian part, putting the administrative centre of the Faith in one country and the holiest spot on earth, the burial place of Bahá'u'lláh, in a separate, hostile county. Unsurprisingly, this did not happen.[46]

The caretakers of the Shrine of Bahá'u'lláh at this time were Salah Jarrah and his mother. Salah was the great-nephew of Colonel Aḥmad Jarráh, the Commander of the Guard during Bahá'u'lláh's imprisonment who had become a Bahá'í. Salah had been serving Shoghi Effendi since 1942 in various capacities. During this time of disturbance, he had been the Guardian's mail courier between Haifa and Beirut, going by way of small boats since the roads were so dangerous. Serving at Bahjí was for him a delight. He nailed pictures on the walls of the Mansion with Shoghi Effendi looking over his shoulder to make sure the position was just so. To every request of the Guardian, Saláh would always reply, 'Yes, my Guardian,' usually without first thinking whether the task could be done. One day Shoghi Effendi said he needed 70 cypress trees that were two metres high. After saying 'Yes, my Guardian', he discovered that the Bahá'í nursery only had three trees available. Finally, he discovered a kibbutz with a huge number of cypress trees. When he explained what he needed, he was told to take as many as he needed – free of charge. All Salah had to do was arrange for them to be dug up and transported.[47] Salah thought that the Guardian would be delighted by the fact that he had managed to procure them, but to his surprise, when Shoghi Effendi saw them he asked quite abruptly, 'Where did you get them?' When Salah told him, Shoghi Effendi's face cleared and he said happily, 'I knew you would be entirely obedient, and it had occurred to me that you might actually dig up the ones we have just planted so as to have them ready for me today!'[48]

For a number of years Shoghi Effendi had not had a car. The old one had been sold during the Second World War because no spare parts for it were available, but Roy Wilhelm had recently sent him a new one. During the early afternoon of 4 May, while Rúḥíyyih Khánum and Gladys were having coffee, a man came to the door. He was the local Haganah chief, Mr Friedman, and he had twenty armed men with him. A local guard had noticed a group of five armed men with a jeep by Shoghi Effendi's garage. When the guard approached them, they pulled out their guns, so he ran for help. By the time help arrived, the armed men had gone.

> But although the padlock on our door was sawn through the door was closed from the inside so they thought it [the car] was still there. I looked through the keyhole and what a ghastly emptiness – no Buick! Poor Gladys rushed around to the little door at the back and, indeed, no Buick! The Haganah Guard implied Jews had taken it (or English) but would not say it outright. Well, Friedman notified the Haganah. Gladys and Mansoor notified the army and Stanton St. Police. I phoned Dr. Weinshall [their lawyer] who advised us to go to the Hadar Hacarmel Police Station. Shoghi Effendi was calmer than anyone else, only said 'How it will rejoice my enemies!' I guess none of us hoped to really see the car again – but how sad it was to have our big lovely Buick, just received after so long a time, gone!

With some difficulty I got a Jewish taxi for the Guardian. The driver said 'If Jews have taken your car you'll get it back again!' I went with Gladys to the Police station and waited outside while she made a report, then we left for Weinshall a description of the car as he had said to give him one so he could help. Then our nice taxi driver took us to another Haganah place and we again reported. Then a strange thing happened! We were walking home tired and dispirited, and in the window of a cosmetic shop on Herzl Street she saw a hand lotion I had tried several times to get. I thought I would not bother, but then I decided to get it and went in. The proprietor has known Dad and me for years so he asked about Daddy and I enquired about his old father, etc. I was not going to say anything about the car as I felt humiliated about it but after paying for my things I started out without them. That looked so foolish that I apologized and said 'I am very upset because our car has just been stolen!' The man said 'But I saw your car today at about 2:15 in the new Business Center! And I was surprised because I wondered how you could sell such a beautiful new car!' It seems he had seen Gladys and me driving by the day before and remembered the car vividly and the U.S. license plates! He said Jews had been in it and a Jew driving it and it was just around the corner from the Savoy Hotel. He also said please not to give his name as a witness, but I said then it won't help us, so he weakened and said we could. Of course we rushed back to the police station and reported what he had said and when I got home I found Mr. Friedman had left his number for me so I called him and told him and he said 'That's all I need to know. Now I know they brought it into our part of town I can get them!' Some time later the Hadar Police Station called and said 'Your car has been located and you will get it back tomorrow so don't worry.' Mr. Friedman also phoned and said the same thing, and sure enough, about 11 a.m. the 4th he phoned and said he could come and get Gladys to get the car and she drove up to Hadar Police Station and got it! My Goodness, were we all happy! The funny thing is, on our way home, before going to that store I had been saying only a miracle could get it back![49]

On 15 May, the day the British Mandate came to an end, Ben and Sutherland returned to Haifa on the S.S. *Argentina*, having missed most of these interesting times.[50]

By June, things had calmed down considerably. Ben wrote that it was quiet in Haifa and that one could move about the city without any problems, though cars could not be driven after eight in the evening. There was petrol rationing, but the stores were well stocked. Travel outside the city, however, was restricted. To go to Bahjí required getting passes because Akka was in the military zone and the fighting front was not far away. For the commemoration of the Ascension of Bahá'u'lláh, the event began in Bahjí, but had to be completed in Haifa because of the 8 o'clock curfew.[51] Shoghi Effendi's Arab driver had scurried away during the fighting, so Ben became the Guardian's driver, which raised some eyebrows. People wondered who it was who had come all the way from America to be Shoghi Effendi's chauffeur, a job normally considered to be very lowly. To be called a chauffeur was a deep insult. Ben, of course, was thrilled to be able to drive the Guardian from place to place. Driving the big car, though, was a challenge in Haifa's narrow streets. Ben noted that the car needed 'a hinge in the middle'. But Ben was really happy to drive because Shoghi Effendi had great enjoyment from it.[52]

One day Ben drove Shoghi Effendi to Bahjí. He later wrote to his friend Carl Krug that he 'went into the Shrine alone with him, where he chanted the Prayer of Visitation. Spent the rest of the morning going over the Mansion and have him tell me of the many things there and about the room Bahá'u'lláh used. We had lemonade on the cool balcony and absorbed the wonderful and very tangible peace which radiates all about Bahjí.'[53]

Ben described life in Haifa:

The work is so different from anything experienced in America and everything you do has such subtle and far reaching effects. I have heard wonder expressed at the fact no teaching is carried on in Haifa . . . It is true that classes are not held nor talks given but you only have to do business in this country a very, very short time to learn that living the Bahá'í life is the greatest bit of teaching that can be used anywhere. To say you are a Bahá'í really means something more than just another religious sect here. It is a way of life and recognized as such. When . . . pilgrims come to Haifa they might bear that in mind and do a little practicing. Here one must not forget for a moment that one is a Bahá'í and that is not too easy but is important. Carl, you have no idea what a thrill it is to see the change that comes to faces when you mention you are doing something for the Bahá'í Faith and Shoghi Effendi.[54]

National Spiritual Assembly of Canada, and more teaching plans

Though surrounded by war, Shoghi Effendi still kept a close eye on the rest of the Bahá'í world, with the Tablets of the Divine Plan uppermost in his mind. Right in the middle of the battle for Haifa in April, he gave the Canadians their own National Spiritual Assembly. Their National Convention was held on 24 and 25 April in the Maxwell House and was attended by thirteen delegates and about a hundred others. Six delegates from the west were unable to attend due to 'flood and three thousand miles'. Five members of the outgoing National Assembly of the United States and Canada (those from the United States) also attended.[55] The new National Assembly was immediately given a teaching plan by the Guardian. Their goals were to incorporate the National Assembly, establish national endowments, increase the number of Local Assemblies and localities with Bahá'ís, and to enrol Eskimos and Native Indians into the Faith.[56]

The National Assemblies of Egypt and Sudan, and Germany and Austria were given five year plans to take them to 1953. In both cases, Shoghi Effendi asked the National Assemblies to make their own goals. Egypt and Sudan decided to increase the number of local assemblies and localities with Bahá'ís, to send pioneers to Tunisia, Algeria and Libya, to acquire land for a Bahá'í school, to start a Bahá'í magazine and to consolidate the Ethiopian Bahá'í community. Germany and Austria's plan was to double the number of local assemblies, to increase the number of localities with Bahá'ís, to deepen on the Administrative Order, to acquire a Ḥaẓíratu'l-Quds in Frankfurt, and to publish literature about the Faith.[57]

The Shrine of the Báb

On 3 July, Shoghi Effendi announced to Sutherland: 'Well, the historic decision to commence work on the Shrine has been taken at 10:15 (p.m.) today!' The Guardian then shook hands with his architect. Rúḥíyyih Khánum noted at the time that she could 'hear explosions in the distance' and thought 'God help this poor country!'[58]

On 2 September, the orders went to the gardeners to begin clearing the site for the ground breaking. This meant removing the tiles around the Shrine, digging up 'many metres of hedging, dismounting huge lead vases & dismantling their pedestals'. Two days later, ground was broken and work begun on the foundation for the arcade.[59]

On 16 November, Shoghi Effendi received a cablegram from Ugo Giachery that read:

> First shipment granite, stone holy Báb's Shrine left Leghorn Sunday November 14th Steamship *Norte* due Haifa twenty-third entrusting safety beloved Guardian's prayer assistance Blessed Perfection ever-present Master's guiding hand.[60]

The *Norte* carried seventy-two wooden cases containing ninety tons of stone from four different parts of Italy. All the ship had to do was run a 'blockade of hostile naval vessels' and work on the superstructure of the Shrine of the Báb could begin.[61]

Finding the right rock had been a challenge, but converting it from mountain bedrock to a carved panel or column required true artisans. Each block of rock in the quarry had to be

> cut to a size prescribed by the plans made by the architect, then carved, finished to a smooth surface, and placed with its neighbouring stones in the actual part of the building erected in the marble works, in sections held together by plaster of Paris. Specialized workers then went over every single stone to eliminate any imperfection to the fraction of a line. The stones were then numbered, the temporary part of the building dismantled, and every piece placed in a strong wooden box made especially for it, to be shipped to Haifa.
>
> A detailed list would give the number of the case and the number of each stone contained in it, while a master key-plan indicated the location of each stone in the building. A fascinating gigantic puzzle.[62]

An Italian journalist claimed that this was the 'largest prefabricated building' to be moved from Europe to any place in the world.

Bahá'u'lláh's cell in the Most Great Prison

A few months after the State of Israel came into being, there were rumours that the barracks in Akka were going to be used as a mental institution and, of course, the Bahá'ís worried about how this would affect the cell where Bahá'u'lláh had been imprisoned. The British had put up a plaque noting that Bahá'u'lláh had stayed there, but what the Israelis would do was not known. One day, a letter addressed to the 'Bahá'í Community' arrived saying that the authorities were willing to put the cell permanently in the care of the Bahá'ís. They wanted someone to come and accept the key. This was a great surprise because usually this sort of thing happened only after lengthy negotiations instigated by the Bahá'ís. Shoghi Effendi appointed Ben, Salah and Gladys to collect the keys. On the day the keys were passed over, the head of the institution and the three Bahá'ís went into the cell of Bahá'u'lláh. Prayers were said in three languages and Bahá'u'lláh's cell in the Most Great Prison was in Bahá'í hands.[63]

1949: Increasing recognition

On 20 December 1948, the main English-language newspaper in Israel carried a long article which favourably described the Bahá'í Faith and stated that Shoghi Effendi was its world head. But a month later, on 28 January 1949, a short note appeared in the same paper that stated bluntly that 'Mr. Rabbani is not the Guardian of the Bahai Faith, nor its World Leader.' The note was signed 'Bahai U.N. Observer.' The note cited the New History Society in New York as the source of its information – a creation of Ahmad Sohrab, the long-discredited Covenant-breaker. It was a desperate attempt by 'Abdu'l-Bahá's former secretary to discredit Shoghi Effendi and it was completely ignored by virtually everyone.[64]

Just a week earlier, Shoghi Effendi had received an invitation to meet Prime Minister Ben Gurion at a reception. The Guardian, however, decided that Sutherland and Ben should go in his place, because it was not befitting that the Head of the Faith should go and be lost in a crowd. Shoghi Effendi said that he was willing to call on the Prime Minister privately, so Rúḥíyyih Khánum telephoned the Mayor of Haifa to try to arrange this, and on 21 January the Mayor called back and said that it had been arranged for Shoghi Effendi to meet the Prime Minister that evening at 7:15. Rúḥíyyih Khánum recounts what happened:

> It is now 7 o'clock and the Guardian and Daddy, driven by Ben have just left . . . As Shoghi Effendi has been trying for twenty-five years to get the Cause here to be recognized as not a local community but a world centre, and he not a local or national head, but a world head, this opportunity to meet the Prime Minister is very important. No doubt Ben Gurion feels he is being very condescending – if only he knew what an honour is being conferred on him and how condescending God is being to him tonight! Such is the smallness of men's lives and the vanity of the world.
>
> Well, the interview is over. Lasted about 15 minutes. When they got there the Guardian found the front door ajar, he went in, saw no one, knocked on the door, went further and found Ben Gurion and wife and host finishing their dessert in one of these small houses where alcoves divide the rooms . . . Ben Gurion got up and took the Guardian into the neighbouring . . . room and courteously offered him the best seat, and so on. Then he asked some questions about the Cause, said he knew about it, that it is a 'social movement', whereupon the Guardian said it was much more than that, divinely inspired from God, etc. He put it not too strongly. Ben Gurion also asked his exact relation to the Faith and was told.
>
> The Guardian did not want to keep him from his dinner and after a short interview rose to go. Ben Gurion took him to the other door and a servant to the car and opened the door. . .
>
> Ben Gurion asked the Guardian if there was a history of the Cause he could read and Shoghi Effendi said he would be pleased to send him a book. [He sent him *God Passes By*.][65]

1950

The year 1950 would bring extraordinary victories: the completion of teaching plans in India, Pakistan and Burma, Iraq, Persia, and the British Isles; the initiation of the first international teaching plan – for the African continent – bringing together for the first time several National Spiritual Assemblies in cooperation; the beginnings of a permanent secretariat at the World Centre, and the completion of the arcade surrounding the Shrine of the Báb.

Even the weather in Haifa seemed to herald change. On 29 January, there was a 'goodly dusting' of snow on top of Mount Carmel, but it was gone within a couple hours after the sun came up. But on 6 February, a foot of snow fell on Haifa with a foot and a half on top of Mount Carmel. The snow was wet and heavy and it brought down many of the power and telephone lines. Ben Weeden wrote that he was having to use a kerosene lamp because of the loss of electricity. The snow broke the branches of many olive trees. For much of the local population, it was the first time they had seen snow and Ben found their reactions to be highly entertaining:

> I was amazed at how the young and old reacted to the snow. They seemed possessed to throw it at someone or something. They got onto roofs and dropped great gobs on passers-by. Automobiles seemed to be the chief mark of every person who could toss a handful of snow. Why, one old fellow who could just about dodder along picked up a double handful of snow and tossed it at the Buick as Shoghi Effendi and I were on our way to the Gardens.[1]

But the challenges were increasingly severe. Shoghi Effendi's secretary had commented on this the previous year in a letter to the struggling British Bahá'í community:

It would seem as if all our tasks, including here at the World Centre, are becoming increasingly more of a challenge to us. As the time approaches for the ending of the various Plans, Six Year ones, Seven Year, Five Year, etc., the obstacles seem to become greater, and the friends are made to realise that very real, hard, often back-breaking effort and sacrifice is involved! . . . He himself, having undertaken at such a disturbed time to raise at least the first story or arcade of the new part of the Báb's Shrine, finds himself beset with worries, problems and complications which have not only underlined his work, but exhaust and harass him all the time. So at least, let the British friends know that when they struggle and feel hard beset, they are not struggling and worrying alone! Far from it!

We must expect these things . . . We must have no illusions about how much depends on us and our success or failure. All humanity is disturbed and suffering and confused; we cannot expect to not be disturbed and not to suffer – but we don't have to be confused. On the contrary, confidence and assurance, hope and optimism are our prerogative. The successful carrying out of our various Plans is the greatest sign we can give of our faith and inner assurance, and the best way we can help our fellow-men out of their confusion and difficulties.[2]

The superstructure of the Shrine of the Báb

The work on the superstructure of the Shrine of the Báb was under way, but there were always problems. During 1948 and 1949 there had been many delays with the shipping of the construction materials. In the spring of 1949, a drought in Italy restricted the availability of electricity needed to cut and work the stones. Then there was a strong earthquake near the shipping port of Leghorn (Livorno) which sent the populace, including those loading the ships, fleeing into the countryside. On another occasion, when a ship was unloading its cargo in Haifa, a plane flew over and panicked the captain, who immediately set sail and returned to Italy with most of his cargo still aboard. Another ship caught fire, but none of the stone was damaged.[3]

At one point, a contractor had submitted a bid of £18,000 for building the arcade, which Shoghi Effendi said was 'terrible'. The building was ready for construction to begin, but the Guardian refused to pay what he considered to be an extortionate amount. In January 1949, heavy rains delayed the delivery of over eighty cases of stone that were sitting on the Haifa dock.[4] A few weeks later, early in the morning, a lighter sank in the port of Haifa carrying a large load of stones. Luckily, the water was not too deep and a salvage company rescued every case of stones undamaged.[5]

Shoghi Effendi spent almost every day at the Shrine directing the work. At the end of one day, Rúḥíyyih Khánum, Ben and Gladys were in the drawing room when the Guardian walked in with mud all over his coat. When Rúḥíyyih Khánum asked what he had been doing, he replied, 'I had a fight with General Mud, only he won!' It had been raining and the work area was very slippery so he had fallen in the mud.[6]

On 14 March 1949, as work on a new drainage system neared completion, the first of the 140 foundation stones, each weighing half a ton, was set into place. There base stones for of the corners followed rapidly.[7]

But on 5 April 1950, tragedy struck. Sutherland Maxwell collapsed, reaching a point where he no longer recognized his daughter. The doctors gave up all hope of recovery for the seventy-five year-old architect. But when Shoghi Effendi would go to see Sutherland and 'although he could not speak, and gave no conscious sign whatever of the Guardian's nearness, a flutter, a tremor, some reaction wholly ephemeral but nevertheless visible, would pass over him because of the very presence of Shoghi Effendi.' This tremor in the presence of Shoghi Effendi was so obvious that the nurse saw it as well. The Guardian decided that it wasn't time for Sutherland to die, so on 16 May he sent him with a nurse to Switzerland and put him under the care of his own doctor. Within weeks, Sutherland was conscious and alert. When Rúḥíyyih Khánum and his Swiss nurse took him for his first car ride, Sutherland invited them to stop at a café they passed and have tea.[8]

By July, Sutherland was back in Haifa and at work. Though much improved, he was still very frail and required a special diet that was difficult to satisfy in Haifa. During the summer of 1951, Shoghi Effendi and Rúḥíyyih Khánum took Sutherland to Switzerland with them. When it came time to return to Haifa, because of Sutherland's dietary problems and his great wish to see Montreal, he left with his Swiss nurse and returned there.[9] He died there on 25 March 1952.

Completion of the Arcade

On 8 May 1950, the last shipment of stone left Leghorn on the S.S. *Maria*. All told, the great project had required seventeen ships to carry 1,800 wooden cases of stone weighing eight hundred tons containing a total of 4,587 pieces over a period of nineteen months. The last ship arrived in Haifa on 20 May.[10] Then, at 3:30 on the afternoon of 29 June, the last piece of stone, a small piece only a foot long, was fitted and the arcade and parapet were completed.[11]

Shoghi Effendi informed the Bahá'í world of its completion on 7 July, and announced the next stage in the work:

> Announce to believers, through all National Assemblies, termination initial stage of construction of domed structure designed to embellish and preserve the Báb's sepulcher on Mount Carmel.
>
> The two-year enterprise launched on the eve of the gravest turmoil rocking the Holy Land in modern times, involving the expenditure of a quarter of a million dollars, necessitating the transportation and placing of almost eight hundred tons of stone and marble mosaic, was consummated on the eve of the Centenary of His martyrdom. My soul is thrilled in contemplation of the rising edifice, the beauty of its design, the majesty of its proportions, the loveliness of its surroundings, the historic associations of the site it occupies, the sacredness of the Sanctuary it envelops, the transcendent holiness of the Treasure it enshrines.
>
> My gratitude is deepened by the miraculous recovery of its gifted architect, Sutherland Maxwell, whose illness was pronounced hopeless by physicians. I acknowledge the valuable service rendered by Ugo Giachery, through his supervision of the work of shipment of consignments to Haifa.
>
> The hour is ripe to undertake the preliminaries for the erection of the octagonal first unit of the superstructure, another milestone in the process set in motion sixty years ago by Bahá'u'lláh's visit to Mount Carmel.[12]

On 1 September, he announced that the architectural plans for the 'octagon', basically an eight-pointed foundational star which would support the dome, were completed and a contract was signed on 21

October for its construction. This was a critical part of the design because the dome, which would weigh about a thousand tons, could not be built on the roof of the original building constructed by 'Abdu'l-Bahá. The major problem was to design a way to support the dome so that the weight did not rest on the old building. Solving this problem fell to Prof. H. Neuman of the Haifa Institute of Technology. He designed a

> very ingenious system to support the entire superstructure by planning to sink eight mighty piers . . . all the way through the original Shrine to reach the bedrock lying under its foundation. It was a truly gigantic and delicate task to break through the masonry of the Shrine without damaging its structure or impairing in any manner the sacred entirety of the Holy Tombs.[13]

The job required a lot of structural steel, eight huge pipes, called Manesmann pipes, and 100,000 pounds of cement. The Manesmann pipes were initially a problem. None were apparently available in Italy, England or Germany, but then eight were found in a neglected collection of building materials in Milan. They had been made before the war in Germany, but never used. Shoghi Effendi needed eight and there were exactly eight, and of the exact length and diameter needed.[14] The cement was particularly troublesome. It was in short supply in Italy and could be exported only with a special government licence. Twice, cement was found only to have its shipment blocked by ever-changing laws. It was not actually shipped until April 1951. A second cement shipment ran into similar problems. An official who was finally authorized to sign the licence said, 'This is an exceptional measure, as no such permit has been granted for months, even to large corporations with world-wide trade.'[15]

Completion of national plans and the beginning of the Africa Plan

The difficulties and challenges of finishing the arcade in time were mirrored by the struggles of the Bahá'ís in those countries where national teaching plans were due for completion in 1950. Perhaps nowhere was this crisis more dramatic than in the British Isles, and the ultimate victory of the small community of believers there was to have far-reaching consequences.

Throughout the last year of the British Six Year Plan (1944–1950), the Guardian sent over twenty cables and letters encouraging and appealing to the believers

> to arise as one soul, to exert one more superhuman effort, to fix steadily their gaze on the pinnacle they are visibly approaching and to disencumber themselves from any burden impeding their arduous climb, in a last and determined attempt to scale and conquer the summit, from which alone they can catch a glimpse of the future glory of their destiny.[16]

What was that destiny mentioned by Shoghi Effendi? The Guardian's cable on the victorious completion of the British Six Year Plan read:

> Heart flooded joy striking evidence bountiful grace Bahá'u'lláh enabling valorous dearly loved Bahá'í community British Isles triumphantly conclude first historic plan half century British Bahá'í history. Herald Author Faith Centre Covenant Concourse on High acclaim superb collective achievement . . . Historic pledge British Bahá'í community nobly redeemed. Tribute memory Martyr Prophet Faith worthily paid. Spiritual potentialities prosecute subsequent stage unfolding mission fully acquired. Triumphant community now standing threshold catching first glimpse still dimly outlined future enterprises overseas . . .[17]

Linking the victorious completion of their Six Year Plan to the acquisition of spiritual capabilities – as he had done earlier in the case of the American Bahá'í community's Seven Year Plan and its implications for the Second Seven Year Plan – the Guardian now launched the first teaching plan to draw on the combined efforts of several National Spiritual Assemblies, to be spearheaded by the National Spiritual Assembly of the Bahá'ís of the British Isles.

> Hour propitious galvanised firmly knit body believers brace itself embark after one year respite yet another historic undertaking marking formal inauguration two year plan constituting prelude initiation systematic campaign designed carry torch faith territories dark continent whose northern southern fringes were successively illuminated course ministries Bahá'u'lláh 'Abdu'l-Bahá. Hour struck

undertake preliminary steps implant banner faith amidst African tribes mentioned Tablet Centre Covenant signalising association victorious British Bahá'í community with sister communities United States Egypt designed lay structural basis Bahá'í administrative order scale comparable foundation already established North South American European Australian continents.[18]

Shoghi Effendi reiterated the link between the sacrificial carrying out of a teaching plan and the creation of new capabilities in his letter of 15 June, in which he further explained that the honour of coordinating the Africa Plan was also linked to the historic links between Great Britain and its colonies and territories:

So magnificent an achievement has . . . endowed the entire community . . . with tremendous potentialities, empowering it to launch on the first stage of its historic overseas mission destined to bring that community into closer and more concrete association with is sister communities in North America and Egypt, for the purpose of promoting the Faith in the vast virgin territories where its banner is still unraised and which constitute an integral part of the territories of the British Crown . . .[19]

Guided by the Guardian in all details, the Plan focused on three countries: Gold Coast, Tanganyika and Uganda. Before the end of the year, the National Spiritual Assembly of Persia – whose national plan had also been completed in 1950 – was also asked to participate.

Things moved fast, and although the Africa Plan was not officially due to start until Riḍván 1951, the Guardian was able to send a cable in December concerning the first pioneer to leave home. This was Claire Gung. She had been born in Germany, but had gone to England in 1930, where she became a Bahá'í and pioneered five times, much of it during the Six Year Plan. She became the 'Mother of Africa', pioneering first to Tanganyika (Tanzania) where she arrived in January 1951.[20] Almost simultaneously, from Persia came Músá Banání and his wife Samíhih, his daughter Violette and son-in-law 'Alí Nakhjavání with their small daughter Bahíyyih, pioneers to Uganda.[21] These first pioneers would shortly be joined by English Bahá'ís Philip Hainsworth, Edward (Ted) Cardell and Eric Manton.

In August 1950 the Guardian specifically directed an appeal to black American Bahá'ís to arise and help in Africa:

Feel moved to appeal to gallant, great-hearted American Bahá'í Community to arise on the eve of launching the far-reaching, historic campaign by sister Community of the British Isles to lend valued assistance to the meritorious enterprise undertaken primarily for the illumination of the tribes of East and West Africa, envisaged in the Tablets of the Center of the Covenant revealed in the darkest hour of His ministry.

I appeal particularly to its dearly beloved members belonging to the Negro race to participate in the contemplated project marking a significant milestone in the world-unfoldment of the Faith, supplementing the work initiated fifty years ago on the North American continent, forging fresh links binding the American, British and Egyptian Communities and providing the prelude to the full-scale operations destined to be launched at a later period of the unfoldment of the Divine Plan aiming at the conversion of the backward, oppressed masses of the swiftly awakening continent.[22]

Two black American Bahá'ís heard the Guardian's call and responded. Ethel Stevens pioneered to the Gold Coast in October 1951. Ethel was only able to stay at her post for a year before she had to return to America. William Foster was ready to pioneer to Liberia in May 1951, but didn't actually reach the country until January 1952.[23]

As always looking to the future and the expected results of this first international collaboration plan, the Guardian explained in a cable dated 16 January 1951:

Fervently praying participation British American Persian Egyptian National Assemblies unique epochmaking enterprise African continent may prove prelude convocation first African teaching conference leading eventually initiation undertakings involving collaboration all National Assemblies Bahá'í world thereby paving way ultimate organic union these assemblies through formation international House Justice destined launch enterprises embracing whole Bahá'í world . . .[24]

By June 1951 India was also a participant, bringing the number of collaborating National Assemblies to five.[25]

A world secretariat

In the second half of 1950, Shoghi Effendi began another historic change. To this time, he had almost single-handedly, with the help of Rúḥíyyih Khánum and a number of dedicated but temporary secretaries, conducted and managed the affairs of the Faith throughout the world. Now, he began to create a Baháʼí World Centre worthy and capable of living up to its name. One day in November, while still in Switzerland, he sent cablegrams to Lotfullah Hakím in England and Ethel and Jessie Revell, Amelia Collins and Mason Remey in America. Lotfullah's cable read: 'Kindly arrange departure Luṭfuʼlláh Ḥakím Haifa for necessary service. Shoghi'.[26] He was the first to arrive in Haifa.

Shoghi Effendi sent another cable to two 'self-effacing little ladies from Philadelphia', Ethel and Jessie Revell. It read simply, 'Welcome your presence Haifa – Shoghi'. There was no explanation, just the welcome. It was obviously an invitation so the two ladies, surprised and puzzled, packed and went to Haifa.[27]

In their youth the Revell sisters had met the Master during his visit to Philadelphia. Jessie, who was barely five feet tall, quickly earned the trust and admiration of the Guardian and became a companion for Rúḥíyyih Khánum. She also became the pilgrims' confidant and helper. Jessie was put in charge of sending and collecting Shoghi Effendi's mail, 'a task to which he attached great importance as during his absences from the Holy Land no one had access to him except his "postman"'. Ian Semple described Jessie as a 'bulldog'. She was in charge of the International Fund, which she kept in a pink toffee tin in her room, which, consequently, was the only room in the Pilgrim House with a Yale lock.

Jessie also greatly enjoyed being with the pilgrims. Ethel wrote:

She loved to look after their comfort and received them with a loving welcome, visiting with them, helping them on their shopping trips. At times the pilgrims arrived very late at night from certain countries. On one occasion a group of dear pilgrims came at about eleven-thirty at night. It was raining heavily. They were shown their rooms and made comfortable by Jessie. The next morning Jessie awakened to find she had slept peacefully all night in a wet raincoat![28]

Jessie later attended the Intercontinental Conference held in the United States in 1958 to represent Shoghi Effendi. She also travelled with Rúḥíyyih Khánum to Australia in 1961 to open the House of Worship in Sydney and, when Rúḥíyyih Khánum fell ill, visited the New Zealand Bahá'í community in her place.[29]

Ian Semple called Ethel 'a saint in every way'. She completed any job given to her that day, even if it meant staying up most of the night. Ethel also had a sense of humour. Mr Semple remembered getting up early only to find Ethel already up and working in the kitchen. As he walked in, Ethel said, with a twinkle in her eye, 'The early bird catches the worm. But who wants a worm anyway?'[30]

Ethel, Jessie and Milly Collins, Shoghi Effendi's 'secret' Hand of the Cause, arrived in Haifa before the end of the year. Mason Remey arrived in early January 1951. What happened next would astonish the Bahá'í world.

1951–1952

The International Bahá'í Council

As we have seen, Jessie and Ethel Revell, Lotfullah Hakím, Mason Remey and Amelia Collins had all arrived in Haifa by January 1951. The Guardian then sat them down with Ben and Gladys Weeden around the table at the Western Pilgrim House and told them that they were the new International Bahá'í Council. Every one accepted his or her fate without question.

Along with the naming of the first group of Hands of the Cause at the end of 1951 and the beginning of 1952, this began a dynamic new chapter in the history of the Bahá'í Faith. For the first time, the Bahá'í World Centre would not consist of just Shoghi Effendi, Rúhíyyih Khánum and whoever he could beg to help him. It would have an organized secretariat to work with the world-ranging Hands of the Cause and set the stage for the establishment of the Universal House of Justice, that God-protected, infallible body that was a major pillar of the World Order of Bahá'u'lláh, along with the pillar of the Guardianship.

On 9 January 1951, Shoghi Effendi sent this historic cablegram to the Bahá'í world announcing the formation of the International Bahá'í Council:

Proclaim National Assemblies of East and West weighty epoch-making decision of formation of first International Bahá'í Council, forerunner of supreme administrative institution destined to emerge in fullness of time within precincts beneath shadow of World Spiritual Center of Faith already established in twin cities of 'Akká and Haifa. Fulfillment of prophecies uttered by Founder of Faith and Center of His Covenant culminating in establishment of Jewish State, signalizing birth after lapse of two thousand years of an independent nation in the Holy Land, the swift unfoldment of historic undertaking associated with construction of superstructure of the Báb's Sepulcher on Mount Carmel, the present adequate maturity of nine vigorously functioning national administrative institutions throughout Bahá'í World, combine to induce me to arrive at this historic decision marking most significant milestone in evolution of Administrative Order of the Faith of Bahá'u'lláh in course of last thirty years. Nascent Institution now created is invested with three-fold function: first, to forge link with authorities of newly emerged State; second, to assist me to discharge responsibilities involved in erection of mighty superstructure of the Báb's Holy Shrine; third, to conduct negotiations related to matters of personal status with civil authorities. To these will be added further functions in course of evolution of this first embryonic International Institution, marking its development into officially recognized Bahá'í Court, its transformation into duly elected body, its efflorescence into Universal House of Justice, and its final fruition through erection of manifold auxiliary institutions constituting the World Administrative Center destined to arise and function and remain permanently established in close neighborhood of Twin Holy Shrines. Hail with thankful, joyous heart at long last the constitution of International Council which history will acclaim as the greatest event shedding luster upon second epoch of Formative Age of Bahá'í Dispensation potentially unsurpassed by any enterprise undertaken since inception of Administrative Order of Faith on morrow of 'Abdu'l-Bahá's Ascension, ranking second only to glorious immortal events associated with Ministries of the Three Central Figures of Faith in course of First Age of most glorious Dispensation of the five thousand century Bahá'í Cycle. Advise publicize announcement through Public Relations Committee.[1]

In March 1952, Shoghi Effendi added Rúḥíyyih <u>Kh</u>ánum, Ugo Giachery and Leroy Ioas to the Council following the departure of the Weedens from Haifa.

Victory after victory

Shoghi Effendi was always trying to acquire places with Bahá'í significance for the Faith, and in December 1950 he was able to add Mazra'ih to the list, where Bahá'u'lláh had lived when he had agreed to move out of the prison city of Akka. The property had been a Muslim religious endowment rented to various parties, such as General and Lilian McNeill, who lived there from 1931 to 1950. The vacant house was then taken over by the new Israeli Government, which planned to turn it into a rest home for officials. At first, the Guardian tried to work through channels to acquire Mazra'ih, but those efforts were unfruitful. Then he appealed directly to Prime Minister Ben Gurion and explained the significance of the site for Bahá'ís as one of Bahá'u'lláh's homes. With the Prime Minister's direct intervention, Mazra'ih was leased to the Bahá'ís. Shoghi Effendi announced the acquisition on 16 December, then followed that announcement up with another on 2 March 1951:

> Announce to friends of East and West the following: furnishing Mazra'ih, completion of restoration of historic house of Bahá'u'lláh in Acre, scene of prolonged afflictions sustained by Founder of Faith, as well as supreme crisis suffered by 'Abdu'l-Bahá at hands of Covenantbreakers. Greatly enhanced international endowments in Holy Land in twin cities of Acre and Haifa, now include twin Holy Shrines situated on plain of Acre and slope of Mount Carmel; twin Mansions of Bahjí and Mazra'ih, twin historic Houses inhabited by Bahá'u'lláh and 'Abdu'l-Bahá; twin International Archives adjoining the Báb's Sepulcher and the resting-place of the Greatest Holy Leaf; twin Pilgrim Houses, constructed for Oriental and Occidental pilgrims; twin Gardens of Riḍván and Firdaws, associated with the memory of the Author of the Bahá'í Dispensation.[2]

The cable also welcomed

> the assistance of the newly-formed International Bahá'í Council, particularly of its President, Mason Remey, and its Vice-President, Amelia Collins, through contact with authorities designed to spread the fame, consolidate the foundations and widen the scope of influence emanating from the twin spiritual, administrative World Centers permanently fixed in the Holy Land constituting the midmost heart of the entire planet.[3]

There followed a series of cablegrams announcing victory after victory. On 2 April 1951, Shoghi Effendi announced the completion of two additional terraces below the Shrine of the Báb. These were part of the Master's desire to connect the Templar Colony at the foot of Mount Carmel with the Shrine of the Báb, in spite of the opposition of the Covenant-breakers:

> Machinations of Covenant-breakers who succeeded in shelving project for more than decade foiled. Hail success of enterprise presaging the day destined to witness, as envisaged by 'Abdu'l-Bahá, pilgrim kings ascending this route to pay humble tribute to Martyr-Herald of Faith of Bahá'u'lláh.[4]

Then during Riḍván, the Guardian sent a cablegram that announced, among other things, the formation of two new National Spiritual Assemblies: for Central America, Mexico and the Antilles, and for South America; that the Administrative Order was now established in 106 sovereign states – 27 of them since the Centenary celebrations just seven years earlier; that the Third European Teaching Conference had been attended by representatives from 22 countries; and that full funding needed to finish the House of Worship in Chicago had been achieved. About the Covenant-breakers, Shoghi Effendi wrote:

> Divine retributive justice is strikingly demonstrated through series of sudden, rapid, devastating blows sweeping over leaders and henchmen of breakers of Bahá'u'lláh's Covenant foiling the schemes, levelling the hopes, and well-nigh extinguishing the remnants of the conspiring crew which dared challenge the authority, succeeded in inflicting untold sorrow and assiduously plotted to disrupt the Will and Testament of its appointed Center.[5]

The War of Independence in 1948 and 1949 had driven many of the Covenant-breakers out of the area. Badí'u'lláh, the youngest son of Bahá'u'lláh and 'chief lieutenant' of Mírzá Muḥammad-'Alí, died in November 1950, leaving those few who remained in disarray. Several other key Covenant-breakers had also died by early 1952.[6]

Shoghi Effendi's relatives refused to help him even when his mother died in 1951. None of his brothers or sisters would help, so he went to the house, made all the funeral arrangements himself and had her buried in the Bahá'í cemetery in Haifa. Shoghi Effendi's father stayed in another room and never came out. One of his brothers only sent a lawyer to find out about any inheritance. Shoghi Effendi gave the whole inheritance to the family.[7]

On 24 September 1951, the Guardian announced the acquisition of a large block of land on the slope of Mount Carmel above the tomb of the Greatest Holy Leaf and on the eastern approaches to the Shrine of the Báb. He explained the significance of this:

Acquisition of area extending from heart to ridge of mountain safeguards precincts of sacred Mausoleum now in process of erection, broadens basis of administrative structure of rising World Center of Faith in Holy Land, may induce civil authorities to abandon project construction of arterial road crossing diagonally Bahá'í international endowments, and facilitates extension of terraces ultimately stretching from foot to crown of God's Holy Mountain.[8]

Announcement of the Holy Year

On 30 November 1951, Shoghi Effendi began to prepare the world for what was to come next. Much had been accomplished during the previous few years. The national plans due to finish in 1950 had been completed. The Africa Plan, the first calling for international collaboration, was under way, and in America, the Second Seven Year Plan was advancing well, with all the necessary funds in place to finish the House of Worship. India had launched a Nineteen-Month Plan in 1951. In the Holy Land, the arcade of the Shrine of the Báb had been finished and work had begun on the dome. The International Bahá'í Council was already functioning.

But in his 30 November cablegram, Shoghi Effendi began to set the stage for the beginning of the most dramatic decade since he began his tenure as Head of the Faith. He announced that a Holy Year would begin in October 1952 to celebrate the Revelation given to Bahá'u'lláh in the Síyáh-Chál. This Holy Year would be marked by four major intercontinental teaching conferences, to be held in Kampala, Uganda (for Africa), Wilmette, United States (for the Americas), Stockholm, Sweden (for Europe), and in New Delhi, India (for Asia), during 1953.[9]

Less than a month later, on 24 December 1951, the Guardian appointed the first group of twelve Hands of the Cause.

Hands of the Cause of God

Amelia (Milly) Collins had been appointed a Hand of the Cause in 1946, but the world had not been told. On 24 December 1951, however, Shoghi Effendi officially named twelve Hands of the Cause of God, including Milly. The others were Sutherland Maxwell and Mason Remey in the Holy Land; Valíyu'lláh Varqá, Ṭarázu'lláh Samandarí and 'Alí-Akbar Furútan in Persia, the cradle of the Faith; Horace Holley, Dorothy Baker and Leroy Ioas in the American continent; and George Townshend, Hermann Grossmann and Ugo Giachery in the European continent.[10]

When Beatrice Ashton was on pilgrimage in 1952, Shoghi Effendi talked about the institution of the Hands of the Cause:

> One evening he spoke at some length about the 'Twin Pillars'. Everything that the Guardian says is uttered with the greatest clarity. One does not wish to miss a single word, for every word, every expression, conveys just the right meaning and is deeply engraved on one's heart and mind . . .
>
> That evening at the table he said that up to this time we had been erecting only one of the twin pillars, the one which is to culminate in the Universal House of Justice – that he had not yet been able to establish the Universal House of Justice but he had appointed the International Bahá'í Council as an intermediary stage. Now, he explained, he had begun to erect the pillar of the Guardianship by the appointment of the Hands of the Cause. Just as the other pillar had its institutions – the local and national assemblies, each with its own subsidiary institutions (the committees and the funds) – so the Hands of the Cause would also have their own institutions revolving about them.[11]

Ian Semple, who was later to serve on the Universal House of Justice, wrote about the effect the naming of the Hands of the Cause had on him:

The real bombshell of the Conference [on 5th and 6th January 1952 in Birmingham], however, was the Guardian's cable announcing the appointment of the first contingent of Hands of the Cause of God. I don't know if you can conceive of what this meant to the Baháʼís of that time. We knew about Hands, of course, from the Will and Testament of ʻAbduʼl-Bahá and we had known of outstanding believers, like Martha Root and John Esslemont, raised to the rank of Hands after their passing. However, to actually have the possibility of knowing and meeting such precious souls had been beyond our wildest dreams. Now, suddenly, this had become a reality. For me personally the greatest joy and confirmation was to know that Hermann Grossmann was among these Hands, for him I had known and he had aroused my intense admiration and esteem and love.[12]

When Shoghi Effendi named the first group of Hands of the Cause on 24 December, Dhikruʼlláh Khádem was the one in Tehran who received the cablegram. He was very excited and exclaimed, 'These are very special people. They have been elevated to the rank of Hands of the Cause!' When he saw the name of his good friend ʻAlí-Akbar Furútan, he couldn't wait to tell him the good news even though it was late at night. His wife, Javidukht, suggested waiting until morning, but Mr Khádem obviously thought his friend would want to know, saying 'For this kind of news, he would be more than happy to get up. He would prefer not to sleep in order to learn of his exalted station.'

It was very late when they arrived and Mr Furútan answered the door in his pyjamas, surprised to see two unannounced visitors at that hour. Bringing them into the house, he hurried off to get dressed. In Persian style, neither could come to the point of the visit without first going through the rituals of courtesy and hospitality. Mr Khádem was enjoying himself and greatly anticipating the delivery of his news. He 'chuckled with glee at Mr Furútan's plight'. Finally, he could hold back no longer and he handed Mr Furútan the cable. The newly appointed Hand of the Cause could only respond with 'stunned disbelief', which brought a big smile to Mr Khádem's face.[13]

Three months later, during the Fast, another cablegram arrived. Mr Khádem had gotten up for breakfast then, after prayers, had gone back to bed. When the doorbell rang, his wife Javidukht answered and was handed a cablegram addressed personally to her husband from Shoghi Effendi. They received many cablegrams, but it was rare that one was addressed specifically to Mr Khádem. She rushed to the bedroom knowing that he would be excited, and said, 'There is a cablegram from the Holy Land with your name on it. It's for you!'

Mr Khádem leaped out of bed and told her to put it on the desk. Before opening it, he had to prepare himself because it was from the Guardian, so Javidukht left. She later saw him in the dining room, reading and rereading the cable. She noted that 'he was trembling and sobbing. The effect of that cablegram amazed and worried me. "Is there bad news?" I asked. He did not reply. I tried again. "Please, please, tell me what has happened!" Still no answer. I approached him, begging him to share the tragic news.'

Mr Khádem was unable to speak, so he numbly handed her the cablegram. It read:

Dhikru'lláh Khádem Teheran
    Moved convey glad tiding your elevation rank Hand Cause . . .

Mrs Khádem was thrilled and congratulated him, but was suddenly concerned when 'his expression of deep concern and anxiety did not change'. His first, very stern, words were of disbelief: 'This is a ruse. The enemies of the Faith are trying to trick me. I don't deserve this. The beloved Guardian knows that. He knows my spiritual capacity. I couldn't possibly be a Hand of the Cause.' It wasn't until another cablegram arrived a couple days later addressed to all National Spiritual Assemblies announcing the elevation of twelve Hands of the Cause that he finally would believe it. That was when he understood how Mr Furútan had felt.[14]

This second group of Hands of the Cause included Siegfried (Fred) Schopflocher, Corinne True, Dhikru'lláh Khádem, Shu'á'u'lláh 'Alá'í, Adelbert Mühlschlegel, Músá Banání and Clara Dunn.

Músá and Samíhih Banání were on their second pilgrimage, coming from their pioneer post in Uganda, when Shoghi Effendi was preparing to announce the second group of Hands of the Cause, but though Mr Banání's name was on his list, he said nothing about it until the night before they were to return home. Exciting things were happening in Africa and Músá Banání was deeply involved in them. Each day during his pilgrimage, the Guardian would give him instructions for the expansion and consolidation of the Faith in Africa.

Initially, Shoghi Effendi wanted to wait until Mr Banání had returned home and then send him a cable, but then decided that he couldn't wait, so, on the night before he left, Shoghi Effendi told him that he had appointed a new group of Hands of the Cause and that he was one of them. Staggered by the news, Mr Banání objected, crying and saying, 'I am not worthy. I cannot read or write. My tongue is not eloquent. Give this mantle to 'Alí Na<u>kh</u>javání who is doing the lion's share of teaching in Africa.' Shoghi Effendi simply stated that 'It is your arising that has conquered the continent. 'Alí's turn will come.' And it did, when he was elected to the International Bahá'í Council in 1961 and then to the first Universal House of Justice in 1963.[15]

Leroy Ioas

Leroy Ioas was so affected by his appointment as a Hand of the Cause that he wrote to the Guardian and offered his services in whatever way the Guardian proposed. On 15 February 1952, Leroy received a letter written on behalf of the Guardian that said:

> What he needs, I might say desperately, is a capable, devoted believer to come and really take the work in hand here, relieve him of constant strain and details, and act as the secretary general of the International Bahá'í Council. If you accept to do this it would be rendering him and the Faith an invaluable service.[16]

To the amazement of everyone, Leroy left everything else behind, arriving in Haifa on 10 March, less then a month after receiving the letter. On his way, he stopped in Chicago and gave a talk in which he related a dream Albert Windust had had. In the dream, Albert saw the Master 'working very diligently, going to and fro, searching the ground, picking up a twig here, a few pieces of straw there, and finally with these bits and pieces making something with a little shape and form.' When Albert wrote to 'Abdu'l-Bahá and asked what the dream meant, the response was: 'I have been commanded to build the Temple of the Lord and I build it with what God gives me!' Leroy concluded his talk by saying, you and I are those twigs . . . and the Master is working to shape something out of us. Why should we, unknown and incapable, be quickened by the power of this great spirit and come alive in this day when millions are dying and deprived of spiritual insight? I don't know, and you don't know, but there is only one thing we can do in return for these great gifts and that is to dedicate our lives, purify our deeds, and allow ourselves to become dynamic vehicles which God can use to quicken society.[17]

Then he went to Haifa. On the way his luggage was stolen and he arrived with only a toothbrush and razor purchased at the airport. He arrived ready for a completely new life.

The gardens at Bahjí

One of Shoghi Effendi's primary goals was to appropriately develop the land around the Holy Shrines. His biggest problem was land. At the beginning of 1952, the Bahá'ís owned no land contiguous to the Shrine of Bahá'u'lláh, so the Guardian could not carry out his plans to beautify the area with gardens. The largest piece of land he needed was a forty-acre plot owned by the Baydún family, Muslims with close ties to the Covenant-breakers, who refused to even consider selling their land to the Bahá'ís. Before the First World War, 'Abdu'l-Bahá had purchased some properties near the Sea of Galilee and the Jordan River for farming. These lands were in the name of Dhikru'lláh, a descendant of Bahá'u'lláh's faithful brother, Mírzá Músá. After the Israeli battle with their Arab neighbours following statehood, the Israelis desperately wanted the property because it was adjacent to Transjordan. During the war between Israel and the surrounding Arab States, many Arabs, including the Baydún family, had fled the country and their lands had reverted to the State of Israel.[18]

Larry Hautz, the first American pilgrim to arrive after pilgrimages resumed, was given the task with Leroy Ioas of negotiating with the State of Israel to exchange the Dhikru'lláh property in Galilee for the Baydún property at Bahjí. Larry took advantage of the fact that Golda Meir, then Minister of Labour, had once been a schoolteacher in Larry's home town of Milwaukee. Meir had been very impressed that the Bahá'ís had not run away during the War of Independence and she helped open many doors.[19] On 12 November 1952, the exchange was completed and 145,000 square metres of land had been added to the Bahjí holdings.

Leroy Ioas immediately notified the Guardian who, that same day, went to Bahjí and made a plan to create widespread gardens.[20] He rented a bulldozer and levelled the northwest quarter of the great circle around the Shrine. To oversee this work, Shoghi Effendi found a small ruined building at the edge of the area which he repaired, creating an office inside and adding a staircase to its roof. From the roof, he had a good view of all the work going on. The levelling process resulted in a lot of earth being moved. From his vantage point on the roof, he directed that the earth be piled into a long embankment from which the area could be viewed. Ultimately, the embankment was moved and became the long, terraced mound we see today. As soon as the quarter circle was level, Shoghi Effendi began laying out his gardens with lawns, flower-beds, paths made with crushed red tiles and lined with lamp-posts. Ninety-nine of the wrought-iron lamp-posts were set at Bahjí and lighted for the first time at Riḍván 1953.[21] The Guardian was reportedly inspired to make paths with the crushed red tiles after seeing garden paths in Torquay, England, which were made of crushed red granite. Shoghi Effendi had spent three weeks in Torquay in August 1921, while a student at Oxford, and visited several of the town's gardens.[22]

Leroy Ioas had hardly arrived in Haifa when Shoghi Effendi sent him to face the Covenant-breakers. These miscreants were always looking for a way to regain part of the Mansion and the Shrine. The preceding December, Shoghi Effendi had the gardener at Bahjí begin to tear down a small house that was in danger of collapse. Two Covenant-breakers who still lived in a shack built against the Mansion immediately filed a lawsuit claiming that, with their one-sixth interest in the Mansion, they should have been consulted. Upon his arrival, Leroy was delegated to meet them and their lawyer and found himself faced not with people trying to solve a problem, but with attacks on 'Abdu'l-Bahá dating back sixty years. Ugo Giachery was brought in to help Leroy and soon the court determined that the issue was a religious one and therefore could not be handled by the Civil Court. The Covenant-breakers then took their claim to the Israeli Supreme Court on a technicality. Leroy and Ugo continued to present the Bahá'í case until Shoghi Effendi appealed to Prime Minister Ben Gurion, who sent his adviser to resolve the issue.

The Covenant-breakers kept up their attacks on the Master and the Guardian until the adviser pointed out that, because of the way they had made their appeal to the Supreme Court, they were now fighting the government and not Shoghi Effendi. The Covenant-breakers quickly dropped their case and within forty-eight hours the house was demolished.[23]

The night before the demolition, Shoghi Effendi called for all available men to go to Bahjí the next day for some intense work. All were ready the next morning to help Shoghi Effendi with his plan to beautify the gardens. Eight truck-loads of plants and ornamental pieces were sent to Bahjí. Shoghi Effendi, aided by his chauffeur who carried a ball of string and wooden stakes, laid out several paths that radiated out from the Shrine of Bahá'u'lláh. With the string and stakes marking the design, gardeners followed and dug trenches in which they planted a hedge of thyme. The main path stretched from the door of the Shrine to the north. The small buildings at the south end of the space between the Mansion and the Shrine were quickly demolished and the rubble was used to create a level area by the gate to the Mansion.[24] Ugo Giachery described the work:

> The word magic cannot well define what was taking place at every moment. It was like a powerful and ever-present force of enchantment creating beauty in a hundred places at the same time. Shoghi Effendi was moving about directing, counselling, cautioning, encouraging, explaining, demonstrating how to do apparently impossible things, and rejoicing in the transformation of the land under our very eyes. In the afternoon a drizzle came down but he would not leave the grounds, determined to accomplish as much as was possible before sunset. Markers and trees placed by the previous owners, who had never permitted either the purchase of the land or extension of the gardens around the Shrine, were removed. Young trees were brought in and planted along the paths; the outer semicircular line was doubled to make a wide tree-bordered avenue. Iron gates, steps, stone decorations, flowering plants, top soil and grass seeds were brought from Haifa, from Mt. Carmel, the Riḍván Garden, and the Master's House to give consistency to the superb embellishment plans.
>
> During the night Shoghi Effendi developed a cold but in the

morning he returned to work, feverish and suffering . . . For three additional days he did not give up; there was ground to level, trees and borders to plant, and a hundred other details, all well established and correlated in his mind, and which only he would be able to accomplish. The sand was disappearing; the stones from the demolished buildings were already covered with good soil; hedges, pedestals and flower-beds were in place . . .

By the end of the fourth day, the sacred precincts of the Qiblih of the Bahá'í world had taken on the appearance of a beauteous, entrancing garden, looking as if it had been there from ancient times, and much as we see today.[25]

A gate, originally planned for the bottom of the terraces on Mt Carmel, was placed on one of the paths radiating west of the Shrine. Early in 1953, the Collins Gate, a gate Shoghi Effendi had purchased with funds supplied by Milly Collins, was erected on the main path to the Shrine. The Guardian had originally planned to pave the main path with Carrara marble, the same stone used for the monuments in the Monument Gardens, but for some reason abandoned the idea and used small white pebbles from the Sea of Galilee.[26]

Another thing that Shoghi Effendi changed at the Shrine of Bahá'u'lláh was the door. The original door was a rather strange thing: two half-doors and unaligned hinges designed, it seemed, to ensure that water drained away. Some years earlier, the Guardian had built a solid entry porch, and now he wanted an appropriate door. He sent Ugo Giachery a drawing of a door and asked him to find a suitable carpenter. In Tuscany, famed for the skill of its artisans, Ugo found Saiello Saielli, who proved to be very good; he selected well-seasoned oak and built the door in layers to avoid the possibility of warping. It was constructed with copper nails, a bronze lock and hinges. There were to be eight identical nine-petal rosettes on the door and, to ensure that each was truly identical, they had to have a sculptor make a model panel which the carvers would copy. When it arrived, Shoghi Effendi was 'overjoyed by its simplicity, perfect execution and highly decorative beauty'. He later had Mr Saielli make the wooden core of the bronze doors for the Archives Building.[27]

With the near completion of the Shrine of the Báb and the ever-developing gardens in both Haifa and Bahjí, the Faith began to receive more attention. On 29 December, the English section of the Israeli radio station 'Kol Zion' broadcast an interview with Rúḥíyyih Khánum and Leroy Ioas at the Shrine of the Baháʼuʼlláh and in the gardens. The announcer began his broadcast by stating that Israel was not just the home of Judaism, Christianity and Islam, but also of the Baháʼí Faith. Rúḥíyyih Khánum then gave a short history of Baháʼuʼlláh's exiles, explained His basic teachings and said that the primary objective of the Baháʼí Faith was the creation of world peace. She then mentioned that Shoghi Effendi was the Head of the Faith and that people from all over the world came as pilgrims to meet him. Following that, Leroy was asked about the gardens and the Shrine of the Báb. To conclude, Rúḥíyyih Khánum talked about the life of the Báb and His martyrdom.[28]

A day in the life of the Guardian

In a recorded talk by Hand of the Cause Leroy Ioas in Johannesburg, South Africa in 1958, Leroy described a typical day in the life of the Guardian:

> Shoghi Effendi usually arose in the morning about 5:30. Then he had his period of prayer and devotions and meditations. After that he would receive . . . piles of mail, and he would start to go through this mail from all over the world. And he would indicate on each letter what should be done with it . . . Shoghi Effendi opened every letter that was addressed to him . . . the letters were opened by the Guardian himself. He took out the letter and read it, then he indicated what should be done with it. Sometimes he gave it to Rúḥíyyih Khánum to respond to, or he gave it to me or at other times he would give it to Dr Hakím if it was from Oriental countries and had to be answered in Persian. So, every piece of mail that came in addressed to the Guardian of the Cause was received by him personally and opened by him personally . . .
>
> Then after going through this correspondence for hours – and don't think it was light – one evening he came over and said that today I have received 700 pages of minutes and records from different parts of the world and I have to read them all . . . Later in the afternoon he went up on Mount Carmel and to the Baháʼí gardens there, which he had built himself, and he met the Oriental pilgrims.

He would walk with them in the gardens, he would talk with them and he had tea with them and answered their questions and would talk about the Cause in all parts of the world . . . Then he would lead them into the Shrine. After a period of prayer and devotion which he would chant for them . . . then he would go down and deal with his mail and the cables that had come in during the day . . .

In the evening he would come over and have dinner with the pilgrims from the western part of the world. He would talk about the Cause with the people from the West . . . and he would talk about the Cause and the different conditions all throughout the world. He would talk with them about the progress of the Faith in their own country. One of the most interesting things that we experienced was when a pilgrim would come from . . . Canada, he would say, 'Well, how is the Cause developing in Canada? How is it progressing? How many centers do you have; how many spiritual assemblies do you have?' 'Well, Shoghi Effendi, I don't know.' 'If you don't know, then I do know. I'll tell you what it was.' . . . He would tell you the number of assemblies or the number of Bahá'ís. Any part of the world; it made no difference. He would talk with each and every one about their own countries, about the conditions there, about the social conditions, about the problems under which they worked and give them hope and encouragement, guidance and instructions.

I give you this as a picture of one day in Shoghi Effendi's life. Remember, it wasn't one day and then he rested for a week. It wasn't two days and he rested. It was three days; it was four days; it was five days; it was six days; it was seven days. And it was week after week, week after week. When he was in the Holy Land there was no rest whatsoever for the Guardian. From 5:00 or 5:30 in the morning to 11 or 11:30 at night . . .

In the West, we have come to associate majesty and greatness with size . . . But Shoghi Effendi was a very delicate and refined man. He was small in stature. He was so refined and delicate in his features, in his nose, his eyes, his hands. Every one of those features was so delicate and so refined and so perfect that you could realize that the power when he spoke was not of the man, Shoghi Effendi, but was of the power of the spirit coming through him. That he was a channel that God used. He was not a man sitting there . . . and yet the power with which he spoke! And when he would speak about the power of the Cause, the room would shake . . . It was a tremendous experience to see how God could use His chosen instrument, to speak through him and to work through him and to disseminate His Will and power throughout the world.

Shoghi Effendi was about the size or smaller than 'Abdu'l-Bahá . . . he looked quite a bit like 'Abdu'l-Bahá; he walked like the Master and he had the same stance as the Master . . .

He had no one to consult with, no one to share his burdens with. He had to decide for himself. He had to consider for himself and had to make a decision for himself, because there was no associate for his divine guidance . . . But what it was we don't know. What it is and how it works, but there it was; we saw it all the time.

One time he came over for dinner and he was rather disturbed because of some cables from America about certain matters and the actions that had been taken. He was a little bit disturbed at the actions . . . He started to talk about it, discuss it and he read the cable he had received. In a minute or two he turned to me and said, 'Roy, you were on the National Assembly in America when this thing happened, when it first came up, weren't you?' I said, 'Yes, sir, I was.' He said, 'Tell me what happened at that first meeting.' So, I started to tell him what happened and he stopped me when I got about one-fifth of the way. 'No, no, no,' he said, 'I will tell you what happened and then you tell me if I'm right or wrong.' He proceeded to discuss that meeting; what had taken place; the spirit behind the actions that had been taken – which was the thing I was trying to convey to him because an action is simple, you know you did this, but why did you do it? That is the important thing – the spirit behind it. He described that in detail. He said to me, 'Am I right or am I wrong?' I said, 'Shoghi Effendi, you are right even in the details.' 'Because, you see, I don't have to have all this information. God gives me a feeling in my heart. When I have that feeling, I have it strong and I know what the situation is and it doesn't make a difference what anybody says.'[29]

The Guardian's correspondence exhausted him. After his passing, Rúḥíyyih Khánum described the huge burden it was:

He had the most extraordinary patience. He used to put up with people indefinitely . . . He used to get letters from people. I dread to think of how many they got back from him. I think one Bahá'í must have had well over a hundred. And she just wrote him practically nothing. Every time she felt like sitting down and writing a nice chatty letter, she wrote it to Shoghi Effendi. And patiently and lovingly, he answered her to the tune of over a hundred . . . He never wanted to hurt the believers. He never wanted to make them cold, to injure their feelings in any way. We used to beg him towards the end, when he had so terribly much work to do, we said, 'Shoghi Effendi, why do you answer all of these individual letters. Can't you stop doing it?' He stopped doing it with the East at the period of the Second World War . . . Previously to that, he had appended to letters written by his secretaries his directions to the Bahá'ís of the East in Persia in Persian and then he gave it all up. Then we used to say to him, when we saw how terribly exhausted he got, how overburdened he was, 'Won't you give this up?' And after all, think of how many letters the American Bahá'ís and the English Bahá'ís have had from him. He said, 'Yes, but now there are new Bahá'ís coming in all over the world and I must act according to principle. If I stop writing to the old Bahá'ís in these well-established communities, then I have no excuse for writing to the new Bahá'ís and I don't want to close that door at this time.' So this love and this tenderness and this solicitude for the feelings of others we could well profit from and emulate.[30]

But when the correspondence was good, Shoghi Effendi could become so animated that he forgot to eat:

Sometimes the beloved Guardian would push away his dinner plate in his enthusiasm to tell us some important news or explain one of his new plans. Then Rúḥíyyih Khánum would ask him to please eat his food while it was hot, doing her wifely duty. She had already told me how difficult it was to get him to eat properly. She had learned during her travels with him that he liked blue dishes, so she would use blue and white tablecloths and blue and white china to tempt him, especially when he had meals in their own apartment.[31]

1952

SOME LAST PILGRIMAGES BEFORE
THE TEN YEAR CRUSADE

Since 1941 and the early part of the Second World War, Shoghi Effendi had allowed almost no one to come on pilgrimage. Through the world conflict between 1941 and 1945 and then the War of Independence from 1947 to 1949, it hadn't been safe. But on 25 December 1951 Shoghi Effendi sent a cable announcing: 'restrictions on pilgrimage being gradually removed'. This electrified the Bahá'í world and within four months one hundred Bahá'ís from East and West were allowed to come. Their visits, however, were limited to nine days because of the great numbers who wished to go and the limited space in the Eastern and Western Pilgrim Houses. By limiting the pilgrimage to just nine days, more people could be accommodated.[1]

The first pilgrim to arrive after the restriction was lifted was Sami Doktoroglu from Istanbul. When he left Haifa after his pilgrimage he was carrying instructions from the Guardian that resulted in the formation of the first Local Spiritual Assemblies in Istanbul, Aintab and Adana and the purchase of a portion of the land on which one of the houses where Bahá'u'lláh had lived was located.[2]

Larry Hautz

The first Western Bahá'í to arrive was Larry (Laurence) Hautz from Milwaukee. When Larry heard that pilgrimage had been reopened, he didn't bother with a letter or a cable. He picked up the telephone and called. He wanted to talk directly with Shoghi Effendi, but the phone was answered by Rúḥíyyih Khánum, who told him that 'nobody called

Shoghi Effendi'. She told Larry to write, but he was too impatient and sent a cable instead.[3]

Larry had a moustache, but before leaving America, he had debated shaving it off, worried about a passage in the Kitáb-i-Aqdas about superfluous hair. In the end, and after noticing that his passport picture showed him with a moustache, he decided to keep it. Shortly after arriving in Haifa, the Guardian came to meet him: 'a short man with a moustache just like his!' Shoghi Effendi told Larry that as the first Western pilgrim, his pilgrimage was a 'great privilege and also a great responsibility'.

Larry noted that the dining table in the Pilgrim House was rectangular and that the Guardian always sat to the right of the head of the table. Rúḥíyyih Khánum sat to his right and the most recent pilgrim sat at the head. The pilgrim would later move to the left and the chairman of the International Council, Mason Remey, would sit at the head. One night Larry was present with Ugo Giachery and Fred Schopflocher when Shoghi Effendi lectured Fred for two hours about the greatness of the Cause in Canada. Then he suddenly told Fred, 'I now make you a Hand of the Cause,' catching everyone present by surprise.[4]

Initially, Larry was only supposed to have a nine-day pilgrimage, but he ended up staying for ninety days.[5] One of his tasks was to drive Shoghi Effendi's car, although Shoghi Effendi didn't ask if he knew how or had a driving licence.[6]

When a government surveyor visited the Bahá'í gardens, he asked how many architects and landscapers worked there. When Larry told him 'None. Just the Guardian,' he exclaimed, 'Impossible! No one man could do this.'[7]

Shortly after Larry's arrival, Shoghi Effendi asked him to work with Leroy Ioas. They were involved in some very difficult negotiations to acquire certain parcels of land at Bahjí,[8] as described in the previous chapter. On 4 March Shoghi Effendi said to him:

If you succeed in getting this land around the Shrine . . . it will be a great blow to the Covenant-breakers. You will not only have dealt them a terrible blow, but you will have paved the way for the construction of what is going to be the intermediate stage between the present structure of the Shrine of Bahá'u'lláh and the final building, which will be on a scale far greater than the Shrine of the Báb.[9]

One of the things that struck Larry about life in Haifa was that they had no refrigerators. When he returned home, he immediately sent a DC-3 full of them to Shoghi Effendi. But the Guardian kept only one, which was placed in the Western Pilgrim House.[10]

In January 1954, Larry sent a shipment of 400 California rose bushes to Haifa. The *Milwaukee Journal*, on the 11th of that month, carried a story which read:

> A shipment of America's choicest rose bushes is bound for Israel as a Milwaukeean's gift to the new Jewish nation. Lawrence A. Hautz, Milwaukee Baha'i leader, ordered the 400 rose bushes sent from California. They will be placed aboard an El-Al air lines plane in New York Monday, bound for Haifa, Israel.
>
> There they will be met at the airport by the mayor of Haifa, who promised recently, while Hautz was visiting there, that he would see that the roses were planted in the public gardens of the Baha'i shrine at Haifa.
>
> To Hautz, the roses are filled with symbolism. They will help to beautify Israel, he believes, and thus fulfil the prophecy from the book of Isaiah, 'And the desert shall rejoice and blossom as the rose.' This will symbolize the friendship and unity of peoples divided by the barriers of different religions.[11]

Spurred on by his pilgrimage, Larry afterwards made a teaching trip that carried him around the world. The *Milwaukee Journal* reported that

> He marched into the Russian embassy in New Delhi and snapped, 'You people think religion is the opiate of the masses, but you're dead wrong.' He sat down and gave members of the staff a lecture on the Baha'i faith and told them religion had come a long way from the corrupt form it assumed in czarist Russia. He said they listened politely and told him when he left: 'You're not such a bad guy.'
>
> He got an appointment with the top Buddhist priest in India. 'What are you doing about your corrupt priests?' he demanded. He detailed stories of corruption from his own observation, and the priest acknowledged that the time for reform seemed to be not too far off.
>
> In an interview with India's Prime Minister Nehru, Hautz

demanded to know: 'What is the difference between a prophet of God and a politician like you?'

Nehru told him politicians must compromise in order to accomplish anything, while religious prophets never deviate from their principles. This impressed Hautz, and they had a 20 minute talk on just what compromises were necessary to guide a superstitious old country like India in the complex world today.[12]

Larry pioneered to Rhodesia (now Zimbabwe) during the Ten Year Crusade at the suggestion of Shoghi Effendi.

Aziz Panahi

Aziz Panahi was at the Tehran Bahá'í centre when the National Secretary said to him, 'You are the luckiest man.' When Aziz asked why, the National Secretary said that they had just received a cable from Shoghi Effendi which announced the reopening of pilgrimage. Aziz immediately went to the post office and sent a cable to the Guardian requesting pilgrimage, and few days later a cable came that simply said 'Welcome'. Aziz quickly organized the journey to Haifa with his wife.

Just before he left, Aziz was given a ring that had belonged to the Báb to take to Shoghi Effendi, so as soon as they arrived in Haifa he entrusted the ring to Lotfullah Hakím, who gave it to the Guardian. Aziz and his family stayed in Haifa for two weeks. Several times, Aziz spent time alone with the Guardian and said his voice was 'very clear, not too loud and, I can't say powerful', but strong. They also had the bounty of spending one night in the Mansion of Bahjí, another night at the House of 'Abbúd and yet another night at Mazra'ih.[13]

One day Shoghi Effendi asked Aziz to come to the House of the Master. When he arrived, Shoghi Effendi's car was parked in front with Larry Hautz, whom the Guardian jokingly called his chauffeur, in the driver's seat. Shoghi Effendi opened the car door and told Aziz to get in. With Larry driving, Shoghi Effendi, Lotfullah Hakím and Aziz drove from the shore to the monastery at the top of Mount Carmel, then down to the Cave of Elijah.[14]

Ugo Giachery

In early February, Ugo Giachery received a cablegram from Shoghi
Effendi reading, 'Welcome to Haifa'. He made 'hasty and feverish prep-
arations', then rushed away 'on wings'.[15] It was while he was in Haifa
that he learned of his appointment as a Hand of the Cause.

On 4 March, Ugo went to the House of the Master, which he
described in a letter to his wife Angeline:

> It is a lovely building with a very large central hall from which one
> can see the door of the room where 'Abdu'l-Bahá passed away . . .
> I sat for a while with Milly . . . in the small sitting-room where the
> Guardian receives visitors. It is an oblong room with two windows; it
> has the type of furnishing prevalent some eighty years ago; of course
> all the rugs are beautiful and the atmosphere is one of great repose.
> One feels happy to enter this room because there is a spirit of great
> holiness that hovers around you. On the wall there is a picture of
> 'Abdu'l-Bahá and a few hangings; the ceiling, as in all other rooms,
> is very high and the walls are painted a warm buff colour. From the
> windows one can see the garden which goes around the house and
> the peacocks strutting in a special pen at the end of the garden.[16]

Rúḥíyyih Khánum took Ugo up to the Shrine of the Báb, where they
arrived just as a group of American tourists came from the cruise ship
Constitution. Ugo thought the gardens at the Shrine to be amazingly
beautiful. Rúḥíyyih Khánum told him that a prominent person had
been so impressed with the gardens that he requested the designer to
lay out his own gardens. Unfortunately for him, Shoghi Effendi didn't
'do' private gardens! Ugo, Milly and Rúḥíyyih Khánum went into the
Shrine and Ugo wrote that his eyes were

> transfixed on the central spot of the central room, where a small rare
> rug marks the sacred spot above the real tomb. Three chandeliers
> give a brilliant light and there are flowers everywhere. We stop at the
> threshold which is covered by an embroidered white cloth, literally
> covered with flowers which the custodian places there fresh every
> morning. We prostrate ourselves on the floor with our faces upon
> the threshold and pray with all our hearts.[17]

When he finally approached the Shrine of Bahá'u'lláh for the first time, he found himself frozen before the building. His guide gently urged him forward and he entered:

> It is not possible to describe the feelings of exaltation and awe which overtook me upon entering the door of that Sacred Sepulchre! The world with all its immensity whirled away into nothingness with the rapidity of lightning. I was alone, relieved of cares and thoughts, free from all attachments, as if suspended between heaven and earth. I could only feel the fast beats of my heart and the humming of infinity. There was nothing but light all around me and a powerful fragrance never known before. As in a dream, transported by the attraction exercised by the mystery emanating from the most Blessed Spot in creation, I reached the portal leading to the inner chamber of the Tomb and fell on my knees and placed my forehead on that hallowed Threshold. I felt the need to conceal my face in the ground, as my whole being was gripped by a strong sensation of guilt – guilt for having arrived so late in my life. I could hear myself saying: Forgive, forgive, forgive . . . for a long time, and then a great peace filled me. My whole past life came before me as an irrelevant episode of eternity, while the present and the vision of the future filled me with unprecedented joy and the lightness of freedom . . . Prayers of thanksgiving and praise came to my lips; streams of unending tears flowed from my eyes . . .
>
> When I came back to the reality of this contingent world, I felt that something had happened to me; my heart was filled with contentment, stability, expectation and unfading certainty . . . Shoghi Effendi was eternally linked to my soul, while the problems of everyday life disappeared as small clouds swept by a fresh wind.[18]

One day, Ugo was shown some large architectural drawings that had been found in 'Abdu'l-Bahá's room in the Pilgrim House at Bahjí. The language on the drawings was Italian, so Ugo could read it. The drawings were of a monumental tomb for Bahá'u'lláh by an engineer and architect from Florence, Henry Edward Plantagenet (a descendant of the Plantagenet dynasty that had ruled England for 300 years). Years before, the former Ottoman Government had contracted him to build the Syrian railroad. The drawings had been commissioned by some member of Bahá'u'lláh's family and showed an edifice in the form of a pentagram, a five-pointed star. 'Abdu'l-Bahá had obviously not followed the design and neither did Shoghi Effendi.[19]

That night, when Ugo mentioned the drawings to Shoghi Effendi, the Guardian laid out his vision for a future monumental Shrine for Bahá'u'lláh. The new structure would leave the existing Shrine untouched, but would surround the whole area. He

> contemplated surrounding the Sepulchre with a colonnade which would dramatize it from far and near: a total of ninety-five monolithic columns of Carrara marble, of Doric design, with capitals inspired by the purest existing examples of that order; all columns arrayed in pairs, two in depth, over a platform of the same marble, accessible by a series of five steps, the whole ensemble 'like arms stretching ready to embrace'.
>
> . . . Each of the ninety-five columns would be six metres tall, supporting a carved capital – the weight of which would come close to a half metric ton – and each shaft, with the base and the capital, would stand up in the air almost seven metres; that, added to the height of the platform, would make an awesome complex whose brilliant majesty would glorify and enshrine the sacred Holy of Holies.[20]

At dinner on 4 March, Shoghi Effendi told Ugo that when the dome of the Shrine of the Báb was completed, his work would not be yet done. Although it was not possible to carry out his plans for the Shrine of Bahá'u'lláh at that time, he wanted to start work on the colonnade. Ugo sent to Italy for scale drawings and estimates. However, the Guardian later abandoned the plan for the colonnade, and instead concentrated on beautifying the surroundings of the Shrine.[21]

Ugo greatly enjoyed the privilege of staying at the Mansion. It offered the opportunity to pray in the Shrine very late and very early. He remembered waking in the morning in the Mansion and hearing Shoghi Effendi's beautiful chanting from the room of Bahá'u'lláh. Shoghi Effendi's room was diagonally opposite Bahá'u'lláh's room across the central hall. One day when he had the bounty of seeing Shoghi Effendi in his room, he noticed that the Guardian had a photo of the first Local Spiritual Assembly of Rome, of which he was a member, by his bed.[22]

Músá and Samíḥíḥ Banání

From their pioneer post in Uganda came Músá Banání and his wife Samíḥíḥ, also arriving in February. It was here in Haifa that Mr Banání learned of his appointment as a Hand of the Cause, as described in the previous chapter.

During their pilgrimage another highly significant event occurred:

> Before they had left Kampala it had been agreed that the pioneers would hold a special meeting for the African enquirers while the Banánís were in Haifa. The meeting was timed to coincide with the hour when Shoghi Effendi usually visited the Shrines. At the appointed time the Guardian and Mr Banání prayed together at the Shrines for the progress of the Faith. The next morning Enoch Olinga declared his belief in Bahá'u'lláh to the pioneers in Kampala. By 21 April 1952 the number of new believers was sufficient to elect Uganda's first Local Spiritual Assembly at Kampala. Enoch Olinga was among the members. By October there were a hundred believers in Uganda.[23]

For Samíḥíḥ Banání, it was a memorable pilgrimage for another reason. On her 1934 pilgrimage, 'Abdu'l-Bahá's wife Munírih Khánum had recognized her and told her a story about her great-grandmother, who had been living in a room in the House of 'Abbúd. One day, her great-grandmother fell down the stairs and landed on 'Abdu'l-Bahá. She was so embarrassed that she moved to another house. During the 1952 pilgrimage, Mrs Banání greatly wanted to ask Shoghi Effendi about the story of her great-grandmother, but was too afraid to do so. One day, the Banánís went to Bahjí and Akka. When they returned, Shoghi Effendi asked: 'Did you go to Akka?' 'Yes,' she said. 'Did you go to the House of 'Abbúd?' 'Yes,' she said again. 'Have you been to that room?' 'Yes,' she said for the third time. Shoghi Effendi then said that 'Abdu'l-Bahá had told him the story of her great-grandmother.[24]

As the Banánís left Haifa, Mrs Banání asked if they would have the bounty of returning to Haifa and Shoghi Effendi said that they would return many times. Rúḥíyyih Khánum added that they would come back with their children, but Shoghi Effendi said, no, they would return with their spiritual children. At the first Conclave of the Hands after the passing of the Guardian, Samíhíh Banání noted that her husband was sitting next to Enoch Olinga, one of his spiritual children.[25]

The pioneers in Africa were overjoyed. Philip Hainsworth wrote:

> The visit of the Bananis was historic and will have far-reaching effects – it is said, 'We sent them to have their batteries re-charged, and the Guardian has changed the whole car.' We did not realise what a man we had in Banani that the Guardian should shower such praise and blessings upon him – & indeed upon Kampala.[26]

Dhikru'lláh Khádem

The newly-appointed Hand of the Cause Dhikru'lláh Khádem made his sixth and last pilgrimage in mid-March. He had been entrusted with carrying with him to Haifa a precious copy of the *Kitáb-i-Íqán* in the handwriting of 'Abdul-Bahá, with annotations by Bahá'u'lláh Himself in the margin. Words could not describe Mr Khádem's joy and gratitude.[27]

One day while he was with Shoghi Effendi, the Guardian

> pointed with his right hand to the Shrine of the Báb and thanked Bahá'u'lláh that the spiritual center of the Faith on Mount Carmel was almost complete. Then he waved his left hand, pointing to the lands of the Monument Gardens, and said, 'From now on we must exert our efforts to build the Administrative World Center there.'
>
> He often remarked that the believers must be waiting anxiously for the realization of the promises of God uttered in the Tablet of Carmel: 'Ere long will God sail His Ark upon thee.'[28]

It was after this that the Guardian started to build an Arc across the top of the Monument Gardens, around which in the future would rise the institutions comprising that 'Ark of God'.

Nell French

Nell French of California made her second pilgrimage in April. At Ridván, Shoghi Effendi talked about the *Tablets of the Divine Plan* and how the world had not been ready to put them into effect immediately after 'Abdu'l-Bahá wrote them. The Guardian said that only a few individuals had arisen when the Tablets were published in America:

Martha Root started on her travels, Mr. and Mrs. Dunn went from Calif. to Australia; you and Emogene went to Italy, but all on an individual basis . . . not organized, not systematic, not continuous; more or less spasmodic, purely on an individual basis. It was not directed towards a definite plan . . . so unlike the present plans the Bahá'ís have formulated throughout the world . . . National Assemblies have each their own plan.[29]

The Administrative Order was necessary to systematically organize such a huge, world-wide teaching effort. Shoghi Effendi said that it had taken the Bahá'í world twenty years to build the institutions of the Faith before it was possible to implement the beginnings of the Divine Plan:

It took us two decades . . . twenty years to do that [develop the administrative order]. As the work progressed some of the Bahá'ís began to wonder whether that was going to be the sole concern of the Bahá'ís . . . to establish these institutions. Some began to doubt, some to criticize. Ahmad Sohrab entirely misunderstood our purpose, for the simple reason that I asked the Bahá'ís to think of nothing else but building these institutions that were to be the means in our hands to achieve a purpose later on. It took us twenty years to establish two stages of this administrative order . . . local and national assemblies. When the local and national assemblies were established and were beginning to function, then I directed the attention of the Bahá'ís to the purpose for which these institutions had been created and were being perfected. For two decades . . . The first part in the plan, the Americas . . . Latin America, So. America, Canada. The second stage in Europe . . . Now we have started in Africa. That is why the Cause is progressing so rapidly. In Switzerland, as you know, Mrs. Lynch worked, and labored for years . . . not on a sound basis, not organized. It could not be, the time was not ripe . . . Worked fifty years in England, but as soon as local assemblies were formed, National assemblies were formed . . . then they began to formulate their own plans. All the attention of the

British believers was concentrated on their plan. Then it began to progress. It took 50 years to establish two assemblies . . . but in five years they established 19 assemblies . . . not only in England, but in Scotland, Wales and Ireland.[30]

Ted Cardell

Ted Cardell also arrived in April, coming from Kenya where he was pioneering. Ted, an Englishman, had become a Bahá'í in Canada in 1949 and was a professional photographer. He had originally pioneered to Uganda. When the Banánís went on pilgrimage they took a message from Ted to Rúḥíyyih Khánum. Not wanting to bother the Guardian, he told Rúḥíyyih Khánum that he was saving money for his own pilgrimage. When the Banánís returned, they brought a message from the Guardian's wife: 'You've got enough money. Come now.'[31]

There was a bit of confusion when Ted arrived in Haifa because he didn't know where Shoghi Effendi lived or where else to go. The driver took Ted to the taxi office, where he first tried the phone book until he saw that it was all in Hebrew. Fortunately, there was a clerk who spoke some English and Ted soon found himself at No. 7 Persian Street, the House of the Master. A maid answered his call, then took him across and up the street to the Western Pilgrim House where he was welcomed by Mason Remey and Leroy Ioas. Ted noted that everyone was very cheery because 'some critical local troubles' had been resolved. Ted also met Ugo Giachery who was acting as the self-appointed nurse for Leroy, who was ill.[32]

Ted quickly learned to appreciate Ugo's sense of humour, which topped even that of Rúḥíyyih Khánum. He also learned that humour was the 'safety valve and protection against the great strain of the business affairs of the Cause at the World Centre'. Ted was surprised by Rúḥíyyih Khánum's youth, her boundless energy and her well-trained mind that did 'without trivialities'. Rúḥíyyih Khánum was, he said, the general of the World Centre's domestic army. She did

> everything from buying food to arranging details of pilgrims' visits to the Holy places (including food and sleeping facilities) and being advisor to each of the International Council in their respective jobs. On top of all this, one must remember she is the liaison between the

Guardian and just about everything, taking as much off his shoulders as possible and organising all things so they may require as little of the Guardian's attention as possible.[33]

Rúḥíyyih Khánum had a wry sense of humour that mirrored Shoghi Effendi's. She described how one day, the International Bahá'í Council could not remember a date important to Israeli affairs. She reported that Shoghi Effendi facetiously threatened that he would 'dissolve the International Bahá'í Council till they found out'! On another occasion, she told about the arrival of a group of Persian women pilgrims. She noted how Persians sometimes let their emotions get out of hand because they confused the station of Guardian with that of the Manifestation. On this occasion, Shoghi Effendi saw what was going to happen, so quickly said, 'Welcome, welcome, but it is forbidden, the laws of the Aqdas, the instruction of the Master, forbid it.' The women, however, paid no attention to his words and threw themselves down and began kissing the ground at his feet.

Ted suffered the honour on his first night of having to sit at the head of the table:

Imagine my embarrassment when at the first lunch of all with the Council & Rúḥíyyih [Khánum] installed me at the head of the table!

It is the custom in the evening for everyone of the Council and western pilgrims to put on dark suits and dresses and await the call to dinner in the main lounge. This call may come any time between 7 and 9:30 according to how busy the Guardian is. When descending to the dining room on the ground floor, we find the Guardian awaiting us. He shakes hands cordially all round with a light but deliberate grip and a slight, quiet smile on his lips. This night I was pushed ahead of all the others and so was greeted first, this time by a momentary embrace on each cheek in the oriental fashion. The Guardian is definitely shorter than I, which was a surprise. He wore nearly always when I saw him a black fez and black long coat a bit threadbare at the front button where I imagine he is always touching the desk. I must admit that when seated facing the Guardian across the table, realising at last that this was no fairy dream such as I had so often had, I was utterly tongue-tied and spell bound. The Guardian with charming informality soon produced a little life from his visitor but I was at once acutely aware (never really forgot) that he is the Sign of God on earth today. Humility and submissiveness and absolute trust cause one to become silent and immensely happy at once . . . Not only does one not even think of saying anything trivial but even one's own deepest thoughts and questions are given a severe dusting over before presenting to him . . .

The first few nights these notes were made just before bed, after leaving the Guardian, but later two American pilgrims, Mr. and Mrs. Harris of Illinois, arrived and enabled me to move further down the table where I could keep a notebook on my knee. This way enabled the saving of many jewelled utterances. I was amused to see that the Revell sisters and even Leroy often did likewise. However when talking directly to the Guardian or listening to one of crystal clear expositions on some aspect of the Cause or Teachings, I never did other than watch his face closely, trying to make indelible in my memory its lines, expressions, mannerisms and above all just drinking in the spirit of divine confidence, radiant awareness and utter single-pointedness which must surely leave its influence on a person to his dying day.[34]

As was almost everyone, Ted was amazed by the power of the Guardian. He said:

As a person, he was very humble. You remember how he always used to say 'You shouldn't celebrate my birthday. I'm just Shoghi Effendi, your true brother.' He wouldn't accept any other commemorations. Although his wisdom and knowledge were obviously far ahead of us, he regarded himself as much the same as one of us. He said, You have to remember the gap separating himself from 'Abdu'l-Bahá was infinitely greater than the gap separating 'Abdu'l-Bahá from Bahá'u'lláh . . .

His official station was a different matter altogether. He knew that he was representing and was the head of an independent world faith. As such, in the eyes of humanity, at least, he had to maintain a position of that nature. This was illustrated in a dramatic way one day, when it was reported to him that the State of Israel was going to celebrate their fifth anniversary of independence by a major parade in Jerusalem. The Bahá'ís had not been offered a place in the parade, so he sent two members of the International Council down to Jerusalem, while I was there, to ask for a place in the parade. He asked, he didn't demand . . . They came back that night in high victory – they had been given place number seven in the parade. The Guardian said, 'Very good. Tomorrow you'll go back and do better. Please tell the minister that unless we get place number one, we won't come.' And he got it! [35]

Ted was British and the Guardian seemed to go out of his way to extol that nation:

The British believers were first extolled with many adjectives; their Poise, Balance, Good Judgment, Perseverance, Persistence, Thoroughness were just some. I was left gasping; the friends said later that he had often commented on these British qualities. Nor was I ever free from this imminent persistent deluge of compliments till I finally left. Frequently, when on any topic pertaining to the lack of these qualities, the Guardian would, with a gleam in his eyes, say 'not like the British now!' . . .

The English are clear thinking, slow to start but sure, notice much. The Americans enthusiastic but not sustained in their effort, easy to start but need frequent reminders. The English 'steady drizzle' is very comforting, also their loyalty, efficiency, quiet determination, steadiness. The British have it par excellence, next the Americans, at the other extreme are the Persians. There is some rain (effort) in America, but in England a steady drizzle. The gleam of high humour in his eye as he said this was too much for us and all burst out laughing . . .

The Guardian was talking of the English weather, its steady drizzle, so unlike the American efforts which were unsteady and spasmodic. He laughed heartily for almost the first time; we were so happy to see it. He said the 'steady drizzle' was much appreciated . . .

The Guardian now read cable from [the] American Convention outlining one-year plan of such colossal goals that we all felt nonplussed. The Guardian pointed out that the plan first is vague, second is ambitious, 'The Americans love experimenting, meanwhile the Cause suffers. Not like the British now, they are deliberate, consider carefully first, then they persevere.' . . .

The Harrises brought news of American plans and the forth-coming 4 conferences were touched upon. Again the Guardian extolled the British Baha'is and said that if the U.S.A. dropped the standard, the British would pick it up. He spoke of Martha Root, May Maxwell, Keith [Ramson-]Kehler, Dr. Susan Moody, Mrs. Dunn, now all buried all over the world, after following the Master's instructions to 'go out into all the world'. He spoke of the World Crusade, the World Order, World Plan, World Faith, World Conception. America the Chief Implementer of the Divine Plan, Canada her Ally [sic], the Latin-Americas her Associates. Rúḥíyyih Khánum said, 'What about Britain?' The Guardian followed his train of thought undeterred, explaining the distinction between ally and associate, then with a twinkle in his eye, 'Great Britain is the Chief Auxiliary to U.S.A.'[36]

Ted arrived at the time when the Guardian was in the middle of a very serious legal case against the Covenant-breakers. They were suing Shoghi Effendi for destruction of some of their property (as described earlier), hoping to get him into the dock and humiliate him. The case dragged on interminably, but eventually the Covenant-breakers, who had started the suit, pushed the judge to take action. They did this in such a rude way that the judge, in anger, threw the whole case out of court and the Covenant-breakers lost everything. These events had not yet happened when Ted was on pilgrimage, and even though the Guardian didn't seem to be affected by this problem, you could see that there was some kind of tension. Ted said that 'Later that night when we were gathered upstairs, Ugo said "Oh, how the beloved was suffering tonight". If you could imagine that the vision that was before him was that there was going to be a really big stink, big law case, and he was going to be the criminal.'[37]

Ted was in Haifa not just for pilgrimage, but also to work. He had been given the task of photographing the Shrines and Holy Places inside and out. This created a dilemma:

How is it possible to both work at the Shrine (taking photos) and to worship? How was it possible to get into the proper state of devotion necessary during a pilgrimage, while there was much work to do also. My mind seemed quite incapable of operating to such vast extremes . . . Millie suggested that it was probably a great bounty that I was confronted with this problem, for one of life's greatest problems is just this, i.e. How to live a practical life and a prayerful one at the same time. I found that it could be done, but one had to be very clear from moment to moment just what was the present objective. Ruhiyyih Khanum had earlier suggested that when I visited the Shrine I should decide first whether it was for work or prayer and if the latter, then leave the camera at home . . . it was one of the big surprises at Haifa to find everyone so intensely practical in their service to the Cause. There was almost none of the dreamy spiritual type of thing. In fact Millie Collins said she had never in her life had so little time for praying and reading as now in Haifa. I recall once again how the Guardian had said, 'It is not enough to pray, one must also think' and then of course act.[38]

One night the Guardian suggested that it was a good time to photograph the inside of the Shrine of the Báb, so Ted put down his prayer book and picked up his camera. He spent three-and-a-half hours photographing the interiors of the Shrines, using four cameras and both black and white and colour film to ensure success. Because of the workload, Shoghi Effendi suggested that Ted stay an additional week so that he could both pray and work. After the Shrine of the Báb, Ted went to Bahjí for several days. He spent a lot of time in the Mansion, looking at all of the treasures on display there. He was particularly taken with photographs on either side of the door to Shoghi Effendi's room. On one side was a photo of the Báb's executioner, while on the other were two photos of National Spiritual Assemblies. Shoghi Effendi said of the executioner, 'I want him to see the result of his handiwork.'[39]

One day, the subject of why only men could be on the Universal House of Justice was raised by Rúḥíyyih Khánum. Shoghi Effendi replied, 'The Master said the wisdom of it will appear in the future.'[40]

From the talks of Shoghi Effendi, Ted also learned that the Guardian thought that the best English Bahá'í writer was George Townshend, while the best American Bahá'í writer was Stanwood Cobb. Shoghi Effendi also mentioned that a woman named Van-Hooten, who was the grand-daughter of Násiri'd-Dín Sháh, was a Bahá'í. One night, someone asked about greeting people with 'Alláh'u'Abhá'. Shoghi Effendi's answer was that the Faith was strange enough to others without people 'Alláh'u'Abhaing everybody'. The Guardian also noted that 400 to 500 Jews a day were visiting the Shrine of Bahá'u'lláh.[41]

Pilgrims from Persia

'Alí Akbar Rafí'í, a relative of Mrs Banání, applied for permission for eleven members of his family to go on pilgrimage, but was told that only five could go at one time from Iran. Only nine Eastern pilgrims were permitted on pilgrimage at one time and only five of those could be from Persia, so the family was divided into three groups. 'Alí Akbar, his wife Sháyistih, and two sons went in the first group. Their two daughters, one daughter's husband and his mother were in the second group and the other daughter's husband was in the third. All three groups heard Shoghi Effendi encourage them to pioneer and open new territories.

The second group included Nosrat Rouhani Ardekani, whose husband, Hussein, stayed home to care for their young daughter. Because of the still recent conflict in the area, there was very little food available. The Guardian asked the pilgrims to buy food in Turkey and bring it with them. They did so and, like the other Eastern pilgrims, brought it to the Guardian's house where everybody ate.

Nosrat was very eager to pioneer, so she prayed in the Shrines and asked Shoghi Effendi for help for pioneering. Her husband was very busy with his business and didn't see how he could pioneer. But Shoghi Effendi said that everyone who could pioneer, should pioneer, and that if one could not pioneer, then he should send someone in his place. If that was not possible, he should contribute to the Fund so someone else could pioneer. And if that was not possible, then the person could at least pray every day for the success of the plan.

While she was there, Nosrat was able to attend the commemoration for the Ascension of Bahá'u'lláh. For the commemoration, the women met with Rúḥíyyih Khánum in a building adjacent to the Pilgrim House, while Shoghi Effendi spoke with the men in the Pilgrim House. After the talks, everyone entered the Shrine, with the men in the room on one side and the women in the room opposite. This allowed them all to listen to the Guardian as he chanted the Tablet of Visitation. The next morning, Nosrat was allowed to go into the Archives in the back of the Shrine to see the photograph of Bahá'u'lláh. Since Nosrat was able to visit the Archives as part of her pilgrimage, she had the inestimable bounty of seeing Bahá'u'lláh's photograph twice.

It was also during Nosrat's pilgrimage that Shoghi Effendi received permission from the Israeli authorities to demolish the house that had been occupied by the Covenant-breakers. A group of pilgrims and other Bahá'ís went with the very happy Shoghi Effendi to remove the blight from the holiest site on earth.

Hussein Rouhani Ardekani, Nosrat's husband, had his pilgrimage next. He was a member of the Persian National Teaching Committee and he relayed the request of the Committee for the Guardian's prayers for the success of the teaching and pioneering efforts of home-front pioneers in Iran. The Guardian replied, 'Yes, yes, they will have success, and', turning to him, said, 'you, also, will be successful in your pioneer post.' As Hussein was busy taking notes, he did not realize what the beloved Guardian had said to him. With all his work obligations, he wasn't planning on pioneering. He and Nosrat had decided to send someone in their place as pioneers. On his return to Tehran after the pilgrimage, one day there was a group of people at his house to hear his pilgrim notes. When he read this statement of Shoghi Effendi, one of those listening exclaimed, 'Hai! You are Rouhani Ardekani. And what did the beloved Guardian say to you? He said you have to be successful in your pioneer post. Why do you sit here and you don't go?' After a thoughtful moment, Hussein turned to his wife and said, 'Nosrat, now we are also pioneers. We have to go and pioneer.' And he did, spending the rest of his life as a pioneer in Morocco, the Canary Islands and Senegal. This change of heart resulted in he and his wife being named Knights of Bahá'u'lláh.[42]

End of year pilgrims

Bahíyyih Ford and Marion Little were on pilgrimage from 17 to 25 November 1952. Much of what they remembered were interesting vignettes: Shoghi Effendi's favourite flower was the jasmine; summer schools would eventually develop into 'great institutes of learning and culture'; and the earth in the little garden in the Shrine of Bahá'u'lláh had been brought by 'Abdu'l-Bahá and those with Him in their cloaks and in pots from the Riḍván Garden. Shoghi Effendi also told them that the German Hands of the Cause would be the historians and the scientists while the gift of the English Hands would be their organizational ability. From the Americans would come the 'saints and heroes'.[43] They also appear to have been some of the earliest to hear Shoghi Effendi warn of the dangers facing America:

> America has potentialities but she must be purged. America is the cradle of materialistic civilization. The Administration symbolizes Divine Civilization. Very probably there will be war on the American continent. If New York is bombed it may be worse than London [in the Second World War] . . .
>
> Americans are slaves of materialism. On the bright side of the American picture they have pure hearts. This is their distinguishing characteristic . . . That is why they have built the Administration. But they must be cleansed and purged. They have not suffered yet. When they do, this will permit them to lead all nations spiritually. 'My calamity is My Providence.' We will share the suffering as others did during the 1st and 2nd wars. The world has to suffer on a still greater scale, particularly in the United States. We must not live in a fool's paradise, that is the Bahá'ís. We [Americans] will suffer even more than other nations. We cannot live on the statement that we are the chief trustees – the suffering that is coming will bring us to the point of being able to fulfil what the Master said 'That America will lead all nations spiritually'. Purity of heart is not enough – we must have discipline. This time we will be caught in the suffering – the sooner the better. Everything that is happening is for the good.[44]

Over the remaining years of his life, this was to be a subject that the Guardian returned to many times and virtually every Western pilgrim heard of it.

Corinne True, who had been appointed a Hand of the Cause in February, and her daughters Katherine and Edna also came on pilgrimage in November. Corinne was 91 years old, so their journey was slow and easy, with stops in Paris and Switzerland, and they arrived just a day after Shoghi Effendi returned from his summer stay in Europe. Corinne was met at the dock, as she had been in years past, by Fujita, who had lived in her house for seven years after 'Abdu'l-Bahá's departure from America. Earlier that very day, Shoghi Effendi had gained a huge victory for the Faith. For thirty years, he had been trying to have the Faith recognized as an independent world religion. The Israeli Government had given him, as the Head of the Bahá'í Faith, a seat of honour at the funeral of Chaim Weizmann, the first President of Israel. News bulletins on national radio had announced that His Eminence Shoghi Effendi Rabbani, world head of the Bahá'í Faith, was among the dignitaries.[45]

That evening at dinner, the Guardian was quite happy. After seating Corinne, he said, with a twinkle in his eye, 'I understand, Mrs True, you had something to do with the Temple in the United States.' She was puzzled because he knew very well that she had. Then he asked, 'Didn't you have something to do with the money?' Even more confused, she replied, 'Yes, I received the money and was the financial secretary.' Shoghi Effendi then brought out a wallet and gave it to her saying, 'This was the purse carried by 'Abdu'l-Bahá when He visited America.' Corinne had spent considerable time with the Master in Chicago and was overwhelmed. Then he told her to open it. Inside was a five-dollar gold coin dated 1907, the year she had made her first pilgrimage.[46]

That night, Shoghi Effendi enthusiastically talked about the upcoming Ten Year Crusade. At one point, he asked Corinne if he was being too ambitions. She replied, 'No, Shoghi Effendi. But I think we should hurry home and get to work; there is so much work to be done.' Then, with that twinkle back in his eye, 'Go ahead and work with your daughters – in Europe, Africa, Asia, and the islands, even Tibet, you can pioneer to any one of those places.' Corinne was momentarily shocked, until she saw the twinkle. The Guardian then suggested that she should direct her efforts into helping other Bahá'ís to become teachers. 'He described Corinne as a "spiritual politician", a term none of the Bahá'ís at the table had ever heard before.' Explaining what he meant, he said to her, 'You have learned to be spiritual and at the same time to get things done.'[47]

About this time, Nura and Nurí Mobine arrived on pilgrimage and stayed at the Eastern Pilgrim House. Half an hour after their arrival, the Guardian arrived and Nura remembered hearing a beautiful voice: 'never before in my life have I heard anything like it, as if this melodious voice was coming from another world, world of love, beauty and perfection.' She described Shoghi Effendi as 'small, but so handsome, his hands are so beautiful and graceful. His eyes are the source of light, love and life.'[48]

In December, Frances Edelstein arrived from Sioux Falls, South

Dakota, on her first pilgrimage. When she first met Shoghi Effendi at dinner, she wrote: 'I had butterflies in the pit of my stomach, and my heart was trembling – in short, I felt like dying rather than being ecstatic over this great opportunity. The inner turmoil was overwhelming and not once in the 13 days of my visit did I ever feel different when I was to sit down at the table opposite Shoghi Effendi.' As awed as she felt in the presence of the Guardian, Frances found she could make a contribution because she had once been a bookkeeper at a frozen-food plant. One day, Rúḥíyyih Khánum showed her the freezer donated by Larry Hautz. Inside were a side of beef, three lamb carcasses and three chickens, all unwrapped and dehydrating. Frances told Rúḥíyyih Khánum that meat had to be cut and wrapped or it would become tasteless and freezer-burned. But she needed waxed paper, and none was available. Rúḥíyyih Khánum, however, said 'I've plenty of candle stubs we can melt down.' Frances described the process:

> We took the huge brown sheets of wrapping paper that had come in on the various shipments, put them on the ironing board, dipped a paint brush in the wax, spread it on the paper, put another sheet of paper on top, took an iron, and made waxed paper.
>
> Then, the process of prying the frozen meat from the deep-freeze began. A few weeks before, someone had sent a complete set of screwdrivers of all lengths and sizes, so I took the largest one and pried the meat out, defrosted the locker, having heated water in every possible cook pot available, and placed three of these hot ones inside which soon melted all the accumulated ice. I washed it thoroughly, put the electricity on again, and left it while I supervised the cutting and wrapping of that frozen meat.
>
> Having taken lots of cutting instructions, I could say more or less where to cut. We had a hacksaw and a butcher knife. To this day, I'll never know how it was accomplished. Lutfullah Hakim and Mason Remey wielding first one and then the other (knife or hacksaw); Sylvia Ioas wrapped and marked it; we tied it with string that had been saved for emergencies whenever any came – same as the brown paper. It was all done in an afternoon and put back in the deep freeze without thawing – another miracle![49]

One night, Shoghi Effendi asked Mason Remey for drawings that

Mason had made for a future Shrine to be built over the existing Shrine of Bahá'u'lláh.

> Mason brought them to the table which had been cleared of dishes. Shoghi Effendi swiftly rolled them out and at one glance and with a sweeping gesture of his hands said 'They won't do.' The drawings were swiftly rolled up and Mason was completely crestfallen. He asked Shoghi Effendi what he would suggest for a design, and the Guardian quickly told him he (the Guardian) wasn't an architect. He said, 'Mason, you are the architect. When you produce what I want, I'll know it.' Mason Remey pressed as to ideas and finally the Guardian said, 'I want columns' . . . Later, Rúḥíyyih Khánum said, 'Mason, Daddy didn't produce anything at first for the Shrine and had to make several attempts before he got what Shoghi Effendi wanted.' [50]

Mason had to learn the same lesson that Sutherland Maxwell had learned. Shoghi Effendi did not visualize the finished design and then ask his architect to create it. He looked at what the architect drew and intuitively knew which parts were right and which parts were not.

When Frances went to the Archives, she greatly anticipated seeing the photograph and the two paintings of Bahá'u'lláh. Afterwards, Shoghi Effendi asked her which one she liked best. Frances groaned inwardly because she had found the paintings to be very stylized and the photograph a poor one. Before she could answer, Shoghi Effendi said, 'The photograph is a poor one, taken in Adrianople after He had suffered greatly.' When the American House of Worship was dedicated the next year, Frances realized why he had asked. As a gift from the Guardian, Rúḥíyyih Khánum had brought a coloured photographic reproduction of the painting of Bahá'u'lláh wearing a red turban.

Marzieh Gail, who was present on that occasion, described this portrait as showing Bahá'u'lláh 'in the bloom of manhood . . . a youthful Personage, still in His thirties, perhaps, or early forties, since the Portrait was done in Baghdad . . . not yet, in this Portrait, the Manifestation Whom the world had forsaken . . . Amatu'l-Bahá spoke of the strong and youthful beauty He had once . . .' [51]

One night, Frances and Rúḥíyyih Khánum both experienced an agonizing moment. The Guardian was going through his mail. He was 'harassed with papers, papers, papers – too many papers'. He said that both Bahá'u'lláh and 'Abdu'l-Bahá had experienced the same thing. The Guardian said, 'On the last days of their lives their papers became too much for them.' Knowing what Shoghi Effendi had to put up with, Rúḥíyyih <u>Kh</u>ánum fled from the table in tears. Frances said that she 'mechanically sat down with unseeing eyes, ate my food, not conscious of what I was eating, finally I felt compelled to lift my head and look up to discover Shoghi Effendi's eyes boring into my inmost being. Then I drew a breath and began to feel alive.' When Rúḥíyyih <u>Kh</u>ánum returned, Shoghi Effendi told her that he had not meant to frighten her. Nine years later, Frances asked Leroy Ioas if the Guardian ever again mentioned his passing. Leroy replied, 'Never again, before pilgrims.' [52]

Frances stayed in the Holy Land for thirteen days. On the night before she left, Shoghi Effendi took her hand and said, 'I will see you tomorrow before you leave.' Frances and the members of the International Council were 'dumbfounded' since it was almost unprecedented. The next day, 31 December, true to his word, Shoghi Effendi sent for her and said:

'Now you have been in Paradise and you must take it back to the friends for, to have it and not to share it – Well!!' and he spread his hands, as if to keep it to oneself is to lose it . . . 'Tell them of the map soon to be printed, also the statistics – impress upon them the vitalness of the Ten Year Crusade. Tell them of the new gardens at Bahji.' [53]

THE NEXT BIG STEP

By Riḍván 1952, all the pieces were in place. Shoghi Effendi had established a world-overseeing secretariat at the Baháʼí World Centre. The International Baháʼí Council had been formed as the preparatory body to the establishment of the Universal House of Justice, lacking, however, its power of infallibility and being appointed instead of elected. The nineteen Hands of the Cause were ready to take up the tasks of propagation and protection, promoting teaching activities and protecting the Faith from a whole range of problems. They also quickly became a buffer between the Guardian and the Covenant-breakers. Shoghi Effendi had to make all the decisions, but the Hands took on all contact and negotiation with those who had forsaken the Manifestation of God.

A Holy Year and four intercontinental conferences

Finally, there were the four intercontinental teaching conferences scheduled for 1953 to focus the world Baháʼí community on what had to be done. Jessie Revell wrote a letter on 9 July 1952 that explained Shoghi Effendi's view of the crises the Faith continually faced and the significance of the forthcoming conferences:

> Recently there have been many problems here but these problems always lead us to victory and our beloved Guardian tells us that the Faith raises up enemies as it expands and grows, it triumphs over them, then a new set of problems arises and eventually it triumphs again. There is no end to the evolution of the righteous and there is no end to the activity of the evil one. After sixty years of opposition since the passing of Baháʼuʼlláh, the enemies can do nothing and this reveals the Power of the Cause. Crisis always leads to victory and never causes a split. Everything that happens in the Baháʼí World

has repercussions here and now. The Cause is entering a World stage in its activities.

Our beloved Guardian tells us that with regard to the Intercontinental conferences to be held during the Bahá'í Holy Year, nothing similar has been attempted since the History of the Faith. It is a World Crusade, utilizing the agencies of a World Administrative Order which is Worldwide in character, to carry out the provisions of 'Abdu'l-Bahá's World Plan, in the service of a World Faith – a Global Crusade in which all National Spiritual Assemblies will take part. The chief task of these Conferences will be the opening up of new territories under their jurisdiction, consolidating the work, on an international scale.

One day at dinner Shoghi Effendi called for a world map and he himself drew circles around the territories under the jurisdiction of the eleven now existing National Spiritual Assemblies, then he drew circles around eleven more territories where new National Spiritual Assemblies are to be made within the next ten years, and he called this THE WHEELS OF BAHÁ'U'LLÁH'S CHARIOT. This World Crusade will last ten years and will culminate in THE MOST GREAT JUBILEE and will include every sovereign state, every chief dependency, every island of the globe. How very fortunate are we all, to have a part in this great crusade! America is the chief executor of 'Abdu'l-Baha's World Plan. In ten years the Bahá'ís of the world will double what has been accomplished since 1844 working through the institutions.[1]

So, after thirty years of carefully constructing the great engine of the World Order of Bahá'u'lláh. Shoghi Effendi was about to turn it on.

On 8 October 1952, Shoghi Effendi announced two world-encompassing events, the first ever Bahá'í Holy Year and the Ten Year Crusade. The Holy Year was to mark the centenary of the Revelation received by Bahá'u'lláh in the Síyáh-Chál in Tehran. Shoghi Effendi wrote that the Revelation of Bahá'u'lláh marked the 'consummation of the six thousand year cycle ushered in by Adam, glorified by all past prophets and sealed with the blood of the Author of the Bábí Dispensation.' He then set the stage for the second announcement by evoking the sacrificial history of the first century of that Revelation and acclaiming

the glorious memory and . . . the immortal exploits of the

Dawn-Breakers of the Apostolic Age of the Bahá'í Dispensation in the cradle of the Faith and the mighty feats of the champion build-ers of its rising World Order in the Western Hemisphere as well as the multitude of valorous achievements of the past and present generations of their brethren in the European, Asiatic, African and Australian continents, whose combined accomplishments during the one hundred and nine years of its existence contributed to the survival of God's struggling Faith, the reinforcement of its infant strength, the safeguarding of the unity of its supporters, the preser-vation of the integrity of its teachings, the enrichment of the lives of its followers, the rise of the institutions of its administrative order, the fashioning of the agencies for the systematic diffusion of its light and the broadening and the consolidation of its foundations.[2]

The Ten Year Spiritual Crusade

When the Guardian announced the Holy Year, he then went on to announce a mind-boggling plan, ten years in length, designed to expand the Faith more in that single decade than had been accomplished in the previous one hundred and nine years:

Feel hour propitious to proclaim to the entire Bahá'í world the projected launching on the occasion of the convocation of the approaching Intercontinental Conferences on the four continents of the globe the fate-laden, soul-stirring, decade-long, world-embracing Spiritual Crusade involving the simultaneous initiation of twelve national Ten Year Plans and the concerted participation of all National Spiritual Assemblies of the Bahá'í world aiming at the immediate extension of Bahá'u'lláh's spiritual dominion as well as the eventual establishment of the structure of His administra-tive order in all remaining Sovereign States, Principal Dependencies comprising Principalities, Sultanates, Emirates, Shaykhdoms, Pro-tectorates, Trust Territories, and Crown Colonies scattered over the surface of the entire planet. The entire body of the avowed sup-porters of Bahá'u'lláh's all-conquering Faith are now summoned to achieve in a single decade feats eclipsing in totality the achievements which in the course of the eleven preceding decades illuminated the annals of Bahá'í pioneering.[3]

The Ten Year Crusade wasn't just another set of national teaching plans. For the first time, Shoghi Effendi had prepared a world teaching plan that summoned the 'entire body of the avowed supporters' of Bahá'u'lláh to arise and do what they had never done before. The Universal House of Justice later wrote that

> the Plan called for the Cause to make a giant leap forward over what might otherwise have been several stages in its evolution. What Shoghi Effendi saw clearly – and what only the powers of foresight inherent in the Guardianship made it possible to see – was that an historical conjunction of circumstances presented the Bahá'í community with an opportunity that would not come again and on which the success of future stages in the prosecution of the Divine Plan would entirely depend. What he did not hesitate to call the 'summons of the Lord of Hosts' was embodied in a message that seized the imagination of Bahá'ís in every part of the world:
>
> 'No matter how long the period that separates them from ultimate victory; however arduous the task; however formidable the exertions demanded of them; however dark the days which mankind, perplexed and sorely-tried, must, in its hour of travail, traverse; however severe the tests with which they who are to redeem its fortunes will be confronted . . . I adjure them, by the precious blood that flowed in such great profusion, by the lives of the unnumbered saints and heroes who were immolated, by the supreme, the glorious sacrifice of the Prophet-Herald of our Faith, by the tribulations which its Founder, Himself, willingly underwent, so that His Cause might live, His Order might redeem a shattered world and its glory might suffuse the entire planet – I adjure them, as this solemn hour draws nigh, to resolve never to flinch, never to hesitate, never to relax, until each and every objective in the Plans to be proclaimed, at a later date, has been fully consummated.'[4]

Thus began the third stage in the Guardian's implementation of 'Abdu'l-Bahá's *Tablets of the Divine Plan*. The Bahá'í world was about to step into a new era – and that is a book all to itself.[5]

BIBLIOGRAPHY

'Abdu'l-Bahá. *The Will and Testament of 'Abdu'l-Bahá*. Wilmette, IL: Bahá'í Publishing Trust, 1944.

Alexander, Agnes. *Notes Taken in the Presence of Shoghi Effendi*, United States Bahá'í National Archives, Ella Cooper Papers, 1937.

— *History of the Bahá'í Faith in Japan 1914-1938*. Osaka, Japan: Bahá'í Publishing Trust, 1977. Available at: http://bahai-library.com/east-asia/history.japan.

Amatu'l-Bahá Rúḥíyyih Khánum *Shoghi Effendi in Scotland*. N.d. Available at: http://bahai-library.com/shoghieffendi_scotland_ruhiyyihkhanum_edinburgh.

— *Tribute to Shoghi Effendi*, Kampala Conference, 26 January 1958. Available at: http://bahai-library.com/rkhanum_kampala_1958_jan.

— 'The Guardian of the Bahá'í Faith', in *The Bahá'í World*, vol. XIII (1954-1963), pp. 59-205.

— Audio recording of a talk at Wilmette, Riḍván, 1960.

— Audio recording of a talk in New York City, 5 June 1960.

(see also Rabbaní, Rúḥíyyih).

Ardekani, Nosrat. Transcript of a phone conversation, 20 August 2013.

Armstrong-Ingram, Jackson. 'Introduction' to Keith Ransom-Kehler and Lorol Schopflocher, 'Haifa Talks'.

Bach, Marcus. *The Circle of Faith*. New York: Hawthorn Books, 1956.

Bahá'í Encyclopedia Project. National Spiritual Assembly of the Bahá'ís of the United States. Available at: http://bahai-encyclopedia-project.org.

Bahá'í News. Periodical. National Spiritual Assembly of the Bahá'ís of the United States and Canada, 1924-.

The Bahá'í World: An International Record. Vol. II (1926-1928); vol. III (1928-1930); vol. IV (1930-1932); vol. V (1932-1935); vol. VIII (1938-1930); vol. IX (1940-1944); vol. X (1944-1946); vol. XI (1946-1950); vol. XII (1950-1952). RP Wilmette, IL: Bahá'í Publishing Trust, 1980, 1981. Vol. XIII (1954-1963),

Haifa: The Universal House of Justice; vol. XIV (1963–1968), Haifa: The Universal House of Justice, 1970; vol. XV (1968–1973), Haifa: Bahá'í World Centre, 1978; vol. XVIII (1979–1983), Haifa: Bahá'í World Centre, 1986; vol. XX (1986–1992), Haifa: Bahá'í World Centre, 1998.

Bahá'u'lláh. *Epistle to the Son of the Wolf.* Trans. Shoghi Effendi. Wilmette, IL: Bahá'í Publishing Trust, rev. ed. 1976.

— *Gleanings from the Writings of Bahá'u'lláh.* Trans. Shoghi Effendi. Wilmette, IL: Bahá'í Publishing Trust, 2nd ed. 1976.

— *The Hidden Words of Bahá'u'lláh.* Trans. Shoghi Effendi. Wilmette, IL: Bahá'í Publishing Trust, 1970; New Delhi: Bahá'í Publishing Trust, 1987.

— *Kitáb-i-Íqán: The Book of Certitude.* Trans. Shoghi Effendi. Wilmette, IL: Bahá'í Publishing Trust, 2nd ed. 1950, 1981.

— *Prayers and Meditations by Bahá'u'lláh.* Trans. Shoghi Effendi. Wilmette,IL: Bahá'í Publishing Trust, 1938, 1987.

Baker, Effie. United States Bahá'í National Archives, Rabb, Box 6: Effie Baker, 1925.

— New Zealand National Bahá'í Archives, letters 1925–1927.

— New Zealand National Bahá'í Archives, 1930.

Bedekian, Victoria. United States Bahá'í National Archives, Alfred Lunt Papers, 1926.

Bishop, Helen. United States Bahá'í National Archives, George Latimer Papers, 1934.

Brigham, Gertrude Richardson. 'A Modern Pilgrimage to Bahá'í Shrines', in *Star of the West*, vol. 18, no. 9 (December 1927), pp. 278–82.

Bolles, Jeanne. 'Haifa Notes'. United States Bahá'í National Archives, Alice Cox Papers, 1936.

Bowditch, Nancy. 'A Visit to Bahjí', in *The Bahá'í World*, vol. IV ((1930–1932), pp. 411–15.

Cardell, Edward (Ted). 'Extracts from a description by Ted Cardell of his Pilgrimage to Haifa' [April 1952].

— United States Bahá'í National Archives, Nancy Bowditch Papers, 1952.

— *Experiences with the Guardian.* Audio recording, August 1988. ARC T- 1199, The Heritage Project of the National Spiritual Assembly of the Bahá'ís of the United States.

Chapman, Anita Ioas. *Leroy Ioas: Hand of the Cause of God.* Oxford: George Ronald, 1988.

Collins, Amelia. *Shoghi Effendi.* Wilmette: Bahá'í Publishing Trust, 1958.

— United States Bahá'í National Archives, Amelia Collins Papers, 1938.

Coy, Genevieve. United States Bahá'í National Archives, Albert Vail Papers, 1923.

de Vries, Jelle. *The Babi Question you Mentioned: The Origins of the Bahá'í Community of the Netherlands, 1844–1962.* Holland: Peeters, 2002.

Dudley, Alice. United States Bahá'í National Archives, Alice Dudley Papers, 1957.

Edelstein, Frances. The Heritage Project of the National Spiritual Assembly of the Bahá'ís of the United States, 1985.

Etter-Lewis, Gwendolyn, and Richard Thomas. *Lights of the Spirit: Historical Portraits of Black Bahá'ís in North America.* Wilmette, IL: Bahá'í Publishing Trust, 2006.

Faizí, Abu'l-Qásim. *Milly.* Oxford: George Ronald, 1977.

Faizi-Moore, May. *Faizi.* Oxford: George Ronald, 2013.

Finch, Ida, Fanny Knobloch and Alma Knobloch. *Flowers Culled from the Rose Garden of Acca* (1908). Available at: http://bahai-library.com/finch_knobloch_flowers_acca.

Ford, Bahíyyih, and Marion Little. United States Bahá'í National Archives, Viola Tuttle Papers, 1952.

'Fred Schopflocher: Hand of the Cause of God', insert in *Canadian Bahá'í News*, November 1953. Available at: http://www.bahai-encyclopedia-project.org/index.php?option=com_content&view=article&id=69:schopflocher-siegfried&catid=37:biography.

French, Nell. *Nellie French Pilgrim Notes,* 1952. Available at: http://bahai-library.com/french_pilgrims_notes.

Gail, Marzieh. *Dawn over Mount Hira.* Oxford: George Ronald, 1976.

— *Arches of the Years.* Oxford: George Ronald, 1991.

— 'Jubilee at Wilmette', in *The Bahá'í World*, vol. XII (1950–1954), pp. 152–3.

Garis, M. R. *Martha Root: Lioness at the Threshold.* Wilmette, IL: Bahá'í Publishing Trust, 1983.

Giachery, Ugo. *Shoghi Effendi: Recollections.* Oxford: George Ronald, 1973.

Grand, Helen F. 'How I became a Baha'i', in *Star of the West (The Bahá'í Magazine),* vol. 15, pp. 363–4.

Greenleaf, Elizabeth. United States Bahá'í National Archives, Vail, Box 8: Elizabeth Greenleaf, 1926.

Guy, Walter. B. 'A Bahá'í Traveler in Palestine', in *Star of the West*, vol. 21, no. 2 (May 1930), pp. 44–6; also in *The Bahá'í World*, vol. IV, pp. 509–12.

Hainsworth, Philip. *Looking Back in Wonder.* London: Skyset Limited, 2004.

Harper, Barron. *Lights of Fortitude.* Oxford: George Ronald, 1997, rev. ed. 2007.

Hassall, Graham. *Ambassador at the Court: The Life and Photography of Effie Baker* (1999). Available at: http://bahai-library.com/hassall_ambassador_court_baker.

— 'Euphemia Eleanor Baker', in Australian Dictionary of Biography, Volume 14: 1940–1980. Ed. John Ritchie. Melbourne: Melbourne University Publishing, 1996.

— 'Obituary: James Heggie', in Bahá'í Studies Review, Vol. 9, 1999.

Hassan, Gamal. Moths Turned Eagles: The Spiritual Conquests of Sabri and Raissa Elias. National Spiritual Assembly of Ethiopia, 2008.

Holmes, John Haynes. 'Haifa – and the Baha'is', in Star of the West, vol. 20, no. 2 (May 1929), pp. 44–6.

Hautz, Laurence. United States Bahá'í National Archives, Beatrice Ashton Papers, 1952.

Hoagg, Emogene H. United States National Bahá'í Archives, H. Emogene Hoagg Papers, 1920.

— 'A Short History of the International Bahá'í Bureau at Geneva, Switzerland', in The Bahá'í World, vol. IV (1930-1932), pp. 257–61.

Hofman, David. George Townshend. Oxford: George Ronald, 2002.

Hofman, Marion. Private collection of papers.

'Imbrie Murder Laid to Religious Hate', in The New York Times, 24 July 1924. Available at: http://bahai-library.com/nyt_imbrie_religious_hate.

Ioas, Leroy. In the Days of the Guardian. Talk given in Johannesburg, South Africa, 1958. Available on iTunes.

Ioas, Sylvia. Interview of Sachiro Fujita, 1965. Available at: http://bci.org/pilgrim/fugita.htm.

Jasion, Jan Teofil. Never Be Afraid to Dare: The Story of 'General Jack'. Oxford: George Ronald, 2001.

Johnson, Edith and Lowell. Heroes and Heroines of the Ten Year Crusade in Southern Africa. Johannesburg: Bahá'í Publishing Trust, 2003.

Joseph, Albert. United States National Bahá'í Archives, Agnes Parsons Papers, 1926.

Kelsey, Curtis. Statement by Curtis D. Kelsey of Experiences in which He Participated, A Part of the Early Days of the Bahá'í Faith in America. United States Bahá'í National Archives, Curtis and Harriet Kelsey Papers.

Kelsey, Olivia. United States Bahá'í National Archives, Olivia Kelsey Papers, 1954.

Kerner Stein, Carolyn. From a Gnat to an Eagle: The Story of Nathan Rutstein. Wilmette, IL: Bahá'í Publishing Trust, 2008.

Khádem, Dhikru'lláh. 'The Beloved of All Hearts – Shoghi Effendi', in The Vision of Shoghi Effendi, pp. 117-127.

Khadem, Javidukht. Zikrullah Khadem: The Itinerant Hand of the Cause of God. Wilmette, IL: Bahá'í Publishing Trust, 1990.

Khadem, Riaz. *Prelude to the Guardianship*. Oxford: George Ronald, 2014.

— *Shoghi Effendi in Oxford*. Oxford: George Ronald, 1999.

Khianra, Dipchand. *Immortals*. New Delhi: Bahá'í Publishing Trust, 1988.

Landau, Rom. *Search for Tomorrow* (1938). Whitefish, Montana: Kessinger Publishing 2004.

Lee, Anthony Asa. *The Establishment of the Bahá'i Faith in West Africa: The First Decade, 1952–1962*. Los Angeles: University of California, 2007.

Lockman, Zachary. *Comrades and Enemies: Arab and Jewish Workers in Palestine, 1906–1948*. Berkeley: University of California Press, 1996.

Marcus, Della L. *Her Eternal Crown: Queen Marie of Romania and the Bahá'í Faith*. Oxford: George Ronald, 2000.

Ma'ani, Baharieh Rouhani. *Leaves of the Twin Divine Trees*. Oxford: George Ronald, 2008.

Martin, Douglas. 'Missionary as Historian: William Miller and the Bahá'í Faith', in *Bahá'í Studies*, vol. 4. Ottawa: Association for Bahá'í Studies, 1978–12. Available at: http://bahai-library.com/martin_missionary_historian_miller.

Maxwell, May. *Conversations with Shoghi Effendi* (1924). Available at: http://bahai-library.com/maxwell_conversations_shoghieffendi.

— United States Bahá'í National Archives, Hannen-Knobloch Papers, 1924.

— and Mary Maxwell. *Haifa Notes of Shoghi Effendi's Words: Taken at Pilgrim House during the Pilgrimage of Mrs May Maxwell and Miss Mary Maxwell, Jamuary, February, March 1937*. 2 vols. Available at: http://bahai-library.com/maxwell_haifa_notes.

McDaniel, Allen B. United States Bahá'í National Archives, Jessie and Ethel Revell Papers.

McKay, Doris. *Fires in Many Hearts*. Canada: Nine Pines Publishers, 1993.

Miller, Rev. William McElwee. *My Persian Pilgrimage*. Pasadena, CA: William Carey Library Publisher, 1989.

Milwaukee Journal. Milwaukee, Ohio.

Mobine, Nura. United States Bahá'í National Archives, Alice Cox Papers, n.d.

Moffett, Ruth. United States Bahá'í National Archives, Roushan Wilkinson Papers, 1927.

— United States Bahá'í National Archives, Charlotte Linfoot Papers, 1954.

Momen, Moojan (ed.). *The Bábí and Bahá'í Religions, 1844–1944*. Oxford: George Ronald, 1981.

Morrison, Gayle. *To Move the World: Louis G. Gregory and the Advancement of Racial Unity in America*. Wilmette, IL: Bahá'í Publishing Trust, 1982.

Murray, W. Smith. *Report to the U.S. Secretary of State*, 10 August 1924. Available at: http://bahai-library.com/imbrie_report_secretary_state.

Nabíl-i- A'ẓam (Muḥammad-i-Zarandí). *The Dawn-Breakers: Nabíl's Narrative of the Early Days of the Bahá'í Revelation*. Trans. Shoghi Effendi. Wilmette, IL: Bahá'í Publishing Trust, 1932.

Nakhjavání, 'Alí. *Shoghi Effendi: Author of Teaching Plans*. Ariccia: Casa Editrice Bahá'í, 2006.

Nakhjavani, Violette. *A Tribute to Amatu'l-Bahá Rúḥíyyih Khánum*. Ontario: Bahá'í Canada Publications, 2000.

— *The Great African Safari*. Oxford: George Ronald, 2002.

— *The Maxwells of Montreal, Middle Years 1923-1937, Late Years 1937-1952*. Oxford: George Ronald, 2012.

Nourse, Catharine. Audio recording, 1963. The Heritage Project of the National Spiritual Assembly of the Bahá'ís of the United States.

Oglesby, Sadie. United States Bahá'í National Archives, Alfred Lunt Papers, 1927.

— United States National Bahá'í Archives, Corinne True Family Papers, 1927.

Paine, Mabel Hyde. 'Notes on Shoghi Effendi's Table Talk' (1931). United States Bahá'í National Archives, Horace Holley Papers. Available at: http://bahai-library.com/paine_notes_table_talk.

— 'Notes Taken at Haifa, November 1931', United States National Bahá'í Archives, Rexford and Sylvia Parmelee Papers, 1931.

— and Sylvia Paine. 'Glimpses of the New World Order: Notes on a Visit to Haifa and Akká', in *Star of the West*, vol. 23, no. 12 (March 1933), pp. 374-7; vol. 24, no. 3 (June 1933), pp. 90-93; vol. 24, no. 4 (July 1933), pp. 126-8; vol. 24, no. 5 (August 1933), pp. 144-6.

Panahi, Aziz. Interview by the author, German Bahá'í Winter School, 31 December 2012.

Pfaff-Grossmann, Susanne. *Hermann Grossmann: A Life for the Faith*. Oxford: George Ronald, 2009.

Pinchon, Florence. 'Haifa Calling', in *The Bahá'í World*, vol. V (1932-1934), pp. 655-7.

Rabbaní, Rúḥíyyih. *The Guardian of the Bahá'í Faith*. London: Bahá'í Publishing Trust, 1988.

— *The Priceless Pearl*. London: Bahá'í Publishing Trust, rev.ed. 2000, together with further corrections, 2010, for a forthcoming edition.

Randall-Winckler, Bahiyyih. *My Pilgrimage to Haifa, November 1919*. Wilmette, IL: Bahá'í Publishing Trust, 1996.

Ransom-Kehler, Keith. 'Excerpts from my Diary', in *Star of the West*, vol. 17, no. 8 (November 1926), pp. 256–60.

— 'On Earth as it is in Heaven', in *Star of the West*, vol. 18, no. 7 (October 1927), pp. 198–202.

— and Lorol Schopflocher. 'Haifa Talks'. Ed. R. J. Armstrong-Ingram. Available at bahai-library.com/ransom-kehler_haifa_talks.

Rassekh, Báhereh. *Promoting the Unity of East and West: The Role of American Women in the 1910 Establishment of the Tarbíyat School in Iran & Remembrances.* 2012. Available at: juttabayani@tango.lu.

Redman, Earl. *'Abdu'l-Bahá in Their Midst.* Oxford: George Ronald, 2011.

Remey, Charles Mason. *A Brief Account of My Eighth Pilgrimage to the Holy Land.* United States Bahá'í National Archives, Charles Mason Remey Papers, Box 1, vol. 3, 1922.

— *The Violation in Chicago.* United States Bahá'í National Archives, Charles Mason Remey Papers, Box 10, vol. 46.

— and others. *Report of the Bahá'í Committee of Investigation 1917–1918.* Available at: http://www.h-net.org/~bahai/docs/vol5/RCI/RCI.htm.

Revell, Jessie. Available at: http://bahai-library.com/revell_letters, 1952.

Rexford, Orcella. 'Alaska, Our New Frontier', in *The Bahá'í World*, vol. 9 (1940–1944), pp. 918–22.

Rives, Isabel. United States Bahá'í National Archives, Leone Barnitz Papers, 1927(?).

— 'Carmel, Haifa and 'Akká', in *Star of the West*, vol. 20, no. 4 (July 1929), pp. 122–3.

Robarts, Audrey. 'Reminiscences about Shoghi Effendi', in *The Vision of Shoghi Effendi*, pp. 164–70.

Rohani, Aziz. *Sweet and Enchanting Stories.* Hong Kong: Juxta Publishing, 2005.

Root, Martha. 'Days in Haifa, Palestine'. Manuscript. United States Bahá'í National Archives, Martha L. Root Papers.

Ruhe, David. *Door of Hope: The Bahá'í Faith in the Holy Land.* Oxford: George Ronald, rev. ed. 2001.

Ruhe-Schoen, Janet. 'Ransom-Kehler, Keith Bean (1876–1933)'. Bahá'í Encyclopedia Project, National Spiritual Assembly of the United States, 2009. Available at: http://www.bahai-encyclopedia-project.org.

Rutstein, Nathan. *Corinne True: Faithful Handmaid of 'Abdu'l-Bahá.* Oxford: George Ronald, 1987.

— *He Loved and Served: The Story of Curtis Kelsey.* Oxford: George Ronald, 1982.

Sabour, Azíz. *In the Presence of the Beloved Guardian*, 1983.

Sala, Emeric. United States National Bahá'í Archives, Mary Lucas Papers, 1938.

— 'Shoghi Effendi's Question', in *The Vision of Shoghi Effendi*, pp. 189–93.

Shoghi Effendi. *The Advent of Divine Justice* (1939). Wilmette, IL: Bahá'í Publishing Trust, 1984.

— *Arohanui: Letters from Shoghi Effendi to New Zealand.* Suva, Fiji: Bahá'í Publishing Trust, 1982.

— *Bahá'í Administration: Selected Messages 1922–1932.* Wilmette, IL: Bahá'í Publishing Trust, 1980.

— *Dawn of a New Day: Messages to India 1923–1957.* New Delhi: Bahá'í Publishing Trust, n.d.

— *God Passes By* (1944). Wilmette, IL: Bahá'í Publishing Trust, rev. ed. 1974.

— *Letters from the Guardian to Australia and New Zealand, 1923–1957.* Sydney: Bahá'í Publishing Trust, 1971.

— *The Light of Divine Guidance: The Messages from the Guardian of the Bahá'í Faith to the Bahá'ís of Germany and Austria.* 2 vols. Hofheim-Langenhain: Bahá'í-Verlag, 1982, 1985.

— *Messages to America, 1932–1946.* Wilmette, IL: Bahá'i Publishing Trust, 1947. Published online by the Project Gutenberg.

— *Messages to the Bahá'í World 1950–1957.* Wilmette, IL: Bahá'í Publishing Trust, 2nd ed. 1971.

— *Messages to Canada.* Thornhill, ON: National Spiritual Assembly of the Bahá'ís of Canada, 1965.

— *The Promised Day Is Come* (1941). Wilmette, IL: Bahá'í Publishing Trust, rev. ed. 1980.

— *Unfolding Destiny: The Messages from the Guardian of the Bahá'í Faith to the Bahá'í Community of the British Isles.* London: Bahá'í Publishing Trust, 1981.

— *The World Order of Bahá'u'lláh: Selected Letters by Shoghi Effendi* (1938). Wilmette, IL: Bahá'í Publishing Trust, 2nd rev. ed. 1974.

— *This Decisive Hour.* Wilmette, IL: Bahá'í Publishing Trust, 1992.

— and Lady Blomfield. *The Passing of 'Abdu'l-Bahá.* Haifa, 1922.

Smith, Peter. *A Concise Encyclopedia of the Bahá'í Faith.* Oxford: Oneworld Publications, 2000.

— *Bahá'ís of the West.* Los Angeles: Kalimat Press, 2004.

Star of the West: The Bahai Magazine. Periodical, 25 vols. 1910–1935. Vols. 1–14 RP Oxford: George Ronald, 1978. Complete CD-ROM version: Talisman Educational Software/Special Ideas, 2001.

Stevenson, Margaret. New Zealand National Bahá'í Archives, 1925.

Suthers, A. E. 'A Baha'i Pontiff in the Making', in *Moslem World*, no. 25 (1935), pp. 27–35.

Taherzadeh, Adib. *The Child of the Covenant: A Study Guide to the Will and Testament of 'Abdu'l-Bahá.* Oxford: George Ronald, 2000.

— *The Covenant of Bahá'u'lláh.* Oxford: George Ronald, 1992.

Taherzadeh, Habíb. 'Meeting Shoghi Effendi'. Audio recording, Northern Ireland Summer School, 1993.

Thompson, Emma and Louise. United States Bahá'í National Archives, Elizabeth Bowen Papers, 1931.

Toynbee, Arnold. *Survey of International Affairs, 1934.* London: Oxford University Press, 1935.

True, Corinne. United States Bahá'í National Archives, Agnes Parsons Papers.

United States National Spiritual Assembly vs. Mirza Ahmad Sohrab, Supreme Court, Special Term, New York County, March 31, 1941. Available at: http://bahai-library.com/sohrab_vs_us-nsa_1941.

The Universal House of Justice. *Century of Light.* Bahá'í World Centre, 2001.

van den Hoonaard, Will C. *The Origins of the Bahá'í Community of Canada, 1898–1948.* Waterloo, Ontario: Wilfrid Laurier University Press, 1996.

— 'Schopflocher, Siegfried'. Available at: http://bahai-library.com/hoonaard_encyclopedia_siegfried_schopflocher.

The Vision of Shoghi Effendi, Proceedings of the Association for Bahá'í Studies Ninth Annual Conference, November 2–4, 1984, Ottawa, Canada. Ottawa: Association for Bahá'í Studies, 1993.

Weeden, Ben. United States Bahá'í National Archives, Charles (Carl) Krug Papers, 1948.

Weeden, Gladys. United States Bahá'í National Archives, Charles (Carl) Krug Papers, 1947–48.

— Unpublished manuscript (memoirs). Marion Hofman Papers, undated.

Weinberg, Robert. *Ethel Jenner Rosenberg: England's Outstanding Bahá'í Pioneer Worker.* Oxford: George Ronald, 1995.

— *Lady Blomfield: Her Life and Times.* Oxford: George Ronald, 2012.

Weinstein, Ilona Sala. *Tending the Garden: The Edited Letters and Papers of Emeric and Rosemary Sala.* New Liskeard, Ontario: White Mountain Publications, 1998.

Weir, Clara. 'The Shrine', in *Star of the West*, vol. 22, no. 2 (May 1931), pp. 56–7.

Whitehead, O.Z. *Portraits of Some Bahá'í Women.* Oxford: George Ronald, 1996.

— *Some Bahá'ís of the West*. Oxford: George Ronald, 1981.

— *Some Bahá'ís to Remember*. Oxford: George Ronald, 1983.

Wilhelm, Roy. United States Bahá'í National Archives, Mary Rabb Papers, 1922.

Woolson, Gayle. United States Bahá'í National Archives, Albert Windust Papers, 1956.

Wright, Louise Drake. United States Bahá'í National Archives, Louise Drake Wright Papers, 1931.

Yazdi, Marion. United States Bahá'í National Archives, Lillian James Papers, 1928.

Zinky, Kay (ed.). *Martha Root: Herald of the Kingdom*. New Delhi: Bahá'í Publishing Trust, 1983.

REFERENCES

USBNA = United States Bahá'í National Archives.

Preface

1. Rabbaní, *The Priceless Pearl*, p. 148.
2. ibid. pp. 229–30.
3. Sala, 'Shoghi Effendi's Question', in *The Vision of Shoghi Effendi*, pp. 190–91.
4. Ida Finch, Fanny Knobloch and Alma Knobloch, *Flowers Culled from the Rose Garden of Acca* (1908).
5. Sala, 'Shoghi Effendi's Question', pp. 189–90.
6. Rabbaní, *The Priceless Pearl*, pp. 80–81.
7. Bach, *The Circle of Faith*, pp. 61–77.
8. Shoghi Effendi, *Directives from the Guardian*, p. 54.

Who Is Shoghi Effendi?

1. 'Abdu'l-Bahá, *The Will and Testament of 'Abdu'l-Bahá*, p. 11.
2. Rabbaní, *The Priceless Pearl*, p. 17.
3. Amatu'l-Bahá Rúḥíyyih Khánum, *Tribute to Shoghi Effendi*, Kampala, 1958, pp. 2–3.
4. Quoted in Rabbaní, *The Priceless Pearl*, pp. 11–13.
5. ibid. pp. 82–3.
6. Shoghi Effendi, *Messages to the Bahá'í World 1950–1957*, pp. 153–4.
7. ibid. p. 154.
8. ibid. pp. 154–5.
9. ibid. p. 155.

The Ascension of 'Abdu'l-Bahá

1. *Star of the West*, vol. 12, no. 15, p. 245.
2. ibid. no. 16, p. 253.
3. USBNA, Bosches, Box 11: John and Louise Bosch.
4. Shoghi Effendi and Lady Blomfield, *The Passing of 'Abdu'l-Bahá*.
5. ibid.
6. *Star of the West*, vol. 12, no. 19, p. 293.
7. Rutstein, *He Loved and Served*, p. 100.
8. Shoghi Effendi and Lady Blomfield, *The Passing of 'Abdu'l-Bahá*.

9. Weinberg, *Ethel Jenner Rosenberg*, p. 187.
10. ibid. p. 188.
11. *Star of the West*, vol. 12, no. 19, p. 303.
12. Quoted in Rabbaní, *The Priceless Pearl*, p. 40.

1922: 'Tell the friends, time will prove that there has been no mistake'

1. Quoted in Gail, *Dawn over Mount Hira*, p. 213.
2. USBNA, Jessie/Ethel Revell Papers, Box 7: Ethel Rosenberg.
3. Gail, *Dawn over Mount Hira*, p. 214.
4. Gail, *Arches of the Years*, p. 223.
5. Gail, *Dawn over Mount Hira*, p. 214.
6. ibid. p. 215.
7. Khadem, *Prelude to the Guardianship*, pp. 170, 174–5.
8. Ma'ani, *Leaves of the Twin Divine Trees*, p. 351.
9. Rúḥíyyih <u>Kh</u>ánum, *Tribute to Shoghi Effendi*, p. 3; Rabbaní, *The Priceless Pearl*, p. 148.
10. USBNA, Rabb Papers, Box 6, Effie Baker, letter dated 9 April 1925, pp. 2–3.
11. USBNA, H. Emogene Hoagg Papers.
12. Weinberg, *Lady Blomfield*, p. 220.
13. ibid. p. 221.
14. ibid. p. 228.
15. ibid. p. 223.
16. USBNA, H. Emogene Hoagg Papers.
17. Catharine Nourse, The Heritage Project, audio recording, 1963.
18. USBNA, H. Emogene Hoagg Papers.
19. Sylvia Ioas, Interview of Sachiro Fujita, 1965.
20. Weinberg, *Lady Blomfield*, p. 228.
21. *The Bahá'í World*, vol. XIX, p. 680.
22. Catharine Nourse, The Heritage Project.
23. ibid.
24. http://www.bahai-encyclopedia-project.org/index.php?option=com_content&view=article&id=69:schopflocher-siegfried&catid=37:biography.
25. Isabel Rives, in USBNA, Leone Barnitz Papers.
26. ibid.
27. USBNA, H. Emogene Hoagg Papers.
28. Gail, *Dawn over Mount Hira*, p. 216.
29. Catharine Nourse, The Heritage Project.
30. Rutstein, *He Loved and Served*, p. 79.
31. ibid. p. 79.
32. Catharine Nourse, The Heritage Project.
33. USBNA, H. Emogene Hoagg Papers.
34. Momen (ed.), *The Bábí and Bahá'í Religions*, p. 457; USBNA, H. Emogene Hoagg Papers.
35. Remey, *A Brief Account of My Eighth Pilgrimage to the Holy Land*, p. 24.
36. Rabbaní, *The Priceless Pearl*, p. 54.
37. Momen (ed.), *The Bábí and Bahá'í Religions*, p. 457.
38. Ruhe, *Door of Hope*, pp. 110–13.

39. See *The Bahá'í World*, vol. XII, pp. 699–701.
40. Letter to Albert Windust, 20 April 1948, quoted in Taherzadeh, *The Child of the Covenant*, p. 298.
41. ibid. p. 297.
42. ibid. pp. 298–9.
43. Rabbaní, *The Priceless Pearl*, p. 120.
44. Taherzadeh, *The Child of the Covenant*, p. 294.
45. ibid. pp. 294–5.
46. Rabbaní, *The Priceless Pearl*, p. 120.
47. Smith, *A Concise Encyclopedia of the Bahá'í Faith*, p. 66.
48. *The Bahá'í World*, vol. III, pp. 53–4.
49. Toynbee, *Survey of International Affairs, 1934*, pp. 120–21.
50. Rabbaní, *The Priceless Pearl*, pp. 94–5.
51. ibid. pp. 95–7.
52. Harper, *Lights of Fortitude*, pp. 110–11.
53. *The Bahá'í World*, vol. X, pp. 532–3.
54. Jináb-i-Fádil (Fáḍil-i-Mazindarání), *Star of the West*, vol. 14, no. 6, p. 181.

1922: A Gathering of the Learned

1. Weinberg, *Lady Blomfield*, p. 232.
2. Weinberg, *Ethel Jenner Rosenberg*, pp. 207–8.
3. Redman, *'Abdu'l-Bahá in Their Midst*, various pages; Redman, *Visiting 'Abdu'l-Bahá*, various pages.
4. Roy Wilhelm, USBNA, Mary Rabb Papers, p. 1.
5. ibid. pp. 1–2.
6. ibid. p. 2.
7. Weinberg, *Lady Blomfield*, p. 233.
8. Roy Wilhelm, USBNA, Mary Rabb Papers, p. 3.
9. ibid.
10. *Star of the West*, vol. 13, no. 4 (17 May 1922), p. 68.
11. Weinberg, *Lady Blomfield*, p. 234.
12. USBNA, H. Emogene Hoagg Papers.
13. Weinberg, *Lady Blomfield*, p. 235.
14. Redman, *'Abdu'l-Bahá in Their Midst*, p. 111.
15. Rutstein, *Corinne True*, pp. 156–8.
16. ibid. pp. 158–9.
17. Weinberg, *Lady Blomfield*, p. 237.
18. ibid.
19. Mason Remey, USBNA, Mary Rabb Papers, pp. 5–6.
20. ibid. pp. 9–10.
21. *Star of the West*, vol. 14, no. 9 (December 1923), pp. 265–6.
22. Rutstein, *He Loved and Served*, p. 68.
23. Mason Remey, USBNA, Mary Rabb Papers, pp. 16–18.
24. ibid. p. 24.
25. Redman, *'Abdu'l-Bahá in Their Midst*, pp. 313, 315.
26. Mason Remey, USBNA, Mary Rabb Papers, p. 19.
27. Remey, *A Brief Account of My Eighth Pilgrimage to the Holy Land*, pp. 41–2.

28. Mason Remey, USBNA, Mary Rabb Papers, pp. 43–4.
29. Mason Remey and others, *Report of the Bahá'í Committee of Investigation 1917–1918*; Remey, *The Violation in Chicago*, pp. 1–4.
30. Remey, *The Violation in Chicago*, pp. 1–4.
31. Remey, *A Brief Account of My Eighth Pilgrimage to the Holy Land*, pp. 7–8.
32. Remey, *The Violation in Chicago*, pp. 1–4.
33. Remey, *A Brief Account of My Eighth Pilgrimage to the Holy Land*, p. 55.
34. ibid. p. 10.
35. ibid. pp. 33–4.
36. ibid. pp. 36–7.
37. ibid. p. 28.
38. ibid. pp. 38–9.
39. ibid. pp. 35.
40. *Star of the West*, vol. 14, no. 9 (December 1923), p. 266.
41. Roy Wilhelm, USBNA, Mary Rabb Papers, p. 2.
42. Weinberg, *Lady Blomfield*, p. 233.
43. Remey, *A Brief Account of My Eighth Pilgrimage to the Holy Land*, p. 43.
44. Rabbaní, *The Priceless Pearl*, p. 55.
45. Remey, *A Brief Account of My Eighth Pilgrimage to the Holy Land*, pp. 21–2.
46. Shoghi Effendi, *Bahá'í Administration*, p. 20.
47. Harper, *Lights of Fortitude*, pp. 137–8.
48. Rabbaní, *The Priceless Pearl*, pp. 90–91.
49. Remey, *A Brief Account of My Eighth Pilgrimage to the Holy Land*, p. 45.
50. Rúḥíyyih Khánum, *Tribute to Shoghi Effendi*, p. 6.
51. Remey, *A Brief Account of My Eighth Pilgrimage to the Holy Land*, pp. 52–3.
52. ibid. p. 45.
53. Weinberg, *Lady Blomfield*, p. 236.
54. ibid. pp. 238–9.

1922: The First Respite in Switzerland

1. Rabbaní, *The Priceless Pearl*, p. 348.
2. Leroy Ioas, *In the Days of the Guardian,* audio recording.
3. Rúḥíyyih Khánum, talk at Wilmette, Riḍván, 1960.
4. Rabbaní, *The Priceless Pearl*, p. 57.
5. ibid.; from *Star of the West*, vol. 13, no. 4 (17 May 1922), pp. 81–22.
6. Ma'ani, *Leaves of the Twin Divine Trees*, p. 351.
7. Rabbaní, *The Priceless Pearl*, pp. 60–61.
8. ibid. p. 62.
9. Rabbaní, *The Guardian of the Bahá'í Faith*, between pages 154 and 155.
10. *The Bahá'í World*, vol. XIV, p. 327.
11. *Star of the West*, vol. 13, no. 10 (January 1923), p. 282.
12. ibid. p. 283.
13. ibid. pp. 283–4.
14. Catharine Nourse, The Heritage Project.
15. *Star of the West*, vol. 13, no. 8 (November 1922), pp. 207–8.
16. ibid. p. 208.
17. ibid. p. 210.

18. ibid. no. 11 (February 1923), pp. 296–8.
19. Rabbaní, *The Priceless Pearl*, p. 63.
20. *Star of the West*, vol. 13, no. 11 (February 1923), p. 315.
21. Letter from Shoghi Effendi to the Bahá'ís of Germany and Austria, 17 December 1922, in *The Light of Divine Guidance*, vol. 1, p. 7.
22. Letter from Shoghi Effendi to 'the members of the National Spiritual Assembly, the elected representatives of all believers throughout the continent of America', 23 December 1922, in *Bahá'í Administration*, p. 27.
23. Letter from Shoghi Effendi 'to the loved ones of 'Abdu'l-Bahá throughout the continent of America', 16 December 1922, ibid. p. 26.

1923

1. Rabbaní, *The Priceless Pearl*, p. 89.
2. *Star of the West*, vol. 14, no. 9 (December 1923), p. 268.
3. ibid.
4. ibid. no. 4, pp. 121–2.
5. Miller, *My Persian Pilgrimage*, p. 91.
6. ibid. p. 101.
7. Quoted by Martin, 'Missionary as Historian: William Miller and the Bahá'í Faith', in *Bahá'í Studies* (Ottawa), vol. 4.
8. Miller, *The Bahá'í Faith: Its History and Teachings*; see Martin, 'Missionary as Historian: William Miller and the Bahá'í Faith'.
9. Letter from Shoghi Effendi to the Bahá'ís in America, Great Britain, Germany, France, Switzerland, Italy, Japan and Australasia, 12 March 1923, in *Bahá'í Administration*, p. 39.
10. Weinberg, *Lady Blomfield*, p. 255.
11. Shoghi Effendi, *Dawn of a New Day*, p. 3.
12. Khianra, *Immortals*, p. 15.
13. Pfaff-Grossmann, *Hermann Grossmann*, p. 30.
14. Shoghi Effendi, *God Passes By*, p. 333.
15. Ian Semple, talk given in London, 28 January 2006.
16. Violette Nakhjavani, *The Maxwells of Montreal: Middle Years, Late Years*, pp. 4–5.
17. Rabbaní, *The Priceless Pearl*, p. 150.
18. Violette Nakhjavani, *The Maxwells of Montreal: Middle Years, Late Years*, p. 8.
19. Maxwell, *Conversations with Shoghi Effendi*, p. 1.
20. Violette Nakhjavani, *A Tribute to Amatu'l-Bahá Rúhíyyih Khánum*, p. 12.
21. ibid. pp. 12–13.
22. Rabbaní, *The Priceless Pearl*, p. 133.
23. Amatu'l-Bahá Rúhíyyih Khánum, talk at Wilmette, Riḍván 1960.
24. Rabbaní, *The Priceless Pearl*, pp. 72–3.
25. Violette Nakhjavani, *The Maxwells of Montreal: Middle Years, Late Years*, pp. 9–10.
26. ibid. pp. 13–14, 17.
27. Violette Nakhjavani, *A Tribute to Amatu'l-Bahá Rúhíyyih Khánum*, p. 14.
28. Maxwell, *Conversations with Shoghi Effendi*, p. 7.
29. ibid. p. 8.
30. Rabbaní, *The Priceless Pearl*, pp. 145–6.

31. Maxwell, *Conversations with Shoghi Effendi*, pp. 2–4.
32. ibid. p. 6.
33. Giachery, *Shoghi Effendi: Recollections*, p. 113.
34. Rutstein, *He Loved and Served*, pp. 167–9.
35. Rohani, *Sweet and Enchanting Stories*, p. 131.
36. Collins, *Shoghi Effendi*, p. 1.
37. Faizí, *Milly*, pp. 3–6.
38. ibid. p. 7.
39. USBNA, Olivia Kelsey Papers.
40. Letter on behalf of Shoghi Effendi to an individual, 9 December 1923, in Shoghi Effendi, *Unfolding Destiny*, p. 18.
41. Genevieve Coy, in USBNA, Albert Vail Papers, p. 1.

1924

1. Genevieve Coy, in USBNA, Albert Vail Papers, p. 5.
2. 'Fred Schopflocher: Hand of the Cause of God', insert in *Canadian Bahá'í News*, November 1953.
3. Grand, 'How I became a Bahá'í', in *Star of the West*, vol. 15, pp. 363–4; see also Whitehead, *Portraits of Some Bahá'í Women*, pp. 42–3.
4. Murray, Report to the US Secretary of State.
5. Rassekh, *Promoting the Unity of East and West*, pp. 29–30.
6. *Star of the West*, vol. 16, no. 10, p. 689.
7. 'Imbrie Murder Laid to Religious Hate', in *New York Times*, 24 July 1924.
8. Rassekh, *Promoting the Unity of East and West*, pp. 30–31.
9. *The Bahá'í World*, vol. XII, pp. 703–4.
10. Gail, *Arches of the Years*, p. 278.
11. ibid. p. 281.
12. ibid. p. 283.
13. ibid. p. 285.
14. ibid. pp. 286–8.
15. ibid. p. 285.
16. Shoghi Effendi, *God Passes By*, p. 246.
17. Gail, *Arches of the Years*, p. 289.
18. ibid. p. 290.
19. ibid. pp. 290–91.
20. ibid. p. 291.
21. ibid. pp. 292–3.
22. *The Bahá'í World*, vol. VIII, pp. 933–4.
23. Letter from Shoghi Effendi, 24 September 1924, *Unfolding Destiny*, pp. 27–8.
24. Letter on behalf of Shoghi Effendi to an individual, 4 November 1924, ibid. p. 31.
25. Shoghi Effendi, *God Passes By*, p. 333.

1925

1. Hoagg, 'A Short History of the International Bahá'í Bureau at Geneva, Switzerland', p. 261.

2. Momen, *Dr. J. E. Esslemont*, pp. 31–2.
3. Martha Root, letter dated 7 April 1925, in USBNA, Agnes Parsons Papers; quoted in Garis, *Martha Root*, p. 210. See also Harper, *Lights of Fortitude*, p. 82.
4. Letter from Shoghi Effendi, 27 May 1925, in Shoghi Effendi, *The Light of Divine Guidance*, vol. 1, p. 24.
5. Momen, *Dr. J. E. Esslemont*, p. 34.
6. Corinne True, in USBNA, Agnes Parsons Papers, p. 1.
7. ibid.
8. Hassall, *Ambassador at the Court*, ch. 3.
9. Hassall, 'Baker, Euphemia Eleanor', in *Australian Dictionary of Biography*, vol. 14.
10. New Zealand National Bahá'í Archives, MS 15.09.01, 1980.
11. Ethel Blundell, ibid. MS 8.11.01, pp. 3–4.
12. Margaret Stevenson, letter dated 20 March 1925, ibid. MS 22.11.04.
13. Effie Baker, in USBNA, Rabb Papers, Box 6: Effie Baker.
14. Margaret Stevenson, letter dated 20 March 1925, in New Zealand National Bahá'í Archives, MS 22.11.04.
15. ibid. letter dated 5 April 1925, MS 22.11.05.
16. ibid. letter dated 20 March 1925, MS 22.11.04.
17. ibid.
18. Martha Root, letter dated 7 April 1925, in USBNA, Agnes Parsons Papers; quoted in Garis, *Martha Root*, p. 210.
19. Effie Baker, letter dated 29 March 1925, in USBNA, Rabb Papers, Box 6: Effie Baker, p. 2.
20. *Star of the West*, vol. 12, no. 11, p. 184; Ruhe, *Door of Hope*, pp. 180–81.
21. Martha Root, 'Days in Haifa, Palestine'; quoted in Garis, *Martha Root*, pp. 208–9.
22. Effie Baker, letter dated 29 March 1925, in USBNA, Rabb Papers, Box 6: Effie Baker, p. 2.
23. Martha Root, 'Days in Haifa, Palestine'; quoted in Garis, *Martha Root*, p. 209.
24. Margaret Stevenson, letter dated 20 March 1925, in New Zealand National Bahá'í Archives, MS 22.11.04.
25. ibid.
26. Effie Baker, letter dated 9 April 1925, in USBNA, Rabb Papers, Box 6: Effie Baker, pp. 1–3.
27. Margaret Stevenson, letter dated 20 March 1925, in New Zealand National Bahá'í Archives, MS 22.11.04.
28. Hassall, *Ambassador at the Court*, ch. 6.
29. Effie Baker, letter dated 9 April 1925, in USBNA, Rabb Papers, Box 6: Effie Baker, p. 6.
30. *The Bahá'í World*, vol. XIV (1963–1968), p. 320; Hassall, *Ambassador at the Court*, ch. 6.
31. ibid.
32. Margaret Stevenson, letter dated 5 April 1925, in New Zealand National Bahá'í Archives, MS 22.11.05.
33. Dr John Esslemont, letter dated 8 May 1925, p. 2, in New Zealand National Bahá'í Archives.
34. Garis, *Martha Root*, p. 214.

35. Rabbaní, *The Priceless Pearl*, p. 107.

36. Quoted in Momen, *The Bábí and Bahá'í Religions, 1844–1944*, p. 455.

37. Letter from J. E. Esslemont on behalf of Shoghi Effendi and the Greatest Holy Leaf, 9 May 1925, in Shoghi Effendi, *Arohanui*, pp. 6–7; Mas'ud Mazgani, personal communication of a story told him by Hand of the Cause Abu'l-Qasim Faizí.

38. de Vries, *The Babi Question You Mentioned*, p. 133.

39. Javidukht Khadem, *Zikrullah Khadem*, pp. 8–11.

40. *The Bahá'í World*, vol. IX, p. 598.

41. *The Bahá'í World*, vol. III, pp. 49–50.

42. Letter from Shoghi Effendi to the National Spiritual Assembly of the Bahá'ís of the United States and Canada, 26 January 1926, in *Bahá'í Administration*, pp. 100–01.

43. Letter from Shoghi Effendi 'To the beloved of the Lord and the handmaids of the Merciful throughout the West', 12 February 1927, in *Bahá'í Administration*, pp. 120–21.

44. *The Bahá'í World*, vol. IX, p. 598.

45. ibid; see also Harper, *Lights of Fortitude*, pp. 50–52.

46. Letter from J. E. Esslemont on behalf of Shoghi Effendi, 28 May 1925, in Shoghi Effendi, *Arohanui*, p. 10.

47. *The Bahá'í World*, vol. XV, pp. 488–9.

48. Armstrong-Ingram, Introduction to Keith Ransom-Kehler and Lorol Schopflocher, 'Haifa Talks'.

49. van den Hoonaard, 'Schopflocher, Siegfried'.

50. Hassall, *Ambassador at the Court*, ch. 8.

51. ibid.

52. Rabbaní, *The Priceless Pearl*, p. 209.

53. ibid. ch. 9; *The Bahá'í World*, vol. XIV (1963–1968), p. 320.

54. See note in Shoghi Effendi, *Arohanui*, pp. 96–7.

55. Shoghi Effendi, *God Passes By*, p. 333; Taherzadeh, *The Covenant of Bahá'u'lláh*, p. 293; Rutstein, *Corinne True*, p. 160.

56. Rutstein, *Corinne True*, p. 160.

57. Shoghi Effendi, *Bahá'í Administration*, pp. 37–41, 45–46, 53, 64–65, 78–80, 83–84, 87–88.

58. *Bahá'í News*, no. 6 (July–August 1925), p. 5.

59. Letter from Shoghi Effendi to the National Spiritual Assembly of the United States and Canada, 24 October 1925, in Shoghi Effendi, *Bahá'í Administration*, pp. 92–3.

60. Letter on behalf of Shoghi Effendi, 27 November 1925, in *Unfolding Destiny*, pp. 40–41.

61. Letter on behalf of Shoghi Effendi, 23 January 1926, ibid. p. 46.

62. *The Bahá'í World*, vol. XVIII (1979–1983), p. 637.

63. ibid. pp. 337–8.

64. ibid. p. 638.

1926

1. Rabbaní, *The Priceless Pearl*, pp. 92–3.
2. *Bahá'í News Letter*, no. 10 (February 1926), p. 5.
3. Albert Joseph, in USBNA, Agnes Parsons Papers, p. 1.
4. Rexford, 'Alaska, Our New Frontier', in *The Bahá'í World*, vol. IX, p. 921.
5. ibid. p. 922. See also her 'In Memoriam' article in *The Bahá'í World*, vol. XI, pp. 495–8.
6. Elizabeth Greenleaf, in USBNA, Vail, Box 8: Elizabeth Greenleaf.
7. Whitehead, *Some Bahá'ís to Remember*, p. 107.
8. Victoria Bedekian, in USBNA, Alfred Lunt Papers, p. 14.
9. ibid. p. 7.
10. ibid. p. 5.
11. ibid.
12. ibid. pp. 5–6.
13. Letter from Shoghi Effendi to the National Spiritual Assembly of the Bahá'ís of the United States and Canada, 11 May 1926, in Shoghi Effendi, *Bahá'í Administration*, p. 108.
14. Victoria Bedekian, in USBNA, Alfred Lunt Papers, p. 14.
15. ibid. pp. 11–12.
16. ibid. p. 12.
17. ibid. pp. 8–9.
18. Amatu'l-Bahá Rúhíyyih Khánum, 'The Guardian of the Bahá'í Faith', in *The Bahá'í World*, vol. XIII, p. 87.
19. Hassall, *Ambassador at the Court*, ch. 8.
20. Ransom-Kehler, 'Excerpts From My Diary', in *Star of the West*, vol. 17, no. 8 (November 1926), p. 256; see also *The Bahá'í World*, vol. II, p. 129.
21. See http://www.bahai-encyclopedia-project.org/index.php?option=com_conten t&view=article&id=73:ransom-kehler-keith-bean&catid=37:biography.
22. Rabbaní, *The Priceless Pearl*, p. 97.
23. *Bahá'í News Letter*, no. 13 (September 1926), pp. 2–3.
24. Smith, *Bahá'ís of the West*, pp. 155, 170.
25. Ransom-Kehler, 'On Earth as it is in Heaven', in *Star of the West*, vol. 18, no. 7 (October 1927), pp. 199–200.
26. Ransom-Kehler, 'Excerpts From My Diary', in *Star of the West*, vol. 17, no. 8 (November 1926), pp. 256–7; see also *The Bahá'í World*, vol. II, pp. 129–30.
27. *The Bahá'í World*, vol. II, pp. 134–5.
28. ibid. p. 135.
29. ibid. p. 133.
30. *The Bahá'í World*, vol. IV, p. 398.
31. May Stebbins, The Heritage Project of the National Spiritual Assembly of the United States.
32. ibid.
33. Hofman, *George Townshend*, pp. 55–6.
34. ibid. pp. 56–7.
35. ibid. p. 57.
36. *Bahá'í Prayers*, p. 66.
37. ibid. p. 60.

38. ibid. p. 50.
39. ibid. p. 196.
40. Amatu'l-Bahá Rúḥíyyih Khánum, 'The Guardian of the Bahá'í Faith', in *The Bahá'í World*, vol. XIII, p. 87.
41. Marcus, *Her Eternal Crown*, pp. 49, 54.
42. ibid. pp. 57-8.
43. Rabbaní, *The Priceless Pearl*, p. 100.
44. Marcus, *Her Eternal Crown*, p. 65.
45. ibid. p. 67.
46. Rabbaní, *The Priceless Pearl*, p. 109.
47. Violette Nakhjavani, *A Tribute to Amatu'l-Bahá Rúḥíyyih Khánum*, pp. 13-14.
48. Violette Nakhjavani, *The Maxwells of Montreal, Middle Years, Late Years*, pp. 67-8.
49. Effie Baker, letter dated 23 May 1925, p. 7, in New Zealand National Bahá'í Archives, MS 2.03.
50. Effie Baker, letter dated 1 August 1926, pp. 2-3, ibid.
51. Effie Baker, letter dated 19 June 1926, p. 1, ibid.
52. Hassall, *Ambassador at the Court*, Ch. 8.
53. Rabbaní, *The Priceless Pearl*, p. 92.
54. 'Hippolyte Dreyfus-Barney: An Appreciation by Shoghi Effendi', in *The Bahá'í World*, vol. III, pp. 210, 214.
55. Letter from Shoghi Effendi to the National Spiritual Assembly of the United States and Canada, 31 October 1926, in Shoghi Effendi, *Bahá'í Administration*, pp. 115-16.
56. Rabbaní, *The Priceless Pearl*, p. 94.
57. Hassall, *Ambassador at the Court*, Ch. 8.
58. ibid.
59. ibid.
60. ibid.
61. Effie Baker, letter dated 11 November 1926, p. 1, in New Zealand National Bahá'í Archives, MS 2.09.
62. Hassall, *Ambassador at the Court*, Ch. 8.
63. Effie Baker, letter dated 11 November 1926, p. 1, in New Zealand National Bahá'í Archives, MS 2.09.
64. *Star of the West*, vol. 17, no. 4, last page (unnumbered).
65. Hassall, *Ambassador at the Court*, Ch. 8.
66. Letter from Shoghi Effendi to 'the members of the American National Spiritual Assembly', 6 November 1926, in Shoghi Effendi, *Bahá'í Administration*, pp. 94-5.
67. Mountfort Mills, in USBNA, O/S Correspondence.
68. ibid.
69. Effie Baker, letter dated 16 October 1926, p. 1, in New Zealand National Bahá'í Archives, MS 2.08.
70. *Bahá'í News Letter*, no. 9 (December 1925-January 1926), p. 1.

1927-1928

1. Weinberg, *Ethel Jenner Rosenberg*, p. 249.
2. Letter on behalf of Shoghi Effendi, 29 January 1927, in Shoghi Effendi,

Unfolding Destiny, p. 62.

3. ibid. pp. 62–3.
4. Hofman, *George Townshend*, pp. 58, 109.
5. Weinberg, *Ethel Jenner Rosenberg* p. 256.
6. ibid. p. 262.
7. *The Bahá'í World*, vol. II, p. 33.
8. Etter-Lewis and Thomas, *Lights of the Spirit*, pp. 76–7.
9. Sadie Oglesby, in USBNA, Alfred Lunt Papers, p. 1; published in Etter-Lewis and Thomas, *Lights of the Spirit*, ch. 19.
10. Etter-Lewis and Thomas, *Lights of the Spirit*, p. 77.
11. ibid. p. 78.
12. Sadie Oglesby, in USBNA, Alfred Lunt Papers, p. 2.
13. Sadie Oglesby, in USBNA, Corinne True Family Papers, p. 1.
14. Morrison, *To Move the World*, p. 179.
15. Sadie Oglesby, in USBNA, Corinne True Family Papers, p. 2.
16. Etter-Lewis and Thomas, *Lights of the Spirit*, p. 79.
17. Letter from Shoghi Effendi to the National Spiritual Assembly of the Bahá'ís of the United States and Canada, 27 May 1927, in Shoghi Effendi, *Bahá'í Administration*, pp. 134–5.
18. Shoghi Effendi, *God Passes By*, p. 335.
19. Letter on behalf of Shoghi Effendi, 27 December 1934, in Shoghi Effendi, *Unfolding Destiny*, p. 101.
20. Faizi-Moore, *Faizi*, pp. 58–9.
21. ibid. pp. 61–3.
22. Harper, *Lights of Fortitude*, p. 381.
23. Effie Baker, letter dated 20 May 1927, pp. 4–5, in New Zealand National Bahá'í Archives.
24. *Bahá'í News*, no. 18, p. 4
25. ibid. no. 19, p. 6.
26. Hassall, *Ambassador at the Court*, ch. 8.
27. Brigham, 'A Modern Pilgrimage to Bahá'í Shrines', in *Star of the West*, vol. 18, no. 9, pp. 278–9.
28. ibid. pp. 279–82.
29. ibid. p. 282.
30. *The Bahá'í World*, vol. IX, pp. 626–7.
31. Letter from Shoghi Effendi to Bahá'í National Spiritual Assemblies throughout the West, 17 October 1927, in Shoghi Effendi, *Bahá'í Administration*, pp. 138–9.
32. Shoghi Effendi, *Dawn of a New Day*, p. 20.
33. Hassall, *Ambassador at the Court*, ch. 8.
34. ibid.
35. Ruth Moffett, in USBNA, Roushan Wilkinson Papers.
36. Ruth Moffett, in USBNA, Charlotte Linfoot Papers, p. 1.
37. Hassall, *Ambassador at the Court*, ch. 8.
38. ibid. ch. 9.
39. Momen, *The Bábí and Bahá'í Religions, 1844–1944*, p. 458.
40. ibid. pp. 458–9.
41. Allen B. McDaniel, in USBNA, Jessie and Ethel Revell Papers, p. 1.

42. Hassall, *Ambassador at the Court*, ch. 8.
43. Allen B. McDaniel, in USBNA, Jessie and Ethel Revell Papers p. 1–2.
44. Letter on behalf of Shoghi Effendi, 6 May 1928, in *Dawn of a New Day*, p. 21; Rowshan Mustafa, email to the author, 12 April 2014.
45. Hassall, *Ambassador at the Court*, ch. 8.
46. Marion Yazdi, in USBNA, Lillian James Papers, pp. 1–2.
47. Hassall, *Ambassador at the Court*, ch. 8.
48. *The Bahá'í World*, vol. III, pp. 37–8; vol. VIII, p. 88.
49. *The Bahá'í World*, vol. VIII, pp. 87–9; Momen, *The Bábí and Bahá'í Religions, 1844–1944*, p. 473.
50. *The Bahá'í World*, vol. XIV, pp. 479–80.

1929

1. Gail, *Arches of the Years*, p. 97.
2. Rabbaní, *The Priceless Pearl*, p. 119.
3. *Baha'i News Letter*, no. 31 (April 1929), p. 6.
4. 'Guardian's Response to Challenges Will 'Abdu'l-Bahá', letter from Rúḥí Afnán, 12 January 1931, Bahá'í Heritage Project of the National Spiritual Assembly of the United States, pp. 1–2.
5. ibid. p. 8.
6. Rabbaní, *The Priceless Pearl*, p. 119.
7. Taherzadeh, *The Child of the Covenant*, p. 300.
8. Letter on behalf of Shoghi Effendi to an individual, 8 April 1931, in Shoghi Effendi, *The Light of Divine Guidance*, vol. 2, p. 17.
9. Rabbaní, *The Priceless Pearl*, p. 120.
10. Horace Holley, 'Introduction', in Shoghi Effendi, *The World Order of Bahá'u'lláh*.
11. Khianra, *Immortals*, pp. 27–8.
12. ibid. pp. 29–30.
13. ibid. pp. 30–31.
14. Rives, 'Carmel, Haifa and 'Akká', in *Star of the West*, vol. 20, no. 4, p. 122.
15. ibid.
16. Giachery, *Shoghi Effendi*, p. 112.
17. Rives, 'Carmel, Haifa and 'Akká', in *Star of the West*, vol. 20, no. 4, p. 123.
18. Holmes, 'Haifa – and the Baha'is', in *Star of the West*, vol. 20, no. 2 (May 1929), pp. 44–6.
19. Harper, *Lights of Fortitude*, pp. 303–4.
20. *Baha'i News Letter*, no. 32 (May 1929), p. 4.
21. Rabbaní, *The Priceless Pearl*, pp. 78–9.
22. ibid. p. 180.
23. Rabbaní, *The Guardian of the Bahá'í Faith*, photos facing p. 163; Robarts, 'Reminiscences about Shoghi Effendi', in *The Vision of Shoghi Effendi*, p. 169.
24. *The Bahá'í World*, vol. XI, pp. 502–3.
25. Rabbaní, *The Priceless Pearl*, p. 86.
26. ibid. pp. 84–5.
27. Amatu'l-Bahá Rúḥíyyih Khánum, talk at Wilmette, Riḍván, 1960.
28. Rabbaní, *The Priceless Pearl*, pp. 86–7.
29. Momen, *The Bábí and Bahá'í Religions, 1844–1944*, p. 458.

30. Rabbaní, *The Priceless Pearl*, p. 284.
31. ibid. pp. 248, 250.
32. Mountfort Mills, in USBNA, O/S Correspondence.
33. ibid.
34. ibid.
35. *Bahá'í News Letter*, no. 31 (April 1929), p. 6.
36. *Bahá'í News Letter*, no. 32 (May 1929), p. 7.
37. Zinky (ed.), *Martha Root, Herald of the Kingdom*, p. 149.
38. *The Bahá'í World*, vol. IV, pp. 237–47.
39. *The Bahá'í World*, vol. V, pp. 354–5.
40. Letter from the Universal House of Justice to the Bahá'ís of the world, 17 July 2013.
41. Garis, *Martha Root*, p. 330.
42. ibid. p. 331.
43. ibid. pp. 331–2.
44. Guy, 'A Bahá'í Traveler in Palestine', in *Star of the West*, vol. 21, no. 2 (May 1930), pp. 44–6; also in *The Bahá'í World*, vol. IV, pp. 509–12.
45. Garis, *Martha Root*, pp. 332–3.
46. Rabbaní, *The Priceless Pearl*, pp. 231–2.
47. Faizi-Moore, *Faizi*, p. 64.
48. Giachery, *Shoghi Effendi*, p. 125.
49. ibid. p. 140.

1930

1. Marcus, *Her Eternal Crown*, pp. 163–6.
2. Rabbaní, *The Priceless Pearl*, p. 113.
3. Marcus, *Her Eternal Crown*, pp. 169–70.
4. Rabbaní, *The Priceless Pearl*, p. 114.
5. ibid. p. 115.
6. ibid. pp. 115–16.
7. Weir, 'The Shrine', in *Star of the West*, vol. 22, no. 2 (May 1931), pp. 56–7.
8. Quoted in Hofman, *George Townshend*, p. 62.
9. ibid. p. 63.
10. ibid. pp. 65–8.
11. Hassall, *Ambassador at the Court*, ch. 10.
12. *The Bahá'í World*, vol. XIV, p. 321.
13. Hassall, 'Euphemia Eleanor Baker', in *Australian Dictionary of Biography*, vol 14: 1940–1980.
14. Hassall, *Ambassador at the Court*, ch. 10.
15. ibid.
16. Effie Baker, in New Zealand National Bahá'í Archives, pp. 4–5.
17. ibid. p. 5.
18. ibid. pp. 5–6.
19. ibid. pp. 6–7.
20. ibid. p. 7.
21. ibid. pp. 8–9.
22. Mabel Hyde Paine, in USBNA, Rexford and Sylvia Parmelee Papers, p. 2.

23. Hassall, *Ambassador at the Court*, ch. 10.
24. ibid.
25. ibid.
26. *The Bahá'í World*, vol. XVIII, p. 751.
27. Hassall, *Ambassador at the Court*, ch. 10.
28. ibid.
29. ibid.
30. ibid.
31. ibid.
32. See *The Bahá'í World*, vol. XV, p. 548.
33. Mason Remey, in *Bahá'í News Letter*, vol. 46 (November 1930), p. 12.
34. *The Bahá'í World*, vol. XIV, pp. 374-5.
35. Hassall, *Ambassador at the Court*, ch. 8.
36. *The Bahá'í World*, vol. XIII, p. 883.
37. Shoghi Effendi, in *Bahá'í News*, no. 46 (November 1930), p. 2.

1931

1. USBNA, Louise Drake Wright Papers, pp. 1, 3.
2. ibid. pp. 4, 6.
3. *The Bahá'í World*, vol. X, p. 523; Jasion, *Never Be Afraid to Dare*, p. 114.
4. Marion Jack, letter to Emma and Louise Thompson, 21 February 1931, quoted in Jasion, *Never Be Afraid to Dare*, pp. 114-15.
5. McKay, *Fires in Many Hearts*, p. 256.
6. Marion Jack, letter to Lorol Schopflocher, March 1931, quoted in Jasion, *Never Be Afraid to Dare*, pp. 117-18.
7. Rabbaní, *The Priceless Pearl*, p. 232.
8. Jasion, *Never Be Afraid to Dare*, p. 120.
9. McKay, *Fires in Many Hearts*, p. 257.
10. ibid. p. 258.
11. Jasion, *Never Be Afraid to Dare*, p. 122.
12. Emma and Louise Thompson, in USBNA, Elizabeth Bowen Papers, p. 1.
13. Marion Jack, letter to Emma and Louise Thompson, undated, quoted in Jasion, *Never Be Afraid to Dare*, p. 121.
14. ibid. p. 122.
15. Marion Jack, letter to Emma and Louise Thompson, 21 February 1931, quoted in Jasion, *Never Be Afraid to Dare*, p. 122.
16. ibid.
17. ibid. p. 123.
18. Rabbaní, *The Priceless Pearl*, p. 161.
19. Jasion, *Never Be Afraid to Dare*, p. 76.
20. Rutstein, *Corinne True*, pp. 173-4.
21. ibid. p. 175.
22. ibid; see also *The Bahá'í World*, vol. XIII, p. 874.
23. ibid. pp. 175-6.
24. ibid. pp. 176-7.
25. *Bahá'í News Letter*, vol. 62 (May 1932), p. 2.
26. Shoghi Effendi, *God Passes By*, p. 333.

27. Hassall, *Ambassador at the Court*, ch. 11.
28. Redman, *'Abdu'l-Bahá in Their Midst*, pp. 164–5.
29. USBNA, Nancy Bowditch Papers, p. 1.
30. Bowditch, 'A Visit to Bahjí', in *The Bahá'í World*, vol. IV, pp. 411–13.
31. ibid. p. 415.
32. Mabel and Sylvia Paine, 'Glimpses of the New World Order: Notes on a Visit to Haifa and Akká', in *Star of the West*, vol. 23, no. 12 (March 1933), p. 374.
33. Mabel Hyde Paine, 'Notes taken at Haifa, November 1931', p. 2, in USBNA, Rexford and Sylvia Parmelee Papers.
34. Mabel and Sylvia Paine, 'Glimpses of the New World Order . . .', in *Star of the West*, vol. 23, no. 12 (March 1933), p. 375.
35. ibid. p. 376.
36. Mabel Hyde Paine, 'Notes taken at Haifa, November 1931', p. 2, in USBNA, Rexford and Sylvia Parmelee Papers.
37. ibid. p. 4.
38. Mabel and Sylvia Paine, 'Glimpses of the New World Order . . .', in *Star of the West*, vol. 24, no. 3 (June 1933), p. 92.
39. ibid. no. 4 (July 1933), p. 127; see Shoghi Effendi, *The World Order of Bahá'u'lláh*, p. 45.
40. ibid. no. 5 (August 1933), pp. 145–46.
41. Mabel Hyde Paine, 'Notes on Shoghi Effendi's Table Talk', pp. 1–3, 5, in USBNA, Horace Holley Papers.
42. *The Bahá'í World*, vol. V, p. 77.
43. USBNA, Alice Dudley Papers, p. 9.
44. *The Bahá'í World*, vol. XIV, p. 333.
45. ibid. pp. 387–8.
46. *Bahá'í News*, no. 52, p. 2.
47. Hassall, *Ambassador at the Court*, ch. 9.

1932

1. Khianra, *Immortals*, p. 191.
2. ibid. p. 194.
3. Rabbaní, *The Priceless Pearl*, p. 135.
4. *The Bahá'í World*, vol. XI, p. 503.
5. Hassall, *Ambassador at the Court*, ch. 11.
6. Website of the National Spiritual Assembly of New Zealand, available at: http://www.bahai.org.nz/what_is_bahai/NZ_timeline.html.
7. Rabbaní, *The Priceless Pearl*, p. 215.
8. ibid. p. 217.
9. ibid. pp. 217–18.
10. Hassall, *Ambassador at the Court*, ch. 10.
11. *Bahá'í News*, no. 61, pp. 3–4.
12. Rabbaní, *The Priceless Pearl*, p. 143; *Bahá'í News,* no. 61, pp. 3–4.
13. Giachery, *Shoghi Effendi*, pp. 109–10.
14. Shoghi Effendi, *Dawn of a New Day*, p. 35.
15. Ruhe-Schoen, 'Ransom-Kehler, Keith Bean (1876–1933)'.
16. *The Bahá'í World*, vol. V, p. 187.

17. Keith Ransom-Kehler and Lorol Schopflocher, 'Haifa Talks'.
18. ibid.
19. *The Bahá'í World*, vol. V, pp. 25-6.
20. ibid. p. 409.
21. Harper, *Lights of Fortitude*, pp. 94-5.
22. *The Bahá'í World*, vol. XVIII, p. 388.
23. Rabbaní, *The Priceless Pearl*, p. 144.
24. ibid. p. 145.
25. ibid. p. 144.
26. Javidukht Khadem, *Zikrullah Khadem*, pp. 292-3.
27. Rabbaní, *The Priceless Pearl*, p. 147.
28. *The Bahá'í World*, vol. V, p. 22.

1933–1936

1. Hassall, *Ambassador at the Court*, ch. 11.
2. Gail, *Arches of the Years*, pp. 303-4.
3. ibid. p. 316.
4. Randall-Winckler, *My Pilgrimage to Haifa*, pp. 81, 85.
5. Pinchon, 'Haifa Calling', in *The Bahá'í World*, vol. V, p. 657.
6. *The Bahá'í World*, vol. XVIII, pp. 769–70.
7. Hassan, *Moths Turned Eagles*, pp. 37–40
8. Suthers, 'A Baha'i Pontiff in the Making', p. 31.
9. ibid. p. 33.
10. ibid. p. 35.
11. *Bahá'í News Letter*, no. 84 (June 1934), p. 3.
12. *The Bahá'í World*, vol. XVIII, p. 389.
13. Rabbaní, *The Priceless Pearl*, p. 269.
14. Audio recording of various speakers, 1985. Available at: http://web.archive.org/web/20090213152355/http://www.bahaistudy.org/audio-talks.html.
15. ibid.
16. *The Bahá'í World*, vol. XV, p. 422.
17. *The Bahá'í World*, vol. VI, p. 42.
18. *The Bahá'í World*, vol. XIII, p. 890.
19. National Spiritual Assembly of the Bahá'ís of Germany, email to the author, 18 August 2014.
20. *The Bahá'í World*, vol. XIII, p. 910.
21. National Spiritual Assembly of the Bahá'ís of Germany, email to the author, 4 September 2014.
22. de Vries, *The Babi Question you Mentioned*, p. 167.
23. Helen Bishop, in USBNA, George Latimer Papers, p.1.
24. Rutstein, *Corinne True*, pp. 178-9.
25. Shoghi Effendi, *God Passes By*, p. 333; *The Bahá'í World*, vol. VI, p. 268.
26. *Bahá'í News*, no. 93 (July 1935), p. 3.
27. Letter on behalf of Shoghi Effendi, 10 January 1935, quoted in Hofman, *George Townshend*, p. 74.
28. *The Bahá'í World*, vol. XVI, p. 528.
29. *The Bahá'í World*, vol. XIII, p. 892.

30. National Spiritual Assembly of the Bahá'ís of Germany, email to the author, 18 August 2014.
31. Hassan, *Moths Turned Eagles*, pp. 62-3, 66-7.
32. ibid. pp. 67-8.
33. *Bahá'í News Letter*, no. 92 (June 1935), p. 1.
34. Momen, *The Bábí and Bahá'í Religions, 1844-1944*, p. 460.
35. Rabbaní, *The Priceless Pearl*, p. 272.
36. See Hofman, *George Townshend*, pp. 123, 126, 132. The paper was published in *The Bahá'í World*, vol. VI, pp. 614-19.
37. Shoghi Effendi, *Directives from the Guardian*, p. 4-5.
38. Hassall, *Ambassador at the Court*, ch. 11.
39. Shoghi Effendi, *Letters from the Guardian to Australia and New Zealand, 1923-1957*, pp. 11-12.
40. ibid. p. 12.
41. Lorol Schopflocher, letter dated 28 May 1936 to Marion Hofman, in Marion Hofman Papers.
42. Shoghi Effendi, *Messages to America 1932-1946*, p. 6.
43. ibid. p. 7.
44. Shoghi Effendi, *This Decisive Hour*, p. 13.
45. Shoghi Effendi, *Messages to America, 1932-1946*, p. 8.
46. Shoghi Effendi, *Messages to the Bahá'í World, 1950-1957*, p. 155.
47. Rabbaní, *The Priceless Pearl*, p. 213.
48. Jeanne Bolles, letter dated 19 May 1936, in Marion Hofman Papers.
49. Jeanne Bolles, 'Haifa Notes', in USBNA, Alice Cox Papers, p. 11; see also Shoghi Effendi's letter to the Chairman of the United Nations Special Committee on Palestine, 14 July 1947, in Rabbaní, *The Priceless Pearl*, p. 288.
50. Gail, *Arches of the Years*, p. 314.
51. May and Mary Maxwell, *Haifa Notes of Shoghi Effendi's Words*, vol. 2, p. 7.

1937

1. Rabbaní, *The Priceless Pearl*, p. 219.
2. Violette Nakhjavani, *The Maxwells of Montreal: Middle Years, Late Years*, p. 252.
3. Violette Nakhjavani, *A Tribute to Amatu'l-Bahá Rúḥíyyih Khánum*, pp. 20-21.
4. ibid. pp. 20-22.
5. Violette Nakhjavani, *The Great African Safari*, pp. 338-9.
6. Letter from Shoghi Effendi to the National Spiritual Assembly of the Bahá'ís of Canada, 1 March 1951, in Shoghi Effendi, *Messages to Canada*, p. 22.
7. May and Mary Maxwell, *Haifa Notes of Shoghi Effendi's Words*, vol. 2, pp. 33-4 (p. 28 in the retyped version).
8. Notes from a talk by May Maxwell, 27 September 1937, Marion Hofman Papers.
9. Violette Nakhjavani, *A Tribute to Amatu'l-Bahá Rúḥíyyih Khánum*, pp. 25-6.
10. ibid. p. 26.
11. Notes from a talk by May Maxwell, 27 September 1937, Marion Hofman Papers.
12. Violette Nakhjavani, *The Maxwells of Montreal: Middle Years, Late Years*, pp. 260, 263.
13. Rabbaní, *The Priceless Pearl*, p. 151.
14. Violette Nakhjavani, *A Tribute to Amatu'l-Bahá Rúḥíyyih Khánum*, p. 28.

15. Rabbaní, *The Priceless Pearl*, p. 151.
16. ibid. p. 152.
17. Notes from a talk by May Maxwell, 27 September 1937, Marion Hofman Papers.
18. Rabbaní, *The Priceless Pearl*, p. 153.
19. ibid. pp. 152-3.
20. ibid. p. 153.
21. Violette Nakhjavani, *A Tribute to Amatu'l-Bahá Rúḥíyyih Khánum*, p. 29.
22. ibid. p. 62.
23. May Maxwell, letter to Katherine Baldwin, February 1939.
24. ibid.
25. *The Bahá'í World*, vol. VIII, p. 263.
26. Rabbaní, *The Priceless Pearl*, p. 153.
27. Violette Nakhjavani, *The Maxwells of Montreal: Middle Years, Late Years*, p. 275.
28. Rabbaní, *The Priceless Pearl*, pp. 60, 134.
29. Violette Nakhjavani, *A Tribute to Amatu'l-Bahá Rúḥíyyih Khánum*, p. 30; *The Maxwells of Montreal: Middle Years, Late Years*, p. 292.
30. Violette Nakhjavani, *A Tribute to Amatu'l-Bahá Rúḥíyyih Khánum*, pp. 30-31.
31. ibid. p. 35.
32. Rabbaní, *The Priceless Pearl*, pp. 81-3.
33. Amatu'l-Bahá Rúḥíyyih Khánum, talk at Wilmette, Riḍván, 1960.
34. Amatu'l-Bahá Rúḥíyyih Khánum, talk in New York City, 5 June 1960.
35. Pfaff-Grossmann, *Hermann Grossmann*, p. 48.
36. ibid. p. 52.
37. ibid. pp. 50-51.
38. ibid. p. 51.
39. Harper, *Lights of Fortitude*, p. 182.
40. Pfaff-Grossmann, *Hermann Grossmann*, p. 52.
41. Alexander, *History of the Bahá'í Faith in Japan*, p. 99.
42. ibid. p. 100.
43. ibid.
44. ibid.
45. ibid. p. 1.
46. Alexander, *Notes Taken in the Presence of Shoghi Effendi*, p. 3.
47. Alexander, *History of the Bahá'í Faith in Japan*, p. 100.
48. ibid.
49. ibid. pp. 100-01.
50. ibid. p. 101.
51. ibid. pp. 101-2.
52. ibid. p. 102.
53. Agnes Alexander, in USBNA, Ella Cooper Papers, p. 1.
54. ibid.
55. Dhikru'lláh Khádem, 'The Beloved of All Hearts – Shoghi Effendi', in *The Vision of Shoghi Effendi*, pp. 120-21; see also Javidukht Khadem, *Zikrullah Khadem*, pp. 47-8.
56. Harper, *Lights of Fortitude*, p. 282.
57. Shoghi Effendi's words as remembered by Dhikru'lláh Khádem, quoted in Javidukht Khadem, *Zikrullah Khadem*, pp. 291-2.

58. ibid. pp. 33–4.
59. USBNA, Amelia Collins Papers.
60. ibid.
61. ibid.
62. ibid.
63. ibid.
64. *The Bahá'í World*, vol. XIV, p. 363.
65. ibid.
66. Emeric Sala, in USBNA, Mary Lucas Papers, p. 1.
67. Sala, 'Shoghi Effendi's Question', in *The Vision of Shoghi Effendi*, p. 189.
68. ibid.
69. ibid.
70. Shoghi Effendi, 'The World Order of Bahá'u'lláh', letter to the National Spiritual Assembly of the Bahá'ís of the United States and Canada, 27 February 1929, in Shoghi Effendi, *The World Order of Bahá'u'lláh*, p. 5.
71. Weinstein, *Tending the Garden*, pp. 61–2.
72. Johnson and Johnson, *Heroes and Heroines of the Ten Year Crusade in Southern Africa*, p. 444.

1938–1939

1. Shoghi Effendi, *The World Order of Bahá'u'lláh*, p. v.
2. ibid. pp. 23–4.
3. *The Bahá'í World*, vol. XIII, pp. 941–2.
4. Landau, *Search for Tomorrow*, pp. 171–2.
5. Momen, *The Bábí and Bahá'í Religions*, 1844–1944, p. 456.
6. Landau, *Search for Tomorrow*, p. 215.
7. Habíb Taherzadeh, 'Meeting Shoghi Effendi'.
8. Ma'ani, *Leaves of the Twin Divine Trees*, p. 354.
9. ibid. pp. 353–4.
10. Rabbaní, *The Priceless Pearl*, pp. 197–8.
11. ibid. pp. 201–02.
12. ibid. p. 222.
13 See for example http://en.wikipedia.org/wiki/1936–1939_Arab_revolt_in_Palestine.
14. Rabbaní, *The Priceless Pearl*, pp. 219–20.
15. Sylvia Ioas, interview of Sachiro Fujita, 1965.
16. *The Bahá'í World*, vol. XII, pp. 316–17.
17. Letter on behalf of Shoghi Effendi to the National Spiritual Assembly of the British Isles, 27 November 1938, in Shoghi Effendi, *Unfolding Destiny*, pp. 122–3.
18. Letter on behalf of Shoghi Effendi to the National Spiritual Assembly of the British Isles, 4 June 1939, ibid. pp. 128–9.
19. Hainsworth, *Looking Back in Wonder*, p. 17–20. The verbatim report of the tribunal proceedings was also published in *The Bahá'í World*, vol. VIII, pp. 84–5.
20. *The Daily Telegraph*, 21 December 2001.
21. Rutstein, *He Loved and Served*, p. 17.
22. Pfaff-Grossman, *Herman Grossmann*, pp. 62–3.
23. ibid. pp. 55, 57, 67.

24. *The Bahá'í World*, vol. VIII, p. 679.
25. Rabbaní, *The Priceless Pearl*, p. 160.
26. Cardell, 'Experiences with the Guardian'.
27. Shoghi Effendi, *Messages to America, 1932–1946*, p. 17.
28. Amatu'l-Bahá Rúḥíyyih Khánum, *The Bahá'í World*, vol. XIII, p. 91; Shoghi Effendi, *This Decisive Hour*, p. 42.
29. Rabbaní, *The Priceless Pearl*, p. 130.
30. Quoted in Momen, *The Bábí and Bahá'í Religions*, 1844–1944, pp. 460–61.
31. *The Bahá'í World*, vol. VIII, pp. 253–7.
32. Letter from Shoghi Effendi, 21 December 1939, 'The Spiritual Potencies of That Consecrated Spot', in Shoghi Effendi, *Messages to America* 1932–1946, p. 31.
33. ibid.

1940

1. 'Alí Nakhjavání, *Shoghi Effendi: Author of Teaching Plans*, p. 67.
2. Javidukht Khadem, *Zikrullah Khadem*, pp. 293–5.
3. Quoted ibid. p. 296.
4. ibid.
5. ibid. pp. 320–23.
6. ibid. pp. 34–6.
7. *The Bahá'í World*, vol. VIII, pp. 641–2; Violette Nakhjavani, *The Maxwells of Montreal: Middle Years, Late Years*, p. 364.
8. Violette Nakhjavani, *A Tribute to Amatu'l-Bahá Rúḥíyyih Khánum*, pp. 37–8.
9. Violette Nakhjavani, *The Maxwells of Montreal: Middle Years, Late Years*, p. 367. See also *The Bahá'í World*, vol. VIII, pp. 631–42.
10. Sabour, *In the Presence of the Beloved Guardian*, pp. 1–2.
11. ibid. p. 1.
12. ibid. p. 2.
13. ibid. pp. 2–3, 5.
14. ibid. pp. 3–4.
15. ibid. p. 24.
16. ibid. p. 9.
17. ibid. pp. 13–14.
18. ibid. p. 23.
19. ibid. p. 24.
20. ibid. pp. 7, 16.
21. ibid. pp. 2, 4, 16–17.
22. ibid. pp. 26–7.
23. Rabbaní, *The Priceless Pearl*, pp. 178–9.
24. ibid.
25. Shoghi Effendi, *This Decisive Hour*, p. 57.
26. Rabbaní, *The Priceless Pearl*, p. 180.
27. Violette Nakhjavani, *A Tribute to Amatu'l-Bahá Rúḥíyyih Khánum*, pp. 41–2.
28. Violette Nakhjavani, *The Great African Safari*, p. 333.
29. Rabbaní, *The Priceless Pearl*, p. 180.
30. Violette Nakhjavani, *The Great African Safari*, p. 307.
31. Violette Nakhjavani, *A Tribute to Amatu'l-Bahá Rúḥíyyih Khánum*, p. 42.

32. Rabbaní, *The Priceless Pearl*, p. 181.

33. ibid.

34. Rowshan Mustapha, email to the present author, 16 May 2014, enclosing a copy of his letter to Amatu'l-Bahá Ruḥíyyih Khánum dated 1 July 1961.

35. Rabbaní, *The Priceless Pearl*, p. 182.

36. ibid. pp. 182–3.

1941–1944

1. Rabbaní, *The Priceless Pearl*, pp. 183–4.

2. ibid. p. 131.

3. ibid. pp. 220–21.

4. Violette Nakhjavani, *A Tribute to Amatu'l-Bahá Rúḥíyyih Khánum*, pp. 44–5.

5. Rabbaní, *The Priceless Pearl*, pp. 196–7.

6. Furútan, *Story of My Heart*, p. 57.

7. ibid. p. 58.

8. ibid. pp. 59–60, 62.

9. ibid. pp. 62–3, 69–70.

10. ibid. pp. 73–4.

11. Shoghi Effendi, *Messages to America, 1932–1946*, pp. 49–50.

12. Taherzadeh, *The Covenant of Bahá'u'lláh*, pp. 355–7.

13. ibid. p. 359; Ian Semple, talk given in London, 28 January 2006.

14. Taherzadeh, *The Covenant of Bahá'u'lláh*, pp. 359–64.

15. Violette Nakhjavani, *A Tribute to Amatu'l-Bahá Rúḥíyyih Khánum*, pp. 31–2.

16. Philip Hainsworth, letter to Marion Hofman dated 5 March 1952, Marion Hofman Papers.

17. Rabbaní, *The Priceless Pearl*, pp. 161–2.

18. Hassall,' Obituary: James Heggie'.

19. Violette Nakhjavani, *A Tribute to Amatu'l-Bahá Rúḥíyyih Khánum*, pp. 43–4.

20. Rabbaní, *The Priceless Pearl*, p. 162.

21. Harper, *Lights of Fortitude*, p. 279.

22. Violette Nakhjavani, *The Maxwells of Montreal, Middle Years, Late Years*, pp. 383–4.

23. ibid.

24. Violette Nakhjavani, *A Tribute to Amatu'l-Bahá Rúḥíyyih Khánum*, pp. 42–3.

25. Rabbaní, *The Priceless Pearl*, p. 238.

26. ibid. p. 239.

27. Amatu'l-Bahá Rúḥíyyih Khánum, talk at Wilmette, Riḍván 1960.

28. Rabbaní, *The Priceless Pearl*, p. 239.

29. ibid. pp. 239–40.

30. Chapman, *Leroy Ioas*, pp. 226–7.

31. *The Bahá'í World*, vol. XIII, p. 837.

32. Shoghi Effendi, *Unfolding Destiny*, p. 160.

33. Hassan, *Moths Turned Eagles*, pp. 76–7.

34. ibid. pp. 77–8.

35. ibid. pp. 78–9.

36. ibid. pp. 77–80.

37. Rabbaní, *The Priceless Pearl*, p. 297.

38. ibid. p. 141.
39. ibid. pp. 163-4.
40. Amatu'l-Bahá Rúḥíyyih Khánum, *Tribute to Shoghi Effendi*, Kampala, 1958, p. 6.
41. Rabbaní, *The Priceless Pearl*, pp. 223-4.
42. ibid. p. 163.
43. Hofman, *George Townshend*, p. 69.
44. ibid. p. 72.
45. ibid. p. 69.
46. Rabbaní, *The Priceless Pearl*, pp. 224-5.
47. 'Alí Nakhjavání, *Shoghi Effendi: Author of Teaching Plans*, p. 92.
48. Rabbaní, *The Priceless Pearl*, p. 382.
49. ibid. pp. 387-8.
50. Shoghi Effendi, *Messages to America, 1932-1946*, pp. 76-7.
51. ibid. p. 97.
52. ibid. p. 74.

1945-1946

1. USBNA, Ella Robarts Papers, Box 7, pp. 1-2.
2. ibid. pp. 2-4.
3. Shoghi Effendi, *Messages to America, 1932-1946*, p. 78.
4. ibid. p. 79.
5. ibid. p. 84.
6. ibid. pp. 97-8.
7. 'Alí Nakhjavání, *Shoghi Effendi: Author of Teaching Plans*, pp. 95-6.
8. ibid. pp. 97-9, 106.
9. ibid. p. 299.
10. Hainsworth, *Looking Back in Wonder*, p. 34.
11. ibid. pp. 34-5.
12. ibid. pp. 35-6.
13. ibid. pp. 36-7.
14. ibid. pp. 38-9.
15. Violette Nakhjavani, *The Maxwells of Montreal, Middle Years, Late Years*, p. 398.
16. Hainsworth, *Looking Back in Wonder*, p. 42.
17. ibid.
18. ibid. p. 46.
19. ibid. pp. 47-9.
20. Faizí, *Milly*, pp. 2-3.
21. Rabbaní, *The Priceless Pearl*, pp. 258-9.
22. Faizí, *Milly*, p. 14.
23. Amatu'l-Bahá Rúḥíyyih Khánum, account available at: http://bahai-library.com/shoghieffendi_scotland_ruhiyyihkhanum_edinburgh.

1947-1949

1. *The Bahá'í World*, vol. XVIII, p. 694.
2. Quoted in Rabbaní, *The Priceless Pearl*, p. 79.
3. ibid. pp. 79-80.

4. *The Bahá'í World*, vol. XVIII, p. 694.
5. Rabbaní, *The Priceless Pearl*, p. 167; Violette Nakhjavani, *The Maxwells of Montreal: Middle Years, Late Years*, p. 402.
6. Gladys Weeden, unpublished manuscript, Marion Hofman Papers, pp. 74–5.
7. ibid. pp. 75–6.
8. ibid. p. 76.
9. ibid. p. 88.
10. ibid. pp. 90–94.
11. ibid. pp. 7–8.
12. ibid. pp. 80–82.
13. *Star of the West*, vol. 10, no. 10 (8 Sept. 1919), p. 196.
14. Lockman, 'Haifa Refinery Riots', in *Comrades and Enemies*. Available at: http://www.mideastweb.org/refriots.htm.
15. 'Alí Nakhjavání, *Shoghi Effendi: Author of Teaching Plans*, pp. 90–91, 97.
16. Rabbaní, *The Priceless Pearl*, pp. 240–41.
17. Gladys Weeden, in USBNA, Charles (Carl) Krug Papers.
18. Rabbaní, *The Priceless Pearl*, p. 188.
19. ibid. p. 168.
20. ibid.
21. *The Bahá'í World*, vol. XVIII, p. 694.
22. Gladys Weeden, in USBNA, Charles (Carl) Krug Papers.
23. Gladys Weeden, unpublished manuscript, Marion Hofman Papers, p. 119.
24. Gladys Weeden, in USBNA, Charles (Carl) Krug Papers.
25. *Bahá'í News*, no. 211 (September 1948), p. 7.
26. Ben Weeden, quoted in Rabbaní, *The Priceless Pearl*, p. 80.
27. Ben Weeden, in USBNA, Charles (Carl) Krug Papers, 21 April 1948.
28. ibid. 22 April 1948.
29. ibid. 8 November 1948.
30. Rabbaní, *The Priceless Pearl*, p. 187.
31. ibid. pp. 241–2.
32. ibid. p. 242.
33. Violette Nakhjavani, *The Maxwells of Montreal: Middle Years, Late Years*, p. 407.
34. Ben Weeden, in USBNA, Charles (Carl) Krug Papers, 22 April 1948.
35. ibid. 22 November 1948.
36. Giachery, *Shoghi Effendi*, p. 8.
37. ibid.
38. Harper, *Lights of Fortitude*, p. 282; Rabbaní, *The Priceless Pearl*, p. 168.
39. Giachery, 'An Account of the Preparatory Work in Italy', in *The Bahá'í World*, vol. XII, p. 240.
40. Rabbaní, *The Priceless Pearl*, p. 170.
41. ibid. p. 188.
42. ibid. pp. 288–9.
43. Taherzadeh, *The Covenant*, p. 363.
44. Rabbaní, *The Priceless Pearl*, p. 171.
45. Gayle Woolson, in USBNA, Albert Windust Papers.
46. Rabbaní, *The Priceless Pearl*, p. 188.
47. *The Bahá'í World*, vol. XX, p. 932.

48. Salah Jarrah, conversation with May Hofman, 1977; emailed to the present author, 28 September 2014.
49. Rabbaní, *The Priceless Pearl*, pp. 171–2.
50. ibid. p. 173.
51. Ben Weeden, in USBNA, Charles (Carl) Krug Papers, 1 June 1948.
52. ibid. 31 Aug 1948.
53. ibid. 1 June 1948.
54. ibid.
55. van den Hoonard, *The Origins of the Bahá'í Community of Canada*, pp. 269–70.
56. 'Alí Nakhjavání, *Shoghi Effendi: Author of Teaching Plans*, p. 106.
57. ibid. pp. 104–5.
58. Rabbaní, *The Priceless Pearl*, p. 173.
59. Ben Weeden, in USBNA, Charles (Carl) Krug Papers, 16 Sept 1948.
60. Giachery, 'An Account of the Preparatory Work in Italy', in *The Bahá'í World*, vol. XII, p. 241.
61. ibid.
62. ibid. p. 243.
63. Gladys Weeden, unpublished manuscript, Marion Hofman Papers, p. 135.
64. Rabbaní, *The Priceless Pearl*, p. 290.
65. ibid. pp. 174–5.

1950

1. Ben Weeden, in USBNA, (Carl) Krug Papers, 6 February 1950.
2. Letter on behalf of Shoghi Effendi, 9 April 1949, in Shoghi Effendi, *Unfolding Destiny*, p. 225.
3. Giachery, 'An Account of the Preparatory Work in Italy', in *The Bahá'í World*, vol. XII, p. 243.
4. Rabbaní, *The Priceless Pearl*, p. 174.
5. Giachery, 'An Account of the Preparatory Work in Italy', in *The Bahá'í World*, vol. XII, p. 243.
6. Rabbaní, *The Priceless Pearl*, p. 176.
7. Ben Weeden, 'Reports on the Construction of the Arcade', in *The Bahá'í World*, vol. XII, p. 248.
8. Rabbaní, *The Priceless Pearl*, pp. 155–6.
9. ibid. p. 157; Violette Nakhjavani, *The Maxwells of Montreal: Middle Years, Late Years*, pp. 410–11.
10. Giachery, 'An Account of the Preparatory Work in Italy', in *The Bahá'í World*, vol. XII, pp. 243–44.
11. Ben Weeden, 'Reports on the Construction of the Arcade', in *The Bahá'í World*, vol. XII, p. 251.
12. Shoghi Effendi, *Messages to the Bahá'í World 1950–1957*, pp. 5–6.
13. Giachery, 'An Account of the Preparatory Work in Italy', in *The Bahá'í World*, vol. XII, p. 244.
14. Giachery, *Shoghi Effendi*, p. 97.
15. Giachery, 'An Account of the Preparatory Work in Italy', in *The Bahá'í World*, vol. XII, p. 246.
16. Letter from Shoghi Effendi, 9 April 1949, in Shoghi Effendi, *Unfolding Destiny*, p. 227.

17. Cable from Shoghi Effendi to the British National Convention, 1950, ibid. p. 245.
18. ibid.
19. Letter from Shoghi Effendi, 15 June 1950, ibid. p. 251.
20. *The Bahá'í World*, vol. XIX, pp. 653–7.
21. Harper, *Lights of Fortitude*, p. 342.
22. Shoghi Effendi, *Citadel of Faith*, pp. 87–8.
23. Lee, *Establishment of the Bahá'í Faith in West Africa*, pp. 97–9.
24. Cable from Shoghi Effendi to the National Spiritual Assembly of the Bahá'ís of the United States, and the National Spiritual Assembly of the Bahá'ís of the British Isles, 16 January 1951, in Shoghi Effendi, *Unfolding Destiny*, p. 256.
25. Cable from Shoghi Effendi, 22 June 1951, ibid. p. 265.
26. Cable from Shoghi Effendi, 14 November 1950, ibid. p. 255.
27. Rabbaní, *The Priceless Pearl*, p. 251; *The Bahá'í World*, vol. XIV, p. 302.
28. *The Bahá'í World*, vol. XIV, p. 302.
29. ibid.
30. Ian Semple, talk given in London, 28 January 2006.

1951–1952
1. Shoghi Effendi, *Messages to the Bahá'í World 1950–1957*, pp. 7–8.
2. ibid. p. 8.
3. ibid.
4. ibid. p. 10.
5. ibid. pp. 10–11.
6. ibid. pp. 24–5.
7. Philip Hainsworth, letter to Marion Hofman, 5 March 1951, in Marion Hofman Papers.
8. Shoghi Effendi, *Messages to the Bahá'í World 1950–1957*, p. 15.
9. ibid. pp. 16–18.
10. ibid. pp. 19–20.
11. *Bahá'í News*, no. 262 (December 1952), p. 5.
12. Pfaff-Grossmann, *Hermann Grossmann*, pp. 110–11.
13. Javidukht Khadem, *Zikrullah Khadem*, pp. 45–6.
14. ibid. pp. 46–7.
15. *The Bahá'í World*, vol. XV, pp. 422–3.
16. Chapman, *Leroy Ioas*, p. 157.
17. ibid. p. 159.
18. ibid. pp. 206–7.
19. Edith and Lowell Johnson, *Heroes and Heroines of the Ten Year Crusade in Southern Africa*, p. 375.
20. Chapman, *Leroy Ioas*, pp. 206–8.
21. Rabbaní, *The Priceless Pearl*, pp. 88–9.
22. 'Haifa's Bahá'í World Centre modelled on Babbacombe', in *Local World*, 16 February 2012.
23. Chapman, *Leroy Ioas*, pp. 188–9.
24. ibid. p. 189; Giachery, *Shoghi Effendi*, p. 127.
25. ibid. pp. 128–9.
26. ibid. pp. 129–30.

27. ibid. pp. 135–6.
28. *Bahá'í News*, no. 265 (March 1953), p. 5.
29. Leroy Ioas, *In the Days of the Guardian*, audio CD.
30. Amatu'l-Bahá Rúḥíyyih Khánum, talk at Wilmette, Riḍván 1960.
31. Gladys Weeden, unpublished manuscript, Marion Hofman Papers, pp. 157–8.

1952: Some Last Pilgrimages Before the Ten Year Crusade

1. *The Bahá'í World*, vol. XII, pp. 42–3.
2. *Bahá'í News*, no. 258 (August 1952), p. 6.
3. Rosalee Skrenes, personal communication, 2013.
4. Laurence Hautz, in USBNA, Beatrice Ashton Papers, p. 1.
5. Edith and Lowell Johnson, *Heroes and Heroines of the Ten Year Crusade in Southern Africa*, p. 375.
6. Laurence Hautz, in USBNA, Beatrice Ashton Papers, ibid. pp. 1–3.
7. ibid. p. 4.
8. Shoghi Effendi, *Messages to the Bahá'í World 1950–1957*, p. 24.
9. Giachery, *Shoghi Effendi*, p. 133.
10. Rosalee Skrenes, personal communication, 2013.
11. *Milwaukee Journal*, 11 January 1954, p. 13.
12. *Milwaukee Journal*, 22 December 1953, part 2, p. 1. Available at: http://news.google.com/newspapers?id=GQYdAAAAIBAJ&sjid=4iQEAAAAIBAJ&pg=4721,503918&dq=hautz&hl=en.
13. Aziz Panahi, interviewed by the author at the German Bahá'í Winter School, 31 December 2012.
14. ibid.
15. Giachery, *Shoghi Effendi*, p. 9.
16. ibid. p. 196.
17. ibid. pp. 196–7.
18. ibid. pp. 121–2.
19. ibid. pp. 131–2.
20. ibid. p. 133.
21. ibid. p. 134.
22. ibid. pp. 145–6.
23. Harper, *Lights of Fortitude*, p. 262.
24. Audio recording of various speakers, 1985, available at: http://web.archive.org/web/20090213152355/http://www.bahaistudy.org/audio-talks.html.
25. ibid.
26. Philip Hainsworth, letter to Marion Hofman, 5 March 1952, in Marion Hofman Papers.
27. Javidukht Khadem, *Zikrullah Khadem*, pp. 48–9.
28. ibid. p. 297.
29. French, *Nellie French Pilgrim Notes*, p. 1.
30. ibid. p. 2.
31. Ted Cardell, *Experiences with the Guardian*, audio tape, The Heritage Project of the National Spiritual Assembly of the United States, 1988.
32. Ted Cardell, 'Extracts from a description by Ted Cardell of his Pilgrimage to Haifa'.

33. ibid.
34. ibid.
35. Ted Cardell, *Experiences with the Guardian*, audio tape.
36. Ted Cardell, 'Extracts from a description by Ted Cardell of his Pilgrimage to Haifa'.
37. Ted Cardell, *Experiences with the Guardian*, audio tape.
38. Ted Cardell, 'Extracts from a description by Ted Cardell of his Pilgrimage to Haifa'.
39. ibid.
40. ibid.
41. Ted Cardell, in USBNA, Nancy Bowditch Papers, pp. 1–2.
42. Nosrat Ardekani, transcribed phone conversation, 20 August 2013, and email to the present author, 30 August 2013.
43. Bahíyyih Ford and Marion Little, in USBNA, Viola Tuttle Papers, pp. 1, 5.
44. ibid. p. 3.
45. Rutstein, *Corinne True*, pp. 202–4.
46. ibid. pp. 204–5.
47. ibid. p. 205.
48. Nura Mobine, in USBNA, Alice Cox Papers, p. 1.
49. Frances Edelstein, in The Heritage Project of the National Spiritual Assembly of the United States, 1985.
50. ibid.
51. Marzieh Gail, 'Jubilee at Wilmette', in *The Bahá'í World*, vol. XII, pp. 152–3.
52. Frances Edelstein, in The Heritage Project of the National Spiritual Assembly of the United States, 1985.
53. ibid.

The Next Big Step

1. Jessie Revell, letter dated 9 July 1952 'to the friends in America'. Available at: http://bahai-library.com/revell_letters.
2. Shoghi Effendi, *Messages to the Bahá'í World* 1950–1957, pp. 40–41.
3. ibid. p. 41.
4. The Universal House of Justice, *Century of Light*, p. 78.
5. To be continued in *Shoghi Effendi Through the Pilgrim's Eye*, Volume 2: *The Ten Year Crusade*.

INDEX OF NAMES

ABOUT THE AUTHOR

Earl Redman is the author of *'Abdu'l-Bahá in Their Midst*, the story of the journeys of 'Abdu'l-Bahá to Europe and North America, 1911–1913, told through the words of those who met Him. He worked as a geologist for the US Bureau of Mines in the Juneau Gold Belt, Alaska, before moving to Ireland in 1999. Much in demand as a speaker and storyteller, he travels widely and has three more books forthcoming.